WIDE AWAKE
in the
WINDY CITY

WIDE AWAKE
in the
WINDY CITY

CELEBRATING A CENTURY OF EXCELLENCE AT
NORTHWESTERN UNIVERSITY'S
KELLOGG SCHOOL OF MANAGEMENT, 1908–2008

By Matt Golosinski

Edited by Richard P. Honack

 Northwestern
University Press
Evanston, Illinois

 Kellogg
School of Management

Front endsheet photograph: Wieboldt Hall entrance © Padgett and Company.
Back endsheet photograph: James L. Allen Center © James F. Snyder.

The publisher has made every reasonable effort to contact all copyright holders
and to obtain permission to use the photographs presented here.
Photographer credits, where available, appear with their photographs.

Library of Congress Cataloging-in-Publication Data
Golosinski, Matt.
Wide awake in the Windy City : celebrating a century of excellence
at Northwestern University's Kellogg School of Management,
1908–2008 / by Matt Golosinski ; edited by Richard P. Honack.
    p. cm.
"Kellogg School of Management".
   Includes bibliographical references and index.
   ISBN-13: 978-0-8101-2504-9 (trade cloth : alk. paper)
   ISBN-10: 0-8101-2504-8 (trade cloth : alk. paper)
1. Kellogg School of Management—History. 2. Business
schools—Illinois—History. I. Honack, Richard P. II. Kellogg
School of Management. III. Title.
HF1134.K43G65 2008
650.071'17731—dc22

                         2008000302

CONTENTS

Matt Golosinski is the editorial director of the Kellogg School, managing a variety of communications initiatives, such as *Kellogg World,* the school's 50,000-circulation alumni journal.

Richard P. Honack is the assistant dean and chief marketing officer of the Kellogg School, where he is also an adjunct associate professor.

PREFACE

The Noble Calling

*Walter D. Scott, Professor of Management and
Senior Austin Fellow*

When Northwestern University founded its School of Commerce in 1908, many of the challenges facing business were quite different from those facing organizations in 2008. Nevertheless, the school's overriding mission remains much the same: to prepare students for leadership by teaching them the best in management theory and practice so that they can succeed. Although the focus of the curriculum and the student body in 1908 was, importantly, on clerical jobs with Chicago banks, the school then, as now, was meeting the needs of students and the business community.

The seeds of what would become the Kellogg School of Management were planted well before the school opened its doors in downtown Chicago. Northwestern at the time was a good, if modest, university whose students and perspectives were mostly midwestern. It did, however, have faculty members whose research and courses were ahead of their time.

A reflection on my grandfather, Walter Dill Scott, suggests this advanced thinking as well as the unchanging challenge of applying theory to practice. In 1908, he was chair of the Psychology Department at Northwestern and the first professor of applied psychology in the country. He was fascinated by the possibilities inherent in his research to meet business needs and improve human performance. He authored or coauthored books such as *The Theory and Practice of Advertising* in 1902; *The Psychology of Public Speaking* in 1906; and, later, *Personnel Management, Increasing Human Efficiency in Business* and *Influencing Men in Business. Personnel Management* was still used as a text when I attended Northwestern in the 1950s. His book *The Psychology of Advertising* had a dedication that suggests the evolution that was ahead: "The author respectfully dedicates this volume to the increasing number of AMERICAN BUSINESS MEN who successfully apply science where their predecessors were confined to custom."

The work of Walter Dill Scott and others like him prepared Northwestern well for its entry into business education. Their creative approaches were matched by strong support and prodding from the business community, which provided a partnership that led to the creation of the School of Commerce. That partnership persists today and is at the heart of the Kellogg story.

Throughout its history, the school has benefited from the leadership of many giants and the dedicated efforts of others who may not have been giants in a traditional sense but who nevertheless contributed significantly to the story on the pages that follow. Their vision, passion and integrity created the foundation for the Kellogg School that exists today.

The story of how Kellogg rose to international prominence is, of course, no mystery. The leadership of its three most recent deans, especially of Donald P. Jacobs, supplies much of the answer. The right leaders have been in place at the right times and have created an environment with excellence and high aspirations as core values. The school has attracted and nurtured a gifted faculty and strong administrators whose skills have benefited generations of students. Kellogg also has created a culture that welcomes the continuous innovation critical to meeting the evolving needs of our customers—our students and their present and future employers.

In the late 1960s and early 1970s, Dean John Barr enlisted the business community under the leadership of Jim Allen of Booz Allen Hamilton to help shape a strategic agenda for change and transformation. Barr's leadership set the stage for the dramatic growth and success that followed. The imprint of Dean Jacobs has been writ large. His transforming deanship expanded the school's vision and made it a reality. He positioned Kellogg brilliantly for the late twentieth and early twenty-first centuries. He led in the creation of a world-class faculty composed of thought leaders dedicated to teaching and mentoring students, including executives attending executive programs. The James L. Allen Center, home to the top-ranked Kellogg EMBA and Executive Education Programs, has provided a window into the professional world of the practitioner and has helped showcase the talents of our faculty. And Dean Dipak C. Jain, the gifted leader of today, is increasingly making Kellogg a global leadership brand with a mission that includes knowledge creation and the development of responsible global leaders. His intellect, marketing skills, integrity and values, matched with his vision and leadership, make him an ideal dean for Kellogg today and tomorrow.

The changes at Kellogg since I joined the faculty in 1988 have been dramatic and critical in positioning the school to meet present and future challenges. Some significant ones include the internationalization of the student body, faculty, curricula and programs. The school has created research centers and dedicated programs for an array of disciplines, including entrepreneurship and innovation, family business, executive women, risk management, biotechnology, technology management and global citizenship and social enterprise, to mention just a few. Kellogg has developed curricula and new courses to meet emerging demands and realities, and it has established joint-degree programs with other schools in the university, including law, engineering, and medicine, as well as with other universities in the United States and abroad. The application of technology has unleashed intellectual power, with the school establishing knowledge creation centers in key locations around the world. And today, Kellogg and Northwestern are partnering to create new certificate programs for undergraduates. The focus throughout is increasingly on preparing "citizen leaders" who can contribute wherever they find themselves in a dramatically changing global society.

The story that follows describes the journey of the last 100 years. The future will undoubtedly bring major challenges, some known and others not even imagined. The school's inherent strengths and character bode well for the future. Some of those strengths are cultural, some organizational and leadership-driven. Most important will be the continued collaborations between our faculty and students, as well as our dedicated staff, supportive alumni and contributing friends and allies. The team culture that has empowered and encouraged cooperative initiative and effort will remain central, as will the school's ongoing reinvention of itself to meet contemporary demands. Indeed, these qualities are ingrained at Kellogg, a place where innovation is continuous rather than sporadic, a fact that encourages quick adaptation, great creativity and refinement—or rejection—of ideas that don't work or become obsolete. The many programs meeting MBA and executive education needs will be important, as will the strengths and resources of an outstanding university. Finally, Kellogg is led by a dean who brings extraordinary passion and focus to the journey, a prerequisite for continued success in the face of increased competition in a dramatically shifting environment.

If the past is indeed prologue, the Kellogg School can look forward to an exciting and rewarding next century. Preparing students for lifelong journeys of growth and social contribution will continue to be our noble calling.

ACKNOWLEDGMENTS

Writing a book seems, and often is, a solitary enterprise, but the effort's outcome also relies upon factors independent of the author's ability (or his stubborn refusal to take up a less taxing pursuit). The truth is, many people have played a role in supporting this text.

I want to thank the current and former members of the Kellogg School, both faculty and staff, who were generous with their time and recollections. Two deserve special mention for their willingness to be interviewed and for the scope of their contributions: Dean Emeritus Donald P. Jacobs and Associate Dean Emeritus Edmund J. Wilson '84. Other colleagues, including Assistant Dean and Chief Marketing Officer Richard Honack '94, Senior Director of Marketing and Communications Thom Duncan and Senior Associate Dean David Besanko '82, also have been key in guiding this project to completion with their encouragement and insights. Then too, the Kellogg School's Office of the Dean has been an unremitting champion of my efforts throughout my tenure. Dean Dipak C. Jain in particular deserves my thanks for his leadership and confidence in me. The staff members of the Northwestern University Library Archives have been allies as well, and the efforts of photo researcher John Morrison were instrumental in helping assemble this book's images.

Personally, my greatest supporter has been my wife, Mary, whose love, enthusiasm and tolerance have truly anchored my efforts and made this project possible. Each day over the last two years, she has been ready to help me move forward, even when challenges proved daunting and when my work resulted in her own objectives being postponed or sacrificed. She continuously inspires me, and I try to be worthy of her.

Of course, my entire family has been a foundation, especially my mother, Arlene, whose great gifts to me included a childhood rich in imagination and education. It was she who, through tireless effort, instilled an ardor for learning that continues to animate my life. Finally, to Ron Carlson and Jay Boyer, mentors and menschen, I owe whatever refinement my writing possesses.

In producing this book, I have been privileged to see the extraordinary character of the Kellogg School. There is no other place like it, nor are there any colleagues as talented and passionate as those who have worked together to create a legacy with global significance. I hope this book serves to honor some of those whose lives have intermingled with this noble institution, growing richer for the experience.

I know mine has.

—*Matt Golosinski*
Evanston, Illinois, September 2007

WIDE AWAKE
in the
WINDY CITY

8831. BOARD OF TRADE, DURING SESSION, CHICAGO, ILL.

The Chicago Board of Trade during session in 1905.

INTRODUCTION

A Century of Innovation and Excellence, 1908–2008

The best way to predict the future is to invent it.
—Alan Kay

What can happen in 100 years?

Ten decades unleash a dizzying array of activity, much of it ephemeral and trivial, some profound and transformative.

A century takes humanity off the back of a horse and onto the moon's surface, an endeavor so startling that other accomplishments seem to pale by comparison. But that journey, like advances in medical science and communications, suggests incremental developments in many related fields, including those spurred by commercial incentives. Such entrepreneurship is responsible for an unprecedented explosion of discovery, some of which may have proven impossible without the market's influence.

If business helped fuel exploration to outer space and into the atom's nucleus, it also helped produce a global culture more connected than ever before, one where commerce effected profound social change. These developments, however, demanded leaders trained by visionary educators, including those at Northwestern University's Kellogg School of Management, which celebrates its centennial this year.

The Kellogg School story is filled with people *working together* and working relentlessly to achieve more and function better in everything they do. This quest for excellence has created enormous benefits in organizations of all kinds, while also improving the larger community. Whether academics or practitioners, administrators or alumni—today numbering more than 50,000, among them CEOs and senior leaders across every industry—members of the Kellogg network are recognized for the fine quality of their intellectual contributions, their ability to bridge theory and practice, their entrepreneurial approach to innovation and the collegial relationships that distinguish them from their peers in any other school. Dedicated to knowledge creation and the development of socially responsible global leaders, the Kellogg School has achieved much in 10 decades. Today, thanks to an unparalleled, evolving curriculum, the best faculty and students and strength across all programs, full-time, part-time and executive, Kellogg is positioned for even greater accomplishments in the years ahead.

The rise of this remarkable institution is a tale of the brilliant and passionate people affiliated with it since the early years of the twentieth century. It is a narrative told best against the backdrop of the times Kellogg helped shape by bringing better ideas and implementation into the world to solve problems and improve lives.

Industrial Expansion Demands Management Leaders

The rise of modern business in the United States was surprisingly fast, surging with the advent of the railroads and communications technology that fostered robust markets on a massive national scale. America essentially went from being an agricultural economy to an industrial power over the span of 50 years, a process that began in earnest after the Civil War. The promise and challenge of harnessing burgeoning energies, particularly new forms in extractive industries like oil, led scholars, usually economists, to contemplate how best to leverage these forces for social benefit. Practice outstripped theory as inventions crowded each other, leading to still more innovation across all fields. Thomas Edison's telephone and electric light altered how people lived and worked. The Victrola phonograph's arrival in 1906 would be a vital part of a new entertainment age. The internal combustion engine reached its apotheosis in Henry Ford's automotive assembly line, which radically altered the idea of space and urban and commercial planning with the introduction of the Model T in 1908. That same year saw General Motors incorporated, while General Electric patented the electric iron and toaster and geologists discovered oil in Persia (modern Iran), starting an oil boom. Theoretical science was making enormous leaps too. Albert Einstein had published four landmark papers on physics in 1905, a few years before Chicago physicist Robert Andrews Millikan calculated the charge of an electron. Perhaps most remarkable was the Wright brothers' invention in 1903, making the dream of flight a reality.

These and other advances allowed enterprises to grow beyond their local communities but required more sophisticated management. Competition also increased, and so tools such as advertising became more important, ultimately producing marketing specialists. Concerns with efficiency became paramount, as evidenced by the influence of the "scientific management" popularized by Frederick Winslow Taylor.[1]

Throughout the twentieth century with its many towering achievements, the Kellogg School framed critical discussions, strengthened the world's managerial skill and produced influential leaders in all areas of public and commercial life. Since it was founded in 1908 with a part-time evening program, the school has been a pioneer in collaborative learning, executive education and general management. Its name is synonymous with marketing leadership, but Kellogg also has contributed significantly to analytical discourse, including the application of game theory. Facilitating these advances has been the school's commitment to forging relationships between practitioners and its professors to solve real problems. Within these partnerships, which date to the school's founding, the perspectives of business leaders are welcomed. For instance, practitioners still serve as advisory board members at the school. Though informal and nonbinding, this arrangement has resulted in the Kellogg administration gaining critical insights into market needs. This partnership, in concert with an organizational structure that encourages agility and creativity over bureaucracy and invites contributions from all members, enables the school to sense and respond quickly to opportunities, adopting an entrepreneurial strategy that has consistently proven rewarding.

The school's alumni and friends also lend support in many other ways—from making financial contributions that advance research and teaching to serving as guest lecturers in classes or at conferences. They may help interview prospective students and recruit Kellogg graduates. As clinical professors, practitioners complement the school's rigorous, research-oriented faculty to create an engaging, balanced approach to theory and practice.

Origin of a Management Leader

As far as Northwestern University president Edmund Janes James was concerned in 1903, the time had come for collegiate management education. "The average business man is ignorant and inefficient and cowardly," said James. "He is helpless in a crisis."

These strong words would be the impetus for the School of Commerce and would influence its mission to apply scientific frameworks to business. Recalled

Willard E. Hotchkiss, the school's first dean: "The immediate purpose in establishing the Northwestern University School of Commerce was to give in evening courses an opportunity for capable and ambitious employees to pursue business subjects from the point of view of foundation principles."

At its inception, the school was part of an elite group of institutions that launched business education in the United States. Early peers included the Wharton School of Business at the University of Pennsylvania (the first collegiate business school, founded in 1881); the College of Commerce and Politics at the University of Chicago (1898); the College of Commerce at the University of California at Berkeley (1898); the Amos Tuck School of Business at Dartmouth College (1900); and the Harvard Business School (1908). Northwestern's commerce program began as a humble, though ambitious, effort at Lake and Dearborn streets in downtown Chicago, a city reborn after the great fire of 1871 and ready to impress the world with its entrepreneurial, rough-hewn spirit. From the start, the commerce curriculum aimed to meet the needs of people eager to advance their careers by putting knowledge to work. The school's faculty members, steeped in economic theory and ready to use their insights to advance social good, reached out to business leaders to combine their talents. As they did, the school grew increasingly sophisticated, quickly adding courses to an initial handful of offerings until the program was recognized as among the most impressive of its kind.

This year, the Kellogg School marks its centennial, a remarkable achievement in an era of transient endeavors and disposable culture. But Kellogg has not merely passed an endurance test; its hundredth birthday is made more exceptional because of the lasting value created by generations of scholars, students, staff and graduates associated with this "jewel in the crown" of Northwestern University, as current Northwestern president Henry Bienen has described the business school.

The Kellogg School per se is a relatively recent creation, begun in the late 1970s as the J. L. Kellogg Graduate School of Management, in recognition of the benefactor whose $10 million gift—a record at the time—set the midwestern academy onto a path that would make it a top-ranked, internationally known management leader. But the institution founded in 1908 was the School of Commerce, one of a handful in the country. Its part-time curriculum, not yet grappling with the sophisticated management issues that would only emerge in the coming decades, was located in Chicago's vibrant Loop district. Study culminated in the acquisition of a diploma of commerce, but the school soon added other, more comprehensive offerings—one that led to a bachelor of business administration degree (1912) and a full-time program on the school's Evanston campus (1919), where a doctoral course also was begun in 1926. Initially, the business world wanted graduates with technical expertise rather than general management skills, so Northwestern produced experts in niches like accounting or marketing. Over time, trends altered to reflect a growing need for holistic managers, developments suggested by the commerce school becoming known as the School of Business (1956) and then the Graduate School of Management (1969). To illustrate management's general utility across a swath of organizations, both for-profit and nonprofit, the school offered a master of management (MM) degree rather than an MBA by 1970. For 30 years, the school retained this distinctive credential, until market conditions indicated that a return to the traditional degree yielded more value for graduates. Each of the decisions behind such changes reflected a larger shift in perception about the objectives of modern business, the tools required to meet those objectives, the types of professionals needed to make the attempt and the role of schools in preparing these people for leadership positions.

Wide Awake in the Windy City

Chicago, the context that gave rise to the School of Commerce, was arguably the nation's entrepreneurial center, a multicultural city where optimism and a hard-scrabble, can-do spirit created many opportunities for economic advancement. Though in the Midwest, parts of which seemed sleepy and provincial compared to older East Coast cities, Chicago churned with commercial activity. Home to Montgomery Ward, the world's first mail-order business, established in 1872, Chicago emerged as a financial and manufacturing power—one reason why the Rotary Club, the first business-related service organization, established its headquarters there in 1905. In 1892, Chicago had introduced the world's second elevated train line. Seven years earlier, it had produced the Home Insurance Building, the world's first skyscraper, albeit only 9 stories tall. In 1900, city engineers completed a remarkable feat begun 13 years earlier: reversing the flow of the Chicago River using a 28-mile canal in an effort to improve the deficient sewer system. By 1907, Chicago had become home to the world's largest department store, Marshall Field's, a 12-story structure on State Street that replaced an earlier Field's enterprise. The city also laid out a wildly ambitious civic agenda in its "Plan of Chicago." Dubbed the "Burnham Plan" after the famous architect who was central to creating the 1909 initiative, it brought together business and government leaders in the cause of community development.

Yet, Chicago was also rife with political corruption and crime. It was a place of economic disparity and labor disputes, as well as the proving ground where fortunes were made. The world of George Pullman and Allen Pinkerton, the Haymarket Square Riot of 1886, the stockyards that became infamous in Upton Sinclair's *The Jungle* (published in 1906 and responsible for stirring President Theodore Roosevelt to investigate the novel's thinly fictionalized content)—all these elements were part of the tumultuous socioeconomic climate of the Windy City.

The metropolis clearly would benefit from enlightened management education, a commodity that Northwestern University was well positioned to deliver. And deliver it did.

Through their leadership in teaching and research, School of Commerce scholars helped transform business. To cite only one example, professors introduced critical elements to marketing, a discipline that would come to academic prominence at the Kellogg School. Indeed, marketing excellence continues to be an institutional hallmark at Kellogg and can be traced back a century to Walter Dill Scott's research into applied psychology and advertising. In their focus on principles, early scholars like Fred E. Clark and Paul W. Ivey would lay the foundations for future Kellogg professors, including marketing guru Philip Kotler, to create an entirely new, expanded conception of what the discipline could achieve.

As business grew more complex over the decades, Northwestern's business school adapted to meet new needs, even sacrificing short-term gain for long-term viability and the chance to be in the vanguard of management education. In 1966, university trustees voted for a proposal by School of Business dean John Barr to dismantle the well-regarded undergraduate business program in favor of creating a graduate curriculum exclusively. The school then turned its energies to cultivating its modern, research-based design, drawing particularly upon mathematical analysis and game theory but also organizational behavior, which would culminate in the school introducing its pathbreaking, team-based learning model. The risk paid off handsomely.

By the mid-1970s, Dean Donald P. Jacobs was continuing the efforts of his predecessors and introducing his own ideas that would prove critical to the school's evolution. In particular, his ability to perceive the value of executive education and lifelong learning resulted in establishing a world-class executive MBA program and facility in the James L. Allen Center, a $5.5 million gamble that few besides Jacobs believed would succeed. It opened in 1979 and remains the industry standard for excellence, emulated worldwide. Then too, the school pursued a unique recruiting strategy for both faculty and students, preferring young, talented individuals who nevertheless may have been overlooked by others and then personally interviewing them all to determine whether they would fit in the "Kellogg culture" being developed on a foundation of collaboration and engagement.

These resources and the foresight of Jacobs—whose tenure lasted 26 years, longer than that of any other business school dean—would help Kellogg achieve number one rankings in national surveys, including the 1988 *BusinessWeek* poll. What's more, the school would repeat the feat multiple times, never placing below third in the magazine's rankings for the next 20 years and having all its programs— full-time, part-time and executive—recognized as being in the top echelon. Research and research centers also flowered during Jacobs's tenure, and the school adopted curriculum innovations that balanced market demand for traditional core management skills with up-to-the-minute offerings to meet emerging require- ments. Jacobs also perceived the importance of global business and the need for Kellogg to have a presence worldwide, so he initiated strategic partnerships with schools like the Sasin Graduate Institute of Business Administration in Bangkok; the Leon Recanati Graduate School of Business in Tel Aviv; the Otto Beisheim School of Management in Vallendar, Germany; the Business School at the Hong Kong Institute of Science and Technology in Hong Kong; and the Schulich School of Business in Toronto, Canada.

These partnerships marked the start of a global portfolio that continues under the current dean, Dipak C. Jain, a scholar whose marketing talents are finding new ways to ensure that Kellogg remains among the world's most prestigious manage- ment educators, able to provide the qualities required to succeed in a hypercompet- itive, global business environment. Dean Jain's commitment to "rigor and relevance" and his vision of global knowledge centers to disseminate Kellogg School thought leadership have already advanced with the 2006 launch of the Kellogg-Miami Program to offer executive MBA training to professionals throughout Latin America. The school's founding principles consist of four key elements: intellectual depth, experiential learning, global perspectives and leadership and social responsi- bility. These aspects are integrated into the Kellogg curriculum, which is itself part of the school's culture of innovation and collaboration. The dean's entrepreneurial insights also drive his strategic plan for the school, as does his belief in the impor- tance of inclusiveness and a governance style of distributed leadership. He also advocates continuous innovation to meet emerging customer and market demands in a world that, in some ways, seems vastly different from that confronting Dean Hotchkiss in 1908.

Perennial Concerns

Yet, for all these changes and alongside all the critical managerial advances introduced by the Kellogg School, some fundamental issues persist. Around 1900, concerns with globalization already were linked with considerations of technological development. Debates about ethics and the proper role and scope of business in the world—and indeed the responsibility of business leaders to society—seemed as animated at the dawn of the last century as they are today.

In fact, were the date obscured and a few details modified, modern readers could be forgiven for thinking that this passage from a June 1900 *Atlantic Monthly* essay was published last week:

"Recent Economic Tendencies"

The Events of the last decade, and particularly of the last few years, have required a readjustment by economic thinkers of many preconceived points of view upon important subjects relating to industry and capital. It is not so much that the maxims of classical political economy have been proved false, as that those upon which stress has been laid during the effort to emancipate industry from mediaeval fetters have become of subordinate importance because their operation has come to be modified by new conditions. The last few years have witnessed a remarkable expansion in trade and industry in nearly every civilized country, which is causing a larger volume of production in proportion to population, and employing a larger capital than any previous development of the kind. . . .

While this revival of industry, following upon the panic of 1893, bears much resemblance to the revivals that have followed earlier periods of depression, an important new element has gradually become a controlling factor. . . . This is the widening of the field of competition. This widening . . . has proceeded with accelerating pace during the last two centuries as the result of labor-saving machinery, swift and cheap methods of communication, and the great accumulations of saved capital resulting from the use of these improved instruments of production and exchange. . . . The condition which now confronts [the commercial professional] is the necessity of seeking new outlets, whether for finished goods or saved capital, in foreign markets where he must compete with other producers from without who have entered the field under the same stimulus as himself.[2]

The article went on to cite trends in the global expansion of commercial ventures, as well as the tools and intellectual acumen that were increasingly demanded to compete. Even then, the need for more rigorous, scientific frameworks was apparent, particularly in finance and banking. This market need would spur a move away from relying upon a rather formless curriculum built out of economics and anecdotes, an approach largely in circulation before 1900 at the few schools that bothered to teach business at all. Just beneath the surface, there was also an argument for the enhanced marketing skills and cross-cultural insights that would emerge at the School of Commerce. One could even glimpse the importance of what would become known as supply chain management:

> The new market opening in the undeveloped countries will be won by the people showing the greatest efficiency in every department of production,—not merely in machinery and labor, but in the organization of their banking and carrying systems and their distribution of the burdens of taxation. Local markets have been merged into a world market, where the operator in goods, money, or securities can place orders and make sales at his will, in London, Paris, Vienna, or New York, according as the news brought by telegraph, telephone, or cable indicates that he can buy cheaper or sell dearer at any given moment.

Complementing these observations was another article from the May edition of the same publication that reflected on the human consequences of these commercial advances. In "A Nation in a Hurry," Eliot Gregory offered a lament that seems strangely contemporary:

> A curious curse has fallen upon our people, an "influence" which tempts us to do in an hour just twice as much as can be accomplished in sixty minutes. "Do as well as you can," whispers the influence, "but do it quickly!" That motto might be engraved upon the front of our homes and business buildings.

With regard to business ethics, too, we find precedent. Dean Hotchkiss considered the matter central. He believed that business education's goal was to give the student a "many-sided survey . . . and a thorough grasp of scientific method . . . [to] prepare the student to think complicated business problems through to the end."[3] But he also contended that such analysis had to be yoked to synthesis, taking a broad view of theory and practice and exercising care to master the "human factor" that would enable managers to work effectively and fairly with others.

"The executive's task is primarily to adjust to human relations" while aligning internal corporate goals with external social ones, creating a "[h]armonizing of social and business motives," wrote Hotchkiss.[4]

"All of these studies," he believed, "would be pursued with constant reference to the fact that *business is carried on in a community* in which certain public policies are enforced in recognition to the fact that business should conform to these policies and help to make them effective in contributing to *public welfare*" [emphasis added].[5]

And just as an effort to balance corporate interests against the interests of the public continues today, similar efforts took place a century ago, with legislation such as the Sherman Antitrust Act responding to public concern that conglomerates were accruing too much power.[6] Government labor policies were intended to offset economic damage caused by actions such as the 23-week Anthracite Coal Strike in 1902 that nearly crippled the nation. Famously, President Theodore Roosevelt's "square deal" speech in 1903 promised Americans that oversight by a sufficiently strong federal government would ensure optimal benefit to corporations, workers and consumers alike by balancing the concerns of all three. (What Roosevelt was calling for might seem uncontroversial today: food and drugs could no longer be mislabeled, nor could consumers be deliberately misled for profit.) "The welfare of each of us is dependent fundamentally on the welfare of all of us," said Roosevelt. "It cannot be too often repeated that in this country, in the long run, we all of us tend to go up or down together."

As president, Roosevelt channeled the spirit of the times, taking action against corporate trusts in 1902 to convince Congress to establish a bureau that oversaw unscrupulous monopolies. He also went after J. P. Morgan's Northern Securities Corporation, a railroad conglomerate, and, eventually, more than 40 other major corporations during his presidency. Collusion and price-fixing among railroads were concerns that legislation such as the Elkins Act and Hepburn Act sought to discourage. Other laws, including the Heyburn Bill and the Pure Food and Drug Act, which regulated food producers and sellers, and the Aldrich-Vreeland Act, designed to correct deficiencies in the banking system that had created a panic in 1907, represented an effort to bolster trust in the overall market system and to safeguard prosperity. In agreement with Dean Hotchkiss and his like-minded peers about the importance of ethics, Roosevelt believed that "to educate a man in mind and not morals is to create a menace to society."

Ethics continues to be an important practical consideration for MBA students, particularly in the wake of corporate scandals such as the Enron debacle that rekindled the debate about ethics in business school education. Government legislation is prominent too. With the Sarbanes-Oxley Act of 2002, the United States sought to correct weaknesses in corporate accounting systems, illustrating how perennial challenges demand continuous innovation.[7] These elements are reflected in a Kellogg curriculum that now includes a comprehensive social enterprise component, recognizing that the intersection of business, government and society will define the challenging new terrain for leaders whose skills will have to span parameters formerly distinct but now converging.

Today, the Kellogg School of Management continues to thrive, dedicating itself to producing leaders whose talents will drive critical social change in arenas ranging from health care to the environment. As Dean Jain noted: "Clearly, management leadership matters more than ever, which is why Kellogg will continue to produce a curriculum that prepares the next generation for success. And we will define this success by challenging students to achieve more and, indeed, to *be* more. An MBA education should engage a person's whole spirit, encouraging them to aspire to greatness in themselves, in their work, and in the community."

The words attributed to urban planner Daniel Burnham capture the vision of Dean Jain and the Kellogg School as it looks to the next 100 years, even while pausing to reflect on the last century of achievement, innovation and excellence: "Make no little plans; they have no magic to strike man's blood."

This Book's Goal

Capturing 100 years in the history of an institution as rich as the Kellogg School of Management is a daunting task. It is also one best considered in light of existing texts, including the fine and detailed effort of Michael W. Sedlak and Harold F. Williamson. Their 1983 book, *The Evolution of Management Education,* is an estimable survey of Northwestern University's contributions to business education up to that time. There is little value in retracing that book's steps in full, as readers interested in comprehensive enrollment figures or curricular minutiae, for instance, can find an abundance of valuable material in this earlier document.

However, that text grew out of Sedlak's doctoral dissertation and was, as might be expected, a chronicle shaped by the academic impetus of the authors. What I have endeavored to present here is a narrative that complements Sedlak and Williamson's, providing additional detail by accenting points that, in some cases, the earlier text did not, including more perspective on the personality and work of the commerce school faculty. That said, revisiting some key moments in the school's history, despite their inclusion in the 1983 book, is valuable and unavoidable. Included in this category are the school's founding as well as details associated with dismantling the school's undergraduate program in favor of a graduate curriculum in the 1960s.

There is also value in emphasizing the development of one discipline in particular that has played a major part in the Kellogg School's success and reputation—marketing—particularly since that field's evolution helpfully frames much of the larger changing business picture. The significance of figures ranging from early marketing professors, such as Fred E. Clark, to famous later figures, such as Philip Kotler, indicates how strongly Kellogg has influenced this field. Exploring some important midcentury assessments of the business school curriculum will demonstrate how certain criticisms (most notably leveled in surveys by the Ford Foundation and the Carnegie Corporation in 1959) helped shape the overall management education landscape since the late 1950s. Such a consideration naturally would include a review of the vaunted Managerial Economics and Decision Sciences (MEDS) Department, particularly its founding, an act that established the importance of analytical rigor at the school and would serve as a magnet to attract scholars throughout all Kellogg disciplines. Complementing MEDS (and developed about the same time) was the school's Organization Behavior Department, now known as Management and Organizations. It too produced remarkable benefits for the school, in terms of academics, reputation and actual culture. Beginning in the early 1970s, this department was central in enhancing the school's team-based learning model, a model that has since influenced nearly everyone else in management education.

In any case, the goal in writing this book has been to add to the existing historical narrative by providing new detail and considering the larger social context influencing the Kellogg School's development—and to do so in a style that engages the interested layperson as well as the curious academician. One way this text varies from its predecessor is in giving more room to the actual contributions of individual leaders associated with the school. In the earlier volume, primary figures such as marketing professor Fred Clark, to take one example, were mentioned only in passing, but here, I attempt to situate Clark and his contribution to the Kellogg School's history in proper context.

Most important, though, this book seeks to relate events not covered in the previous history of the school, having occurred after that text's publication. Some of the most exciting developments in Kellogg history have taken place since the 1980s, including the school's ascension into the top ranks. Meanwhile, the business world has continued changing in ways that place extraordinary demands on management educators. The Kellogg School has been meeting these needs while also helping lead management education's future.

Given the school's achievements to date, the accomplishments that will come in the next stage of the Kellogg School's journey will undoubtedly prove as fascinating and influential as anything seen thus far.

A typical scene in downtown Chicago circa 1905, near the location where
Northwestern's School of Commerce would open in October 1908.

Chapter 1

A MANAGEMENT LEADER
EMERGES

Chicago's vibrant commercial scene inspires Northwestern University's new commerce school to "broaden the horizon, increase the efficiency, and promote the progress of its students towards positions of greater responsibility and influence."

By 1900, the United States had become the world's commercial leader, leveraging the recent developments in mass production to manufacture nearly a third of the globe's consumer goods. Heavy industries, including oil and steel, had become enormously important, and transportation and communications advances had contributed to the rise of national markets, bringing previously isolated parts of the country into the larger, gradually more homogenous socioeconomic matrix. One indication of how quickly technology conquered distances could be seen in the railroads' expansion. Before 1871, some 45,000 miles of track crossed the United States; in the century's last three decades, the country added another 170,000 miles of rail service.[1]

This revolution brought increasing cultural, economic and geographic interdependence to a nation that had, since its birth, valued individualism above nearly all else.[2] Although clear benefits accrued as a result of these changes, complex social challenges, including racial and ethnic strife, demanded to be addressed and would significantly alter the country's identity.

In concert with these trends came the rise of big business—exemplified by vertically integrated conglomerates such as John D. Rockefeller's Standard Oil and Andrew Carnegie's Carnegie Steel Company, though not limited to ventures of this massive scale.[3] These entities created new workplace models, emphasizing speed and efficiency within a context of large-scale productivity. Standardization and greater mechanization became prominent. Whereas earlier workers often labored either as artisans, farmers or entrepreneurs, mass production began changing how America's commercial life functioned. In particular, these circumstances created demand for a new professional class—the managerial class—whose members were neither manual laborers nor owners of the enterprises they oversaw. These managers found themselves in a rapidly shifting environment that tested their abilities to adapt while using the limited assortment of tools then available. Frameworks to address business challenges were few, in part because only a handful of schools existed at the time to teach business in an academically rigorous way.

In 1902, it was this paucity that led Northwestern University's new president, 47-year-old Edmund Janes James, to declare: "The average business man is ignorant and inefficient and cowardly. He is helpless in a crisis." To counteract the problem, he advocated a business curriculum composed of courses in banking, accounting, finance, insurance and railroad management. He also proposed that adjunct lecturers, including members of the city's professional community, could join forces with full-time faculty members to deliver courses balanced in theory and practice. Among those supporting the president in this initiative were two professors from Northwestern's Department of Economics, Frederick S. Deibler and John Gray, who helped create a plan to establish the commerce school. The school would become a reality only later, in 1908, with the support of figures such as Earl Dean Howard, economics professor, and Seymour Walton, president of the Illinois Society of Certified Public Accountants and among the school's first adjunct faculty members drawn from the working world.[4]

James, a Jacksonville, Illinois, native born in 1855, studied at Northwestern and Harvard before earning his doctorate in 1877 at Germany's University of Halle. He had come to Northwestern from the University of Chicago, where, as professor of political economy, he had helped establish the College of Commerce and Politics in 1898. Prior to that, from 1883 until 1896, James had served on the faculty at the University of Pennsylvania's Wharton School of Business, where he was largely responsible for its early direction.[5] These experiences were predicated on his earlier responsibilities as principal of Evanston Township High School (1877–1879) and the Model High School in Normal, Illinois (1879–1883).[6]

James's complaint about the average businessman came on the heels of several economic panics, including that of 1896, which resulted in the failure of Chicago's National Bank of Illinois. Similar trouble struck in 1902 and would strike again in coming years. Soon after his arrival at Northwestern, James proposed a number of enhancements to the university's curriculum and facilities, including expanded offerings in education, engineering and business. He also presented several ideas to improve student life, such as building new residence halls, a dining hall, a student center and a chapel. After two years of efforts to raise funds for these plans, including an unsuccessful attempt to attract the philanthropy of Andrew Carnegie, who had begun turning much of his attention to giving away the fortune he had acquired as an industrialist,[7] James grew frustrated both with the meager results and with the time he was required to spend on "petty administrative matters rather than on building a 'new Northwestern.'"[8] When the University of Illinois offered him its presidency in 1904, he left Northwestern, later saying that he felt the opportunities to do "large things" were slipping away each year. His successor, interim president Thomas Franklin Holgate, did not display the same enthusiasm for building the School of Commerce. A professor of mathematics and dean of the College of Liberal Arts, Holgate mostly focused on the needs of his college. The university trustees, meanwhile, were concentrating their efforts on fund-raising to support the schools of law and medicine.[9]

But James's inclination to develop a commerce school at Northwestern proved prescient; Chicago was too important to lack such an educational resource.

The City of Big Shoulders Supports, and Needs, Business Education

Few places exemplified the commercial promise unfolding at the dawn of the twentieth century as vividly as Chicago did. At the middle of a continent, situated between the traditional industrial and banking centers of the East Coast and the still-young western frontier,[10] Chicago had grown with remarkable speed as a result of playing a central role in the nation's development. "Between 1850 and the 1920s, Chicago was transformed—or more accurately and actively, it transformed itself—from an earnest little regional trading node in the interior of the United States into the nation's second-largest city. Served only by the Galena and Chicago Union in 1850, the city was the greatest railroad center in the world by 1856."[11]

But Chicago offered more than railroads. Over that 70-year span, the city had a major part in a host of industries, including meatpacking, steel, iron, lumber, furniture and tool manufacture, as well as publishing, finance and wholesaling. The city's commercial life and its relentless, outsized ambitions inspired Carl Sandburg's famous homage that begins:

> Hog Butcher for the World,
> Tool Maker, Stacker of Wheat,
> Player with Railroads and the Nation's Freight Handler;
> Stormy, husky, brawling,
> City of the Big Shoulders

"Come and show me another city with lifted head singing so proud to be alive and coarse and strong and cunning," wrote Sandburg, adding that the city is a "tall bold slugger set vivid against the little soft cities" as it piles "job upon job."[12]

A few notable examples help establish the scale and scope of Chicago's commercial life and suggest why the School of Commerce was positioned to make a strong impact there. On Christmas Day in 1865, the city opened the Union Stock Yards, a development that eventually sprawled over a square mile, from 39th Street to 47th Street and from Halsted to Ashland. The yards would inform Sandburg's rough-hewn conception of the city and provide the infamous backdrop to *The Jungle*, Upton Sinclair's 1906 novel detailing the working conditions of immigrant laborers.[13] In 1872, Aaron Montgomery Ward established the first mail-order house at Clark and Kinzie. The company's inaugural catalog consisted of a single page, but the venture would eventually grow into a major business, thriving for nearly 100 years.[14] In 1885, the world's first skyscraper, the 9-story Home Insurance Building, appeared in Chicago at LaSalle and Adams streets, the first of many architectural marvels that would establish Chicago as a modern and cosmopolitan city in subsequent decades. The city also gave birth to the world's second elevated rail line, in 1892, joining New York, which had begun construction on its system in 1867 and started service the following year. And in 1907, Marshall Field's opened the largest department store in the world on State Street, replacing an earlier building with a new, 12-story edifice.

From its earliest days, beginning with its discovery in 1673 by explorers Jacques Marquette and Louis Jolliet, Chicago had repeatedly jumped hurdles to create itself, attracting those with entrepreneurial leanings—hardy souls who would brave the elements and run against the odds to build a world-class city out of little more than a reeking swamp.[15] It was hardly a foundation upon which to erect a metropolis, but the city would thrive, in part due to the old portage, a spit of marsh that extended some 10 miles between the Chicago River and a prairie waterway called the Des Plaines, from which traders ultimately could access the Mississippi River.

When it was incorporated as a town in 1833, Chicago boasted a population of only 350, making its growth over the next few decades stunning.[16] Officially becoming a city in 1837, Chicago attracted young, self-made individuals hoping to improve their economic and political prospects, often despite a lack of social pedigree. Among these were people like Gurdon Saltonstall Hubbard, an insurance underwriter and land speculator who first visited Chicago in a 50-foot freight canoe in 1818.[17] He remained influential in the city's development until his death in 1886. The city's first mayor (1837–1838), William Butler Ogden, arrived in Chicago as a real estate speculator, originally overseeing a $100,000 investment made by his brother-in-law Charles Butler—a purchase Ogden initially thought dubious given the primitive conditions he encountered, such as buildings set directly on the marsh, making sewers or cellars impossible and streets hopelessly muddy. In fact, only in 1855 did the city's drainage commission decree that structures henceforth would be built on grades of between four and seven feet above the river. This regulation helped somewhat, but another half century would pass before Chicago enjoyed something approximating proper sewage.

But Ogden, like Hubbard, could see past the initial impediments and soon discovered that the area offered promise to those willing to work hard and take risks. Such individuals would eventually become part of an unpolished "prairie aristocracy" that "admitted into its ranks anyone who managed to push his way to the top." For the members of this aristocracy, "money remained the one and only measure of acceptance. Blood and background counted for little, since so few members of the inner circle came from well-connected families."[18] (It must be said that a later public official, five-term mayor Carter Harrison [in office from 1879 to 1887], went to Chicago from Lexington, Kentucky, because he saw the city as a land of opportunity. Harrison, though popular with working-class people—as evidenced by the 200,000 mourners who paid respects at his casket in city hall after his assassination in 1893—was also accused of cultivating close ties with Chicago's vice lords, particularly those engaged in prostitution and gambling.)[19]

The vision of these early Chicagoans helped stimulate the city's population boom from an initial 350 people to nearly 4,500 in 1837 and then 1 million in 1890, making Chicago the third U.S. city to reach that mark. By 1908, the year Northwestern opened its commerce school, Chicago was home to some 2 million inhabitants, including an estimated 587,000 immigrants.[20] Many of these people had set out for the United States from Germany, Italy, Poland and Ireland. Nationally, some 8 million immigrants were living in the United States by the end of the twentieth century's first decade. In 1901, the growing numbers and socioeconomic conditions of the immigrants helped give rise to the Socialist Party. As the School of Commerce opened, ethnic and racial tensions were contributing to labor unrest in a context that had already been marked by violence: an alleged anarchist's bomb in the Haymarket Square Riot of 1886 had killed one police officer immediately, and seven others later died from their injuries. Precipitating the riot, labor unions had organized a strike three days earlier, calling for an eight-hour workday in the city. Some 80,000 people marched down Michigan Avenue in what became the first May Day parade. Over the next two days, 70,000 workers went on strike at more than a thousand factories. On May 3, a fight broke out at a picket line near the McCormick Harvesting Machine Company, and as a result, police killed four people and wounded several others. The Haymarket rally began as a peaceful reaction to these developments, but, sadly, it devolved into mayhem.[21]

Two decades had done little to assuage concerns that some similar conflagration might spark at any time. In fact, since the Haymarket Square Riot, the city had banned all anarchist rallies. Proposed lectures in Chicago by Emma Goldman, to be held in March, were officially prohibited by Mayor Fred Busse. Complicating matters further were the questionable circumstances surrounding the killing of alleged anarchist Lazarus Averbuch on March 2, 1908, in the home of Chicago's police chief, George Shippy.[22]

Such was the backdrop to the School of Commerce's founding. Despite labor and ethnic frictions, however, Chicago was undoubtedly the seat of much entrepreneurship and a vigorous working class that was ready to fuel such business. This dynamic could not but help influence the city's commercial growth and the development of the area's educational institutions that supported this growth.

"In establishing the School of Commerce, business men and educators are uniting to meet the urgent need for a broad and fundamental training for the business career," declared a July 1908 Northwestern University bulletin announcing the venture. These commercial and academic partners believed that "business . . . is rapidly acquiring, and ought to acquire, a recognized professional standing," necessitating training for practitioners that would raise standards of business efficiency "in the broadest and best sense of the word." The school's chief aim was to "broaden the horizon, increase the efficiency, and promote the progress of its students towards positions of greater responsibility and influence." Students would obtain an education at Northwestern that enabled them to "look beyond the routine duties . . . and grasp the broader principles upon which business success is founded."[23]

As if to underline the ways that business would shift, requiring the talents of sophisticated managers, the same year that saw the School of Commerce open also witnessed the founding of General Motors Corporation and the introduction of Henry Ford's Model T, which was priced at $825 and launched the mass-market automobile age. In 1908, the commercial and consumer finance company CIT was formed, and Congress created the precursor to the Federal Bureau of Investigation—a Justice Department branch designed to investigate corporate greed and organized labor. Advertising, too, soared to new heights, literally taking to the skies in a campaign that, for the first time, used aircraft (to promote a Broadway play). Business was booming, but it was becoming obvious that society needed talented managers to handle the increasingly complex business world.

Down from the Tower:
Academics and Practitioners Create a New Program

The committee planning the school stated that Northwestern could perform "no greater public service" than to train intelligent, civic-minded young men to understand and appreciate the social responsibility of business.[24]

Among those most influential in launching this endeavor were Willard Eugene Hotchkiss, a 38-year-old economics professor who would serve as the commerce school's first dean, and Northwestern University's president, Abram Winegardner Harris, a former director of the Jacob Tome Institute of Port Deposit, Maryland. Another key figure was Earl Dean Howard, a 1905 graduate of the University of Chicago doctoral program in economics who had collaborated with Hotchkiss as early as 1904, prior to the arrival of Harris in 1906.[25] The two had met with the interim university president, Thomas Holgate, but made little progress on the commerce school's plans.

Born in Amber, New York, in 1874, Hotchkiss earned his doctorate from Cornell University in 1905, building upon his 1897 undergraduate degree from the same institution. He was awarded a President Andrew D. White Fellowship for the 1902–1903 academic year and another fellowship for the next year. Before going to Northwestern in 1905, the professor of economics was a teacher and later assistant supervisor at George Junior Republic School in Freeville, New York, from 1897 to 1900. Between 1904 and 1905, he was an instructor in political science at the Wharton School of Finance and Commerce,[26] before being recruited to Northwestern by Professors Deibler and Gray, whose enthusiasm for the commerce school was also important to its creation.

Deibler would remain on the faculty at Northwestern until his retirement in 1942. Born in 1876 in Deputy, Indiana, Deibler began his academic career as a high school principal in Illinois after earning a bachelor's degree from Hanover College in 1900, another AB degree from Harvard in 1903, an AM from Harvard in 1904 and finally a doctorate from the University of Wisconsin in 1909. While working toward his doctorate, he served as instructor in history and economics at Northwestern, beginning in 1904. After 1905, he became assistant professor of economics, and in 1911, he was named assistant professor in the School of Commerce. The next year, he was promoted to associate professor, a post he held until his appointment with the commerce school ended in 1916; at that time, he became chairman of the Northwestern Department of Economics, an appointment he held until his retirement. Deibler also served as secretary-treasurer of the American Economic Association, and his text *Principles of Economics* was published in 1929, with a second edition appearing in 1936. In addition to his teaching, Deibler was influential as a mediator in the newspaper/printing, shipping and footwear industries. "His teaching inspired students to think for themselves—objectively and not selfishly. His healthy influence left a mark on students and associates alike."[27]

John Gray would leave Northwestern for the University of Minnesota in 1906, and his doing so created an opportunity for the university to hire Earl Dean Howard from the Wharton School. Prior to that, a 1904–1905 fellowship had taken Howard from the University of Chicago, where he was earning his doctorate,[28] to the University of Berlin,[29] where he completed his thesis on "The Cause and Extent of the Recent Industrial Progress of Germany" before returning to the United States as an instructor in banking and economics. In 1907, the 31-year-old scholar and Fayette, Ohio, native arrived at Northwestern as an assistant professor. Howard's thesis earned the inaugural Hart, Schaffner & Marx Prize (which awarded him $600) for distinguished economic essays, and it was published in 1907 by Houghton, Mifflin & Company. Tracing the transformation of Germany from little more than a medieval commercial state into a modern industrial power, Howard illustrated how a nation could quickly shake off a "feudal class despising trade" (in the words of Professor O. D. Skelton, who reviewed the book in the *Journal of Political Economy*). Howard would go on to play influential roles as a personnel mediator, including serving as vice president of labor relations and director for Hart, Schaffner & Marx from 1911 until 1931.[30] In 1918, he was also executive secretary of the U.S. Chamber of Commerce Bureau of Industrial Relations; from 1933 to 1934, he lent his abilities as deputy administrator of the Roosevelt administration's National Recovery Administration, part of the president's New Deal program to help Americans recover from the Great Depression.

Howard, along with Sidney Hillman,[31] president of the Amalgamated Clothing Workers of America, would prove central to helping resolve a massive strike by garment laborers in Chicago. Among other things, he helped negotiate an arbitration agreement with workers—eventually numbering as many as 8,000—at Hart, Schaffner & Marx, where the dispute had begun before spreading to other companies. Overall, some 40,000 workers struck throughout the city between September 22, 1910, and February 18, 1911.[32] Joseph Schaffner, an early benefactor to Northwestern and the School of Commerce, was a pioneer in the manufacture of ready-made garments for an emerging middle class, and his factories were large, helping Chicago produce about 15 percent of the nation's clothing for men. By the end of the nineteenth century, Chicago had become the second-largest production center for menswear (after New York), leveraging a manufacturing system that employed vast numbers of immigrants from the ethnically diverse city.[33] When labor strife hit Schaffner's facilities, he turned to Professor Howard and Northwestern for advice, saying: "The great trouble is that I don't really know my own men. I don't really know what is going on in my shops." Howard's investigations revealed that fair employment practices could be built upon "accurate knowledge and a common understanding" between management and labor. "When the original arbitration agreement in 1911 provided for 'a method for settlement of grievances, if any, in the future,' nobody had any conception of the important consequences which would flow from it," Howard recalled in a 1924 interview.[34]

A Christian Scientist and a man with a strong moral compass[35]—he once referred to World War I as "a great fermentation of the corruption of materialistic belief"[36]—Howard endeavored to bring management and labor together equitably. "As matters have stood for a number of years, each side, the union and the management, can afford to make very great efforts to preserve industrial peace; on both sides there is much to lose and little to gain by warfare," he wrote in a 1928 essay. "Therefore, it is worth while to make labor policy and administration a function equal in importance to any other in management." What's more, Howard elevated this managerial efficiency to a "social duty" that was "essential to prosperity and human welfare."[37] Along with Hotchkiss, Deibler and other professors and practitioners, he would help the School of Commerce create a strong portfolio of offerings in the areas of labor and employment management. By 1921, the school presented an array of classes taught by top faculty. Course titles included Howard's "Industrial Relations," which surveyed the organization of the labor department, dealing primarily with "fundamental principles underlying industrial relations," as well as "Trade Unionism," "Factory Management," "Personnel Administration," "Business Psychology" and "Sociology—Modern Social Reform Movements," among others. These one-credit-hour classes convened at the university's Loop building either on Saturday afternoons or during the evenings after work.[38]

Given his views, it is not surprising to discover that Howard, with Hotchkiss, continued "pounding away at the idea" of a commerce school immediately after Harris assumed the university presidency in September 1906.[39] In the new president, they found an able administrator and a kindred soul. A Philadelphia native born in 1858, Harris was an 1880 graduate of Wesleyan University who brought with him considerable teaching experience from that institution and from Dickenson Seminary; he also had served as assistant director of the U.S. Department of Agriculture and as president of Maine State College from 1893 until 1901, when he assumed leadership of the Tome Institute. A mathematician by early training, Harris studied in Berlin and Munich, developing expertise in political economy. During his five-year tenure at Tome, the school's objectives were clearly defined, its departments were coordinated and the founder's financial resources were channeled in ways that "won for the school a place among the great secondary schools of the country."[40]

To make a formal determination regarding the viability of a Northwestern business curriculum, which initially was to include both full- and part-time study, President Harris convened an exploratory committee in 1906. Members of the business community expressed greatest interest in a part-time evening program, leading Harris to request a second proposal from the committee that would articulate the specific benefits of the evening school. "In proposing a part-time evening school, the committee's basic objective had originally been to develop a program that would enhance Northwestern's reputation and increase its visibility by stressing the university's contributions to public service."

Hotchkiss was attuned to this sense of public-spiritedness. He believed the professional business student should master the fundamentals of organization and management, including functional subjects such as accounting and finance. But these elements, valuable as they were, were to be marshaled under yet another, overarching framework. "All of these studies would be pursued with constant reference to the fact that business is carried on in a community in which certain public policies are enforced and in recognition of the fact that business should conform to these policies and help to make them effective in contributing to public welfare," wrote Hotchkiss in 1918, reflecting on his tenure as dean of the commerce school.[41] Among the dean's publications reflecting this attitude were "Chicago Traction: A Study in Political Evolution," "Recent Phases of Chicago's Transportation Problem" and "Recent Trust Decisions and Business."[42] (The latter article included this balanced assessment, tacitly rebutting conventional laissez-faire economic theory: "It is possible to set forth certain definite favorable results of government trust activity. In the first place, the trust movement has been subjected to a large amount of publicity, the net result of which has been to break the spell of the trusts in the public mind. This publicity has made us realize . . . that the bureaucracy of capital may be as dangerous to national productivity and progress as a bureaucracy of public officials.")[43]

In their report, members of the president's committee stated that because of its location and resources, Northwestern would be "in a position . . . to assume absolute leadership . . . to meet the crying intellectual and moral needs of a highly developed industrial metropolitan community. No university in the land is, or can be, in a position to surpass her in this line of work; only a few can hope to equal her."

When these academicians solicited support for a commerce school from the Chicago business community—whose advice and financial backing they recognized as vital to the initiative's success—the professors found that many practitioners shared a desire to advance business education.[44] In fact, in late 1907, several of these men met informally for dinner in the Old Union Restaurant at 68 West Randolph Street,[45] followed by a session in the Northwestern University building in Chicago. Among these early proponents was Arch Wilkinson Shaw, editor and publisher of *System*, a business periodical. Like the others, Shaw expressed an interest in bringing an academic focus to business, without neglecting the challenges facing practitioners. To meet the intellectual needs of these professionals, albeit in an informal way rather than through a program that produced an academic credential, Howard was asked to lecture to them on the subject of finance. These evening discussions proved sufficiently popular that the "student" ranks grew, with more and more practitioners clamoring for seminars in accounting, practical economics, commercial law and management.[46] According to Hotchkiss's recollections, "Howard and Shaw were conjuring up a revolution in university training for business."[47]

Soon, Seymour Walton introduced his accounting course, and then a formal finance offering appeared. Business leaders from throughout Chicago attended these sessions, their enthusiasm suggesting a real need for an organized commerce school in the area.

To refine their conception for such a school and to obtain additional practitioner insights, the Northwestern faculty continued reaching out to professionals in a variety of industries. They met with members of the Chicago Association of Commerce, the Illinois Society of Certified Public Accountants and the American Institute of Banking, among others. As they did, their plan sparked interest in more people, including the cofounder of Hart, Schaffner & Marx.

At Northwestern, Joseph Schaffner had already financed a scholastic award named after his firm;[48] however, he expressed concern that the research associated with the prize might do more to develop teachers rather than business leaders. To create what he believed would be a more beneficial balance, Schaffner thought a school that melded practice with theory would prove invaluable. So strong was his conviction that he attracted the interest of many prominent corporate executives, such as members of the Chicago Association of Commerce—including its president, Richard C. Hall, a well-known manufacturer. Among the others were Harry A. Wheeler, banker and president of the Credit Clearing House; L. W. Messer, general secretary of the Chicago Central Young Men's Christian Association; John W. Scott, of the retailer Carson, Pirie, Scott & Co.; and Stephen Tyng Mather, a newspaperman turned chemist and vice president of a firm of industrial chemists. (Mather would serve as assistant to the U.S. secretary of the interior from 1915 to 1917 and then became director of the National Park Service in 1917, a year after Congress passed the Organic Act that created the service.)[49]

Schaffner's belief in the importance of the university's role in training professional managers led him not only to support the School of Commerce with his leadership and philanthropy but also to join Northwestern's Board of Trustees in 1910.[50] Schaffner's importance to Northwestern was significant. Upon his death in April 1918, the School of Commerce faculty issued a condolence letter to his spouse that cited his "friendly counsel and the ideals for which he stood in business relations." Schaffner's appreciation of business education "as a necessary step in elevating his vocation" was described as a "constant inspiration" to the school's administration and professors. The condolence concluded: "The name of Joseph Schaffner will always be revered in this community as a man who stood for justice in all his business relations."[51]

One particularly powerful way in which Schaffner, along with several dozen other community and business leaders, agreed to facilitate the School of Commerce's creation was by entering into an arrangement with the university to serve as the school's "guarantors." The plan of organization for the school indicated that the guarantors, "though an Executive Committee, shall supervise the finances of the School of Commerce . . . authorize all expenditures" and review all financial statements annually. Executive members included President Harris as chairman ex officio, Richard Hall, Schaffner, and Messer. In addition, several members from the Illinois Society of Certified Public Accountants served on the board, among them John Alexander Cooper, vice president of the society; Allen R. Smart, manager of Barrow, Wade, Guthrie & Company; J. Porter Joplin, of Buchanan, Walton and Joplin; and William A. Dyche, Northwestern University business manager.

Another influential business leader involved with the School of Commerce as a guarantor was Edward Burgess Butler, cofounder of the department store wholesaler

Butler Brothers. Butler also served the school as a "special lecturer," one of a dozen listed for the 1908–1909 academic year. Born the son of a retail grocer in Lewiston, Maine, in 1853, Butler would, at age 16, build on the skills he learned in his father's store and secure a position as "bundle boy" in a wholesale dry goods firm. Over time, he advanced through the organization, becoming a traveling salesman throughout New England until he founded his own firm in 1877 with his brother, George. Originally located in Boston, the enterprise grew to include locations in Chicago, St. Louis, Minneapolis and Dallas. A landscape artist, Butler displayed his own works under an assumed name in 1908, and he would eventually donate 23 masterpieces by the American landscape painter George Innes to the Art Institute of Chicago. An 1892 biography of Butler called him "one of Chicago's most charitably wealthy men"; he erected a building containing a gallery, a library and a reading room and donated it to Hull House, the civic center created in 1889 by Jane Addams and Ellen Gates Starr to aid the city's poor.[52] "One man has enthusiasm for 30 minutes, another for 30 days, but it is the man who has it for 30 years who makes a success of his life," Butler was known to say. Along with fellow guarantor Adolphus C. Bartlett, president of Hibbard, Spencer, Bartlett & Company, he was also part of the Commercial Club of Chicago's committee in support of the famous 1909 Plan of Chicago (better known as the Burnham Plan, after its chief architect, Daniel Burnham). The plan was an ambitious initiative to beautify Chicago and, in the words of its authors, create a "well-ordered and convenient city" as a means to counter the "chaos incident to rapid growth, and especially to the influx of people of many nationalities without common traditions or habits of life."

Other noteworthy guarantors included Elijah Watt Sells, an accountant born in Muscatine, Iowa, in 1858. Sells had been selected by a joint congressional commission in 1893 to effect a revision of the U.S. government's accounting system, with the mandate to make public business more streamlined and efficient—an undertaking considered among the most extensive and important to date. After concluding the two-year process, Sells established his own accountancy and later, from 1906 to 1907, was president of the American Institute of Public Accountants. Serving the commerce school as guarantors with Sells were David Robertson Forgan, a Scottish banker who was president of National City Bank of Chicago and wrote about his industry in publications such as "Banking as a Profession," and Joseph DeFrees, a 50-year-old attorney from Elkhart County, Indiana, who had arrived in Chicago in 1888. DeFrees went on to establish his own law firm and would serve as director of the Chicago Legal Aid Society from 1912 to 1913, while president of the Windermere Company. In 1914, he was president of the Chicago Association of Commerce.

Offering academic support inside the classroom, special lecturers, in addition to Butler, included: Frederick Adrian Delano, president of the Wabash Railroad Company; John Henry Gay, professor of economics and political science at the University of Minnesota; C. F. Hulburd, president of the Elgin National Watch Company; George B. Caldwell, manager of the bond department at the American Trust & Savings Bank; Joseph French Johnson, dean of the school of commerce at New York University; L. Wilbur Messer, general secretary of the Chicago Central Young Men's Christian Association; George E. Roberts, president of Commercial National Bank and director of the U.S. Mint from 1898 to 1907; William A. Scott, director of the commerce course at the University of Wisconsin; Arch Shaw, editor and publisher; Towner K. Webster, president of the Webster Manufacturing Company; and Harry A. Wheeler, chairman of the executive committee of the Association of Commerce.

There was also a financial burden assumed by the guarantors, although it was relatively modest and the school soon was self-sustaining. Hotchkiss noted that the total demand on the guarantors did not exceed $4,000 during the school's first three years, although the group was prepared to deliver up to $5,000 if necessary. "The direct financial contribution of the guarantors, therefore, was perhaps the smallest element of their support," wrote Hotchkiss in 1913. "Of far greater importance was the benefit of their counsel and the facilities offered by several of them for securing business material. Their moral support, moreover, was a large influence in bringing students to the school."[53]

Hotchkiss recalled the impetus for the enterprise: "The immediate purpose in establishing the Northwestern University School of Commerce was to give in evening courses an opportunity for capable and ambitious employees to pursue business subjects from the point of view of foundation principles. . . . An ultimate and more fundamental purpose was to develop, as rapidly as resources and the advance of business science would permit, a course for students not yet employed, with standards and professional aims comparable with those of the older professional schools."[54]

Unlike medicine and law, for example, business had few rules to establish conduct among practitioners or frameworks to govern strategy, as perhaps evidenced by a number of banking and business crises that occurred in the last decade of the nineteenth century and into the twentieth century.

To produce graduates capable of leading increasingly complex organizations, the School of Commerce developed its educational policy based on three key aims— "to give students a comprehensive, many-sided survey of business facts and experience; . . . to develop a power of accurate analysis which will prepare the student to think complicated business problems through to the end; [and] to maintain an atmosphere in which large business problems will be regarded in a public-spirited way."[55]

Indeed, from the very first day, students, faculty and the business community demonstrated an auspicious enthusiasm that would serve the school well in coming years.

"Where Hast Thou Wandered, Gentle Gale, to Find the Perfumes Thou Dost Bring?"—William C. Bryant

The school's location, in downtown Chicago at Lake and Dearborn streets, also proved greatly beneficial, particularly as students were attending classes part-time after working during the day in offices around the Windy City. "The university's facilities for advanced work in commerce" were ideally situated in the "heart of the commercial center of the country,"[56] contended the school's advocates.

Down the block from the school, at the corner of Randolph and Dearborn, stood the Real Estate Board building, an eight-story Italianate structure that contained a number of offices and businesses, including a cigar shop, a barber's shop and grocers. Just around the corner, at 24–28 West Randolph, was Hyde and Behman's Music Hall, a vaudeville house that had been constructed on the same location as the Iroquios Theater after the Iroquios caught fire on December 30, 1903, during a matinee.[57] The Northwestern University Building was also a short walk from City Hall, the public library, the Art Institute, Marshall Field's and other State Street merchants. A block away was South Water Street and its markets, filling the sidewalks with all manner of goods and produce. The street hugged the south side of the Chicago River and brimmed with activity as merchants brought their wares in wagons and on carts. The entire area was ringed by an elevated rapid transit system completed in 1897, connecting the outlying neighborhoods with the downtown area. North of the city, in Evanston, a new rail line, the Northwestern Elevated, had been completed in May 1908, connecting the suburb with the Loop.

Many believe that Chicago earned its Windy City moniker in 1890 thanks to an insulting column by Charles Dana, editor of the *New York Sun*, criticizing the city's vociferous politicians and civic boosters during a bidding war between the two metropolises to host the World's Columbian Exposition of 1893. Chicago would win that contest thanks in significant part to support from business leaders.[58]

Evidence suggests an earlier usage of the city's nickname, dating at least to 1876 and linked to the locale's meteorological conditions,[59] giving the name wider currency during the 1880s when efforts to promote tourism highlighted the "refreshing lake breezes of the great summer resort of the West."[60] But the story persists that Chicagoans' bold municipal entrepreneurship—and their willingness to boast about their efforts to rebuild bigger and better after the great fire of 1871 destroyed the central business district[61]—marked Chicago as blustery in more ways than one.

On October 6, 1908, almost 37 years to the day after the famous fire, Chicago was living up to its reputation. A 30-mile-per-hour fresh wind swept out of the west during the afternoon. Newspapers raised concerns about political tensions in the Balkan Peninsula, and the seeds of what would, four years later, become the First Balkan War and bring the dissolution of the Ottoman Empire had already been planted. TURKS INCENSED; WAR SEEMS NEAR read a headline in the *Chicago Daily Tribune* that day. Locally, the media gave some attention to the city's two baseball teams, each battling for a postseason berth. On the Evanston campus, the Northwestern football team was scrimmaging in preparation for a contest against the school's alumni squad. And later that day, Northwestern University would make news of its own by launching the School of Commerce, an ambitious venture that would prove enduring.

The day's unseasonably mild weather had cooled only slightly from a high of 74 degrees as 165 part-time business students streamed into the old Tremont House Hotel at Lake and Dearborn streets in Chicago that evening. Horse-drawn carts and carriages filled the business district. Streetcar tracks encroached on the narrow sidewalk around the six-story building purchased by Northwestern in 1902, during the tenure of interim president Daniel Bonbright,[62] to house the dental, law and pharmacy schools.[63] The building, acquired for $800,000, stood on the spot where the Frink, Walker & Company Stagecoach Office was established in 1837 and where Abraham Lincoln and Stephen Douglas addressed crowds in 1858 from the balcony of what was then a hotel, one of the most prestigious in the city but eventually among the fire's casualties. From the ashes, in 1873, arose the Dickey Building, once the temporary quarters for the Chicago Public Library. Now the building would serve as a training ground for modern business, too.

A day earlier, university and School of Commerce leaders, along with students and members of the Chicago business community, had formally convened to mark the school's launch at 8 p.m. in the Northwestern Building's Booth Hall. They were celebrating the inauguration of an institution whose central premise was that business could and should be pursued scientifically, while at the same time retaining a healthy respect for actual commercial circumstances. The curriculum would serve part-time evening students, rather than full-time scholars, and focus on giving young practitioners the refined skills they needed to advance in their careers.[64] Many of the commerce school's early students, in their midtwenties, worked as accountants or bookkeepers,[65] or else they worked in industries such as banking or as clerical support. By 1915, the commerce students' occupations were segmented by the school's administration into four categories: "clerical positions of routine character," "clerical positions of responsible character," "positions of professional character" and "managerial positions." The majority of students (50.7 percent) held routine clerical posts, such as ledger clerk, stenographer or general clerk, but a significant number (38.6 percent) held "responsible" clerical occupations, such as general bookkeeper, sales, accounting and auditing, "credit man" or buyer. Much smaller numbers of students held positions such as high school instructor, office manager or general manager. More students, nearly 10 percent, identified themselves as working in marketing roles. The eclectic nature of the commerce school's student body was perhaps best evidenced by the fact that, in 1915, it included a "dress maker" and a "beef cutter" alongside an attorney, a reporter, a nurse, a company president and a vice president.[66] The vast majority of these students came from Chicago and its suburbs or elsewhere in Illinois, although by 1915, the school had attracted some international notice and had, for example, more than a dozen students from Russia.[67]

Upon paying the $75 annual tuition (in 1908) and signing a certificate attesting to good moral character, along with a statement detailing his experience and preparedness for academics, a student could enroll in the School of Commerce, determining whether to pursue a path leading to the diploma of commerce or simply to attend classes on an ad hoc basis. Students satisfactorily completing study in the evening program—which ran from 7 p.m. to 9 p.m. three nights a week over eight months for four years (or four nights a week for three years), working toward a total of 48 semester hours—would earn the diploma. Initially, however, few students saw the value in completing the diploma course: only 78 students did so between 1911 and 1917, with most others interested only in attending a handful of classes that would improve their immediate professional lives.[68] To be sure, early print advertisements for the School of Commerce accentuated the financial opportunities that business study could afford students, who, on average, garnered about $450 a year in salary. A typical newspaper pitch from 1910 unabashedly framed the situation:

· YOU EARN?

Is it $12.00, $15.00 or $20.00 a week? What are your chances of earning more than $25.00 a week? Are you worth more?

Do you know that an expert accountant earns from $1,500 to $6,000 a year? A superintendent, foreman or manager earns from $2,000 to $10,000?

Do you know that you have this opportunity to make yourself an expert accountant, or a business specialist—a man trained in the most advanced business methods?

Do you want to qualify for those positions higher up—where men are scarce?

To know how—send us your name on a postal.

Given such financial considerations, it was not unusual for some students to take one or two classes and then "find themselves unable to carry the required work and so drop to the classification of special students."[69] Indeed, 1911 is the first year the School of Commerce produced graduates who earned the diploma, and only seven names are listed in the commencement announcement as having achieved that distinction.[70] Subsequent years saw little increase in these numbers: diplomas were granted in the single digits until 1914, when 16 were bestowed; the number was the same in 1915.[71] Although one woman was among those registered for courses in finance and accounting at Northwestern for the 1907–1908 academic year (before the School of Commerce opened), it was not until 1911 that the school could claim female enrollment, with 23 women listed on the registrar's roll. The number of female students would remain modest during the school's first decade, with 32 women enrolled in 1912, 35 the following year and 42 in 1914; a similar trend continued until 1918, when women accounted for 172 of the school's total student enrollment of 1,016. In 1914, the first female graduate, Flora Alfaretta Voorhees,[72] was granted the diploma of commerce.

In addition to Northwestern president Abram Harris, guests at the inaugural ceremony for the School of Commerce included L. A. Goddard of the Fort Dearborn National Bank of Chicago; Professor Joseph French Johnson, dean of the New York University School of Commerce and Finance; Professor J. H. Gray of the University of Minnesota; Edward M. Skinner, manager of Wilson Brothers, member of the school's Board of Guarantors and chairman of the Chicagoland Chamber of Commerce in 1909;[73] and John A. Cooper of the Illinois Society of Certified Public Accountants, a member of the Board of Guarantors' Executive Committee. Following several addresses by these guests, the school hosted an informal reception for prospective students and their friends.

Both academicians and practitioners seemed to understand the value their counterparts brought to the endeavor, although at least one speaker, Dean Johnson, argued more strenuously for the importance of theoretical frameworks to advance the fledgling business school. "A science must be developed and learned by thinking, not by doing," Johnson told those assembled, his words recorded by the *Chicago Daily Tribune* the next day.

Those who saw optimal benefit arising from a combination of academic and professional insights—including the 56 Chicago business leaders whose names appeared on the school's Board of Guarantors—did not universally share Johnson's view. Yet Johnson, like Edmund James, could be forgiven his zeal for establishing commercial principles, particularly given yet another financial panic in October 1907. That panic was initiated by a run on the Knickerbocker Trust Company in New York, and it lasted into December. Several Wall Street businesses and broker-ages went bankrupt, and stock market prices plummeted as the nation's banks were assailed by depositors seeking their money. Banks in Chicago were also seriously affected.[74]

"The laws of business are as relentless as the laws of nature," said Johnson, who was also among the school's coterie of special lecturers during its inaugural year. A Harvard graduate who had studied in Germany, he traced the nation's economic panics in part to "inadequate banking and unscientific business systems" and pre-dicted even more perilous economic times within five years if "the men in power do not master the science of business and the science of banking." To his mind, theory rather than practice would have to guide the development of essential commercial frameworks, and the times gave urgency to this mission.

Urgency would prove a stimulus, rather than a deterrent, to the young com-merce school's ambitions. The exhilaration of meeting challenges head-on by using a combination of intelligence and midwestern grit would inform much of what the Northwestern scholars and students would achieve over coming decades. And in contradistinction to Johnson's view, many members of the Chicago business world were prepared to offer their resources—both financial and intellectual—to ensure the new school balanced theory with practice.

Indeed, the commerce school's mission, as articulated in its July 1908 bulletin announcing the new course of studies, practically spelled out the importance of bringing academics and practitioners together. The school would try "to meet the needs of those men who desire to enlarge their opportunities by systematic study." This goal, driven by the demand for greater business efficiency—in part a result of increased mechanization and the advent of "scientific management"—would be met by providing students with the tools to "see business problems in all their relations." Many of the first courses focused on the technical, functional aspects of business operations, culminating in the granting of the commerce diploma. It would be another four years before the school offered a five-year course of study leading to the bachelor of business administration (BBA) degree. The BBA would be built on two years of liberal arts study followed by three years of evening courses at the downtown facilities.

Of the early supporters, Arch Shaw is noteworthy for advocating, with Dean Hotchkiss, the expansion of the commerce curriculum into a full-time undergraduate program on the Evanston campus in 1911. A good friend of Hotchkiss's, Shaw had returned to Chicago that year from Harvard Business School, where he had been auditing courses; he particularly enjoyed those of Professor F. W. Taussig,[75] who was teaching advanced economic theory—content that would influence Shaw's subsequent marketing writing. Shaw was intrigued by the academic proposal as well as other ideas, such as the one Hotchkiss introduced in May to bridge theory and practice by bringing the real-world experiences of practitioners into the classroom in the form of a textbook—a strategy that bore some similarities to the case method that Shaw would help create at Harvard about the same time.[76] It would be nearly a decade, however, before the full-time program became a reality (in 1919, during the tenure of the school's third dean, Ralph E. Heilman), as the trustees and President Harris were unconvinced of its financial viability—despite a pledge by Joseph Schaffner to contribute $5,000 per annum for five years, provided that $20,000 in additional funds were raised each year. Instead, the trustees in 1912 approved the creation of a five-year curriculum leading to the bachelor of business administration degree.

Something of a compromise from the more ambitious program Hotchkiss intended, the BBA regimen nevertheless was designed to provide the young businessperson with the insights and training that would solidify his or her professional standing. Candidates for the course of studies would complete a two-year liberal arts program, with a business focus, in Evanston. Then, they would pursue three years of full-time evening study in business administration, being awarded a bachelor of science (BS) degree by the College of Liberal Arts at the conclusion of their fourth year.[77] The first graduate of the School of Commerce to earn this distinction was David Himmelblau, in 1914, although he already had earned a diploma in commerce in 1911 after graduating from the State University of Iowa with a bachelor's degree in 1909. The 25-year-old Dubuque, Iowa, native had joined the commerce school as an accounting instructor in 1913, teaching a class on cost accounting and working closely with faculty peer Arthur Andersen, who arrived in 1909, to produce a multivolume work in accounting that would eventually find wide use at universities. Himmelblau would work his way up to full professor at Northwestern by 1919, serving as chair of its Accounting Department from 1922 until 1952, while also starting his own firm in 1922 and publishing a number of respected texts, including

Fundamentals of Accounting (1924), *Principles of Accounting* (1924), *Advanced Auditing* (1928) and *Financial Investigations* (1936). He retired from teaching in 1955, receiving the university's Merit Award in 1952 for his accomplishments and services.

For his part, Shaw, born in 1876 in Jackson, Michigan, brought enthusiasm and educational insights that proved helpful to the school's overall mission. He saw the value in establishing and understanding frameworks to practical experiences, such as those he had been documenting in his publications *Factory* and *System: The Magazine of Business*, which began as a company newsletter for the office furniture venture he cofounded at age 23 in 1899 with L. C. Walker, the Shaw-Walker Furniture Company of Chicago. He "devoted himself . . . to advancing the interchange of ideas among businessmen, who, he felt, were retarding business progress by the narrow isolation of their individual interests and experiences."[78] Shaw would step away from the business in 1903 to establish a publishing enterprise that produced books on salesmanship and management, eventually selling the concern to McGraw-Hill Company in 1928. A year later, McGraw-Hill launched *Business Week* magazine, inspired by Shaw's earlier publications. Despite being a college dropout, Shaw interrupted a successful publishing career in 1910 to investigate the "academic cloisters" in Cambridge, Massachusetts, demonstrating a natural curiosity to bridge theory and practice, especially in areas of economics and marketing.[79] He was among those who influenced the way business schools, including Northwestern's, approached marketing studies. After his 1910–1911 stint as a lecturer at Harvard, he would publish on the subject of "marketing functions." His 1912 article entitled "Some Problems in Market Distribution" drew upon his "laboratory method," which included direct observation, statistical data and historical analysis—what today might be considered part of an ethnographic approach.[80]

The insights of Shaw and other early supporters, combined with the vision of Northwestern's faculty and administrators, helped create a valuable curriculum for students, even from the school's beginning.

Early Curriculum and Faculty

A total of six classes were offered in the School of Commerce's initial year, presenting four subjects: economics, finance, accounting and business law. Of these, accounting proved the most popular, followed by business law and then finance, all with enrollments ranging from 110 to 165 students. Economics garnered a comparatively modest 78 students in the 1908–1909 academic year.[81] Faculty members numbered five—one full professor, one assistant professor and three lecturers.

Economics professors Earl Dean Howard and Frederick S. Deibler were accompanied by Seymour Walton, Henry G. Phillips and Alfred William Bays. Walton and Phillips lectured on accounting, and Bays, a 1904 graduate of Northwestern's School of Law, brought his expertise in commercial law into the classroom. The school's initial enrollment by the end of the first year stood at 255, exceeding expectations.

Indeed, as Hotchkiss recalled,[82] the early curriculum of the school remained a work in process, and the administration's initial design sought to establish academic underpinnings that diverged as little as possible from those of other schools in the university.

"[A] greater part of the material for teaching business proper was still to be assembled and . . . methods of instruction had still to be worked out," the dean reflected in 1913. He also noted the faculty's concern from the beginning with promoting extracurricular activities as a way of attracting students and developing loyal alumni, a particular challenge in a part-time program, for, as Hotchkiss observed, "the esprit de corps characteristic of day students develops more slowly among men who come together for evening sessions only."[83]

Of the overarching curricular approach, Hotchkiss noted: "We were not inclined at the start to emphasize too strongly the 'practical' or 'fact' side of courses, or, as teachers, to disturb any more than necessary our moorings with general college work and college standards." Such an agenda, said the dean, meant that the school's faculty and staff would come mostly from a pool of "university-trained men."

However, the practical world was hardly omitted from consideration. Another goal from the school's inception was to encourage camaraderie among the students and between students and instructors. This objective not only created a desirable collegiality and stimulating culture but also enabled faculty members to gain a better understanding of what skills and tools students were seeking in order to advance their professional lives. Coincidentally, this knowledge also proved helpful in making clear the needs of employers in the larger business community.

"From our standpoint the service a university can render in assembling facts and in describing through class instruction the processes of business appears of comparatively little value except as the facts illustrate principles and as the principles in turn furnish the basis for a practical rule of action," wrote Hotchkiss.

So, from the start, commerce school faculty members refused to be trapped in academe's ivory tower but instead contributed their talents in ways that effected change by solving real business challenges. Extraordinary scholars soon enlarged the initial faculty numbers. Among these luminaries was Northwestern University professor Walter Dill Scott. Trained as a psychologist—practically at the dawn of that field—Scott was a pathbreaking researcher who applied psychology to business practices, including advertising and personnel selection. The future president of Northwestern shared this knowledge in courses on advertising and in his seminal textbooks, joining the commerce school in 1909 and immediately helping expand the academic offerings.[84]

Indeed, despite few early graduates and the practical concerns of those enrolled in the school, courses increased each year in the school's first decade, indicating the administrators' long-term vision to create a portfolio that met the emerging demands faced by business professionals as well as the expectations of increasingly ambitious second- and third-year students. The number of courses jumped from 6 initially to 13 in 1909 with the addition of offerings that included a psychology class taught by Scott and John Lee Mahin, an advertising executive.[85] This class helped students understand and frame the psychology of salesmanship, building on Scott's detailed research that incorporated considerations of human perception, association of ideas, emotions and appeals to customer sympathy and the power of suggestion. In fact, Dean Hotchkiss cited Scott's 1909 psychology course as "a signal that this school was headed away from the path of a trade school into that of an institution of learning. For this reason psychology had a significance in those early years even beyond that given to it by President Scott's outstanding personality and his great personal contribution."[86]

Born in 1869 in Cooksville, Illinois, the son of a manufacturer and farmer, Scott earned an undergraduate degree from Illinois State Normal School in 1891 and then a bachelor's degree from Northwestern in 1895. He attended McCormick Theological Seminary between 1895 and 1898, before pursuing his doctorate in psychology and educational administration at the University of Leipzig, Germany, one of the oldest universities in Europe. In his writings, he noted the importance of avoiding "chance, luck, haphazard undertakings . . . rule-of-thumb action" in favor of "theories, systems, ideals, and imagination," since the expense and competition confronting business professionals had resulted in "the great liability of failure," which in turn had "awakened the advertising world to the pressing need for some basis of assurance in its haphazard undertakings."[87]

This conviction about the role and benefit of scientific frameworks appeared throughout Scott's writings, including his *Contribution to the Psychology of Business* (1923), where he explored various means (competition, loyalty, concentration, wages, etc.) to increase human efficiency. Writing during a time that saw remarkable expansion in production's technological means, Scott nevertheless realized that "as the functions and limitations of machinery have become clearer in recent years, business men have generally recognized the importance of the human factor in making and marketing products." Furthermore, he believed that the time had arrived "when a man's knowledge of his business, if the larger success is to be won, must embrace an understanding of the laws which govern the thinking and acting of the men who make and sell his products as well as those others who buy and consume them."[88]

Although it was not explicitly a "marketing" course, Scott's applied psychology class provided significant insight into an area of fundamental concern for the emerging marketing specialists: consumer motivation and wants. His writings at the time presented a sophisticated and indeed prescient awareness of ideas and trends that only decades later would emerge fully in marketing. Scott ranked ideas with the "greatest suggestive power" as those witnessed through others' actions, but he noted that advertisements seen frequently enough were "difficult to distinguish in their force" from ideas suggested by friends or via word of mouth. In understanding the "social service of advertising," Scott also may have anticipated a powerful marketing trend that would transform the discipline some 60 years later in the research of Northwestern marketing scholars Philip Kotler and Sidney Levy: they introduced the then-radical ideas that "everybody markets," not just corporations and, further, that marketing could serve as a useful public service when applied to such efforts as antilitter or antismoking campaigns. Scott seemed to understand, early on, the power of advertising to shape public opinion. "The best advertising campaigns of to-day are founded on the assumption that the confidence of the public can be won by service rendered and when secured is the business man's most valuable asset," he wrote. "Modern advertising has the important and difficult task of overcoming the prejudice created by the exploiters of the past generation and perpetuated by the few disreputable advertisers of the present time."[89]

Scott's teaching and research would lay a foundation for later courses in marketing, such as that introduced in the 1912–1913 academic year by Arthur E. Swanson, an economist educated at the University of Illinois (he earned his doctorate in 1911), or those delivered by economist Fred Emerson Clark, who would, upon joining the Northwestern faculty in 1919, help pioneer the marketing field.[90]

Other courses introduced at the School of Commerce in 1909 included a business English class, another focused on resources and trade, a transportation class, and 2 insurance courses. Additional offerings in these categories increased the total number of classes to 15 for the 1910–1911 school year. The following year, the school introduced 2 foreign language classes and 1 course on organization and management—an offering that would prove sufficiently popular to encourage the school to add 4 more sections in 1912, when total course offerings rose to 24. By 1915, the school's robust academic life was evidenced by the existence of 12 departments and some 40 classes, including a new statistics offering and the continuation of a course in public speaking, first presented during the 1912 school year.[91]

Later, Dean Hotchkiss would reflect upon the time from 1900 until 1918 as a period of discovery for commerce schools as they learned that "there are certain fundamental principles which are alike for all lines of business . . . substituting the principle of likeness for diversity as the starting-point of business analysis." This understanding, he noted, would have "far-reaching consequences not only for education and research but for management as well."[92]

Among the courses consistently attracting the most student attention during the commerce school's early years was accounting: some 165 students enrolled in this class in 1908, a number that rose to 202 in 1909 and 335 in 1910. By 1914, 529 students were enrolled in accounting, an increase that the administration noted "emphasizes the importance which the School places on the more general courses in its curriculum."[93] Also popular was business law, with 152 students in 1908, increasing to 237 by 1914.

In the same year that the prodigious Scott joined the commerce school faculty, so too did Arthur Andersen, the future accounting giant. The son of Norwegian immigrants, Andersen exemplified the indomitable spirit of Chicago, a "city of dreamers and doers."[94] He began his career working as a mail boy during the day and taking classes at night. Orphaned at 16, he become the youngest certified public accountant in Illinois at the age of 23, after graduating in 1908 from the University of Illinois. From 1912 until 1922, he was an accounting professor at Northwestern, helping establish the new profession and, among other things, devising its first centralized training program.[95] Before founding his own accounting firm on West Monroe Street in 1913 at the age of 28, he worked for a Chicago accounting business and served as controller for the Schlitz Brewing Company in Milwaukee, commuting to teach his evening classes at Northwestern. In 1927, he would be elected to the Northwestern University Board of Trustees. Like Shaw, Andersen demonstrated a faith in education as the foundation for developing business-related disciplines, and he had a reputation for generously committing himself to educational and civic organizations. Andersen's mother had taught him to "think straight, talk straight," advice he used to build a legendary accountancy. During an early lecture at the School of Commerce, he told students, "To preserve the integrity of the [accounting] reports, the accountant must insist upon absolute independence of judgment and action." Andersen famously displayed this attitude in an early dealing with a railroad client who, in 1914, demanded the accountant approve a corporate ledger with suspicious numbers. Andersen refused, losing the client but building a reputation for ethical conduct as he advanced his firm's goal of "designing and installing . . . new systems of financial and cost accounting and organization."[96]

Another influential faculty member, economist and statistician Horace Secrist, joined the commerce school in 1912, having earned a doctorate at the University of Wisconsin in 1909. Among the 32-year-old professor's first tasks was developing a transportation course that would analyze the history and impediments associated with the U.S. distribution system. Subsequently, Secrist was asked to create a program in statistical analysis in 1915, at which point his transportation courses were assumed by Homer B. Vanderblue, a Northwestern alumnus who returned to his alma mater as an assistant professor after earning a doctorate in economics at Harvard.[97] Vanderblue would eventually serve as the commerce school's fifth dean, his tenure extending from 1939 to 1949, during which time he would advance the school's liberal arts focus rather than indulging a curriculum of technical specialization. A fellow Harvard economics doctorate, Ralph E. Heilman, joined Vanderblue at Northwestern in 1916, as a professor of social science and economics. From 1919 until 1937, Heilman would lead the School of Commerce as its third dean, introducing several important advancements, including establishing a full-time undergraduate program on the Evanston campus.[98]

Secrist would lead Northwestern's Bureau of Business Research upon its creation in 1919, an endeavor that Dean Heilman regarded as one of the most significant activities ever undertaken by the school.[99] The bureau was the nation's second such institution (Harvard had organized one earlier) and was tasked with conducting studies on business principles and practices, using data analytics. Results could also be used in classroom study. Among the early subjects that the bureau investigated were the Franklin Typothetae, a Chicago printer, and Hart, Schaffner & Marx. Findings from the investigation of the latter entity, conducted in tandem with the National Association of Retail Clothiers and with the support of the firm at a cost of $50,000, were subsequently published in six volumes, offering insight into how merchants would control prices and improve distribution.[100]

A rigorous scholar and demanding teacher who advocated a scientific approach, Secrist "firmly believed that truth must be discovered from an analysis of factual data and he had little patience with 'armchair' economics," in the words of colleague Frederick Deibler.[101] He produced several texts, including *An Introduction to Statistical Methods, Readings and Problems in Statistical Methods* and *The Triumph of Mediocrity in Business,* in addition to monographs and articles. In a 1920 paper read before a meeting of the Association of Collegiate Schools of Business, Secrist argued for the importance of sound research methods in commerce schools, lamenting that "not all teachers of business subjects, however, have met the tests imposed by an extended period of rigorous educational training, and not infrequently these same individuals are teaching courses the subject-matter of which is largely descriptive." He added: "There is a strong demand for instruction in practical and vocational subjects, and not always a supply of teachers nor a body of knowledge with which to meet this demand in a satisfactory and scientific manner."[102] Secrist contended that the scientific method, to date, had been "little understood" by students and "little appreciated" by business professionals. To counter this, he outlined the standards to which business research should conform, as well as the problems facing commerce schools hoping to resolve these challenges. "Business education is only in its infancy," wrote Secrist, "and the possibilities of organized research by schools of commerce almost untouched. Business constitutes an operating laboratory to which schools of business should have free access." The author included a summary of a questionnaire he submitted to deans of leading commerce schools, soliciting their views on the proper scope and method of business research and the comparative needs and benefits for various constituents, including practitioners, faculty and students.

Other key educators who joined the early School of Commerce included Walter E. Lagerquist, an expert in finance and investment banking who earned a doctorate from Yale University and had taught at Cornell University. Arthur Swanson, who would serve as the second dean of the School of Commerce, from 1917 to 1919, arrived at Northwestern in 1911 fresh from the University of Illinois, where he earned an economics doctorate. He was instrumental in developing courses in industrial administration and commercial organization, as well as teaching the school's initial marketing course in 1912, where he employed a "problems method" to teach the content.[103] Swanson's initiative also helped create a course on management policy—the school's first—to complement most of the other offerings whose focus tended to be on a functional analysis of business operations.[104] He was also a founding member of the American Association of Collegiate Business Schools (AACBS), an organization that had among its objectives the establishment of national professional standards in business education.[105]

Bringing expertise in factory management to the School of Commerce was Henry P. Dutton, who joined the faculty in 1915. An engineer by training, Dutton had attended the University of Michigan. As professor of factory management, he produced several texts, including *Factory Management* (1924), *Business Organization and Management* (1925) and *Business and Its Organization* (1929). The second of these works was published by Arch Shaw's company and received favorable reviews: "The book constitutes perhaps the most complete survey of the field. . . . The writer . . . appears eminently qualified for his task."[106]

As indicated earlier, Earl Dean Howard was another whose contributions to the early School of Commerce—and the larger business community—proved invaluable. The sophistication with which he and his commerce school peers approached business study stood in sharp contrast to much of the contemporary material passing for educational resources. Howard was exploring underlying economic drivers for the commercial world, including critical labor dynamics, stripping bare conventional wisdom that had informed business study up to that time. Theoretical economics, as taught from textbooks, "is not the basic science of business as physics is of engineering and chemistry of medicine," wrote Howard in 1917. Rather, he contended that the "objective of business practice is not production but acquisition, not social service but private profit. Production is incidental. The assumption in economics that the direct objective of business is production is the source of error and futility."

Reducing the matter to its core, the Northwestern professor noted that "the science of business is the science of profit-making. Efficiency in acquiring the maximum gross profit is the objective."[107] Anticipating criticism of such a stark analysis that disregarded community concerns, Howard, who personally was an advocate of social service, admitted that his clinical professional perspective had to uncover the facts surrounding the matter of business. In doing so, he compared business with military science as being a "system of action designed to secure certain definite results most efficiently" and an "organized instrument of great power for both good and evil" depending upon the wisdom of practitioners who employed the tools. He likewise declared that "science does not concern itself with the application of the principles which it formulates,"[108] though he acknowledged that the intersection between business and society was a concern of "highest importance," albeit one that "belongs to the political economist and sociologist" and not the business scholar.

Instead, he believed this science should formulate principles to determine the most efficient establishment and administration of business relationships, describing the "interrelations of business organizations among themselves" and explaining the factors that determine prices and valuations. "In short, it should present all the principles and data necessary for business efficiency," stated Howard.

Despite his ability to bracket scientific considerations of business and economics, Howard noted that "the gravest problems with which this country is now struggling concern the proper use and control of this powerful instrument, the business system, so that its social effects may be beneficent rather than evil." He believed that increasing the general understanding of the business system would be a powerful help in achieving benevolent control of market dynamics. As for students learning this discipline, Howard asserted that all business graduates should learn political economy during their studies but that the subject should be presented near the end of a curriculum that developed foundational skills progressing from "the simple to the complex."

The sophistication of even these early School of Commerce courses is better appreciated when viewed against the typical educational backdrop of the time, which included primers along the lines of Walter D. Moody's *Men Who Sell Things* (1907). Written in hyperbolic style with prose extolling the importance of the "Commercial Ambassador . . . the Ambassador Extraordinary and Plenipotentiary," Moody's book presented the salesman as an underappreciated hero whose value included the commercial spark he lent to the modern market. The book was full of earnest wisdom about a range of topics that spilled over chapters with titles like "True Grit" and "The Knocker." Evangelical boosterism masquerading as scientific practice, Moody's text elevated the salesman to a diligent Everyman who employed relentless enthusiasm and a psychological force alternately termed *soul power* and *personal magnetism.* Adversity was not shunned, as "few battles are ever finally won. There are always positions to be held and new ones to be conquered."[109]

Short on scientific frameworks, the book relied on a kind of cheerleading to offer succor to these commercial travelers. Yet, even there, the author acknowledged "the new era" and its "coming conditions" of greater competition that would require more than the "unorganized ways and methods" of the past. Because of the "creeping foe . . . that only newer, better, and quicker methods can halt . . . [t]he salesman must be modern—up to date—as much as men in other professions" who were now using "ideas" and "educated enthusiasm" to succeed.[110]

And as late as 1921, texts such as Norris A. Brisco's *Retail Salesmanship Source Book* seemed more in touch with the nineteenth century than the twentieth. With brief essays ranging over an impossible list of topics—chapters covered "The Development of the Modern Store and Salesmanship" as well as "The Health and Diet of the Salesperson," "Speech and Voice" and "Development of Character and Intellect," among other matters—the book sought to provide an overview of the field that suggested a scientific framework yet proved so eclectic and shallow as to seem anecdotal despite the effort to bring dozens of experts into this edited text.[111]

At the School of Commerce, however, academic rigor and high expectations were established early for students. Indeed, during the school's first decade, the tougher admissions standards that were introduced in 1912 and required all students under 21 years of age to be high school graduates only strengthened the quality of the student body. The school would interview closely all students older than 21, making individual determinations regarding admittance to the program. Tuition also rose from $75, the rate charged from 1908 through 1912, to $100 in 1912 and $110 the following year. Such facts did nothing to diminish the student body's enthusiasm or its overall numbers, which rose steadily from 255 in 1909 to more than 1,000 by 1917, making Northwestern's among the largest business programs in the country. By 1915, nearly 14 percent of the students enrolled in the commerce school had some formal college training. Hotchkiss expressed his pleasure that Northwestern was recruiting students "who had positions of trust and responsibility in many branches of the business world, men who know considerable of the practical side of business life as well as the theoretical."[112] From an initial 6 courses in the first year of operation, the school had added 34 new offerings by 1915, with more added each year. Faculty members, including Hotchkiss, Deibler, Howard, Andersen, Himmelblau and Bays, produced well-regarded and influential publications on subjects ranging from social reform and welfare to labor movement dynamics, antitrust matters, business organization and commercial law. Heilman and Vanderblue also produced a significant body of work on the subjects of public utilities, transportation and government regulation.[113]

The school was doing well financially and in terms of national recognition,[114] but Hotchkiss and some faculty members were disappointed in the evening program, particularly in the students' reluctance to embrace a management curriculum rooted in the liberal arts. The dean believed that a "new atmosphere" demanded that business executives cultivate "those fine qualities of mind and spirit, and the ability to command these qualities for a given task."[115] He saw in the university a rich intellectual setting uniquely able to meet this educational challenge. It was his view that a commerce school should give students a "many-sided survey of business and a thorough grasp of scientific method" to prepare them to analyze problems to a satisfactory conclusion.[116] But in addition, Hotchkiss recognized the importance of moving from scientific analysis to synthesis, when "all the facts and conclusions must be assembled . . . into a working plan."[117] This synthesis effort included developing "an intelligent and sympathetic approach to questions of human relationship,"[118] which would ultimately allow the executive to "harmonize" internal corporate goals with external societal goals. Aligning business and society was increasingly important, according to Hotchkiss: "Directly or indirectly [business] development in any country sets limits upon what people may or may not have, and what they may or may not do. . . . Business has gone far in organizing society with the world, instead of the locality, the region, or the country as the unit of operation. The very nature of the problems created by this organization on a world scale has placed a heavy social responsibility on business, and made it, willy nilly, an important auxiliary of government, both within nations and between them."[119]

Despite the dean's views on liberal education's importance, market pressures played a vital role in shaping the school's curriculum. Early efforts to emphasize analytical tools could not stave off the market's demand for commerce schools to provide specialized offerings in a variety of areas, circumstances that confronted nearly all business schools in the country.

By 1915, as admissions standards continued to tighten, the school's administration wanted to ensure that students were prepared for the academic rigor of business study at Northwestern. To that end, the dean's office advised faculty members to articulate clearly the school's expectations during the first class session. Among the recommendations given was an exhortation that students begin working hard immediately, attending every lecture and consulting with their professors on any part of the curriculum demanding additional explication. Faculty members were to counsel students so they understood that the academic career was a journey demanding patience. The administration's view was that education was inherently a slow process and that it was unrealistic to expect quick results.

In addition, in September 1915, the school distributed a document originally created by Frank Cramer, a member of the Northwestern School of Engineering faculty; it was titled "How to Study." Adapted from Cramer's "Talks to Students on the Art of Study," the mimeographed guide offered a range of advice and insights, even inculcating the habit of study in near-Pavlovian terms: "With every repetition of an act, the ease of performance increases and the attention required diminishes. With sufficient repetition it becomes almost impossible to refrain from performing that act whenever the appropriate conditions arise." The guide encouraged students to discover their own passion for inquiry, though it stopped short of advising them to choose subjects they themselves found compelling. Rather, the school sought to instill a more general spirit of investigation. "What YOU should do is to make up your mind to DO GOOD WORK, however hard or distasteful you may find a subject, and then you will find that YOU ARE INTERESTED IN EVERY SUBJECT. If you supply this DETERMINATION to down all difficulties, you will find the difficulty of interest entirely disappears."[120]

The study guide also addressed how to cultivate the powers of attention, discrimination, association and will, before concluding with a call to seek knowledge in something of an entrepreneurial fashion and as a skeptic: "In reading do not accept the author's statements as correct until you have held them off at arm's length to see if YOU LIKE THEM. Perhaps you can improve upon them. . . . All second hand information should be verified at the earliest opportunity—preferably by personal observation. . . . You will find it pleasanter to BE YOURSELF and THINK YOUR OWN THOUGHTS than to act somewhat the part of a phonograph, repeating the thoughts of others."

One external acknowledgment of the school's progress came during a May 9, 1914, speech by Franklin MacVeagh, a former U.S. Treasury secretary. "If I only had attended such a school as yours," he told commerce school students during a visit, "I would have been a much better business man and merchant. In the past there was no close relation between business and academic education. In the former days the 'high brows' didn't believe in us 'low brows.' Yet, notwithstanding our disadvantages, we have made commerce blaze the way of civilization. Commerce is not only great and powerful in material ways, it is perhaps the greatest spiritual force of all great social movements."[121] Tacit approval of the commerce school's approach to theory and practice also seemed to come from the nation's highest office, in the form of Woodrow Wilson's presidency. Wilson, a leading intellectual of the Progressive Era, had served as president of Princeton University before venturing into politics. After winning the U.S. presidency in 1912, he brought economic theory into practice by working with a Democratic Congress to pass legislation that established the Federal Reserve System and the Federal Trade Commission, as well as the Clayton Antitrust Act, among others.

Despite the many advances made in the first years of the commerce school's existence, Dean Hotchkiss resigned in 1917, frustrated with trying to establish what he perceived to be a superior managerial program—in particular, his dream of a day program in Evanston, a goal arrested by Northwestern trustees as well as by the entry of the United States into World War I. Hotchkiss left to become the University of Minnesota's first director of business education, and in 1925, he became the first dean of Stanford University's business school. From 1932 to 1937, he was president of Armour Institute of Technology (today the Illinois Institute of Technology), and from 1938 until 1944, he taught at Carnegie Institute of Technology, after which he retired to California. Hotchkiss died in an automobile accident in 1956 at the age of 83.[122]

Deans Swanson and Heilman
Advance the Academic Mission

Professor Swanson assumed the school's deanship briefly (1917–1918) before being called away to New York to serve on the War Shipping Board, which built noncombatant ships and helped coordinate arms shipments. Swanson had previously served as acting dean in 1916 while Hotchkiss was teaching at Stanford. After the war ended, Swanson moved into private business, becoming senior partner in Swanson, Ogilvie and McKenzie.

During his short tenure, Swanson and his administration demonstrated the school's continued desire to bring practitioners and academics together. To that end, the school offered a series of public lectures on business organization in February 1917 and 1918. These were hosted in the university's downtown Chicago building and covered an array of topics. Factory management, foreign exchange, industrial relations, marketing methods and the wartime economy were just some of the lectures delivered by School of Commerce faculty members in conjunction with practitioners from the Chicago area. Typically 90-minute sessions that could be scheduled at any time of the day, the lectures were designed to offer surprisingly rigorous insights for business leaders. For instance, on February 4 and 5, 1917, J. L. Jacobs of J. L. Jacobs & Company presented a lecture on public budgets, leading sessions on budgetary principles and procedure and associated problems of practice. The lecture was described as offering insights into scientific aspects and theory; the fundamental problems and purpose of budgets, including those attending the finance of governmental needs; and the growth of municipal activities, among many other points. Professor Alfred Bays brought his legal talents to bear in lectures on business law that offered details about credit and debt in Illinois. "Remedies of Creditors" provided practical and detailed information about how creditors could recover money owed them through legal means such as garnishments, judgments and levies. A session on bankruptcy illuminated the details of that strategy. Other lectures covered language skills for businesspeople and ways to build a better vocabulary, the nature of business cycles and conflicts associated with industrial relations.[123]

However, the most important action taken during Swanson's administration was the decision in late 1917 to establish a separate bachelor of science in commerce program on the Evanston campus. World War I prevented implementation of the plan until 1919, at which time Ralph Heilman was nominated as the school's new dean. Recommended by Hotchkiss and Deibler, among other influential faculty members, Heilman was an authority on labor relations and public utility management who had been an economics professor at the University of Iowa and the University of Illinois from 1913 to 1916, at which time he moved to Northwestern. He assuaged trustees' concerns after Swanson's abbreviated tenure, stating that, if appointed, he would dedicate himself to the school with "loyalty and enthusiasm,"[124] a pledge he began fulfilling on February 17, 1919.

Heilman distinguished two objectives in the mission of commerce schools: one was to train business technicians and specialists; the other was to train executives. Later, in an essay titled "Personal Qualities Requisite for Success in Business and the Role of the School of Business in Their Development,"[125] he would lay out his view regarding the factors required for business leadership. Among these were tools, information and character traits:

Tools: "The business executive must posses, if not a mastery, at least an understanding of how certain tools or techniques are used. Hence the necessity for training in accounting, statistics, salesmanship, English—written and spoken—etc."

Information: It is "essential that the prospective business executive shall have an adequate understanding of the operations of the economic and business system in its various ramifications. . . . Hence the necessity for instruction in the descriptive fields of economics, marketing, organization, law, finance, labor, etc." Heilman admitted, however, that the information imparted in these courses soon became "obsolete" but the training nonetheless offered "the necessary beginning point" that would enable the executive to remain informed about new developments in the field and in economic life.

Personal qualities: Heilman described these qualities as being among the "vital factors in the equipment of the prospective business executive." Such traits and characteristics, he said, were important for any professional, but they were especially critical for business success. This area had been neglected by business schools, according to the author, who went on to reference the framework of Earl Dean Howard, noting that the four most important personal attributes for the effective business executive were, in priority order, judgment, a sense of responsibility, delight in accomplishment and ingenuity. He explicated some of these points as follows. *Judgment* involved deciding rightly or wisely, and it was seen by Heilman as "the primary function" of executives. "Intellectual poise and emotional stability" were among the qualities that enabled good executives to judge discriminately, without being led astray by "intriguing or fanciful ideas." He admitted he was not entirely sure that classroom training could develop this quality, but he suggested that the case method, with its focus on specific business problems, could be helpful in advancing the objective. On *delight in accomplishment,* he observed, "It is one thing to decide what should be done and quite another to do it." Executives had to develop this trait, and schools might contribute to this quality by revisiting grading systems as well as the way in which they structured courses, giving students more opportunities to exercise initiative and creativity. Heilman even entertained the notion of discarding standard letter grades in favor of general "Pass/Fail" (and "High Pass") designations that he said might "eliminate this false emphasis . . . on outside standards and rewards . . . and promote the development of a sense of delight or satisfaction in accomplishment." He also proposed independent study as another potential way to encourage student initiative. On *ingenuity,* he noted that "the power of ready invention—quickness or acuteness in forming new combinations . . . is of the utmost importance." A person might be highly skilled in doing the old things in the old way, but, he said, "in this rapidly changing economic and business world, it is essential that the executive shall be able to meet new situations in new ways." Specifically, these executives had to find time- and labor-saving devices, new methods of using manufacturing by-products and new labor management methods as well as new ways of financing the venture, contended Heilman.

Such ambitious and searching considerations did not remain ideas divorced from action for Heilman. Indeed, his deanship was distinguished for several important developments at the School of Commerce, not the least of which was the establishment of a full-time undergraduate commerce program in Evanston in 1919. This offering, leading to the bachelor of science in commerce degree, was designed to be less technically oriented than the curriculum in either the evening diploma program or the bachelor of business administration program. Tuition for the day program was $150. The precommerce curriculum, lasting two years, required students to learn subjects such as English, economics, economic history, mathematics, psychology and business psychology, money and banking and sociology.[126] The 1921–1922 course bulletin indicated the rationale for this sequence: students were to gain "knowledge of the scientific essentials which affect the physical operations and the human relationships in business."[127] The trustees' records indicated there was considerable discussion about curriculum particulars, including a spirited debate between Roy C. Flickinger, dean of the College of Liberal Arts from 1919 to 1923, and Dean Heilman.[128] According to the trustees' minutes, Flickinger argued that details of the precommerce course were "nowhere defined with sufficient exactness." He also expressed concern that once the bachelor of science in commerce degree was approved by the university, commerce school faculty members would "feel free to modify the conditions at pleasure," in the trustees' words. Dean Heilman responded that the School of Commerce recognized a "moral obligation" to refrain from adjusting specific requirements except as these were modified by the college faculty for its own degree. He assured Flickinger that the commerce school had no intention of undercutting the specific requirements of the College of Liberal Arts.

Still, in a letter dated October 25, 1920, Flickinger wrote to Heilman as follows: "I have received apparently authentic information to the effect that the School of Commerce Faculty has voted that the minimum in foreign language, science, mathematics, and English for the degree of Bachelor of Science in Commerce shall be reduced to one year of science instead of two, an A-course in one foreign language instead of two, English A instead of A1 and B1, and no mathematics . . . I hope you can find time to inform me whether the report of this action is correct."

The following day, Dean Heilman replied, saying: "I do not understand the inferences in your letter of October 25th. The School of Commerce has never 'reduced' its requirements to one year of science, 'instead of two,' since it never has had the two year requirement. Likewise, its requirements in language and English for the degree of Bachelor of Science in Commerce have not been 'reduced,' but rather clarified. The School of Commerce faculty, of course, is the legislative body with regard to the specific requirements to be met by students who are candidates for this degree."[129]

Behind Flickinger's concerns was an aggressive recruiting campaign by Clarence S. Marsh, commerce school educational adviser at the time. Accused by Flickinger of "raiding" undergraduate departments for Northwestern students and inducing them to enroll in the commerce curriculum, Marsh had produced recruitment materials that suggested undergraduates who were slow in indicating their desire to pursue business education might lose the opportunity to register at the School of Commerce. "The liberal arts faculty also characterized the recruiting materials prepared and distributed by Marsh as unethical and irregular 'propaganda.' The absence of such criticism after the mid-1920s suggests that faculty complaints compelled the commerce school to modify its recruiting efforts."[130] Enrollment at the School of Commerce at that time was healthy, and numbers in the evening program gradually rose from about 1,000 in 1918 to nearly 5,700 by the end of the 1920s. Female students represented about one-fifth of all those enrolled during that decade.

In the spring and summer of 1919, the School of Commerce faculty discussed details of the curriculum for the four-year course leading to the bachelor of arts (BA) or BS in commerce degree. Among the courses noted as being required in the third year of study were corporation finance, business organization, accounting, marketing and distribution and business law, with electives offered in advertising, sales correspondence, introductory cost accounting, labor, transportation, investment securities, business psychology and advanced business organization.[131]

Heilman's administration also introduced other academic innovations; for instance, the Bureau of Business Research was created in 1919, designed to help increase Northwestern's national presence as a research-based institution that focused on theoretical and applied study. The bureau would encourage faculty research that would benefit practitioners as well as refine professors' teaching. Heilman also recruited faculty members who could deliver a curriculum that emphasized functional and technical subjects, and starting in April 1920, he began to reorganize the school into eight departments to reflect business specialization, bringing the proposal to the commerce school faculty. A committee composed of Professors H. P. Dutton, Walter E. Lagerquist and Walter K. Smart subsequently explored recommendations to develop the idea, proposing on May 27, 1922, that "the effectiveness of the work of the school will be increased by departmentalization," especially given that more than 80 instructors and lecturers were involved with delivering courses. "Many of these men work alone in detached fields with no supervision other than that possibly of the dean," wrote Dutton in a report. The committee believed that departmental grouping would make possible "greater uniformity of teaching method, much more effective coordination and prevention of overlap, and a more balanced and effective consideration of budget and other general needs of the group."[132] The committee recommended early adoption of the proposal, acknowledging that "certain readjustments and a measure of sacrifice of personal prerogatives in the interest of greater effectiveness of the school as a whole may be necessary." On June 16 of that year, Dean Heilman announced the following departments and their chairs:

Economics (Professor Deibler)
Psychology (Professor Scott)
English (Professor Smart)
Journalism (Professor Harrington)
Accounting (Professor Himmelblau)
Organization, Management, and Merchandising
    (Professor Swanson)
Finance (Professor Lagerquist)
Law (Professor Bays)

The Heilman deanship also oversaw the establishment of a master of business administration degree in 1920 and a doctorate in commerce in 1926. The MBA curriculum required 20 hours of postbaccalaureate study as well as a thesis based on original research. The school felt it necessary to add this offering in part because of the perception that BBA graduates were at a disadvantage in the market compared with peers from other schools that offered the popular MBA credential, including Columbia and Wharton. Michael Sedlak and Harold Williamson noted the "troubled career" of the BBA at Northwestern, specifically the fact that only four such degrees were awarded between 1912 and 1920, at which time the program lapsed before being reintroduced in 1922.[133] The MBA curriculum at Northwestern was an option open to both full- and part-time students, although full-time study tended to encourage completion of the program. During the first decade of the MBA's existence at Northwestern, an average of 25 degrees were granted each year.

The impetus for the school's doctoral program came in part from market demand for more educators with advanced commerce training. Heilman noted that this trend served as an early indication that Northwestern would have to meet the challenge and need for graduate education in commerce.[134] Students pursuing the doctorate had to meet the Graduate School's language requirements as well as pass written examinations in economic theory and history and statistics; they also had to choose a business concentration and defend a dissertation approved by the faculty. In the first decade of the program's existence, the school granted 24 doctorates.[135] Paul L. Morrison earned Northwestern's first doctorate in commerce in 1927, with his dissertation examining equity trading associated with public utility holding companies. He would go on to serve as part of the school's Finance Department, coauthoring the books *Accounting for Business Executives* (1928) and *Advanced Accounting Problems* (1932).

Other significant moves during Heilman's tenure included changes in the facilities. The School of Commerce moved its administrative offices in Evanston from Harris Hall,[136] where they had been located since the building's construction in 1915, to Memorial Hall in 1923. Heilman had reported to Walter Dill Scott, university president since 1920, that the quarters in Harris Hall were inadequate, partly because the commerce school had "no building space whatever under its control."[137] Memorial Hall, which became known affectionately as the Little Red Schoolhouse, had stood near Sheridan Road and Foster Avenue since 1887, first housing the Garrett Theological Seminary and then, after a $100,000 facelift, opening its doors to accommodate Northwestern's burgeoning School of Commerce. A two-story construction, the building included a belfry and would serve as the school's home until 1970.

Wieboldt Hall and the Chicago Campus

Facilities downtown on the Chicago campus also underwent a transformation during Heilman's deanship, with the School of Commerce moving into a new building in October 1926. The groundbreaking for the facility occurred on May 8, 1925, with cornerstones laid on June 11, 1926. At the groundbreaking, major donors used engraved silver spades to mark the occasion, which created the Alexander McKinlock Memorial Campus,[138] a site that would support several other university buildings in addition to the commerce school. Among those present that Friday were Mrs. Montgomery Ward, donor of the Ward Medical-Dental Center; Mrs. Levy Mayer, the benefactor providing funding for the Levy Mayer Hall of Law; Mrs. George R. Thorne, who made possible the Thorne Auditorium; Elbert H. Gary, who contributed the E. H. Gary Library of Law;[139] and William A. Wieboldt, representing the Wieboldt Foundation, whose philanthropy would directly impact the School of Commerce. (Incidentally, Wieboldt's son, Raymond, served as the general contractor for the building.)

Fund-raising for the construction generated solid results early on, with students pledging more than $100,000 toward what would be a $1.1 million building.[140] Alumni contributed another $50,000, and thanks to his relationships in the business community, Heilman secured an additional $450,000—but he was still short of the goal by $500,000. The shortfall was made up by the philanthropy of the Wieboldt Foundation, and as a result, the new facilities were named after the Chicago merchandiser who founded his Chicago-area chain of department stores in 1883. (By 1910, the store on Milwaukee Avenue employed about 700 people and grossed $3 million in annual sales.)[141] The eight-story Wieboldt Hall, constructed from Indiana limestone with a slate roof, featured a central tower that rose an additional six stories. Inside was sufficient room for the commerce students (some 5,000 at the time), as well as features such as a library, two research institutes affiliated with the school—Ely's Institute for Research in Land Economics and Public Utilities and the Bureau of Business Research—and the new Medill School of Journalism, which Heilman helped to organize. The James B. Forgan Room of Finance, named after an early commerce school guarantor and the president of National City Bank of Chicago, was one of several rooms dedicated to special benefactors. Others included the Clement Studebaker Room of Manufacturing and the John G. Shedd Room of Merchandising—each containing a portrait of the donor and dedicated by President Scott.

The school celebrated the move into Wieboldt Hall with a dedication on June 16 and 17, 1927, that featured academic sessions addressing the state of business education. During the conference, Heilman noted the transformation that higher education had undergone in the previous two decades. In particular, he noted, these schools were no longer merely for the affluent but were now also instrumental in training others for "creative accomplishment, for constructive achievement and for definite leadership in *every* important field of human activity and of human endeavor."[142]

Heilman also stated his conviction about the mission of commerce schools. "Training young men merely to increase their earning capacity does not constitute adequate justification for the inclusion of business instruction in university curricula," he told those gathered on June 16 for an evening lecture by Harvard professor of economic history Edwin F. Gay on "Social Progress and Business Education." Heilman expressed the view that all colleges and universities were primarily "public service" agencies whose offerings had to contribute to the public good. "Schools of Commerce are therefore to be judged by precisely the same standard as are schools of art, science, medicine, theology, engineering, education."[143]

These were ideas Heilman would revisit later, including in his 1932 article "Can Business Be Taught?"[144] There, he answered the question in the paper's title in the affirmative: "In the highly complicated, intricate, and interdependent labyrinth which we call the modern economic and business system," wrote the dean, "there are constantly in operation certain fundamental economic laws, basic principles, and tendencies. . . . There can be no doubt as to the basic character of these extrinsic forces, and there is no doubt as to their teachable character."

For Heilman, business education was predicated on the same principles that provided the foundation for all professional and technical education—as in medicine, law, theology and engineering. Classroom lessons were best complemented by action-oriented practica that gave students hands-on opportunities.[145] "University training in business offers a substitute for the old trial-and-error method," he wrote. "Its purpose is to enable the student to profit through the study of the experience of hundreds and thousands of business men, firms, and organizations, and thus to learn what principles of organization, management, finance, and accounting have proven most effective." The strength of such schools, contended Heilman, lay in their ability to teach underlying business principles, such as basic economic laws and business problems that operate throughout the business system. In this way, schools helped students "to think straight" and grow familiar with management methods that had proven most effective, ultimately preparing them for rapid advancement and increased responsibility.

Despite these merits, Heilman believed business schools could justify their existence "only in so far as the training and instruction which they offer [was] socially desirable" and contributed toward increasing the "productive capacity of society and toward the equitable distribution of the products and fruits of industry." Further, the business professional had to learn more than simply the internal operations of his business ("how to make and sell his product"); he also had to learn about the "external forces which lie outside his own business . . . to which he must adapt."

According to Heilman, there were also certain things schools of commerce could not do, such as teaching the "technique and routine of the countless jobs which our students and graduates will occupy." Neither could these schools "eliminate the necessity for our graduates to begin at the bottom. Nor . . . guarantee that they will all arrive at the top."

At the Wieboldt Hall conference, the dean went on to detail the "peculiar problems" facing the relatively new professional schools (commerce schools included) as they tried to develop curricula that complemented the content of traditional arts and sciences colleges. Discussants, including Professor of Economics William Kiekhofer of the University of Wisconsin and Professor Raymond A. Kent, dean of the College of Liberal Arts at Northwestern University, considered the frequently tenuous relationship between commerce schools and the larger universities.

Among the panel's discussants was Professor Frederick Deibler, whose view was that specialization had created some disadvantages for undergraduate students in general, as well as those who were thinking of going into business. "I am thoroughly convinced that there has already developed a degree of specialization in the courses given during the first two years, that is not justified on the ground of the welfare of students," he stated. "How far the professional schools should go in specifying the courses which those entering shall have taken during their preliminary years is a grave educational problem. They are, of course, within their rights in specifying their own entrance requirements, but when they reach down into the college curriculum and begin to specify what work should be taken by students enrolled in this school then I am inclined to believe that their proposals should be carefully scrutinized."[146]

Adding to this discourse, Homer Vanderblue, then a professor at Harvard University, stated that the objectives of undergraduate and graduate study in business were quite similar and, in fact, "extremely difficult" if not "impossible" to differentiate: "Except that the graduate school offers its opportunities to men of more advanced years, with a wide variety of background, it cannot have very different objectives from the undergraduate school."[147] Vanderblue bemoaned the challenges facing undergraduate business instructors in those schools where the students' focus was distracted by "outside activities," such as athletics or "what the undergraduates call 'society.'" He extolled the virtues of graduate business education, at one point discussing the matter from the educator's vantage point: "Only one who has experienced the feeling can fully appraise the relief when one no longer has 'prominent' undergraduates in his classes," he said. "I feel quite secure in my statement that all of you must occasionally envy the instructor who can look at a football team or a baseball team at practice . . . secure in the knowledge that he will not be visited by some prominent alumnus or even colleague who will tell him how good—though quite unappreciated—some worthless loafer is. . . . I believe that the educational objectives of business training can best be gained in a graduate school."

Arch Shaw's remarks at the dedication echoed some of Vanderblue's words. Speaking on "A Suggested Plan for a New Type of Graduate School of Business," he noted the tendency, reinforced by salary incentives, for professionals to specialize rather than cultivate the broader training "requisite for high administrative positions." What's more, he noted, these positions were increasingly important in contemporary organizations, due to dynamics influencing the business world of the late 1920s. Comparing business in 1927 to that of a generation earlier, he observed: "We are in many ways in a different business world. American business is affected by changes even in the remote countries. Even more directly, business is affected by the quickening of research and invention, by substitution of materials and processes better or more economical than those used previously, and by the speeding up of management procedure. There are a thousand influences at work in the business world today, external to the individual enterprise, that affect its internal affairs."[148] Shaw cited the fact of business cycles (what he termed "rhythms") confronting business leaders. "Sagacious" administrators learned quickly to sense and respond to such changes, he said—for example, lending rates and the implications for securing financing. Business students also had to be "schooled in the importance and the nature of the trend," and the problems of business "must be met by formulating policies." Even brilliant administrators had to recognize that business was "inert until policies are formulated, and then put into execution through methods and systems," according to Shaw.

Tough Times and Brilliant Ideas

As the 1920s came to an end, the School of Commerce introduced still more innovations, in addition to enhancements in the facilities, to bring practitioners and academics together. These initiatives included Earl Dean Howard's Institute for Executives, a 1929 proposal to invite select businesspeople to study and discuss business problems with their peers and commerce school faculty and students. Professors and students would benefit by their proximity to real-world issues, and they would have a chance to help solve the challenges, while the practitioners, who would pay no tuition for participating in the program, would gain insight from academic perspectives.

Some years earlier, in February 1922, Howard had sketched a plan for something he called the Institute of Business, which he described as providing "intellectual guidance of men of business affairs . . . who desire contact with the University but for whom hitherto there has been no accommodation." Howard envisioned the institute conveniently situated in the Loop and accessible as "a sort of mental gymnasium for intellectual exercise, prescribed by experts to fit the individual case." Informal study groups would address specific questions, directed by an expert guide, presumably a faculty member. The setting was to resemble an attractive club, with a proposed membership fee of $200 per year. "It would be a sort of graduate school of business guiding the work of the student while he was on the job."[149]

Despite the obvious possibilities of such endeavors, neither proposal gathered sufficient support to become a reality. Actually, the later plan's dissolution was largely the result of the Great Depression, whose advent altered university initiatives significantly after the Wall Street crash of 1929. Northwestern's income, for instance, was reduced by about 37 percent from more than $677,000 in 1930 to less than $430,000 in 1934. And the commerce school's budgeted expenditures declined almost 57 percent as the university sought to reduce operational deficits during the economic downturn.[150]

Not surprisingly, given these circumstances, another ambitious idea fell victim to the disastrous economy, too. The F. C. Austin Scholarship Foundation began with great promise on January 23, 1929, but it experienced a long hiatus after its first few years. Designed in response to criticism that business schools were producing increasingly technical graduates whose specialization prepared them for more narrow roles, not leadership situations or general management positions, the Austin Scholars sought to integrate liberal arts and technical training in a way that produced exemplary leaders.[151] Frederick C. Austin, a self-made businessman, provided financing for the program by donating a building in Chicago's Loop to Northwestern, the income from which would support the program bearing his name. The building was valued at about $3 million but carried a $1 million mortgage. Office rentals in the building, however, were expected to continue producing revenue.[152] In addition, Austin agreed to leave the remainder of his estate to Northwestern, and in the meantime, the university was to pay him $160,000 for life, with his beneficiaries also receiving specified payments.[153]

Meanwhile, Austin's funds, which he calculated would gradually grow to $50 million, would support several hundred scholars—talented individuals whom he hoped would eventually have a profound impact on the character of American business. He envisioned the endeavor as a "business fraternity on a national scale." The initial class, however, numbered only 10, despite the fact that the program attracted a considerable number of talented students to Northwestern (even if the majority did not meet the exacting academic standards of the scholars' program).

Not a college graduate himself, Austin, born on a farm near Skaneateles, New York, in 1853, had made a commercial success as a manufacturer of road machinery, such as dump trucks and graders. Though horse-drawn, this equipment "incorporated the most advanced technology of [the] day and played an important part in building the pre-automobile highway system of [the United States] and several other countries."[154] In 1920, Austin sold this business and invested most of the proceeds from the fortune in Chicago real estate, including the 11-story building on Jackson Boulevard that was designed by the renowned architectural firm Burnham and Root. About this time, he developed what his biographer, James C. Worthy (an Austin Scholar himself), called a special interest in higher education. He also had a lively interest in the arts and culture. For instance, Austin was a life member of the Art Institute of Chicago, and he was active in the Chicago Historical Society and the Chicago Yacht Club. Worthy, among the program's first 10 scholars, graduated from Northwestern in 1933 and went on to serve as vice president of Sears, Roebuck & Co. and, later, as a professor of management at the Kellogg School. He wrote, "It is clear that there gradually began to form in [Austin's] mind a conviction that the business system could no longer generate the caliber of leadership . . . required for its own and the country's future needs."[155]

In his history of the Austin Scholars, Worthy recalled the program's official launch on September 29, 1929, in Evanston's North Shore Hotel. Impeccably dressed, complete with cane and spats, Frederick Austin arrived by chauffeured Rolls Royce to meet the initial class of scholars, as well as university administrators such as President Scott and Professor Delton T. Howard of the psychology faculty, who would be given responsibility for administering the program. Austin told those gathered: "Business has progressed too far in its technique to be mastered by merely good and native talent. The executives of the future must have these, plus the best training [they] can get."[156]

At the School of Commerce, that training featured the experience of a collegial atmosphere—perhaps the forerunner of the school's vaunted team-oriented leadership focus—created by the scholars living together in what Worthy called a "social-professional fraternity." The Austin Scholars resided in their own facility, initially Hinman House, an on-campus dormitory, and then, in the program's third year when their numbers had grown large enough to justify it, in a new $115,000 dorm constructed for their use.[157]

In the classroom, the Austin Scholars were treated to some rather ambitious experimental courses. Among the class offerings in the program's first year, though, only one was specifically designed for these scholars—"Economics A2," known as "Business Concepts" and taught by Earl Dean Howard (no relation to Delton). The course promised an explanation of the U.S. economic system and an understanding of business phenomena. Howard would teach this class for more than a decade. The program's inaugural year also saw a great deal of informal interaction between the students and faculty; in particular, each of the Howards opened his home as a kind of academic salon.

The year following the program's founding, three other classes were offered: "Social Science AX," the "Integrated Study Plan," and the "Independent Study Plan." "Social Science AX" was an eight-credit course taught by Earl Dean Howard, with support by D. T. Howard and Elias Lyman, assistant to President Scott. The course was not intended to address business topics per se but to "provide a broad conceptual background for Commerce School courses and for the business life to follow."[158] Heilman, in 1932, remarked that the class was "in reality a course in dialectics—the process of making ideas clear through discussion—with the concepts chosen largely from the field of the social sciences" in an effort to introduce students to ideas such as wealth, contracts, property, socialism, individualism and so forth.[159] The class featured extensive daily readings—for example, selections from the Bible, Plato's *Dialogues*, Ralph Waldo Emerson's *Essays*, William James's *Pragmatism*, Francis Bacon's *Essays* and H. G. Wells's *Outline of History*, among others. Students participated in daily discussion groups and were responsible for producing both individual written reports as well as group reports. Howard led the sessions by employing the Socratic method. The results were mixed. Some students "found [the course] exciting and looked back on it years later as one of the high points of their college careers; others found it tiresome."[160] The course lasted one semester, but Howard continued to hold informal, noncredit evening discussions in his home for those wishing to participate.

The next formal innovation was the "Integrated Study Plan," a nine-credit offering that sought to combine functional courses like marketing and finance into a single coordinated course that would highlight the interconnected relationship of such disciplines—a fact best understood by those seeking executive roles. The program focused on the connections between business, government and society in a way designed to stimulate civic leadership. The course's ambitious nature also proved to be its Achilles' heel, as administrators found it exceedingly challenging to incorporate so much diverse material in one class. Over time, however, its valuable content was integrated into several regular courses.

Finally, the nine-credit "Independent Study Plan" was offered to help students, during the sophomore and junior years, create individualized curricula under the advisement of a faculty member. However, the plan was never set in motion: by 1932, the Depression's economic effects were making it obvious that the scholars' program would have to be suspended indefinitely.

Rents in the Loop building donated by Austin declined significantly in that period. From more than $300,000 in 1928, the rental income plummeted to $222,000 in 1931. By 1936, rents were only at about 25 percent of their previous high-water mark. Northwestern's business manager outlined the reasons for the decline to university trustees in 1932: "The building is old. The loop is full of new and thoroughly modern structures. Offices in the Austin Building which were rented three years ago at $3 a square foot have been rented more recently at $2 or $2.50, and now as leases expire it is difficult to renew them at $1.50."[161]

As a result, the F. C. Austin Scholarship operated in the black only two years out of its first eight, "despite the fact that Austin reimbursed the University for the costs of the scholarships during his lifetime, i.e., the first three years of the program."[162] Forty scholars participated in the program from 1929 through 1932; after the last class of 10 graduated in 1936, no new candidates were admitted until the fall of 1959. At that point, the sale of the Austin Building produced sufficient capital (about $321,000) to reinstate the scholarships, resulting in another 54 graduates through 1966, by which time the school eliminated its undergraduate program in favor of graduate study.[163] The preparations for reinstating the program were noted in the faculty's November 17, 1958, minutes, which referenced scholarships of $2,000 a year for four years being given to outstanding young men entering the school to prepare for business careers. The plans called for seven Austin Scholarships in the 1959–1960 school year, with five new awards given in each of the next three years for an estimated total expenditure of $116,000. Official university approval came in a letter dated December 16, 1958, from Payson S. Wild, vice president and dean of faculties for Northwestern, to the associate dean of the School of Business, Ira D. Anderson.[164]

The nation's economic pressures during the Depression also resulted in Dean Heilman striving to assist graduates in finding employment. "We . . . have a real responsibility to our students, beyond mere impartation of knowledge and instruction," he said. "Beyond that we have some obligation to 'follow through' with them, to assist in their entrance into the field of business activities so that they will not find themselves in blind alleys, up against a stone wall. . . . We have some obligation to help obtain at least a reasonable opportunity for advancement and promotion to larger responsibilities. And we surely have some obligation to the business public from which we derive, in large part, our support, to try to provide an adequately trained personnel for business."[165]

Between 1932 and 1933, the Depression hit its nadir. The stock market had lost about 90 percent of its 1929 value. School of Commerce enrollment (undergraduate and part-time) mirrored the disastrous national economy, dropping to about

4,400 students from more than 6,700 two years earlier. Financially, the school was operating at a deficit, although it was smaller than some deficits associated with the program during most of the 1920s.[166] So bad were the circumstances that Northwestern and the University of Chicago briefly considered pooling their resources to create a merged business school. The idea came from University of Chicago president Robert Maynard Hutchins to President Scott, who would form a semisecret investigatory body called the Special Committee on an Important Problem to explore the option.[167] Although the trustees of both institutions devised a proposal for consolidating the two schools, Northwestern invited faculty and alumni to offer their opinions on the matter. Concerns ranged from whether the venture would be academically desirable to whether Northwestern could retain its charter's tax-exempt status as a religious institution. Rumors swirled, including one fomented by an anonymous writer in the *Evanston Review* who claimed that the Rockefeller Foundation would offer a $25 million endowment if there was only one university in the Chicago area.[168] Growing resistance soon spread among the Northwestern community, alumni and the city of Evanston, which felt the deal would result in a devastating economic loss for the suburb. The proposal died in February 1934, with the presidents of both schools lamenting a missed opportunity: Hutchins regarded the outcome as "one of the lost opportunities of American education," whereas Scott noted in a letter to the Northwestern board, "The more I studied the merger the more desirable I found it to be. It is a great regret to me that conditions were such that it could not become a reality. In my judgment the merger will become a reality at some future date."[169]

This change in fortunes was a stark contrast to the optimism that only a few years earlier had induced Walter Dill Scott, writing on "The New Energies and the New Man" in *Society Today,* to note the enormous increase in power available to advance civilization, particularly in the United States. "The accumulation of power, and particularly of mechanical power, is resulting in profound industrial changes in our people," he wrote in 1929. "We are told that the coming of the machine has destroyed the dignity of labor; that the monotony of tending a machine deadens the interest and initiative of the workers. Such an interpretation is unwarranted. The machine relieves the worker of the monotony of toil. It enables the machine tender to accomplish in eight hours what would otherwise necessitate the drudgery of many workers from ten to fifteen hours a day. The machine converts many workers from drudges into artisans, and converts a few from drudges into artists."[170]

The times would demand management leaders who could harness both the power of these marvelous machines as well as the full talents of the workers operating them. This would prove a challenge for commerce schools to meet, since many of them had pursued more narrow, technical curricula that produced skilled specialists rather than true leaders.

During the second decade of its existence, the School of Commerce had begun developing away from merely technical or functional lines. But important though such specific skills still were, market pressures made it difficult to take truly revolutionary steps. Even early in the school's history, its administrators glimpsed the future. In the words of Dean Hotchkiss, "A new type of executive [was] appearing on the scene," one who discovered the value and necessity of successfully managing "broader responsibilities" in the "field of human relations."[171] Hotchkiss also noted the fact that some of the school's early students were "highly responsible executives," such as John McKinlay, vice president and general manager of Marshall Field and Company; John J. Mitchell Jr., of Illinois Merchants Bank; and Mark Cresap, who would become president of Hart, Schaffner & Marx.

In reality, though, financial pressures during most of the 1930s would prevent the School of Commerce from making significant strides in its goal of emphasizing the management functions of business and decreasing the focus on technical specialization. Dean Heilman voiced his concern to President Scott in 1935, saying, "We have economized so drastically for such a long period that our educational standards have become seriously impaired" and indeed risked "deteriorat[ing] into [those of] a 'trade school' or 'vocational school.'" Class sizes had ballooned, and faculty teaching loads had grown increasingly untenable.[172] These circumstances would begin to be remedied in favor of a more liberal arts approach advocated by Homer B. Vanderblue, who assumed the school's deanship in 1939 following Heilman's death in 1937 and the brief tenure of Dean Fred D. Fagg Jr., a member of the university's School of Law who resigned to become vice president and dean of faculties for Northwestern.

Welcomed back to Northwestern in 1939 as a professor of economics, Vanderblue, a 1912 alumnus, was soon appointed dean, a move that elicited some controversy among his colleagues, including Frederick Deibler; Deibler feared that faculty members would retain their earlier impressions of the new boss, who had earned a reputation for being abrupt and harsh. As it turned out, the apprehension was only partly warranted, as the new dean, though "personally intimidating . . . established an excellent working relationship with the school's staff."[173]

Vanderblue, born in Hinsdale, Illinois, on December 24, 1888, had returned to the commerce school after a career as a consultant and executive; in addition, he was an occasional instructor at Northwestern and Harvard, where he had earned a doctorate in economics. This eclectic experience would serve both Vanderblue and the commerce school well, for he helped keep the school running during his 1939–1949 tenure despite the economic pressures of World War II that forced many competing institutions to shut down. Notably, the dean would concern himself less with maintaining intimate ties with the local business community despite his personal experiences as a practitioner, including his service as vice president of Tricontinental Corporation, a major investment firm, from 1929 until 1937. Instead, his focus was on beating back a trend that he found worrying—the growing technical specialization of business education, which had been a hallmark of the commerce school's early days, particularly under Dean Heilman.[174] Years before a landmark survey by the Ford Foundation and Carnegie Corporation reported serious shortcomings in management education,[175] Northwestern, starting under Vanderblue's leadership, would pursue a more "managerial" approach to business study that emphasized advanced concepts rather than functional training. Other top schools, including Harvard and Stanford (then headed by former School of Commerce dean Willard Hotchkiss), had also recognized the market indications pointing to a significant transformation in management needs and were starting to shape their curricula accordingly.

The tension between theory and practice would continue at business schools through the middle of the twentieth century, with many experts seeking the balance between the economic frameworks bolstering commerce study and the practitioners' needs for more realistic and immediate solutions. As J. C. Bonbright noted as early as 1926, citing an example found in Vanderblue's 1924 *Problems in Business Economics* text, two kinds of problems informed the business context, one associated with economics, the other with business itself. "The *economist* wants to know why business conditions are so bad and what can be done to improve them," wrote Bonbright. "On the other hand, the business student is interested in a very different set of problems. The economic situation being what it is, how should this business man meet the emergency?"[176]

Although the School of Commerce had, since its earliest days, acknowledged the importance of both theory and practice, the complexity of modern business by the middle of the twentieth century would place dramatically new demands upon management education. Earl Dean Howard, always in touch with the social context of commerce, foresaw the need for commerce schools to train the "true professional man . . . who is more interested in performing his function competently and with distinction than for immediate profit." By 1935, Howard had written about an evolving social landscape that would demand capable business administrators who were also willing and able to contribute to public service. He observed that the "risks of specialization increase as social change accelerates," and he called for more

schools, such as the School of Commerce at Northwestern, to offer "multiple professional training with administration as the basis."[177]

During the 1940s and 1950s, James Worthy was also among those voicing their
observations regarding the American corporate world and its relationship to society as a whole, as well as the effectiveness of management educators in preparing
their students for leadership roles in corporate America. The School of Commerce
graduate was, like Vanderblue and Howard, concerned about specialization. In
"Education for Business Leadership," Worthy asserted that many organizations had
reservations about hiring commerce students. "It has been the experience of many
businessmen that, by and large, what people learn in business school is of little value
to them in business—often quite the contrary. One reason for this is an undue
emphasis on techniques." The schools, continued Worthy, did a decent job of "teaching business methods but not in preparing men for leadership. . . . It is far easier to
develop a course in, say, credit management than to develop one dealing with the
role of business in modern society."[178]

And Worthy, along with a growing number of educators and practitioners,
believed it was critical for management schools to understand that social context.
Worthy would go on to write several books espousing his philosophy of management, highlighting his experiences as vice president of Sears, Roebuck & Co. during
a tenure from 1938 until 1953 that encompassed leadership roles in the company's
personnel office. In *Big Business and Free Men,* he articulated his view that corporate
leaders needed to contribute their talents not only to business but also to civic life,
in a way that "strengthen[ed] the basic values of American society, which are strongly democratic." Doing so demanded that "businessmen . . . operate their businesses
on democratic principles, and that they assume their share of the broader responsibilities of citizenship in a free society," an obligation that Worthy feared too many of
his corporate peers had neglected in favor of enhancing profit exclusively.[179]

Worthy had long advanced this perspective, even noting in a 1949 review of
Alexander Heron's *Why Men Work* that "American management, in attempting to
think through its problems, particularly in the field of human relations, is turning
more and more to the basic democratic ideals and is seeking, in an ever more
rewarding effort, to give them more effective expression in the administration of its
daily affairs."[180]

Over time, commerce schools would become more aware of the sophistication
of what they were attempting. Further, they would play a central part in producing
not only functioning (and functional) technicians but also well-rounded managers
whose values and talents would, in Worthy's view, "stimulate a sense of personal
worth and individual freedom" while also supporting the nation's economic life.

Northwestern's School of Commerce would be chief among those pointing the way forward for business. Its curriculum, though constantly improving, was already ahead of its time, anticipating trends that others would only realize as late as 1960. One discipline in particular—marketing—would help build the school's academic reputation and influence. Indeed, the Kellogg School would revolutionize marketing, becoming its international leader and leaving an indelible mark on an area that was to become integral to business strategy in all organizations.

Northwestern marketing students in 1952 analyze the effectiveness of advertisements.

Chapter 2

GROWTH OF A MARKETING TITAN: THE "HIDDEN PERSUADERS" COME OUT OF HIDING

Marketing was among the School of Commerce's early strengths, as scholars articulated the principles of an emerging field that would bring the school acclaim. Marketing's development mirrored the way business itself grew more sophisticated over the century, offering perspective on concerns facing practitioners and academicians.

Marketing's flowering as a discipline and Northwestern University's role in advancing this field are the substance of a narrative that extended through the twentieth century and continues today. When scholars recall the discipline's origins, they note the part played by Midwest universities in the United States, including the Kellogg School of Management and its predecessor schools dating to 1908, which produced some of marketing's foundational research and teaching. Of particular value was the way in which these schools, between 1910 and 1920, integrated marketing thought from the century's first decade. In so doing, they emphasized initial principles and functions, "treating the subject with a fullness which has since characterized the central body of marketing literature," according to historian Robert Bartels.[1]

As a function, marketing serves as a lens through which to observe the ways business shifted, growing larger and more technologically complex over the last century or so—tendencies that have their roots in the Second Industrial Revolution (1871–1914). By 1900, the factory system's success had instilled unbridled confidence in economic theories erected on a sanguine perspective, such as that of Adam Smith.

Indeed, "at the onset of the twentieth century, students of marketing were equipped with a general philosophy of optimism, a vision of new frontiers of progress, a businessman's viewpoint of confidence in the free play of the market and widespread agreement that consumers acted rationally in the market."[2] Progressively larger markets, a result of the U.S. population jumping from 31.4 million in 1860 to 91.9 million in 1900, meant that production—increasingly standardized—occurred on a larger scale than ever before, circumstances that placed new importance on information systems and promotion. As School of Commerce professor Homer Vanderblue remarked in 1921: "Probably no [marketing] function has greater ramifications than has standardization. Known grades and qualities are the basis of contracts of sale; they are the basis of warehouse receipts and bank loans; . . . also the basis of the growth of advertising . . . [since] standardization is essential for sale by brand in order that all purchasers, guided by satisfaction from an original purchase, shall not be disappointed because of uncertain quality."[3]

This situation also encouraged the rise of specialists who could bring buyers and sellers together. Demographics and technology, including transportation and communication, created conditions that no longer allowed the easy assumption that these parties knew each other, as had been the case traditionally. Consequently, middlemen gained significance, and over time they took such diversified forms as department stores, mail-order houses and chain stores, leading to new concepts of value that encompassed services as well as products and challenged classical economic theories. The new system of production and distribution would contribute to novel social problems, such as the insecurity of buyers as nonlocal markets became prominent. Insecurity would vex consumers too, as they no longer interacted directly with producers, whose goods they could experience immediately and personally, but only through distributive intermediaries.[4]

Since 1900, marketing has become gradually more sophisticated and central to business strategy. Although commodity markets have existed since at least ancient Sumerian times when livestock and other items were traded, the use of refined marketing techniques as a social and managerial function to enhance transactions between producer and consumer is a relatively modern invention. Kellogg School professors have played a vital role in marketing's evolution, and the school itself has earned acclaim for its marketing leadership.

Walter Dill Scott, Fred Emerson Clark and Paul W. Ivey were among the school's marketing trailblazers in the 1920s and earlier, producing seminal works that established the principles of advertising and marketing. But Northwestern boasted other faculty members who were also important to establishing the discipline and the school's reputation. In the process, these figures drew upon knowledge in a variety of academic areas, from economics and mathematics to anthropology and psychology. Lloyd D. Herrold joined the school in 1923 and continued a line of inquiry based on Scott's applied approach to psychology and advertising, with titles such as *Advertising for Retailers, Advertising Copy: Principles and Practice,* and *Advertising Real Estate.*[5]

Delbert J. Duncan arrived at Northwestern in 1930 and, along with Ira D. Anderson, founded and directed the school's Retail Service Scholarship Program, beginning in 1936.[6] The initiative placed graduate interns with prominent Chicago retail stores, including Sears; Wieboldt's; Carson, Pirie, Scott; and Marshall Field's. The program's success was measured in part by the quality of its students, such as future School of Commerce marketing scholars Ralph L. Westfall and Harper W. Boyd. Duncan (with coauthor C. F. Phillips) also produced the influential textbooks *Retailing: Principles and Methods* and *Marketing: Principles and Methods.*[7] Anderson, meanwhile, published *Principles of Retailing* (coauthored with Clare W. Barker). Lyndon O. Brown made contributions to marketing research, and his peers Herrold and James R. Hawkinson did the same for advertising and sales management, respectively.

By midcentury, the school could claim Richard M. Clewett's expertise in distribution channels—an area whose importance another Kellogg colleague, Louis Stern, would amplify and articulate brilliantly as a behavioral and interorganizational relationship, beginning in the early 1970s. From the 1960s on, Kellogg professors such as Philip Kotler and Sidney J. Levy truly began transforming marketing's definitions and scope. Levy may be credited with helping give rise to modern "branding" theory with his research, as in his "Symbols for Sale" (1959). And "Broadening the Concept of Marketing" (1969), coauthored by Levy and Kotler, shook the field by declaring that "everyone markets," not just businesses. "The article was really revolutionary, but it also was threatening to some," recalled Kotler.[8] The research built on foundations laid by other scholars, among them many at Northwestern's School of Commerce.

Other Kellogg professors have also distinguished themselves since the midtwentieth century, such as Boyd, Westfall, Steuart Henderson Britt and Gerald Zaltman. More recently, Bobby Calder, Brian Sternthal, Alice Tybout, Lakshman Krishnamurthi, Dipak C. Jain, Anne Coughlan, Andris Zoltners, Greg Carpenter, James Anderson, Angela Lee and Alex Chernev, among others, have contributed their intellects to the Kellogg School's Marketing Department.

From its inception in 1908 and earlier, under the aegis of Northwestern, Kellogg has contributed critical insights to marketing, a discipline that arose as an academic subject only after 1900 but developed relatively quickly—fast enough that, by 1957, Vance Packard's *Hidden Persuaders* could conjure "the chilling world of George Orwell and his Big Brother" to describe the "use of mass psychoanalysis to guide campaigns of persuasion . . . [as] the basis of a multimillion-dollar industry."[9] The advent of another young field, psychology, and the established area of economics were vital to the way in which early marketers taught and practiced their craft.

The Roots of Marketing Research

One of those at the forefront of applied psychology was Walter Dill Scott, who graduated from Northwestern in 1895. There, he studied psychology, which was then a subdivision of philosophy. Among the most influential of Scott's teachers were George A. Coe and Robert M. Cumnock. Coe encouraged in his pupil a profound appreciation for the practical application of knowledge, including human relations and potential. Cumnock's lessons sparked Scott's interest in public speaking.[10] In 1895, Scott enrolled at McCormick Theological Seminary. Upon graduation in 1898, he married a Northwestern classmate, Anna Marcy Miller, and both pursued additional advanced studies in Germany that year—Walter at the University of Leipzig, working under Wilhelm Wundt, who is frequently credited as the father of experimental and cognitive psychology,[11] and Anna at the University of Halle, where she earned a doctorate in philology. They returned to the United States in 1900, and the following year, Northwestern appointed Scott assistant psychology professor and made him director of its psychological laboratory.

In 1901, Scott accepted an invitation by Thomas L. Balmer, western advertising manager for Butterick magazines, to lecture on advertising psychology to the Agate Club of Chicago. His topic was "The Psychology of Involuntary Attention as Applied to Advertising," and during his presentation, he detailed six principles of human attention, noting the limits of the attention span and reporting that experiments had indicated a person could typically observe no more than four objects simultaneously. Among Scott's key points were the concepts that pictures were more effective than words and that the best advertisements appealed to the emotions and intellect. The lecture impressed the attendees, including John L. Mahin, who owned his own advertising company and agreed to publish a monthly essay by Scott in *Mahin's Magazine,* a trade journal that advocated scientific advertising.[12] Though Professor Harlow Gale,[13] of the University of Minnesota, had already investigated the application of psychological principles to advertising study, Scott was one of the first psychologists to challenge publicly the traditional academic view that it was inappropriate to apply social science to business. This position entailed some risk for him, since it broke with convention.

His research produced several influential texts, including *The Theory of Advertising* in 1903—the first such book in its field and partially subsidized by Balmer[14]—and *The Psychology of Public Speaking* in 1907. He followed this with the 1908 publication of *The Psychology of Advertising in Theory and Practice,* which established principles rooted in empirical science to analyze the stimuli that encourage people to buy.

In 1906, Scott became chair of the university's Psychology Department before joining the School of Commerce three years later, where he delivered what, in terms of content if not name, could be considered the institution's first marketing course. Though "Psychology of Business, Advertising and Salesmanship" focused on advertising and psychology, rather than marketing in a strict sense, the course introduced critical ideas related to mental function (such as attention, idea association, illusions and perception) in a way designed to aid practitioners. The psychological laws Scott taught were not novel, but the context in which he applied them—business—surely was. Bartels noted that Scott was among the writers of the time who "typified the close relationship that existed . . . between the business of advertising and the social science of psychology, a relationship that faded in later years as emphasis on technical knowledge of marketing increased."[15]

Evidence of advertising dates to ancient Egypt and Greece and Rome, where papyrus posters were common. But advertising's importance at the turn of the twentieth century is especially appreciated, given that business then was "weighted with products for which there was no apparent market, and disposing of them was a problem," according to Bartels. (A related challenge would arise after each world war, for the increased manufacturing rates necessitated by the conflict would have to be adjusted to peacetime markets. But the wartime efficiencies resulted in the production of many goods whose distribution relied, in part, upon marketing to create a demand for the relative surplus.) Professional advertising in the United States was still just a few decades old; it was only in 1841 that Volney Palmer had opened the nation's first ad agency in Philadelphia. Ten years later, print advertising began increasing. Robert Bonner is credited as running the first full-page ad in a paper when, in 1856, he promoted his own publication, a literary organ called the *New York Ledger.* In 1864, William James Carlton founded an ad agency that was renamed the James Walter Thompson Company in 1877; today, known as JWT, it is the world's fourth-largest advertising firm and the oldest continuous U.S. ad agency. Interest in advertising prompted the launch of trade journals, including George P. Rowell's *Printer's Ink* in 1888, the oldest and most prestigious magazine dedicated to advertisers and copywriters. The following year, James B. Duke spent $80,000—20 percent of the gross sales of his tobacco company—on advertising. (That tactic seemed to work: by 1890, Duke's American Tobacco Company, formed after a bitter dispute with four other principle manufacturers who ultimately agreed to the consolidation with Duke as its president,[16] controlled some 40 percent of the American cigarette market. It maintained that position until 1906, when it was forced to split into three companies after officials were found guilty of antitrust violations.)

The advertising field was growing significantly, though without an academic framework to support it. Since advertising was enjoying ever greater success, its practice stimulated interest in understanding—and manipulating—customer desire. Psychology seemed to offer great insight into this mysterious terrain, and the dynamics of the selling process—attention, interest, desire, action—"were a formula to be applied."[17]

The formula depended upon cross-disciplinary study. From about 1900 until the early 1920s, advocates of scientific advertising used experimental data to improve marketing and to plan and prepare ad copy. "At the turn of the century American advertising, with other emerging industries and professions, sought to redefine itself by acquiring the prestige accorded the sciences," observed artist and design historian Ellen Mazur Thomson. "This does not mean . . . that the theoretical basis for advertising was superficially elaborated. Science in the form of experimental psychology provided organizing principles for many activities in the advertising industry, including the design of advertising art."[18] By 1910, some $600 million would be spent on business advertising, representing 4 percent of the national income.[19]

For Scott, the practical implications of his research became apparent. "I have never seen or heard any reference to anything except psychology which could furnish a stable foundation for a theory of advertising. . . . Ordinarily the business man does not realize that he means psychology when he says that he 'must know his customers' wants—what will catch their attention, what will impress them and lead them to buy,'" wrote Scott in his 1908 text,[20] a book whose concepts would find a receptive audience the following year when the author included them in his Northwestern course. Other marketing-related courses at the school included merchandising, advertising and salesmanship. Of particular interest for Scott was synthesizing the various strands of psychology and presenting them in a practical way. He noted that advertising psychology had, in less than a decade, "reached a stage . . . where all that has thus far been accomplished should be reconsidered," with "worthless" material being discarded in favor of the valuable insights. What's more, these ideas represented exactly the material Scott wanted to present in "systematic arrangement" so that it would be of "distinct practical value to all who are interested in business promotion."[21] In fact, it was Scott who encouraged Joseph Schaffner to adopt the symbol of a man on horseback for Hart, Schaffner & Marx advertising in 1909. The image was to suggest "rugged yet refined manliness," and the exercise itself indicated one way the professor tried to integrate his teaching and his practical work. When the advertisement was published, Scott brought a stack of the newspapers to his classroom to test his students' responsiveness to the design.[22]

Examples from Scott's work suggest the scope of his thinking and its implications for melding theory with practice, "For the science of psychology is in respect to certain data merely common sense, *the wisdom of experience, analyzed,* formulated, and codified" (emphasis added).[23] One of his goals was to create a framework that would be useful for prediction and explication, and Scott was optimistic about his discipline's contributions for practitioners. His perspective, though not entirely embraced by his peers, was in tune with the excitement of the times, particularly given the discoveries and inventions that had transformed everyday life. "By the application of known physical laws the telephone and the telegraph have supplanted the messenger boy," he wrote. "By the laws of psychology applied to business equally astounding improvements are being and will be secured."[24]

For his students, Scott dismantled preconceptions associated with the priority given to reason in advertising. He illustrated the importance of other psychological tools, such as suggestion. "It was once supposed that suggestion was something abnormal and that reason was the common attribute of men," he wrote in *The Psychology of Advertising.* "To-day we are finding that suggestion is of universal application to all persons, while reason is a process which is exceptional, even among the wisest. We reason rarely, but act under suggestion constantly."[25]

Scott's insights were discriminating. For instance, he distinguished between persuasion and suggestion, noting that even though some customers were indeed persuaded to make a purchase, they more often did so due to a well-timed suggestion. In practice, he taught, "suggestion should not be subordinated to persuasion but should be supplemented by it. The actual effect of modern advertising is not so much to convince as to suggest."[26]

Both Scott's texts and his classes offered biological details related to cognition so that the students gained an appreciation for the mechanisms involved, increasing the likelihood that they could devise more effective advertising strategies. Scott's chapter on perception, for example, emphasized the mind-body connection, offering a gloss on the nervous system ("nerve fibers are white, threadlike bands, which connect each nerve ending with a particular part of the brain"; "function of the nervous system may be likened to the transmitter, connecting wire, and receiver of the telephone. . . . If air waves of a certain quality and of sufficient intensity strike against the transmitter of a telephone, electric currents are set up . . . propagated along the line till they reach the receiver").[27]

A Force for Social Good

Aware of the stereotypes still surrounding advertisers (the "bombast, hyperbole, and deceit" of the world's P. T. Barnums), Scott noted a gradual change in public perception from 50 years earlier, when the advertiser was "one of the least respected members of one of the least respected classes of society [that is, business]." By the 1921 edition of *Psychology of Advertising*, however, the author could state that advertisers and business professionals in general were in the most highly respected social strata. Such a "remarkable change" could not be accidental, he added, but only the result of "a psychological law that will continue to control the further evolution of advertising." Scott contended that this transformation indicated society's "profound respect and confidence" in regard to a professional segment rendering the "most vital" service.[28]

Like others involved in the School of Commerce, Scott believed that business could and should be a force for social good, as well as a profitable enterprise. He reflected upon the rapid industrialization of America between 1865 and 1900, pointing out that the "capitalist was the American ideal" because of the great advances in transportation and industry he brought about. "We looked up to him and permitted him to dictate our laws and our national policy," said Scott. Two decades into the twentieth century, the Northwestern president believed a sense of civic pride should inform the advertiser's profession too. Although common perceptions of the field held that "no man goes in for advertising unless he expects to find it profitable, the only way to make money in advertising is to *render social service*" (emphasis added).[29]

Scott, educated in Germany under the influence of the Historical school of economic thought, believed this social awareness was important. Like former Northwestern presidents Harris and James and School of Commerce colleague Earl Dean Howard, Scott had studied in Germany during a time when a new economic view had emerged, concerned with applying theory to solve real problems, including poverty. Proponents of the Historical school, which arose about 1850 in reaction to dominant laissez-faire market thought, charged that their classical economic counterparts had done little to assuage social ills. This progressive framework was distinctive for its historical, statistical methodology and for its pragmatism and ideals, rather than for theoretical ideas divorced from action. Advocates of the Historical view believed that cultural context, more than mathematical logic, was a valid starting point for economic analysis. They also prized empiricism rather than abstraction, and so, "during the 1880s and possibly even earlier, students in economics often went on excursions to various industrial establishments to study firsthand the institutional forces in the economy."[30]

The Historical school influenced the development of economic education in the United States in large part because of its influence on scholars who returned to America and integrated the thought into universities and business schools, among them Northwestern's School of Commerce. Schools whose curricula were similarly shaped included the University of Wisconsin–Madison, Columbia, the University of Pennsylvania, Harvard, the University of Michigan and a number of others. In addition to Scott and his Northwestern colleagues directly exposed to study in Germany, other School of Commerce faculty would have views indirectly shaped by the Historical approach, notably marketing professors Fred Clark and Paul Ivey, whose contributions will be noted later.[31]

This practical focus encouraged Scott to pursue research beyond advertising. Although he continued to explore the role of psychology applied to advertising (including in his 1911 work entitled *Influencing Men in Business: The Psychology of Argument and Suggestion*), he also turned his attention to problems of personnel selection, seeking to establish a science in an area that, until then, had been dominated by employment managers whose methods were intuitive and erratic. Scott developed vocational aptitude tests, revising the products in the university's laboratory until they comprised a systematic technique—one that would influence military decisions in World War I, when Scott offered his services to the nation's War Bureau. There, despite initial skepticism by some army members, Scott devised a method for identifying potential officers using psychological tools. The work was ultimately hailed as a success. When Scott was discharged from the bureau in 1919, it was with a colonel's rank. By then, he had also earned the Distinguished Service Medal.[32] That year, he founded the Scott Company Engineers and Consultants in Industrial Personnel, with offices in Chicago, Philadelphia and Dayton. In 1920, Northwestern University offered Scott its presidency. Despite the Scott Company's promising future and the university's challenging financial circumstances, Scott indulged his passion for education and took up the presidency, a post he would retain until his retirement in 1939.

Commerce Faculty Members Help Launch
American Marketing Association

Scott's influence, along with that of other School of Commerce faculty members, proved instrumental in creating the American Marketing Association. Founded in Chicago in June 1915 as the National Association of Teachers of Advertising (NATA), the AMA continues today as the preeminent professional group for marketers, with some 38,000 members worldwide.[33] Along with commerce school dean Willard Hotchkiss, Scott was among the organization's 28 initial scholars seeking to determine "what constituted advertising and what should be included in a study of advertising."[34] From this discussion, the AMA went on to define traditional marketing as a process of planning and executing the conception, pricing, promotion and distribution of ideas, goods and services to create exchanges that satisfied individual and organizational objectives. A more updated definition from the group described marketing as "an organizational function and set of processes for creating, communicating and delivering value to customers and for managing customer relationships in ways that benefit the organization and its stakeholders."[35]

The group's first gathering was attended by Ralph Starr Butler, J. W. Piercy, Harry Tipper, Martin Pierce, Harry D. Kitson, George Burton Hotchkiss and Hugh E. Agnew, among others.[36] The members decided to name their organization the National Association of Teachers of Advertising not only because that name directly reflected the vocations of most of those involved but also because marketing remained nascent at the time. "The teaching of marketing had not yet emerged as of great importance," noted Agnew. "The techniques of advertising, however, were being extensively explored, particularly the application of psychology to advertising which had been advanced by Dr. Scott in his excellent books."[37] Those gathered at this meeting elected Scott as their first president.

But this was not the only association interested in the emerging marketing field. As Bartels noted, "It is apparent that between 1915 and 1918 interest in marketing, and the number of marketing-interested teachers, had increased to the point that they began to meet each other at meetings of other professional societies." One such instance involved marketing professor Fred E. Clark, who would join the School of Commerce in 1919. The year before, Yale professor L. D. H. Weld, another marketing pioneer, approached Clark at an American Economic Association meeting to solicit his interest in forming a semiformal association of scholars interested in marketing.[38] The group, consisting originally of about a half dozen men, met annually and "grew fairly rapidly," according to Weld. In 1924, this association was invited to merge with NATA; many members made the change, and the larger organization changed its name to the National Association of Teachers of Marketing and Advertising. Fred Clark would become president of the group in 1928, based on his important contributions as a pioneer in the marketing field.

Clark, along with his colleague Ivey, would prove instrumental in advancing marketing thought during what Bartels termed the discipline's "period of integration," a time spanning from 1920 until 1930 during which the principles of marketing were postulated and a general literature on the subject was compiled.

Although earlier scholars made initial discoveries (between 1900 and 1910) about distributive trades using theory borrowed from economics and then later peers devised concepts and defined terms (from 1910 to 1920), figures such as Clark and Ivey, both graduates of the economics program at the University of Illinois, played a critical role in synthesizing such material to allow marketing study to move beyond its rudimentary form.[39] This contribution is noteworthy because early marketing thinking was driven by those who did not intend to create a "body of thought," according to Bartels. They did strive to develop practical approaches that could solve real problems; any contributions that presented a structured or unified framework were secondary considerations in the service of "describing, explaining, and justifying prevailing marketing practices and institutions, particularly newer ones . . . [and] were offered to clarify misconceptions held among the public, such as the belief that the wholesaler was parasitic and would disappear from the distributive system, fear of the annihilation of small stores by chain organizations, and dismay at the plight of consumers before the ruthless practices of vendors."[40]

Bartels's 1974 article, "The Identity Crisis in Marketing,"[41] nicely traced the general transformations that the discipline had undergone over seven decades. He noted that early marketing was almost entirely subsumed by economics and conceived primarily as a technical process focused on physical distribution and the legalities of the transaction. Starting in the 1920s, the discipline became defined more by the functions and problems of institutions and their operations.

Marketing "Principles" and Integration Advance the Field

In his major publication, *Principles of Marketing,* published in 1922 and revised in two volumes in 1929,[42] Clark defined the activity of marketing as "those efforts which effect transfers in the ownership of goods and their physical distribution," reflecting an understanding of marketing's economic foundations, as Bartels noted. But Clark, a 1916 graduate of the University of Illinois doctoral program in economics, also appreciated the ways that marketing was creating new conditions that classical economic theory was less prepared to address. Specifically, he observed that competition as understood by traditional economic models—for instance, one centered on price and price-cutting—was complicated by advertising and marketing practices based on the antithesis, which was "demand development" at a price. "That is, if goods do not sell in the desired volume, prices are not necessarily cut," he wrote, "rather an effort will be made to increase the demand at the price at which the supply was first ordered."[43]

Clark made similar observations in an earlier publication, where he critiqued marketing efficiency in ways that seemed to challenge traditional laissez-faire economic models.[44] He suggested that facile notions of competitive markets, a cherished economic fundamental, could no longer serve as the entire theoretical foundation in a system increasingly driven by middlemen whose interactions between producer and consumer created complexity. He was concerned with marketing from a social perspective and would defend advertising for its educational value and for sometimes providing a cheaper method of selling than personal salesmanship would provide. "He placed hope in the chain store as an efficient method of merchandising . . . [and] advocated more standardization of consumer goods but questioned the desirability of branded staples."[45]

Clark believed that scholars and practitioners had "long since reached a point where a large group of investigators take it for granted that the competitive regime imputed to the classical economist's mind is and must be supplemented or abandoned." He believed that "something more"—government assistance and private cooperation—was required to augment existing economic theory and "bring about a proper correlation between individual activities, particularly between . . . producers or consumers of specific products." These elements would increase "general efficiencies" variously, he thought, including by improving market information, limiting or increasing production based on market demands, improving transportation and standardization of products, eliminating unnecessary middlemen and controlling excess profits.[46]

In his research, Clark addressed the way in which marketing affected modern distribution. He acknowledged prevailing criticisms of marketing and suggested that, on balance, it was a productive, value-added force, though one that admittedly created new challenges. For example, Clark noted five common criticisms of advertising that indicated how problematic the young field was for those still viewing the market through a nineteenth-century glass. Marketing's detractors typically called the practice expensive and even socially wasteful, said Clark. It was also an activity that "emphasize[d] the purely acquisitive features of business . . . [and] increase[d] the demand for luxuries, variety, style, and create[d] fictitious values." Critics also charged that marketing was ineffective and, perhaps most important, that it tended to increase product differentiation (e.g., branded goods) and thus increased the cost of distribution.[47]

Although branding became a desired practice and strategy as marketing developed, it was initially viewed with suspicion, as something that created inefficiencies in the distribution system. Clark acknowledged that the rise of individualized, branded staple commodities "eliminates many of the economies of commodity standardization, and so renders comparisons more difficult for the buyer to make, and consequently increases the cost of exchange."[48] Nonetheless, advertising and branding exerted another effect, one beneficial to cost efficiency, Clark believed—the development of broad markets suitable for goods produced on a large scale and in specialized (regional) areas. Advertising also helped improve efficiencies in sales, making them more economical.[49]

With respect to the complaint that advertising increased desires for luxuries and fostered empty values, Clark noted the subjective quality of this value judgment. But he also believed that advertising's influence in creating demand was overstated, although he noted its role in conveying information to consumers. Perhaps most important, he revealed that marketers had forced a fundamental change in the competitive emphasis, shifting the focus from classical economic models and their attention to straightforward supply/demand based on price and instead introduced more subtle values that were rooted in the consumer's psychology.

His framework for *Principles of Marketing* took a functional approach, breaking down marketing practice into three main categories: Functions of Exchange (demand creation, assembly), Functions of Physical Supply (transportation, storage), and Auxiliary or Facilitating Functions (financing, risk taking, standardization). This structure emulated to some degree a structure presented by L. D. H. Weld in "Marketing Functions and Mercantile Organizations," an article that appeared in the *American Economic Review* in 1917—which was not surprising, since Clark identified Weld as a significant influence;[50] moreover, he would, in 1932, collaborate with Weld on a second major publication, entitled *Marketing Agricultural Products in the United States,* a text that would be a prominent reference work in agricultural marketing for years.[51] But Clark intended his treatment to offer readers a base from which "to develop the functional approach," as his preface indicated. He also wanted the work to blend theory and practice, a lifelong objective; this was attested by a retrospective tribute delivered in 1957 by Richard Clewett, who also remarked that *Principles* "succeeded in bringing . . . readers and students a greater appreciation of the potentialities of and need for more analysis in a field characterized for the most part by description."[52] Clark's approach was exhaustive, with 26 chapters covering material ranging from marketing and wholesaling farm products (a topic that captured Clark's attention early on due to his growing up on a farm in Albion, Michigan, and a subject reflected in his master's thesis, "Cooperative Grain Elevator Movement in Illinois"[53]) to distribution, financing, marketing efficiency and much more.

With respect to value creation in marketing, Clark built on ideas articulated by Weld and Arch Shaw (specifically as found in Shaw's "Some Problems in Market Distribution" and *An Approach to Business Problems*). He also cited the value of the Bureau of Business Research established at the School of Commerce in 1919 and directed by Professor Horace Secrist, who oversaw a survey of the clothing industry that was published in six volumes after an 18-month study.[54] Clark thought that demand creation, something that "has probably always been associated with marketing," had grown especially important in modern commerce, which, because of its increased production capabilities, resulted in "a larger number of products than the public has been in the habit of consuming." Some of these were staples, others were luxury goods. Clark noted that new products were especially challenging to market because "little or no general desire exists" for them.[55]

Clark's colleague Paul Ivey actually published his *Principles* first, in 1921, although Bartels noted that others had previously used the word in titles in conjunction with advertising and retail, though not marketing. Ivey earned his bachelor's degree at Lawrence College and then received his master's credential at Illinois in 1913, concurrently with Clark. Afterward, several teaching assignments took him to Michigan, Iowa and Nebraska universities and then to Northwestern's School of Commerce in 1923, where Clark had been on faculty since 1919 after teaching at the University of Michigan.[56] Both men approached marketing from a "functions" perspective, dissecting the practice into its constituents (such as assembling, grading, storing, transporting, financing and selling) and claiming a sort of universality for the functions performed by middlemen.

In addition to his marketing contributions, Ivey also was among those advocating that salesmanship could be taught. By the middle of the 1920s, his *Salesmanship Applied* outlined an approach that he had also presented on the paid lecture circuit as "The Paul Ivey Salesmanship Institute." He described what he called "the selling personality" and emphasized the importance of persuading the customer "to accept your viewpoint in the sale and purchase of goods." He also claimed that "everyone is a salesman," a view that contrasted sharply with earlier ones averring that only a special few could attain the skills to sell.[57]

Retail Training: A Partnership between Academics and Practitioners

As Louis W. Stern and others have observed, the growth of urban markets in America after 1850 "followed the spreading railroad network [and] had a profound effect on the marketing of consumer goods,"[58] resulting in many practical innovations, like the growth of department stores. A subset of the School of Commerce marketing curriculum offered classes in retailing, with courses covering all aspects of this enterprise available to students in the evening and day programs. Faculty designed the curriculum to prepare students for "positions of responsibility in the retail field" through training that took a "broad outlook on the entire field of business and economics."[59]

Ira Anderson's *Principles of Retailing* (coauthored with Clare W. Barker) was written in 1935 while he was an assistant professor of economics and business administration at Ohio Wesleyan University, a position he held from 1933 to 1935, following yearlong stints teaching merchandising at the University of Notre Dame (1931–1932) and Indiana University (1932–1933). From 1935 to 1937, he served as assistant chief of retail trade of the U.S. Bureau of the Census, before returning as an assistant marketing professor to Northwestern, where he had earned an MBA degree in 1930. He would become the associate dean and director of the undergraduate school of business at Northwestern in 1953 and provide leadership in the American Marketing Association.[60] His *Principles of Retailing* surveyed the retail landscape, noting that rapid changes had transformed the way in which merchandise was distributed—especially the retailing of merchandise—and making it imperative for those entering the retail trades to gain an understanding of its modern dynamics. "Neither the manufacturer nor the wholesaler can be successful unless the retailer succeeds in selling the goods," Anderson wrote in the book's preface. "Thus, we find the manufacturer and wholesaler, as well as the retailer, vitally interested in studying the principles underlying successful retailing."

The book offered a detailed overview of all of retailing's elements, from a survey of the field's early development to modern store layouts and locations. The authors noted the erosion of distinct traditional merchandising lines in favor of "scrambled retailing" that provided an array of goods under one roof, circumstances driven by the consumer desire for convenience. "Although additional lines are being added in nearly all retail stores, the greatest change is taking place in the drug, grocery, cigar and 5-and-10-cent stores," wrote Anderson and Barker, making reference to Fred Clark's 1933 text *Readings in Marketing*, which included a section on the convenience phenomenon. "Practically all the items being added by these stores are in the group of convenience articles."[61] The authors also made an important point that later marketers would amplify, namely, the way retailers anticipate consumers' unarticulated needs. "It is only when we try to visualize a world without the retailer that we realize how much he does for us. Before we become aware of our own needs, he has foreseen them and has searched the world to get these things."[62]

In their historical account of retailing, Anderson and Barker traced its rise from ancient barter 5,000 years ago through Greek and Roman times into the Middle Ages and up until the contemporary day. In colonial America, general store keepers rarely had to contend with tastes that changed quickly but instead made only one annual trip to the city to secure stock for the next year—a journey that was both treacherous and arduous before the advent of railroads. By the end of the Civil War, however, retailers faced growing demands from customers "wanting a greater variety of merchandise" and better service. Fashion likewise began to change more rapidly, placing additional demands on retailers, a situation, the authors noted, that only grew more prevalent in the decades leading to the publication of their text.[63]

Consumers, as much as retailers, were changing the commercial dynamic, creating additional complexity from which Northwestern faculty would draw much insight for teaching and research. By 1941, marketing professor James R. Hawkinson '29 was noting this trend. In a discussion about distribution issues published in the *Journal of Marketing,* he observed: "Apparently, consumer groups are becoming aware of their potential influence on the retailer and are exerting that influence better to serve their needs." Retailers should pay attention, he advised, although too few of them seemed to do so. However, he continued, "consumers seem skeptical of what some retailers have done to meet their requests . . . the consumer needs some training in and understanding of retailing problems." Hawkinson enumerated the problems, such as challenges in training temporary personnel, the cost of returns and decreasing sales "when costs do not decrease proportionately." He saw the work of the National Consumer-Retailer Council as finding ways to bring the two groups together in mutual understanding.[64]

The School of Commerce was doing its part to enhance retail education at the collegiate level. The school saw "abundant opportunity" in the retail arena for those with sufficient foresight to obtain the necessary education. Instruction ranged from the principles of marketing and retail store management to personnel management,[65] merchandise control, fashion merchandising, advertising and retail layout construction that focused on "balance, movement, contrast, rhythm, harmony, and appropriateness" of newspaper ads and direct-mail pieces.[66] In addition to commerce school faculty members Clark, Lloyd Herrold, Delbert Duncan, Anderson and Elizabeth Paine, a number of special lecturers from leading area retailers contributed their talents in the classroom. These included representatives from Marshall Field and Company; Carson, Pirie, Scott & Co.; Wieboldt Stores, Inc.; Sears, Roebuck & Co.; Montgomery Ward & Company; Chas. A. Stevens and Company; and others. Among the more noteworthy lecturers was Wieboldt president Elmer F. Wieboldt, son of the store's founder, William. Elmer was also among a dozen major executives serving as the retailing program's advisory committee, providing the school with recommendations for projects and information about the retailers' practical needs, which could then contribute to refinements in the program.[67] Other lecturers included Frederick H. Scott Jr. and Archibald MacLeish, who represented Carson, Pirie, Scott. MacLeish, a modernist poet and writer who had already earned one of his three Pulitzer Prizes, would serve as librarian of Congress from 1939 until 1944. His connection with the retailer came through his father, Andrew MacLeish, a prosperous Chicago dry goods merchant who helped Samuel Carson and John T. Pirie establish the firm's retail department store in 1867 and remained its head until he died in 1928.[68]

Chicago could claim one of the world's foremost retailers in Marshall Field, who would found the store bearing his name in 1881 after earlier experience operating dry goods establishments in partnerships with Potter Palmer and Levi Leiter (in fact, most early department stores were primarily dry goods merchants).[69] Other retailers would join Marshall Field and Company in establishing stores in Chicago's Loop. Among these were Carson, Pirie, Scott & Co., Mandel Brothers and Schlesinger & Mayer. The stores posed a threat to smaller retailers, but most customers flocked to the new way of shopping. Field's in particular garnered a reputation for excellent quality and service—even sending its elevator operators to charm school. Most impressive was the sheer size of the Field's buildings. The company's State Street location, which opened in 1907, featured 76 elevators, 31 miles of carpeting and 23,000 fire sprinklers. The 12-story building's centerpiece was its Tiffany dome, a glass mosaic covering 6,000 square feet and rising 6 floors.[70] At the time, Field's employed about 10,000 people. The company would also open two stores outside the Loop: in October 1929, the retailer launched its Oak Park branch, and in November of that year, a replica of the downtown flagship store opened in Evanston at Sherman and Church streets on a site formerly occupied by an old grammar school.[71] The cornerstone for the Evanston location was laid on July 10, 1929, in a ceremony that featured speeches by Dean Heilman and the city's mayor, Charles H. Bartlett. The Evanston shop was in a landmark art deco building and had a five-room model apartment, a formal women's apparel department, a beauty salon and a large inventory of toys. Both the Oak Park and Evanston stores would close at the end of 1986, for a reason that has affected department retailers in general: customer demographics shifted away from centralized urban areas into more suburban locations.

Recognizing the power of such retailers and the retail shopping experience, the School of Commerce incorporated an initiative designed to provide its graduate students with practical experience that would allow them to excel in this booming sector. From 1936 until 1948, the Retail Service Scholarship Program placed students deemed "potential executive material" as interns with prominent Chicago stores. Administered chiefly by Delbert Duncan and Ira Anderson, the program was intended, according to the purpose set forth by its advisory committee in June 1937, to train students "cooperatively—at school and at work—so that they will become valuable to the stores which train them and useful citizens in the retail world."[72] The initial group of students in the program were known as the "guinea pigs" because of the experimental nature of the work-study arrangement.[73] Typically, students worked 30 hours a week for 11 months with the retailers, receiving a salary (at the program's start, the figure was $15 a week; by 1942, it averaged $16.50 per week). In addition, they carried a full load of course work for the master's degree while also writing a thesis. "The service scholars are a small and carefully selected group of college graduates—both men and women—brought to Northwestern from every part of the United States," wrote Ira Anderson in describing the program. Each year, the school chose between 20 and 30 students from a total of 90 applicants. Among that select group would be future School of Commerce professors Ralph Westfall '40 (PhD '52) and Harper Boyd '41 (PhD '52).[74] Store managers rated the student interns using a form produced by the School of Commerce; skills and attributes such as appearance, tact, poise, dependability, initiative and promise of executive ability were among those assessed.[75] Despite the program's successes—driven in part by Duncan's insistence that students pursue "analytical thinking relative to business problems"[76]—the school decided to discontinue the graduate service by 1947. The postwar enrollment boom was creating significant challenges for the school, straining its resources and forcing Dean Homer Vanderblue to use many part-time instructors to meet the demand. Registration at the school quadrupled between 1944 and 1949, rising to more than 12,000. Female enrollment, however, plummeted from 58 percent in 1944 to only 5 percent by decade's end.[77] The curriculum also underwent a major review, one that had begun before the war. As part of this review, the faculty instituted a core curriculum. "This major reform, completed in 1946, introduced a comprehensive, coherently organized sequence of sixteen courses in the basic introductory fields of accounting, finance, production, marketing, business law, and business writing; additional theoretical work in statistics and economics; and a senior course in the problems of business administration, identified as 'business policy.'"[78] The work-study retailing program was terminated despite Professor Duncan's appeal to Vanderblue on behalf of the program in a letter dated September 16, 1946.

"In my judgment it would be most unfortunate to discontinue the graduate service program in retailing," wrote Duncan, who left that year to help Cornell University establish its School of Business and Public Administration, which would open in 1948. "It has attracted numerous students of high quality to Northwestern and should continue to do so. Moreover, it has served as an excellent source of junior executive material for the leading Chicago stores and also as a good point of contact between the University and Chicago business executives." He went on to note four administrative modifications to enhance the program, including adjusting the academic/vocational requirements. The letter concluded by stating the program's strengths: "Our Retailing Program has earned a favorable nation-wide reputation since its establishment in 1936. The quality of the material taught as well as the instruction have equaled or exceeded that of any other institution."[79]

The entreaty was not sufficient to save the program, though no document seems to exist to explain Vanderblue's rationale for dismantling it. Some have speculated that the postwar decline in female enrollment was a factor in his decision and that the dean was not overly fond of women pursuing full-time MBA studies.[80]

But marketing as a profession was only becoming more prominent, a point made by Fred Clark in 1942 when he assessed current trends in the discipline. Looking beyond World War II, Clark observed the coming need for trained professionals. "Business men realize that marketing problems will be increased when the war is over. Many are now searching for post-war markets for the products of enlarged plants operating on a basis of increased efficiency, and many of them will encourage their employees to study marketing." Clark recalled a similar dynamic after World War I and predicted that the demand for marketing would require more teachers. He also saw a role for academics in helping the government with "procurement, allocation of supplies, and the control and manipulation of prices."[81]

Postwar Marketing: New Ideas Lead to Many Models

Chicago was a good place for marketing studies given the city's commercial life. It also attracted those seeking to specialize in advertising and marketing. The Leo Burnett Company, for instance, was formed in Chicago in 1935, during the Depression. The company's founder was noteworthy for many innovations in that field, in particular for trying to capture the "inherent drama" of a product, rather than using long, detailed arguments to induce people to buy. "When you reach for the stars you may not quite get one," Burnett once said, "but you won't come up with a handful of mud either." He believed in the importance of getting a product noticed but felt that "the art is getting noticed naturally, without screaming and without tricks."[82]

At the time, however, there were few rigorous analytical tools to help achieve Burnett's objectives. According to James Smith, marketing research into the late 1930s could be characterized as a matter of playing "20 Questions." "Advertising campaigns rode largely on intuition and faith," he wrote. "Researchers used the same broad approaches to build questionnaires that probably elicited as much misinformation as fact."[83] Then, a young Northwestern University School of Commerce professor, Lyndon O. Brown, published *Market Research and Analysis* in 1937, a text that indicated how marketing research could benefit from more rigorous scientific frameworks.[84]

But despite such occasional efforts, marketing was still trying to find its modern path in the aftermath of World War II. In 1948, Brown declared that "in any developing field of human endeavor, progress to a professional level is earmarked in large measure by the extent to which critical thought has shifted from a descriptive basis to one which is primarily analytical . . . the foundation of marketing management is marketing research."[85] Brown, who earned a master's degree from Northwestern in

1931 and then a doctorate in economics four years later, was a professor in the commerce school's Marketing Department until 1943. Despite his own academic efforts, Brown flatly stated that marketing was not yet a profession, as it lacked the rigorous analytical foundation associated with true professions. Rather, he said, it was "still too largely in the descriptive phase." He reflected on the accomplishments of another Northwestern marketing scholar from the previous generation, Fred E. Clark and his *Principles of Marketing,* published some 25 years earlier. "It did an essentially adequate descriptive job," said Brown, who was teaching a course in radio advertising at Northwestern in 1933—a new field, for commercial radio had made its debut only seven years earlier, in 1926.[86] "It is unfortunate that so much of the energy of the leading thinkers in the field has been devoted to restating and amplifying these descriptive aspects instead of breaking new ground analytically."

One way that marketing could achieve professional status, he claimed, was by gaining necessary perspective on the field's total scope and import. In addition, scholars needed to move away from mere "hunch, guesswork or enthusiasm" in favor of more scientific approaches, and they were urged to consolidate research methods rather than devise "new gadgets for research." Professional standards and ethics would have to rise, and the field would have to develop more basic knowledge—"a constantly expanding body of precise marketing facts on a scope far beyond present availabilities."[87]

Brown's lofty expectations for marketing eventually would be fulfilled by Northwestern professors. By the middle of the 1940s, School of Commerce faculty members were driving the discipline toward its modern incarnation, though their work's full fruition would require time.

The seeds planted in the school's retail program would produce lasting value in this respect, especially in the form of professorial talent that returned to the school as professors. Westfall, who joined the Marketing Department in 1946, and Boyd, who arrived in 1952, the year he earned his doctorate from Northwestern, were graduates of the retail program. Westfall had entered the school in 1939 on a retail management scholarship and would continue in the doctoral program until he was called for active duty with the U.S. Army in August 1941. He served for five years, including almost four with the 37th Division in the South Pacific.[88] After the war, he joined the marketing research department of Standard Oil Company of Indiana before receiving his doctorate from the School of Commerce in 1952. Boyd would serve as Marketing Department chair and director of the school's graduate division before leaving Northwestern in 1963 to join the Stanford School of Business.

Other colleagues also played key roles in expanding the department's expertise: Richard M. Clewett arrived in 1948 from the Wharton School, where he had been teaching and earning his doctorate. He would make special efforts to strengthen the department's overall talent, including mentoring junior faculty. He also advanced scholarship in the area of marketing channels, as did some of his doctoral students, such as: Louis P. Bucklin '60, who developed a channel structure theory grounded by economic theory; Louis W. Stern '62, who based his theory in economic and behavioral principles and applied them to designing and managing distribution channels; Stanley F. Stasch '64, who put channels into a systems analysis context; and Frederick D. Sturdivant '64, who developed new concepts and raised questions about channel effectiveness and efficiency from a social perspective.[89]

Stasch recalled entering the MBA program in 1957 for a year and then taking a full-time job at Motorola while continuing his studies on a part-time basis. He completed the program in 1961, after which he entered the school's doctoral program, then chaired by Clewett. Stasch would earn his doctorate in 1964, having become a part-time marketing instructor in Northwestern's School of Business the year before. He received an appointment as assistant professor at the school and remained on faculty there until 1977, when he moved to Loyola University in Chicago as the Charles H. Kellstadt Professor of Marketing.

"As an MBA student in marketing, I was greatly impressed by how Northwestern University's marketing faculty dominated the authorship of textbooks," said Stasch, noting the accomplishments of Boyd, Clewett, Westfall and others who joined the department later, such as Levy and Kotler. Soon, the department would become "clearly the leading marketing faculty in the country, and in the world," according to Stasch. By the late 1960s and into the 1970s, its doctoral program, which had undergone an enhancement in 1961 to add course work in advanced quantitative methods and computer technology, was producing significant numbers of marketing doctoral students, further enhancing the school's leadership in this area.[90] "Dick Clewett's contribution to this accomplishment was serving as chairman of the department," said Stasch. "I believe he helped each and every faculty member in marketing achieve their goals. He had a fantastic skill for seeing to it that every faculty member could continue to develop themselves to the fullest."[91]

Indeed, Clewett and his peers helped build the school's reputation in this discipline, which was evolving to encompass a variety of research paths. Some of these paths emphasized the social sciences and drew upon an "explosion of knowledge" that produced much specialization among marketing thinkers, according to Bartels.[92]

Traditional marketing thought was rooted in economics, but after World War II, a number of other disciplines, such as psychology, anthropology, mathematics and statistics, began playing a larger part and expanding marketing's possibilities. Paul

Converse noted the field's relative infancy and its principal influences: economics, scientific management, psychology and accounting. The "classified body of knowledge which we call the science of marketing," he wrote, "has evolved during the past 50 years—to a very considerable extent during the past 35 years—and it has been developed very largely by persons still living."[93]

Similarly, Bartels segmented the decade from 1940 to 1950 as the "period of reappraisal," in which traditional explanations were reconsidered in light of new needs for marketing knowledge and from a more scientific perspective. This was a time "identified with the refinement of statistical techniques and the growing interest in research methodology . . . [with] attention . . . given to sampling theory and to multivariate and correlation methods."[94] The period from 1950 to 1960 was associated with "reconception," when traditional approaches were supplemented by more emphasis on managerial decision making and on societal aspects of marketing and quantitative analysis. Many new concepts were introduced, some of which were borrowed from management and other social sciences, particularly the behavioral sciences. Advanced mathematical techniques also became more valuable for marketers.[95]

At the School of Commerce, these larger trends were already taking root in the 1950s, producing a more holistic view on the subject and one that looked beyond U.S. borders: Latin America, Asia and the Middle East were among the regions that captured the marketing faculty's attention. Boyd's 1961 collaboration with Egyptian colleagues, for example, examined distribution in that nation, describing it as especially important in the economic life of an underdeveloped country, since manufacturers "typically delegate their marketing activities to them." Drawing upon Boyd's 1960 visit to Egypt as project director of the Egyptian Management Development Institute's first training program in business administration, the study considered the importance of the region, "a vital area in the world-wide conflict between the West and the Soviet block."[96]

In the important area of channels, for instance, Northwestern faculty members were also early contributors, with Clewett producing *Marketing Channels for Manufactured Products* (as well as many journal articles and a survey of product managers in consumer packaged goods industries). With Boyd, he compiled the edited text *Contemporary American Marketing: Readings on the Changing Market Structure* in 1957. Westfall and Boyd would offer *Cases in Marketing Strategy* in 1961, an indication that the case approach remained prominent even as the department began extending the parameters of marketing research and teaching. The book offered a collection of 80 cases for use in a first course in marketing. "The authors succeed in stripping away unnecessary descriptive matter. . . . The cases provide provocative vehicles for realistic consideration of current issues," said a reviewer in the *Journal of Marketing*. "Marketing problems facing management at all levels of distribution from manufacturer to retailer are included."[97]

A 1954 review of *Marketing Channels* praised it as a "distinct contribution" to an area—the study of the various strategies and incentives a firm employs to take products to market—that was garnering considerable interest at the time. In part, the reason for this attention was that the channel represented a structure that embraced the "complete marketing 'cycle' for a product, and which, therefore, provides one of the best means for integrating [a] perspective of distribution."[98] The book, said one reviewer, offered special value for three prime segments: practitioners, who would find within its pages "suggestions and clues" for solving their own channel problems; teachers of marketing, whose horizons would be broadened by the book's timely research, affording them "a wealth of illustrative material for the class-room"; and students, who could use the book as a "means of integrating . . . marketing knowledge, [since the text's subject was the channel]—a mechanism that spans the entire gap between producer and consumer."[99]

As the 1950s wound down, Boyd, Clewett and Westfall were collaborating on another collection of marketing research that would be well received. *Contemporary American Marketing* consisted of 42 selections focusing on business examples rather than traditional material, according to a *Journal of Marketing* reviewer, Harry Lipson. "This book reflects the editors' thinking that the beginning course in marketing needs current materials which will help students understand the marketing problems faced by businessmen and also the interrelationships between marketing and other areas such as finance or production."[100] These relationships were an indication of a more modern appreciation for marketing's role within the organization, although the book's case study structure still offered mostly "descriptions and explanations of the marketing operations of particular companies." The text also contained articles from 11 publications, such as *BusinessWeek, Printer's Ink, Fortune, Journal of Business* and *Sales Management.* The articles, "which appear to have been selected with care and with a definite objective in mind," in Lipson's view, were all timely—nearly all having been published since 1955.

Equally important was the administration's willingness to hire professors from nontraditional disciplines, including the social sciences, and then cultivate in them a sense of scholarship and "Northwestern" affiliation. Westfall would remain pivotal in developing talent at the school throughout his tenure into the mid-1970s, especially as the business school sought to bring more analytical rigor to a faculty that was increasingly research-based. His efforts in the late 1960s, after he became associate dean for academic affairs under Dean John Barr, for instance, would attract world-class mathematicians and game theorists to Evanston, including figures such as Stanley Reiter, Morton Kamien, Haskel Benishay, David Baron, Nancy Schwartz and others who would create the outstanding Managerial Economics and Decision Sciences (MEDS) Department. But earlier, in the late 1950s and early 1960s, Westfall and his colleagues helped bring prominent professors to the Marketing Department, including Steuart Henderson Britt in 1957, Levy in 1961 and Kotler in 1962.

Britt's hiring signaled the direction in which marketing, and the department, was going. Trained both in law and psychology—he earned a PhD in psychology from Yale—Britt was a member of the Missouri and New York bars. He taught psychology at Columbia and George Washington University and worked as an advertising executive in New York and Chicago before joining the School of Business at Northwestern as a marketing professor, a position he held until his retirement in 1975. Thereafter, he devoted more time to the nationwide consulting firm Britt and Frerichs, Inc., which he started in 1971 with a former student.[101] From 1942 until 1960, he served as codirector of the Westinghouse Annual Science Talent Search,[102] and from 1951 until 1964, he edited the McGraw-Hill Series in Marketing and Advertising. Elected to the Hall of Fame in Distribution in 1963 and named one of America's "Leaders in Marketing Thought" by the American Marketing Association, Britt produced more than 200 articles and 15 books on psychology and marketing, including *The Social Psychology of Modern Life* (1941), *Selected Readings in Social Psychology* (1950), *Advertising Psychology and Research* (1950), *The Spenders* (1960), *Consumer Behavior and the Behavioral Sciences: Theories and Applications* (1966) and *Consumer Behavior in Theory and Action* (1970). A review of *The Spenders* hailed it as a "major, fresh and distinctly original contribution to the field of marketing" that was "profound and sound" in its efforts to educate both the layperson and the marketing professional about a host of techniques employed to advantage advertisers.[103] An article in the *New York Times* referenced the book as a "must-read for enterprising, sales-oriented business men" hoping to understand the surprising power of the growing population of middle-class consumers.[104]

Britt's 1970 text on consumer behavior built on the work he had presented four years earlier in another book, but it took the exploration in new directions, compiling dozens of articles from experts in psychology, sociology and marketing and business education. Chapter sections laid out the foundations of consumer behavior; cultural, group and economic influences on that behavior; business organizations and the consumer; and consumer decision making, among other topics. Britt's colleagues Kotler and Levy were two of the contributors. In a chapter addressing personality and personality differences, Levy provided a selection on "Contrasting Styles of Life," wherein he considered the individual's "real and ideal life styles." The selection introduced the value of ethnography in marketing as well as how self-reporting could offer insights into the customer's mind and motivation. Levy's wry humor and penetrating intellect were apparent: "Two students writing class autobiographies conveyed the contrasting sense of focus each felt about what he sought to achieve in life—one summing up that he wanted to live in accordance with 'intelligence, truth, and justice,' while the other said his aims boiled down to 'thrift, security, and cleanliness.' Presumably, the former young man represents a better potential market for books, the latter is possibly more geared to soap."[105]

Yet for all this intellectual output, "no books [could] be found in the Britt office at Northwestern University(!)—only a display of perceptual illusions."[106] Britt was not formally trained as a marketer, though he clearly understood the field's importance. "Doing business without advertising is like winking at a girl in the dark," he once said. "You know what you are doing, but nobody else does."[107]

Britt was born in 1907 in Callaway County, Missouri. He developed into a kind of Renaissance man, and as an academic, he was eager to put his considerable knowledge into action. After the entry of the United States into World War II in 1941, he served in four positions concurrently: as an expert consultant to the War Manpower Commission, as executive director of the Office of Psychological Personnel, as executive secretary of the Emergency Committee in Psychology, and as executive director of the Office of Psychological Personnel of the American Psychological Association. In addition, he became a lieutenant commander under Admiral Ernest J. King, commander in chief of the U.S. fleet. In that capacity, Britt used his abilities to develop psychological warfare tactics and personnel selection and training methods.[108]

Levy recalled Britt and the circumstances surrounding the school's Marketing Department shortly before his own arrival at Northwestern. "In the Marketing Department there was this small group of excellent, traditional people, so [to develop additional strengths] they hired Steuart Britt, not a traditional marketer . . . but a very qualified person and a bright man. He came in and began to study and teach consumer behavior, which hadn't been on the curriculum before."[109]

Kotler remembered Britt as one of the most colorful figures he had seen at the time. "He was a true gentleman-scholar, British looking and dressed to kill with a bow tie," said Kotler. "He would drive a Rolls-Royce and was very prominent in advertising circles, including at Leo Burnett. He helped run the annual *Advertising Age* Creative Workshop [from 1958 to 1970] and was editor of the *Journal of Marketing* [1957 to 1967]."[110]

The diverse intellectual pursuits of Britt and his marketing colleagues had created a dynamic environment that attracted other brilliant young minds, including some who would go on to create a revolution in marketing thought.

New Leaders Create a Marketing Revolution

He may not have invented marketing, but Philip Kotler has done more than any other person to reinvent the discipline and place it at the heart of business education. In the process, he has helped lead the Kellogg School to international prominence.

With more than a half century of academic leadership and dozens of hugely influential books and articles—including the pathbreaking "Broadening the Concept of Marketing"[111]—to his name, the Kellogg School marketing expert is preeminent and has remained active well into his seventies. Kotler's prodigious and widely recognized contributions—in 2005, the *Financial Times* ranked him as the fourth most influential business leader ever[112]—have made his name nearly synonymous with the field, particularly as it has developed since the 1970s, a period in which Kotler's intellectual input has helped redefine marketing and its possibilities.

His intellect was formed early. Kotler recalled sitting under his parent's kitchen table in Chicago's Albany Park neighborhood as a child and reading voraciously from an array of books, including the encyclopedia and the dictionary. The son of Russian and Ukrainian immigrants and merchants, Kotler would pursue an academic career, studying economics with Milton Friedman at the University of Chicago, where he earned a master's degree in 1953 before going on to add a doctorate from MIT in 1956, absorbing insights from the renowned Paul A. Samuelson. He would subsequently pursue postdoctoral research in mathematics and behavioral science at Harvard and the University of Chicago.[113]

In the late 1950s, Donald P. Jacobs, Kellogg School dean emeritus but then a finance scholar in the Northwestern University School of Business, encouraged Kotler to bring his rigorous economic insights to bear on advancing the marketing curriculum in Evanston. The two men met during a prestigious, yearlong program sponsored by the Ford Foundation at Harvard University. The program was designed to encourage more analysis in business, a field that some believed lacked the necessary scientific rigor to address the emerging management needs. Among the notable critics holding this view were scholars who undertook a massive Ford Foundation survey of management education, the results of which were published in 1959. An equally dreary survey was published in the same year by the Carnegie Corporation, with similar recommendations to bolster business education.

"One of the things missing on the part of those teaching business was mathematics," recalled Kotler, who was teaching at Roosevelt University in Chicago at the time. "So Ford advertised a program that would be very selective. A couple thousand professors wanted to go, and there were maybe 50 or 60 of us actually chosen to attend."[114]

During the program, Jacobs told the young economist that marketing needed good professors who could bring analysis to the discipline. "Don gave me two good pieces of advice," said Kotler. "He said, 'Look, a lot of people can teach managerial economics; it's marketing that really has to be fortified.'" Jacobs also told Kotler that Northwestern had a strong marketing department but one whose traditional strengths could be improved greatly by a scientific approach to research and teaching. Though he had not taught marketing, Kotler was receptive to the idea. He admitted he had already been concerned about certain aspects of economics that troubled him, and so he was willing to look beyond that discipline's boundaries for ways to apply his knowledge.

"I had some misgivings about economics during my training," remembered Kotler. "One was that economists were neglecting two of the main drivers of sales. They only focused on price, and price as influencing demand and supply. They neglected the intense amount of advertising and sales promotion going on and sales force activity. They were flattening out—reducing to one—the real drivers of demand and output."[115]

The other concern he had involved the simplistic price-oriented model of the market in traditional economic thought. He, by contrast, perceived a broad and dynamic marketplace with several competitors engaged in complicated interactions and customer relationships, not mere "buy-sell" transactions. "I saw a whole value-adding chain of events going from the manufacturer to the wholesalers to the retailers to the customers, including agents and brokers and advertising agencies," he said. And supplying the manufacturer was a whole chain of firms selling their inputs to companies. "All that was being flattened out by economic theory."

Kotler's ambitious ideas would find fertile ground in the Marketing Department at Northwestern, where stars like Boyd, Clewett, Westfall and Levy were "systematizing the fields of marketing research, marketing management, channel management and consumer behavior," said Kotler. "Their example had a great influence on me."

But there was no doubt he was entering a field that, overall, was tethered to older models and cursory surveys. The widespread perception of marketers as manipulators only added to the challenge of revamping the discipline. "It was the age of books like *The Hidden Persuaders*," remembered the Kellogg professor, referencing the 1957 Vance Packard title. "It still happens today, with people who believe marketing creates needs that don't need to exist."

The public sees only "the trappings" of marketing in commercials and promotions, leading them to believe that marketing and sales are synonymous, "but they don't see the homework" done to identify opportunities, find unsatisfied needs and design and price products, said the marketing guru.

"Nobody ever asked for a Walkman," Kotler said by way of example. Marketers had to plumb people's subconscious depths to help create such a product. "Most people can't even give you the information on why they bought what they bought," he added, noting research that claims up to 80 percent of purchasing may be subconsciously motivated, which is why he said depth psychology is a good tool to "uncover layers of desire."

"What I think great companies are doing is becoming workshops in which the customer can participate in designing and developing what they want out of a [product]," said Kotler.

"Many people think of marketing as being all about selling. Our big concept has always been that when you do great marketing you don't need much selling," observed Kotler, who, among other distinctions, earned the American Marketing Association's Paul Converse Award for his contributions to the field and the AMA's inaugural Distinguished Marketing Educator Award.[116]

But at the time he entered the profession, little rigorous analytical marketing research was being done. Kotler recalled the dearth of academic resources addressing the subject in anything other than a superficial way.

"All the marketing textbooks were highly descriptive, like 'an effective salesman has five traits' and 'a wholesaler does the following,'" he said. He would go on to remedy the situation with more than 100 articles and nearly 50 books,[117] including his landmark 1967 text, *Marketing Management,* now in its thirteenth edition. His seminal 1969 article, "Broadening the Concept of Marketing," coauthored with Levy, was published to acclaim in the *Journal of Marketing* and would engender a vigorous discourse that significantly advanced the discipline's theoretical underpinnings, as well as its horizons.

Levy arrived at Northwestern in 1961, one year before Kotler, also intent on broadening the perspective of marketing practice at the school. Trained as a psychologist at the University of Chicago, where he earned a doctorate in 1956 and began his teaching career as a lecturer in the 1958–1959 school year, Levy brought a far-ranging intellect to his marketing studies. "You study marketing, that's kind of a narrow part of the world," he reflected. "But in reality, the tools, and the implications of consumption, can also have broader ramifications."[118]

Levy's doctoral dissertation explored the psychodynamics of interpersonal relations, a topic that would launch inquiries that resulted in his seven books and dozens of scholarly articles, many of which are compiled in *Brands, Consumers, Symbols and Research: Sidney J. Levy on Marketing* (1999). The book's editor, Dennis W. Rook, a student of Levy's and a 1983 graduate of the Kellogg School's doctoral program in marketing, identified some of the text's characteristic themes and qualities, calling it interesting, engaging, provocative and fun to read. The work also drew on many fields to produce a distinguishing gestalt. "Levy's thinking eclectically dances and weaves across behavioral disciplines, and by mixing things up, he offers original, polyfocal perspectives to marketing situations that are commonly construed much too narrowly," wrote Rook. "Another enduring quality of his work is an emphasis on the role of interpretive analysis in marketing management. This idea materialized in his 1950s landmark *Harvard Business Review* articles about products, brands, and symbols."[119]

Even a glance at Levy's publication titles indicates his eclectic and innovative approach to marketing studies: "Cigarette Smoking and the Public Interest," "Psychosocial Reactions to the Abundant Society," "Symbols for Sale," "Brands, Trademarks, and the Law," "Consumer Behavior in the United States: The Avid Consumer" and "Hunger and Work in a Civilized Tribe: Or, the Anthropology of Market Transaction," among many others.

Born in 1921, Levy was instrumental in bringing a renewed energy and curiosity to the school, an approach that saw value in pursuing behavioral and qualitative research alongside the quantitative methodologies that were also coming into vogue at the time.

"There had been the traditional marketing approach as exemplified by the Northwestern School of Business, and some outstanding people of that earlier tradition, like Ralph Westfall and Dick Clewett, who were well known and prepared books that had to do with case studies, which was the main approach at the time," said Levy, who would also serve on the mid-1970s search committee that selected Dean Donald P. Jacobs (see chapter 4). But, he added, a "new wave" was influencing management education too, which embraced social science and went beyond mere description.

"Scientific study might be brought to bear on marketing," he recalled. "So with that, all the schools began to change, though not all at the same rate. Northwestern happened to be one of the more leading and alert schools ready to face up to this change." Admittedly, the change did not happen overnight, he noted. Some students and administrators had to be convinced that the new paradigm was indeed the future of marketing.

"Almost everything at first is a harder sell, because you have to change people's minds and people can have resistant minds," said Levy, who would serve as the Marketing Department's chair from 1980 to 1992.[120] "If it doesn't seem conventional and expected, they may not accept it. You don't just [automatically] get agreement, but you persevere."

However, Levy noted that the Marketing Department was committed to recruiting an array of bright, creative scholars eager to work together toward a common goal of excellence. "We were hiring people from social psychology, economics, anthropology," he said. "This provided a kind of diversity of backgrounds and interests that made our department a very lively and interesting place."

This interdisciplinary structure was rare at the time. Even more rare was the fact that the department's members, despite their varied backgrounds and interests, all got along well. Kotler provided some context indicating how impressive this fact was:

> In marketing we normally fall into some groupings. You have the behavioral people, the quantitative people and the managerial group. What is so exceptional about the history of our department is the warm feeling we've all had for each other. I thought this situation was normal, because that's what I'd experienced here. But then I started hearing stories about several other places where the faculty would clash. At [X] University, two of the leading marketing researchers don't speak to each other. They just think the other's philosophy of marketing is awful and ridiculous. One of the things that should be emphasized is that the atmosphere has been warm and reinforcing of everyone's self-respect and the respect of others. Of course [Dean Emeritus] Don Jacobs was sort of the mother figure in that sense. He would serve tea to all of us. He was the head honcho and he was looking out for us. That warm feeling, which I think that [current dean] Dipak Jain has definitely carried forward, is rare in a lot of schools.[121]

Another way the school was building enduring value—not only in marketing but also in management research and teaching overall—was through its doctoral program, which Levy described as "critical" to the school's success. "We began to get great students, and then we found we had these Northwestern School of Business graduates all over the world who were associated with this great marketing department," he said. The students arrived at Evanston from around the globe, bringing diverse cultural and academic backgrounds, and after graduation, they would work in far-flung countries, from Thailand and India to France and England, noted Levy. "They were a testament to our glory," he said. The department's latter-day stars— among them Bobby Calder, Brian Sternthal, Louis Stern and Alice Tybout—were all products of the doctoral program. The department's lasting reputation "all began with these really outstanding people," said Levy.

Broadening the Marketing Concept

But this perennial marketing strength also had much to do with the efforts of scholars like Levy and Kotler, who in particular helped propel the School of Business to international fame with their publications at a time when marketing as a discipline was undergoing creative ferment that some scholars attempted to describe and codify. Bartels's 1968 *Journal of Marketing* article, for example, outlined a general theory of marketing, something to consolidate the various theories that had emerged in the discipline in the six decades of its development. He cited several "lines" of marketing thought: the early traditional school rooted firmly in economics; a behavioral school that emphasized the noneconomic motivations influencing marketing; another theory that emphasized decision sciences—including E. J. McCarthy's postulation of the Four P's, product, place, promotion and price; and lastly, the theory of comparativism, which related marketing to the larger cultural setting.[122]

With Kotler's 1967 landmark text, *Marketing Management,* it was clear that the marketing faculty at Northwestern University was working to take these various theoretical strands and combine them in new and inventive ways that would drive the discipline forward. In the book, Kotler marshaled the strengths of several disciplines to create a new model with greater breadth and comprehension. The author expressly noted his desire to introduce "three distinct emphases": economics, behavioral sciences and mathematics. A review in the *Journal of Marketing* described the text as "a decision-oriented book, with an analytical approach" and a "felicity of style that is all too rare."[123] The review noted that a "major contribution" of the "first-rate" text was its focus on the management perspective, with little concern for traditional marketing frameworks or treatments. Instead, the reader could find in Kotler's work "a refreshing foundation of fundamental concepts and techniques" grounded in quantification—including an "excellent chapter on marketing models . . . [that] includes a section on the computer's role," which was especially noteworthy given the book's publication date.

Kotler's graduate training in economics, mathematics and behavior sciences was noted for its unusual breadth, and his ability to draw upon each discipline adeptly made the combination even more formidable. Gerald Zaltman, a Northwestern University colleague, observed that "a man having a broad interdisciplinary range would ordinarily be expected to be intellectually restless and dissatisfied. Professor Kotler has discovered, as have most scholars, that for every question answered several more appear. Yet unlike some scholars he is undaunted by the encounter of an ever expanding body of unanswered questions and unsolved problems. On the contrary, he seems to thrive on them."[124]

The sophisticated frameworks Kotler advanced built upon the Four P's marketing model (alternately called "the marketing mix"), which highlighted the importance of product, price, promotion and place. *Marketing Management* was the first text to make marketing into a "respectably analytical subject," according to a glowing 1967 review in the *Journal of Business.*[125]

"I elected to take a new approach and base marketing on the concept of decision making," Kotler explained. "Everything is decision theoretic, from determining how much should be spent on advertising to setting price and discounts and allocating resources, including how many sales people you should have."

Despite his clear analytical bent, Kotler also warned his readers of the limits of mathematics to communicate, writing that math "as a language suffers from one great limitation; it lacks nuance . . . a good marketing executive uses a verbal model of his markets that cannot be expressed in any set of mathematical equations, however complex." As such, quantifiable analysis, including that of the computer, was not "to be embraced uncritically . . . [since] results give an aura of precision which should be guarded against." The book's lasting value in shaping the marketing discipline is obvious in both its content and the number of editions published—to date, no less than thirteen. "The book took off marvelously," said Kotler. "What is amazing is that it has had no successful competitors, even today. So far I've been lucky."[126]

Only a few years later, in 1971, Kotler produced another book, *Marketing Decision Making: A Model Building Approach*, hailed by one reviewer as "a landmark and a masterpiece in the marketing literature."[127] The book brought together both micro- and macroeconomic perspectives, discussing decision models and market behavior models while also relating theory to practice. "The theory accounts for the facts that marketing is an open system, human, nonlinear, lagged, interactive, and stochastic," the review noted. "The material, though sophisticated, is presented in a simple and comprehensible manner." Considerations of various marketing policy variables included distribution, pricing, sales and advertising. "Marketing students who are distracted by the abstraction of economic theory can readily see economic theory in marketing practice in this book . . . economics and quantitative analysis are used as . . . tools rather than as the focus."

But in between these two important books was a seemingly more modest journal publication that would rock the entire marketing discipline.

With their 1969 article "Broadening the Concept of Marketing," Kotler and Levy proposed expanding the frameworks for what marketing could do and where it could operate. They started from a premise that "marketing is a pervasive societal activity that goes considerably beyond the selling of toothpaste, soap, and steel." It could also support the efforts of nonbusiness organizations, they contended.[128] The authors defined their terms, saying that marketing was typically seen as finding and motivating buyers for a company's product or service. Product development, pricing, distribution and communication were among the key areas of concern for marketers.

"Whether marketing is viewed in the old sense of 'pushing' products or in the new sense of 'customer satisfaction engineering,' it is almost always viewed and discussed as a business activity," the authors stated.[129] For them, this seemed a narrow limit for such a robust and ambitious—indeed, universal—activity. "Political contests remind us that candidates are marketed as well as soap; student recruitment by colleges reminds us that higher education is marketed; and fund raising reminds us that 'causes' are marketed."

The authors predicted that marketing would either meet the challenge to "take on a broader social meaning or [else] remain a narrowly defined business activity." Nonprofit organizations were starting to take on a more prominent social role, despite for-profit businesses retaining an important place. "Many of these [nonprofit and public] organizations become enormous and require the same rarefied management skills as traditional business organizations." Groups such as the United Auto Workers, the Ford Foundation, the World Bank, the Catholic Church and universities were all examples of contexts in which marketing skills could play a significant role, according to Kotler and Levy. Each of these organizations performed the classic business functions, they noted: raising and managing money and performing proper budgeting, "arranging inputs to produce the outputs," personnel management, purchasing functions and so forth. Perhaps more surprising, nations also were found to engage in marketing: Kotler and Levy cited the example of a Greek junta that hired a New York PR firm to help manage their image—including taking out full-page newspaper ads with the headline GREECE WAS SAVED FROM COMMUNISM.

All this was too much for some traditional minds to absorb.

Kotler and Levy's visionary marketing framework is now obvious when noting the criticism initially leveled at the "broadening" approach, such as that by David J. Luck.

In "Broadening the Concept of Marketing. Too Far," Luck seemed unable to grasp how the actions taken by nonprofit organizations, public agencies or political campaigns could be labeled marketing, even though most people today would clearly recognize that the American Heart Association, for example, must compete for philanthropy in a marketplace, just as for-profit companies must. Although Luck flatly declared that a "church does not sell its religious and redemptive services" and "political parties do not sell specific services (unless corruptly committing illegal acts)," the marketing revision advanced by Kotler and Levy today is everywhere proven valid. For Luck, it was enough that "marketing is performed by three million business firms, in addition to many nonbusiness enterprises in the United States alone."[130] He considered that capitalistic guilt might have been underlying the motives of those who would have broadened the marketing conception, shifting marketing to include, in the words of Kotler and Levy, "an increasingly interesting range of social activity."[131] Luck was quick to point out what he saw as the folly of that view: "If such logic were followed, it could be determined that the Post Office Department is a 'societal activity' and United Airlines is not. The former is (notoriously) a nonprofit institution, while the latter earns substantial profit in providing its services." What's more, he believed that social welfare "largely depends . . . on the private enterprise system and its marketing activities than on nonprofit institutions."

Kotler and Levy presented their response in the same edition of the *Journal of Marketing* in their essay "A New Form of Marketing Myopia: Rejoinder to Professor Luck."[132] There, they noted that all disciplines occasionally face challenges to their traditional structure and that those who are active in the discipline will respond with a range of feelings, from hostility to enthusiastic acceptance. "Whether a particular challenge is accepted depends on its ultimate contribution as a new perspective," stated the authors. They appreciated Luck's desire to retain marketing's more narrow identity as a market transaction, for such a focus "[is] in line with the widely understood meaning of the term and has the virtues of clarity, closure, and comfort. . . . However, there are severe limitations associated with such a viewpoint."

These limitations included denying the expertise of marketers to support "the most rapidly growing institutional sectors of the society" while preventing business from benefiting from examining marketing practice in a new context that could reveal insights as valuable in a for-profit setting as in a nonprofit setting. "Our position starts with the fundamental awareness that marketing-like activities take place in nonbusiness organizations as well as in business organizations. Churches, schools, and museums all engage in product development, pricing, distribution, and communication. For what purpose? To serve the needs of their 'customers.' These institutions seek to cultivate a long-term relationship with well-defined groups in much the same way that the modern business firm seeks to develop loyal customers."[133] That these groups frequently produced services rather than products per se was no proof against the broadening concept, said Kotler and Levy, since traditional marketing has also included services within its framework (e.g., insurance, repair work, beauty treatments, or entertainment). Thus, they stated, "there is no basis for distinguishing these services from religious, protective, or educational services . . . offered in the nonbusiness sector."

"What happened was interesting," said Kotler. "When we wrote the article, which was really revolutionary, we said that marketing was done by places and persons and nonprofit organizations, and not just commercial organizations."

He produced a definition of marketing as a "social process" through which individuals and groups obtain "what they need and want through creating and exchanging products and value with others." This framework must be understood before a company actually attempts to do marketing. Despite the seemingly straightforward nature of his definition, marketing actually is complex, having a number of activities associated with it—"research and analysis, environmental scanning, forecasting of potential demand, identification of marketing segments and the needs of customers in those segments, development of new products which will better meet those needs, product life cycle planning, marketing strategy, pricing strategy, establishment and maintenance of distribution channels, communications and promotion, among others."[134]

Such complexity, said Kotler, was threatening to a lot of marketers who thought marketing involved "payment and money and a market that's commercial." As he noted, "[The 'broadening' concept] created a debate, and we won the debate."[135]

But his audacious vision went further. He built on the framework introduced in 1969 with what he called a "generic concept" of marketing, which he described in a 1972 article. There, he once more expanded the parameters for the field, declaring that marketing was defined as "the disciplined task of creating and offering values to others for the purpose of achieving a desired response." He recalled marketing's evolution, first as a branch of applied economics, next as a management discipline and then as applied behavioral science "concerned with understanding buyer and seller systems involved in the marketing of goods and services."[136]

Kotler observed that marketing traditionalists would "relegate this discipline to an increasingly narrow and pedestrian role in a society that is growing increasingly post-industrial."[137] He noted three stages of marketing "consciousness" that emerged over its history as a subject, both academic and practical. The traditional consciousness was aware of marketing only as a business subject, a perspective that continued to define the field for many practitioners and the public. Then, an expanded consciousness appeared, which conceived of marketing as appropriate for all organizations that have customers. By 1972, Kotler believed that even this broadened view was insufficient to encompass marketing's true scope, which is why a "third consciousness" evolved to acknowledge marketing as relevant for all organizations in their varied relationships with customers but also with their diverse publics.

It is worth noting that Kotler and Levy provided the breakthrough in marketing scholarship that others had been calling for as early as the 1940s but no one had delivered.

Power Player: Channels Run Deeper

But Kotler and Levy extended their framework even further. They argued that it was possible to apply their value principle of marketing to noncommercial exchanges, such as services and products that were provided in a nonprofit context or even offered for free. They even discovered that it was possible to apply them to situations where no formal transaction took place at all, as in marketing candidates for political election. As a result, they applied their marketing model in many kinds of institutional settings, from hospitals and schools to museums and sports. Those who created public service announcements trying to convince a public *not* to do something (such as smoking) were suddenly marketing, according to the Northwestern scholars.

This re-vision exemplified what Bartels identified as marketing's "period of differentiation," extending from 1960 until 1970. During that time, he said, new concepts assumed a substantial identity as marketing thought expanded. Elements of managerialism, holism, environmentalism, systems and internationalism all defined this period. After 1970, the discipline made the transition into what Bartels called a time of "socialization," with social issues becoming important in marketing and the field's influence upon society increasingly becoming a point of focus.[138] Kotler and Levy were among those ushering in these developments. But they were not alone.

Another colleague shared a curiosity and passion for pushing academic boundaries by bringing analytical frameworks to bear on marketing questions, ones that had never before been fully articulated. Of marketing's Four P's, Louis Stern's research has focused most on "place," or the way firms deliver their products. What to the layperson may initially seem straightforward is anything but.

Stern arrived at Northwestern's Graduate School of Management in 1973, coming from Ohio State University, where he had served as a professor of marketing for 10 years; he assumed that position after earning his doctorate from Northwestern in 1962 and working in the industrial research firm of Arthur D. Little, Inc. From January 1965 until June 1966, he was a principal economist for the National Commission on Food Marketing in Washington, D.C. As a young student at Harvard University, Stern had grown interested in the richness and power dynamics of commercial relationships. "The genesis of my academic life was really an undergraduate economics major and a course called *Industrial Organization*," recalled Stern,[139] who is also an expert on antitrust and consumer protection issues. The course included discussions about ideas such as John Kenneth Galbraith's countervailing power, a theory of the political modification of markets by such entities as trade unions and citizens' groups.

But power struggles were also part of the dynamics between a manufacturer and a major supplier, for instance. "These kinds of issues, where there would be power at one end of the chain and power at the other end, were fascinating to me," said Stern.

These dynamics also had significant implications for how organizations would bring goods to market and perfect their chosen channel. "For example, do they want to use intermediaries, or do they want to go through retailers? Will they have their own sales force, set up a public warehouse or have their own logistics system?" he asked.

Because no business today is likely to go to market using only a single channel but instead employs multiple ones, considerable competition can emerge among channels. "There can be a lot of cross purposes," Stern explained. "You have to tailor your channels so they don't blow up on you. You do this by aligning incentives, making sure the system is adaptive enough."

Stern, whose honors include being named one of the 12 best teachers in U.S. business schools by *BusinessWeek,* has earned the AMA's Irwin Distinguished Marketing Educator Award and its Converse Award. In addition, he served as Marketing Department chair from 1977 to 1980, and he has spent much of his career trying to articulate the complexities of channels. The subject can be remarkably subtle. "While business folk often look for the 'ready, fire, aim' stuff, we say hold the fort—there are too many interactions going on and you have to look closely at them," he remarked.

Just as Kotler noted there were few examples of research-based marketing materials when he began studying the subject, Stern's area of interest—marketing channels, or the various strategies and incentives a firm employs to take products to market—lacked substantial research, which left this complex and fascinating subject stalled at a rudimentary stage.

"For years, there was no theoretical base," recalled Stern. The discussion rarely advanced beyond "the benefits of one- versus two-story warehouses, or how many wholesalers could you fit on the head of a pin." Stern would help to radically change channels research through a series of scholarly articles and books, including *Marketing Channels* (in its seventh edition) and "Distribution Channels as Political Economies: A Framework for Comparative Analysis" (coauthored with Torger Reve), which was published in the *Journal of Marketing* in 1980 and earned that periodical's award as the best paper of the year.

The paper was important in part because it offered a way to integrate existing approaches to marketing channel study, thereby allowing comprehensive empirical research, something Stern said had not been available previously. To get at the true complexity of channels, his research has provided a much-needed unifying framework to an otherwise ad hoc array of analyses. "Distribution Channels as Political Economies" argued convincingly for the need to "encompass both economic and sociopolitical determinants" of channel member behavior. The emergent framework offered in the paper provided "a basis for future research by isolating the critical dimensions determining transactional effectiveness and efficiency in distribution," while also providing a "conceptual mapping" that was useful for those hoping to understand channel relationships.[140] And texts such as *Marketing Channels,* which he coauthored with Kellogg professor Anne Coughlan, have brought a strong theoretical perspective to channel design and implementation.

"I've drawn upon all sorts of literatures to do this," said Stern, "but the main thing has been understanding one of the big primary forces, which comes out of economics: the 'make or buy' decision. Do you do things for yourself, or do you go to an open marketplace and buy the services? These are central questions."[141] Answering such questions forces one to examine points of power and conflict—critical issues in the management of distribution. To magnify that political economy perspective, Stern has drawn upon a good deal of social psychology and sociology.

A Tradition Continued

The example and inspiration of Levy, Kotler and Stern, as well as their predecessors, continue to provide direction for other Kellogg School marketing peers.

"In a sense, the marketing field might be divided into two periods: BK (Before Kotler, along with Sid Levy) and AK (After Kotler)," said Alice Tybout, the Harold T. Martin Professor of Marketing and former chair of the Kellogg Marketing Department. "Phil and Sid shaped the field by defining marketing as a strategic activity, and one that was universally applicable to all situations related to exchange. This was radical."[142]

Tybout also praised Stern, a person she has known for most of her academic life, and cited his "dauntingly" high standards for performance and his passionate and disciplined approach to his work. Tybout recalled that as a doctoral student at Northwestern when Stern arrived in 1973, she was inspired by his rigorous theoretical methodology; since then, she said, she has "tried to follow in Lou's footsteps and pursue a similar strategy in my own work."

Coughlan has also been influenced by his work, although the Kellogg professor of marketing was quick to note that "Lou's research has shaped many academics' work in the field, not just mine." Coughlan said that Stern was instrumental in her decision to join the faculty of the Kellogg Marketing Department. "I have learned an enormous amount from Lou over the years," she said. "He has always had a great gift for speaking about channels to audiences of all sorts, from academics to MBA students and practitioners."

Stern said he learned early on at Northwestern that collegiality and mentorship were expected as part of the Marketing Department's culture. The department owed a considerable amount of its success to those leaders who set the standards a decade or more before Stern arrived. In particular, he cited Clewett's beneficial influence, saying the department enjoyed a special cohesiveness under his leadership.

"He was incredible," recalled Stern. "He was a great teacher and one hell of an administrator. What he did was make it so that people understood what this was as a *department,* making this an enjoyable place to work, and making it clear that we all had certain obligations to the department, no matter who you were."

For instance, Stern said that every professor felt the importance of nurturing the department's doctoral students. When students presented their dissertation proposals, they did so to the faculty as a group. Such occasions were always very well attended, he noted, and "the discussions would be absolutely first rate."

> I remember sitting in these presentations and saying, "What a wonderful place to be." It was so intellectually stimulating, no matter what the person was presenting—even if it was something totally outside your area of expertise. You had a curiosity about it and could hear others talk and debate about it. This culture didn't necessarily mean that everyone was always great friends, but it did mean that there was a cohesiveness and collegiality here that I attribute a lot of to Dick Clewett. It was remarkable, because in many departments in a lot of schools they tear each other apart like they're in "Whose Afraid of Virginia Woolf?" That didn't happen here.

Today, the Marketing Department's leadership continues driving the discipline forward through interdisciplinary strategies that address contemporary marketing issues in a global business environment. As it makes substantial contributions to the marketing field, the department has been ranked number one consistently in prestigious surveys, including those in *BusinessWeek* and *U.S. News & World Report.* Moreover, its faculty members have been highly honored with top awards for teaching and research, including the Paul Converse Award for Outstanding Contributions to Marketing; the John D. C. Little Award; the Paul Green Award; and the William F. O'Dell Award, given by the American Marketing Association to recognize outstanding contributions to marketing. Kellogg faculty have produced leading textbooks in key areas of marketing, among them marketing management, channel distribution and sales promotions. Three faculty members (current and past) have won the prestigious marketing educator of the year award from the American Marketing Association, and the doctoral students in the Marketing Department have won more first-place and honorable mention awards from the AMA in its dissertation competition than students at any other school.

The department's knowledge is disseminated in dozens of books and hundreds of publications, including *Kellogg on Marketing, Kellogg on Integrated Marketing* and *Kellogg on Branding,* to name only three. Much of this work is rooted in quantitative analysis. Figures such as Kotler and current dean and marketing scholar Dipak C. Jain have produced a body of research about marketing on the global stage—including the branding of countries. Meanwhile, professors like Angela Lee bring insight into areas such as consumer learning, cross-cultural information processing and metacognition. Bobby Calder is a renowned expert in marketing planning, marketing research analysis and consumer behavior; his work has covered industries from health care and electronics to food and financial services. The current department chair, Gregory S. Carpenter, is an award-winning expert in marketing strategy and has served on the editorial boards of several leading peer-reviewed journals. Andris Zoltners's research into sales force management and marketing strategy has been groundbreaking and has helped him succeed as a practitioner with ZS Associates, the global market research consultancy he founded in 1983 with former Kellogg School marketing professor Prabhakant Sinha. Meanwhile, Coughlan's expertise in channels management and design and quantitative models has garnered her multiple forms of recognition, including for her outstanding teaching. In Lakshman Krishnamurthi, a former Marketing Department chair, Kellogg has an expert in marketing strategy and research, as well as pricing and multivariate statistics. Tybout has studied branding, marketing management and consumer information processing. Robert C. Blattberg brings his long experience and scholarship in the area of category management, sales promotions and marketing strategy. Brian Sternthal's research incorporates his deep insights into advertising and consumer information processing. Others in the department have also contributed to the discipline in important ways and have helped bolster the Kellogg School's leadership in marketing for decades.

The department's history and reputation are sources of strength as the school looks forward to making continued contributions in the field of marketing. Understanding the past offers insight into the possibilities of the future and affords the faculty a chance to build on the work of earlier peers—something that Levy has found critical in his work as a pioneer in the area of brand image.

Brand image remains a central subject for academics and practitioners, though it derives from research begun at least half a century ago, including Levy's "The Product and the Brand" (1955) and "Symbols for Sale" (1959). But Levy recalled the origins of his own thinking on branding and noted the importance of historical perspective. For some students and young faculty looking to produce new insights, said Levy, it can be disconcerting when they discover the precedents for their work. Understanding this history, though, may help them explore uncharted territory.

"It can be irritating to have someone like me say, 'Oh yeah. I wrote about that in 1963,'" Levy observed. "But this never bothered me [as a young scholar]. Our work on brand image, this idea had a tremendous impact that's pervaded the world. But at the time I was writing these early articles on brand I was thinking, 'Well, this is a version of what Plato said in the *Dialogues*.' I studied that in college. . . . There's no harm in referring to your forebears, your intellectual predecessors."

Analytical models, including game theory, would increasingly influence
business education during the latter half of the twentieth century.

Chapter 3

MANAGEMENT EDUCATION
MUST CHANGE

Fifty years after its inception, the School of Commerce had become the School of Business, and like its peers, it was swept up in a reassessment of its mission and methods in the face of growing market complexity. The school found itself on the brink of dramatic changes—taking risks that would prove pivotal to its fortunes for decades.

"The traditional approach to business education described in most catalogs today is outdated," declared Richard Donham, dean of Northwestern's School of Business, in a 1957 *Nation's Business* article.[1]

As if to underscore his remarks by indicating a few of the ways in which business was changing, Toyota that year introduced the first Japanese car sold in the United States. And IBM made its scientific computer programming language, FORTRAN (FORmula TRANslation), available to customers who were starting to use the company's breakthrough processing products, like the IBM 704, released in 1954. Financial institutions were also pushing innovations: Bank of America launched its pioneering BankAmericard in 1958, a credit card that would eventually evolve into the Visa system.[2]

All in all, reported *Time* magazine, a new economy had emerged out of capitalism's rapid adaptation to meet the "vast, growing needs of the population it serves so well." Though 1958 brought economic recession, business had expanded at "fantastic rates" since the end of World War II, and some even viewed the downturn as a necessary pause to allow the economy to "digest all the new capacity," including plant expansion that had risen to $37.8 billion in 1957.[3] This temporary dip did little to dampen the spirits of a relatively new class of investors who poured $14 billion into an increasingly diversified market through mutual funds that year.[4] Many of the rules of classical economics no longer seemed to apply, as the consumer was finding that a third of his or her income was discretionary, "money that could be and was used to power continuing booms in industries that were once termed luxury," according to *Time*. And buy consumers did—purchasing some 5.2 million television sets, 8.9 million radios and nearly 2.75 million automatic washing machines in one year alone. Business professionals, too, were no longer running for cover at the first sign of inclement economic weather. Instead, they continued to plan for long-term expansion.[5] Figures from the Federal Reserve indicate the remarkable overall economic progress. The gross national product (GNP) for 1946 totaled $210.7 billion; by 1957, it had jumped to $440.3 billion. Over that span, investment in nonfarm residential construction rose from $4.6 billion to $17.0 billion, and personal income doubled.[6]

Keeping up with these changes was a daunting task for many business schools.

Donham's statement, appearing in an article on management education and changes under way in the field, anticipated the findings of two major studies then being conducted by the Ford Foundation and the Carnegie Corporation. Robert A. Gordon of the University of California–Berkeley and James E. Howell of Stanford University produced the Ford study, *Higher Education for Business,* and Frank C. Pierson of Swarthmore College produced the Carnegie survey, *The Education of American Businessmen.* The voluminous results—unfavorable to business schools, whose work, in general, was called "sorely deficient,"[7] with serious problems plaguing both admissions standards and curricula—would not be published until 1959. But Donham and his colleagues had already been studying the challenges facing their industry; indeed, such problems had attracted their attention for the better part of a decade, despite the fact that there was no widespread remedy at their disposal. In 1954, for instance, Donham had addressed a conference on "The Challenge to Education: Dilemma or Opportunity?" where he noted that the most significant hurdle confronting undergraduate business schools was that "modern industry requires both specialists and generalists; and in its upper echelons, at least, requires the same men to be both."[8] He had, in fact, broadcast this view earlier, at the faculty meeting announcing his deanship on March 6, 1953. At that time, he told his colleagues that he would seek a balance between the quality and quantity of students enrolled and between general training and training in specific functions, believing that "tomorrow's business leaders should have a broad base [of] training requiring greater integration of the different [academic] departments toward developing a 'rounder' man." He also questioned the wisdom in teaching students to be overly cautious, rather than entrepreneurial, and he called upon the faculty to consider the merits of "training with a view to creating a zest for business and the desire to take risks," qualities that he said had made the United States an economic power.[9]

The *Nation's Business* article, informed by other critiques that had emerged after World War II, predicted that undergraduate business programs could eventually dwindle, to be replaced by more rigorous graduate work, as was the case in law and medicine. Students might also expect fewer lectures and textbooks and more case studies and group interaction. With more assurance, experts claimed that within 10 years, schools would train business students in a way that melded functional expertise and general management skills. In addition to making decisions and collaborating with others to achieve organizational objectives, graduates would come to demonstrate new talents such as "imagination, logic and insight into human nature, a familiarity with electronic data processing equipment and the ability to communicate lucidly. . . . Skill in many trades, mastery of at least one."[10]

Administrators of the School of Business had not waited for survey results before taking the actions necessary to consolidate the school's already respectable position and better prepare its students for modern careers. They had begun to reshape the curriculum in 1954, integrating general education in the arts and sciences with general and specialized business training, Donham recalled.[11] But even this move was predicated on an earlier effort, in 1946, when the school established an undergraduate "core curriculum" of 16 courses designed to provide a comprehensive and coherent sequence in accounting, finance, production, marketing, business law and business writing. Students also took theoretically oriented courses in statistics and economics, along with a senior offering in business administration and policy challenges.[12] Shortly thereafter, the graduate MBA program was also examined (primarily by Donham and Paul Morrison, professor of accounting) with an eye to the future. However, increasing postwar enrollments—nearly 1,000 students entered the program by the late 1940s, up from 550 in 1943—largely curtailed significant developments in revamping its core curriculum of 11 courses in policy formation and analysis, operations and control and reappraisal. These requirements were in addition to eight basic courses in accounting, statistics, economics, finance, production and marketing.

"We are trying to educate a man broadly for life in a world growing smaller, more interrelated, and infinitely more complex," Donham said. "We are trying at the same time to give him the depth of understanding necessary to function effectively within his field."[13] The school was attempting to provide a "new kind of liberal education" at the undergraduate level, said the dean in another interview a few years later. "We are concerned about evolving a habit of searching out relationships and a capacity for seeing things as wholes, with engendering humane feelings and a facility for sound judgments, with cultivating a talent for continuing growth. We are concerned, also, with transferring business knowledge and with developing administrative skills."[14]

In 1956, three years after Donham became dean, the School of Commerce changed its name to the School of Business; its graduate division, located in Wieboldt Hall on the Chicago campus since 1950, was now known as the Graduate School of Business Administration. The changes reflected a desire to adhere to nomenclature being used widely among other schools of business, which were increasingly dropping the word *commerce* from their names. But more important, the shift helped to differentiate the school's undergraduate program from its graduate offering, which was growing more rigorous thanks to recruiters' efforts to attract a higher caliber of student. (This effort was furthered in 1952 when Northwestern and eight other schools, including Harvard, Wharton, Columbia and Chicago, collaborated to produce a standardized graduate admissions exam.) The undergraduate program was considered a success, having about 700 students enrolled annually during the last years of the 1950s, but student numbers actually had fallen steadily since 1949, when 1,903 were enrolled in the full-time undergraduate curriculum and another 7,605 were in the program's part-time undergraduate offering.[15] The declining enrollment seemed to affirm the concerns of those educators who questioned the undergraduate program's validity in the context of a modern business world whose complexity argued for graduate training. Nevertheless, Donham was unwilling to abandon the four-year program and had been addressing its defects—primarily its excessive specialization—since the start of his tenure.

Education for a "New Kind of Person"

Lawrence "Gene" Lavengood, professor of business history and ethics, arrived at Northwestern in 1953, the year he graduated from the University of Chicago's doctoral program in history. He recalled Northwestern's efforts to refine its curriculum, with much of the initial focus on revamping the Evanston-based program.[16] "Dean Donham outlined a vision for the undergraduate school," said Lavengood. "He hoped to make it the premier undergraduate program in the country."

To do so, Donham's administration overhauled the curriculum, streamlining courses so that, by 1957, offerings such as accounting, statistics and finance were integrated because, as one observer noted, "at the action level in business all three are often used simultaneously."[17] Donham encouraged professors to take an active role in this endeavor. Said Lavengood: "The practice of management generated a great many new kinds of demands, and actually seemed to call for a new kind of person. And a new kind of person had to have a new kind of education. [Beginning in 1953], the faculty was put to work designing this curriculum, being guided by the dean's commitment to integration, to what he regarded as true professionalism and to academic excellence." Lavengood remembered several courses that faculty members retooled: "Human Problems in Business," he recalled, approximated modern organizations behavior, with an additional emphasis on personnel; "Quantitative Methods" melded economics with applied mathematics, particularly with utility in finance and production; and a top-level general management capstone course underwent comprehensive review.

Lavengood's courses focused on management's social environment. His graduate-level "Policy and Environment" combined history, the humanities and social science. Its undergraduate version, "Competition of Ideas in an Industrial Society," introduced seniors to a similar intellectual mélange and was noted by Frank Pierson as a particularly worthy and ambitious attempt to enhance the business curriculum in ways that met modern challenges.[18] His class in business history would attract as many as 150 students at a time and fill an auditorium in Memorial Hall, also known as the Little Red Schoolhouse—a cramped facility in Evanston near Sheridan Road and Foster Avenue originally built, in 1887, for the Garrett Theological Seminary.[19] After a $100,000 facelift in 1923, Memorial Hall opened its doors to accommodate the burgeoning School of Commerce, which had operated out of nearby Harris Hall since 1915.

Lavengood's class presented an overview of American history from colonial times forward, concentrating on economics and business but also venturing into political and social history. His colleagues in business history included Richard C. Overton and Howard F. Bennett, both Harvard-educated historians.[20] Bennett's objectives for the course were to have students emerge from the experience with an appreciation both for the environment of commerce and for the businessman functioning in that environment, "trying to see how he reacts to it in terms of accepting the unchangeable factors within it, of taking advantage of its opportunities, of developing institutions and practices to overcome or modify limitations it presents." Developing such insights, he noted, formed the "essential task of business history."[21] The professors assigned students an eclectic reading list, including *The Roosevelt I Knew* by former U.S. secretary of labor Frances Perkins and Matthew Josephson's *The Robber Barons*, a book whose perspective on nineteenth-century industrialists like Andrew Carnegie, J. P. Morgan and John D. Rockefeller was presented to students as a kind of cautionary tale, one designed to reveal the power of public opinion with regard to business, Lavengood said.[22]

"It was a richly textured course," recalled Lavengood, who retired in 1994 and died in 2006 at age 82 after a career in which he also helped improve minority race relations at Northwestern and in Evanston through such initiatives as Leadership Education and Development (LEAD), a national program to encourage promising high school juniors from diverse backgrounds to seek business careers. "I regarded the classroom as a kind of theater, and the students—not as the audience—but, along with me, the players, giving shape and substance to our discussions. Some of the best organizing concepts that I was able to incorporate into my courses came from students during our vigorous discussions. I learned a lot from them, and . . . they from me. I always tried to make it clear that we were in this learning together."

In January 1957, Dean Donham made an announcement that spurred additional changes to the curriculum. He had obtained a $250,000 Ford Foundation grant to assist in planning and course development for the undergraduate program. The Ford Foundation's annual report for that year noted this effort: "Programs in business education, which now attract approximately one out of eight college students, face a forced growth to accommodate an ever-increasing enrollment. . . . A few undergraduate schools of business [including Northwestern's] are moving away from excessive specialization in traditional business functions and toward an integrated curriculum emphasizing relevant training in the social sciences and humanities."[23] An additional $250,000 grant from Ford would arrive three years later and prove helpful in furthering those curricular changes as well as others, including a 1960 revision of the MBA program, that would emphasize more analytical training coupled with behavioral approaches to management.[24]

In general, a move was also under way to encourage the business community to play its part in strengthening the rigor and relevance of the business schools' curricula, increasing the chances that the schools' products would meet market demands. Firms were encouraged to support teachers by setting up yearly fellowships for those working toward doctoral degrees in business administration. Further, they were asked to provide grants to assist schools in developing programs and meeting salary requirements and to cooperate with schools to create research that blended theory and practice. In addition, by having business leaders serve on advisory committees at the management schools—an arrangement that would bring about startling changes at Northwestern by 1965—companies could be confident that their needs were understood when management educators made decisions.

Donham was comfortable engaging the business community and saw the value in doing so immediately upon assuming the deanship in 1953. During the faculty meeting announcing his appointment, he emphasized the importance of maintaining a direct connection with the corporate world, citing recent initiatives by the school for this purpose, such as projects associated with the Business History Department, a research council involving regional executives, a committee on eco-

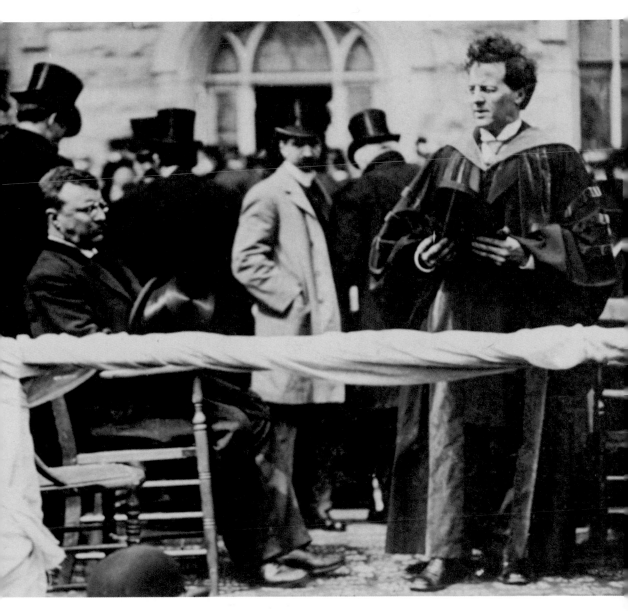

Northwestern president Edmund Janes James (right) with U.S. president Theodore Roosevelt during a 1902 visit to Evanston. James saw a dire need for business education at the university, declaring the average practitioner "ignorant and inefficient and cowardly."

Northwestern University president (1906–1916) Abram Winegardner Harris was instrumental in supporting the creation of the School of Commerce, convening an exploratory committee to investigate the viability of business studies at Northwestern.

Economics professor Earl Dean Howard joined the Northwestern faculty in 1907 and immediately began building relationships between the university and the Chicago business community. His enthusiasm for combining theory and practice contributed greatly to the development of the School of Commerce.

From left: Attorney Levy Mayer, Joseph Schaffner, and Harry Hart (of Hart, Schaffner & Marx) walking across a street in Chicago in 1910. Schaffner was a catalyst who helped establish the School of Commerce. He, along with a few dozen other business leaders, formed a "board of guarantors" that provided support to Northwestern's efforts in commerce education.

The Northwestern University Building at Lake and Dearborn Streets in Chicago, first home of the School of Commerce, 1908 to 1926.

Economics professor Frederick S. Deibler was an early advocate of business education at Northwestern, working in 1902–1903 with university president Edmund Janes James and others to draft a plan in support of such an initiative.

Economist John Gray. Although he left Northwestern in 1906, Professor Gray along with colleague Frederick Deibler were enthusiastic advocates for a business school at Northwestern. In 1905, the two recruited Willard E. Hotchkiss, who would serve as the first dean of the School of Commerce.

Among those lending their support to the early School of Commerce was businessman and publisher Arch W. Shaw, a friend of the school's first dean, Willard E. Hotchkiss, and an occasional lecturer at the school. One of his publications, *System: The Magazine of Business,* would be sold to McGraw-Hill Company in 1928, where it became *BusinessWeek.*

An economist and statistician, Horace Secrist joined the School of Commerce in 1912. He would later direct the school's Bureau of Business Research, an initiative begun in 1919 to produce scholarship on business principles and practices.

Harris Hall was the initial home of the School of Commerce on the Evanston campus, from 1915 to 1923.

Memorial Hall, the second home of the School of Commerce in Evanston from 1923 to 1970. The building was nicknamed the "Little Red Schoolhouse" and had "surprising nooks and crannies and sudden turns," according to Professor Lawrence "Gene" Lavengood. This architecture, he said, "preached a useful moral lesson: be sure you know where you are going."

David Himmelblau was the first graduate of the School of Commerce's bachelor of business administration program, earning the degree in 1914. In 1911 he had earned a commerce diploma from the school. As an early faculty member in the school's Accounting Department, Himmelblau coauthored a multivolume accounting series with colleagues Eric Kohler and Arthur Andersen.

Marketing professor Fred E. Clark joined the School of Commerce in 1919 and would prove to be among the significant early figures who built the school's marketing strength.

Wieboldt Hall, circa 1930s. Constructed in 1926, Wieboldt was the second home of the School of Commerce in Chicago. Today it remains the site of the Kellogg Part-Time MBA Program.

Students in the Commerce Library, Memorial Hall, 1927.

During a 1939 visit to Northwestern University, Prince Olaf of Norway *(center)* was greeted by education leaders, including Northwestern president Walter Dill Scott *(left)* and Arthur Andersen '17, former School of Commerce accounting professor.

THE DAVID R. PHILLIPS COLLECTION

Office machines class, Gregg Division, 1953. The Gregg Division was a commercial and secretarial education program established in 1952. Named for John Robert Gregg, founder of the McGraw-Hill Book Company, which provided the funding, the Gregg Division proved a lucrative addition to the School of Commerce. However, the program was dissolved in 1959 because Dean Richard Donham, among others, felt it detracted from serious business study.

EVANSTON PHOTOGRAPHIC STUDIOS

Classes in shorthand were part of the curriculum at the School of Commerce during the 1940s.

Students at Wieboldt Hall on the Chicago campus participate in a salesmanship class in 1949.

The first Institute for Management class, 1951. The program was designed to provide intensive residential business education for executives. Sessions were held in Evanston over the summer for four weeks.

Experiential learning has long been a hallmark of business education at Northwestern, as indicated by this student's field research circa 1950s.

Students combine practical insights with classroom theory at Kellogg, an approach that goes back decades at the school.

As associate dean and marketing professor, Ira Anderson '30 was among those who carefully assessed the viability of shifting Northwestern University's business program from the undergraduate to the graduate level.

Theory and practice have each been integral to the Kellogg School approach. In this photo from a business management seminar in the early 1960s, professors contribute their insights alongside a panel of practitioners (not shown).

The Kellogg School Marketing Department has redefined its discipline through the efforts of many exceptional professors. In this photo from the 1960s, Professor Steuart Henderson Britt, with the help of an unlikely prop, appears ready to reveal another insight into consumer motivation.

Stanley Reiter, professor of Managerial Economics and Decision Sciences (MEDS), joined Northwestern in 1967 and was tasked with building a department that brought greater analytical rigor to business study. The success of MEDS has left an enduring mark throughout the school, enhancing its overall curriculum and offering a research-oriented foundation.

Nancy L. Schwartz was the Morrison Professor of Decision Sciences and the Kellogg School's first woman faculty member appointed to an endowed chair. She joined the school in 1970, chaired the Managerial Economics and Decision Sciences Department, and served as director of the school's doctoral program until her death in 1981. Today, an annual memorial lecture in her name brings illustrious guest speakers—including several Nobel laureates—to Kellogg.

Professor of business history Lawrence "Gene" Lavengood *(left)* regales a class in the 1960s with the ready assistance of finance professor Donald P. Jacobs. Note the ashtrays and cigarettes on desks and the pipe in Lavengood's hand.

The popularity of the Evanston-based Institute for Management created a demand for an international version of the executive program, which the school launched in 1965 in Lucerne, Switzerland. Instrumental in this initiative were, *from left,* Thomas McNichols, Donald P. Jacobs, John Barr, Pierre Tabatoni and Ralph Westfall.

OFFICIAL PHOTOGRAPH, THE WHITE HOUSE

Finance professor Donald P. Jacobs *(right)* served as costaff director of the Presidential Commission on Financial Structure and Regulation (The Hunt Commission) in 1970 and 1971. Among those seated are, *from left,* Reed Hunt, chairman; President Richard M. Nixon; Paul Volcker, undersecretary of the U.S. Treasury; and Alan Greenspan, chairman of the Council of Economic Advisors.

ULDIS SAULE

Richard Clewett (holding papers) was a catalyst in developing the Marketing Department at Northwestern's School of Commerce. From his arrival in 1948 and for some 30 years afterward, Clewett was regarded by peers as a mentor, particularly for his efforts to help junior faculty members achieve their potential.

Finance professor Corliss D. Anderson leads a discussion during a graduate business class in 1965.

Vennie Lyons '72 counsels a student in the Part-Time MBA Program in 1973. Since then, Lyons has been the program's director, working with his staff to distinguish the Kellogg part-time curriculum. Today, the program attracts talented students from across the United States.

Louis Stern, the John D. Gray Professor Emeritus of Marketing, in 1978. An expert in marketing channels, Stern joined the school in 1973 and has been an integral part of the school's illustrious Marketing Department.

Marketing professors Stanley F. Stasch '64 *(left)* and Sidney J. Levy lead class discussion circa 1975. Levy produced seminal marketing research, including his 1959 article "Symbols for Sale" and his 1969 publication (coauthored with Philip Kotler) "Broadening the Concept of Marketing."

Professor Robert Neuschel teaches the tenets of "servant leadership" in 1981. The former McKinsey & Co. executive joined Kellogg in 1979 and designed and taught its first course on managerial leadership. "Serve your troops first, so that you can lead them better," said Neuschel, who died in 2004.

Dean Donald P. Jacobs shares a laugh with students during a 1976 phone-a-thon that raised funds for the school.

Kellogg students meet informally with Dean Donald P. Jacobs circa 1980s. Jacobs's "open-door" policy, which continues in the Office of the Dean today, brought students and administrators together as partners to create a vibrant culture.

Mr. and Mrs. Nathaniel Leverone, the benefactors who provided the majority of funding for
Leverone Hall, the third home of the Graduate School of Management on the Evanston campus,
look on while Northwestern president J. Roscoe Miller indicates the location of the new
construction. Also present, *from left:* William S. Kerr, Northwestern vice president and business
manager; Franklin M. Kreml, Northwestern vice president for planning and operations; and
John Barr, dean of the Graduate School of Management.

An aerial view of Leverone Hall under construction in August 1971. The building would open the following year and serve as the new home for Northwestern's Graduate School of Management. Chicago industrialist Nathaniel Leverone provided $5 million of the building's total $7.1 million cost, though he died before the project was complete.

With construction on Leverone Hall nearly complete, Associate Dean Ralph Westfall surveys the progress circa 1972.

Game theorist David Baron was a founding member of the Kellogg Managerial Economics and Decision Sciences (MEDS) Department, a highly analytic team that brought mathematical rigor to business studies. MEDS began in 1968 and would subsequently influence every other area of the school, contributing to the institution's research-oriented approach to management education.

Brian Sternthal, the Kraft Foods Chair in Marketing, explaining consumer information processing in class circa 1979. Sternthal has been a member of the school's faculty since 1972.

Philip Kotler teaches a class of executive students circa 1970s. Kotler, who joined the Northwestern business faculty in 1962, has been enormously influential in advancing marketing as a discipline, bringing to it an analytical rigor and an innovative perspective that has made him, and the Kellogg School, international leaders in that field for decades. Today, Kotler is the S.C. Johnson & Son Professor of International Marketing.

Edmund J. Wilson '84 and Mary Corbitt Clark '75 outside Leverone Hall in the late 1970s. Over a tenure that began in 1972, Wilson helped create a collaborative culture at the Kellogg School. He served in several key administrative capacities, including associate dean for master's degree programs and student affairs, and dean of admissions and financial aid. Clark began working in the admissions office in 1973 as a graduate assistant while earning her MBA. In 1977, she became admissions director, after Wilson shifted roles.

John L. Kellogg, son of cereal magnate W. K. Kellogg. It was a $10 million gift from the John L. and Helen Kellogg Foundation in 1979 that led to Northwestern University's business school being renamed the J. L. Kellogg Graduate School of Management that year.

Attorney and Northwestern University trustee Dale Park Jr. was central to securing a $10 million gift from the J. L. and Helen Kellogg Foundation in 1979, money that would support an array of academic initiatives and result in the business school being renamed the J. L. Kellogg Graduate School of Management.

Dean Donald P. Jacobs, James L. Allen and Northwestern University president Robert Strotz pose in front of the Allen Center cornerstone in 1978. The facility would redefine excellence in executive education, proving highly influential.

Kellogg School benefactor and Booz Allen Hamilton cofounder James L. Allen surveys the 1986 construction of an atrium at the executive education facility that bears his name. The addition significantly expanded the building, which originally opened in 1979.

The McManus Living-Learning Center, a facility in Evanston designed specifically for Kellogg students and their families. The property was purchased in 1979 using part of the $10 million Kellogg Foundation gift. The building, named in honor of benefactor and alumnus James R. McManus '56, reopened in September 1981 after being renovated.

Bulletin boards preceded the Kellogg Intranet as a popular forum for communication.

Bala Balachandran, the J.L. Kellogg Professor of Accounting Information and Management, teaches an executive MBA class in 1985.

"The Wizard of Biz" was a satiric skit performed by Kellogg students during Special K Revue in May 1982. Kellogg students write, direct, produce and perform all the material for the sketch comedy and dance revue. Since 1980, the event has been a favorite with alumni and students, one reason why the show is scheduled to coincide with Reunion each spring.

Experiential learning has long played a part in how the Kellogg School prepares its students for leadership positions. *Above,* a team of Kellogg students receive an award in 1982 from F. James McDonald, president of General Motors Corporation, after winning the General Motors Marketing Competition. The contest required the team to solve real-world business challenges. *From left:* Betsy Holden, Mark DaSilva, Lawrence Benders, Mary Bolyard, Glen Madeja (all '82) and McDonald.

Conceptual Issues in Management (CIM) began in 1969 as a way of introducing new students to the school. Since then, the annual orientation has developed into a way for second-year students to pass along the Kellogg culture to the incoming class. Combining academic and social events, CIM was designed to encourage rapid camaraderie among students.

After signing a 1982 joint agreement between their schools, members of the Kellogg School and the Sasin Graduate Institute of Business Administration at Chulalongkorn University in Bangkok, Thailand, celebrate. Sasin was the first of several global partnerships and alliances undertaken by Kellogg. *From left:* Toemsakdi Krishnamra, Sasin director; Khun Kasem, Chulalongkorn president; Suthi Ekahitanonda, Sasin deputy director; Robert Duncan, Kellogg professor of organization behavior; and Donald P. Jacobs, Kellogg dean.

nomic development and the Institute for Management, the executive education program begun in 1951.[25]

A pioneer in executive education, the Institute for Management was the second such program in the United States. (Harvard had introduced its Advanced Management offering in 1945.)[26] As early as 1929, however, Northwestern had considered ways to encourage executives to return to campus for short-term courses designed to enhance their skills. But limited resources and economic conditions exacerbated by the Depression curtailed such efforts until midcentury, when the school introduced a four-week summer immersion program in business management on its Chicago campus.

"In recent years, many businesses have recognized the need for executive development," said Donham, explaining the initiative's rationale. "Some companies have instituted programs, others have been unable to do so. Our Institute for Management will serve both in providing for concentrated study while the executives are free from regular responsibility."[27] Further, the institute's aims would be to broaden the education of executives for general management, with companies paying $1,000 to enroll one individual in the program. The tuition would be used in part to support the initiative itself, but it would also help to develop cases for the four-week executive program, material that would find its way into the school's graduate division as well.[28]

The school's timing was propitious: as a result of widespread unemployment and limited development opportunities, the Depression's legacy meant, among other things, that there was a greatly reduced number of qualified professionals for senior management—a paucity whose impact was still being felt when World War II further disrupted the workforce, sending some 9 million Americans into battle between 1938 and 1946. In many instances, midlevel employees were promoted to serve at more senior levels when their superiors were called away to duty. These circumstances, coupled with an "unexpected and almost unprecedented increase in business activity" starting during World War II and continuing afterward, increased the number of jobs to be filled and resulted in a demand for training targeted to executives.[29]

Donham was keenly aware of these developments, as was clear in a statement he made during a 1958 roundtable discussion reviewing executive programming. There, he cited the challenges of global trade, larger and more complex organizations and a need for sharp executives with general skills: "If, in the old days, managers in sufficient numbers had matured in the natural course of business, and replacements for top positions were always ready for the picking, such was no longer the case. Nor was the top executive of yesterday sufficient unto the new day. Science, with its customary irresponsibility toward the social consequences of its discoveries, had fashioned a need for managers with a quality of vision, foresight, and wisdom hitherto thought to be outside the requisites for managers."[30]

Executives from 28 corporations attended the inaugural Institute for Management, reported Donham. At the time, he was the director of the graduate commerce division, heading the program with assistance from Leon A. Bosch '48, business administration; Frederick A. Ekeblad '47, business statistics; and Charles I. Gragg, business administration at Harvard. Students at the institute lived together in Abbott Hall and studied in Wieboldt Hall for 12 hours each day during the intensive session, the camaraderie being an integral part of the experience. Faculty members also maintained close contact with the executives, eventually residing with them on campus for the program's duration. Classes featured seminar-style interaction, with the professors leading the discussion but the participants drawing significantly on their own experiences and challenges; case studies were used as pedagogical tools.

The program had five objectives: to give executives a comprehensive business perspective, rather than that of a departmental manager; to help executives develop the ability to recognize problems arising from changed conditions; to foster the ability to think problems through rather than to jump at conclusions; to build confidence in making decisions; and to cultivate facility in motivating employees to generate results.

These goals were in line with foundational objectives advanced by pioneering French management theorist Henri Fayol (1841–1925). Most business schools, however, had been unable to teach these lessons, in part, Fayol said, because of an early prejudice toward practical experience rather than theory. As a result, he believed, management lacked a coherent theoretical framework, and schools tended to teach what they *could* easily master: technical skills and a narrow curriculum. To counter this and because he believed that future leadership would require managerial, rather than technical, training, Fayol had posited five functions of management: planning, organizing, leading, coordinating and controlling. His seminal paper on the subject was published in 1908 and incorporated an early list of 14 management principles.

Taking a comprehensive view of management and executive development, the Institute for Management proved popular. Enrollment grew from an initial 28 students to 66 in the program's second year, when an extra session was required to meet demand. Two formal subjects emerged: "Top Management Policy and Administration," which analyzed current case histories, and "Managerial Responsibilities and Their Limits," which considered the social, economic and political problems in a free enterprise society. The formal curriculum was also supplemented with lectures from executive guests, such as James F. Oates Jr., chairman of the Peoples Gas Light and Coke Company.

In 1957, Donham would hire Donald P. Jacobs, an assistant economics professor at City College of New York and the National Bureau of Economic Research, to help bolster the curriculum. Jacobs would be among those tasked with instilling analytical rigor into the business program. To that end, the young professor was at Harvard for the 1959–1960 academic year, participating in the Ford Foundation–sponsored Institute for Mathematics. The foundation earmarked $500,000 for the initiative, which drew an elite group of 41 teachers of business administration from 32 universities for the one-year institute, whose purpose was the intensive study of mathematics and statistics in business education and research. "This training institute—composed of men who have a key part in the preparation of future business teachers and who are active in research—is intended to have a rapid and widespread effect on business education," according to the Ford Foundation's annual report for 1958.

The school expected Jacobs to devote a significant part of his summer at the institute to devising a strategy for sharing his experiences in the Harvard program with his Evanston peers. "Part of Mr. Jacobs' assignment for 1960–1961 will be held open for the purpose of instructing the faculty in connection with this program."[31]

Jacobs would not lose his love of academia, but his early experiences with the executive education program opened him to the practitioner's viewpoint, and that represented an epiphany for him. "That's where I learned business, because my academic emphasis is as an economist," he said. "I didn't know anything about management. I never took a management course in my life."[32] Jacobs said he learned "an enormous amount" from the executives. He would lecture them about theory, and they in turn would offer him insights about the real business world. This experience would prove extremely important for Jacobs and the school when, nearly two decades later, he spearheaded the development of the James L. Allen Center, a state-of-the-art facility dedicated to lifelong learning and executive education (see chapter 5).

"This was a good education for me," said Jacobs of his early exposure to practitioners at the institute. "You sit around talking to executives and you really learn what they're thinking about. This is where the Allen Center came from, this notion that there's a two-way learning [between practitioners and academics]. That's where I got the idea, and that changed management education. It was really sort of interesting what came out of that."

Going International: Roots of the Kellogg Global Network

Jacobs's support for the program grew, and by the early 1960s, others shared his enthusiasm. Colleagues like Thomas McNichols, a faculty member in the School of

Business, and John Peterson, a Harvard MBA who was not on the faculty but was recruited by Donham to help run the executive education program, thought its success could be replicated in Europe. "We didn't have anything to do with overseas. We were just focused domestically," recalled Jacobs. "But we understood that the world was globalizing."

One night in 1965 during a discussion in Abbott Hall, the three men decided to approach the dean with a plan for an international version of the executive program. Peterson, "a kid from North Dakota who worked his way through Harvard by stoking the furnace in the dean's house," according to Jacobs, was an "extraordinary character" whose experiences in the U.S. Air Force during World War II placed him in company close to the "Whiz Kids"—a group of military veterans who became Ford Motor Company executives in 1946 and brought their management science and logistics skills with them. As a result, Peterson had a network of influential business and political contacts, people he could solicit to help develop the school's executive education presence in Europe.

The importance of this early international effort would help position the school for later global partnerships in Asia, Europe and the Middle East. But initially, a receptive Donham was concerned about how the program would attract students, particularly senior executives from prestigious companies. Peterson, with his rich network of contacts, assured the dean the school could meet this objective.

"So Donham gave him a budget and he went around Europe and actually filled up a class with senior people from Unilever, from Royal Dutch Shell, from Exxon— big, big players," said Jacobs, who was enthusiastic about teaching in the program. Students came from many sectors, including banking and the pharmaceutical industry. But the school still had to decide on a location for what would be called the Institute for International Management. Peterson found what he considered the perfect place for the three-week residential program: the top of a mountain above Lake Lucerne in Switzerland.

"He comes up with a place called the Bürgenstock," remembered Jacobs. "It was a gorgeous place where royalty used to come. Big international stars, like Sophia Loren, would be there. It was really a fabulous place. I thought this would never work, but [Peterson] gets the class running."

Because the faculty, though motivated and talented, lacked expertise in international business—"neither Tom McNichols nor I were international economists," said Jacobs—the school looked to European colleagues for help. Soon, they had respected academics from France, Germany and Britain serving on the faculty for the Institute for International Management, including a management theorist from the Sorbonne named Pierre Tabatoni,[33] as well as a young professor in Bonn named

Horst Albach who had graduated from Bowdoin in 1956. Each would become distinguished in his own right.

"So these are people I've known for 40 years now," said Jacobs in 2006. "Albach becomes chairman of the Council of Economic Advisers in Germany and a major figurehead of the National Science Foundation. Later in life, Tabatoni ends up being cultural minister and director of the Sorbonne, and the chancellor of all the universities in Paris, and a member of the Academie de France."

With this support in place, the program would attract some 30 international businesspeople each year. More important, said Jacobs, the seeds of the Kellogg School's international reputation were sown in this program, and it helped influence the current executive education curriculum at Kellogg.

"When I became dean [in 1975], if I had not had this background it would be a different world. We would have been a different school," Jacobs declared.

He also explained how the program ended. "When the Allen Center opened [in 1979], the companies that had come to the [Bürgenstock] program year after year said, 'We'd be better off sending our people to Evanston where we'd get the whole faculty, not just a couple professors.'"[34]

Donham's Values Lead to the Midcentury Academic Push

But the Allen Center had its roots in the efforts made during the 1950s by Dean Donham, who valued academic performance and had a well-formed philosophy of education—especially as it pertained to teaching. He sought to bolster the MBA program, launched in 1920, and to enhance the school's executive education program. To help him achieve these goals, Donham turned to his colleagues. He appointed three faculty members to key positions in his administration: Leon Bosch, a professor of business administration, became associate dean and director of the graduate division; Ira D. Anderson, a professor of marketing, became associate dean and director of the undergraduate division; and Frank T. Hartzfeld, an assistant professor of business administration, became the dean's assistant and later the graduate program's assistant dean.

The son of the founding dean of the Harvard Business School, Donham had earned three credentials from that institution: a bachelor's degree in 1927, an MBA in 1930 and a doctorate in commercial science in 1934. He joined Northwestern as a professor of business administration in 1940 at the behest of Dean Homer Vanderblue, going on to become director of the school's graduate division in 1950 and then dean in 1953, following the brief deanships of Joseph M. McDaniel (1950–1951) and Ernest C. Davies (1951–1953).[35] Born in 1905 in Newton

Highlands, Massachusetts, Donham had taught management at Harvard and at Yale Law School before his Northwestern tenure. He also had ample and privileged opportunity to understand the challenges of business education, particularly since his father, Wallace, had grappled with the matter years earlier.[36]

Not surprisingly, Donham tried to import his Harvard perspective—including that school's emphasis on the case method as a teaching tool—to Northwestern. He departed, however, from his alma mater's approach by placing case study within a broader context of action, analysis and lecture, in part because midwestern circumstances discouraged a wholesale transfer of an Ivy League model.[37] The University of Chicago, meanwhile, adopted an almost entirely theoretical framework for business study and seemed to demonstrate an antipathy for cases, whereas Harvard embraced the case method to the exclusion of much else. Northwestern would use the case study as one tool among several in its MBA curriculum.[38]

Whatever the merits of the case study, it provided only a partial response to the gathering challenges confronting business and business educators after World War II. By 1960, the business world was far different than it had been a half century earlier when the School of Commerce opened. Technological advancements coupled with increased global trade and much larger, multidivisional enterprises were demanding a trained professional who could handle many challenges—some still emerging—that were barely glimpsed in 1908.[39]

Yet the frameworks and methods of many business schools seemed chained to ideas from that earlier age. Their mission appeared confused, as if they had been only partially aware of the dramatic ways that commerce had changed after years of economic depression and then a second world war. This slowness did not go unnoticed.

Among their other recommendations, the Ford Foundation and Carnegie surveys were calling for schools to develop ideas that were already present in some forms, dating back to Fayol and Frederick Taylor and scientific management. But the critiques also encouraged using new tools, like the increasingly sophisticated operations research thought (also called management science) that had come to prominence during World War II. Using interdisciplinary approaches such as mathematical modeling, stochastic processes, statistics and graph and game theory—a form of applied mathematics that came about in 1944 with the publication of *Theory of Games and Economic Behavior* by mathematician John von Neumann and economist Oskar Morgenstern—operations research brought technical frameworks to decision making in complex real-world situations involving the coordination and execution of operations within an organization.[40]

The Ford and Carnegie surveys' detailed and scathing indictment of U.S. management education initiated sweeping reforms. The researchers in each study pursued their investigations independently (though they did share some information) but came largely to the same conclusions: most business schools outside the top ranks needed considerable repair if they were to contribute meaningfully to modern commercial life. Some 1,200 pages in total, the studies called into question many of the assumptions and practices of the majority of the schools of business in that era.[41]

Among their complaints, the researchers found that despite the proliferation of business schools between 1920 and 1960,[42] the institutions' purposes often were ill defined—in part because the wildly eclectic and numerous business careers made curriculum development challenging. *Which* business leaders would a school educate? The ones hoping to run billion-dollar corporations, or those managing hardware stores or gas stations?[43] More troubling, claimed the researchers, was the fact that schools were teaching the wrong subjects in the wrong way to students whose needs were not always being served properly. Curricula were loaded with specialized courses, like accounting or marketing, that encouraged functional dexterity at the cost of more general managerial ability—something increasingly demanded by the corporations to which these graduates were headed. Both the Ford and Carnegie surveys discovered that few schools offered the sort of analytically rigorous courses necessary to cultivate the executive leadership required by an increasingly international commercial world that had become more reliant than ever on sophisticated communications technologies. To make this situation especially problematic, corporate recruiters frequently paid lip service to the notion of wanting graduates with general management training but then hired people who could fill positions that rewarded functional talent rather than managerial acumen. In the process, students were short-changed. Said Pierson, "The vast majority of students receiving undergraduate degrees from these institutions today have had little or no work in any of the humanities outside English, in college mathematics, in any of the sciences outside economics and possibly history."[44]

What's more, the studies uncovered what researchers saw as a fundamental flaw in the claims put forth by the schools—namely, that business was a professional pursuit. By comparing business with other professions, such as medicine and law, the studies contended that business had not yet achieved much in terms of meeting the four prerequisites for professionalism. Robert Gordon and James Howell suggested the following criteria:

> First, the practice of a profession must rest on a systematic body of knowledge of substantial intellectual content and on the development of personal skill in the application of this knowledge to specific cases. Second, there must exist standards of professional conduct, which take precedence over

the goal of personal gain. . . . A profession has its own association of members, among whose functions are the enforcement of standards, the advancement and dissemination of knowledge, and, in some degree, the control of entry into the profession. Finally, there is some prescribed way of entering the profession through the enforcement of minimum standards of training and competence.[45]

The authors claimed that business, though it was beginning to develop a literature to meet the first criterion, actually failed to meet the other three, meaning that much work remained to be done before business could become a true profession. The first step in achieving that goal, they said, was to bolster the business curriculum to increase quantitative rigor while accenting the importance of general, rather than specific, knowledge. The liberal arts should play a key part in this reassessment, with mathematics and the social sciences becoming more prominent, they said. Contemporary business leaders would need to solve complex problems using the scientific method and quantitative analysis. At the same time, a new emphasis on organizational theory, interpersonal relationships and managerial principles would arise.

The studies were concerned primarily with schools outside the top tier—the better programs, in many cases, had already been aware of their deficiencies and taken certain steps to address these problems, though not necessarily entirely satisfactorily. Even Northwestern, though near the top of the business schools' ranks, retained more of its traditional curriculum than Donham thought ideal.[46]

School of Business Adapts for Success

The Ford and Carnegie surveys had a lasting influence at the Northwestern University School of Business. There would be more quantitative analysis, more emphasis on organizational behavior, and a more global focus that recognized the relationships among business, labor and government.

Discussion of the reports was widespread and included a business school summit held early in 1960 at Michigan State University. Northwestern University marketing professor Richard Clewett, along with economics professor Dascomb Forbush and Leon Bosch, the associate dean, attended the event, which drew some 200 people from schools in Illinois, Indiana, Ohio and Michigan.[47]

In Clewett's report to the faculty, he observed that the reaction to the Ford and Carnegie studies "was not antagonistic." Indeed, he said, one or another of the business educators had previously suggested all the ideas presented in the surveys, and there was value in bringing the strands of thought together in one place. Still, he reported, some raised concerns, wondering whether the surveys were asking for more than schools could deliver and if the assessments could spark conflict among the schools. Would professors be inclined to go along with the surveys' recommendations? If so, "a certain re-training of the faculty is required," contended one school's dean, who also voiced a warning about the tendency to treat the reports as "some kind of authoritative reference" rather than mere suggestions. Nevertheless, the consensus at the summit was that it "probably would be wise to give more attention to economic analysis, behavioral sciences and mathematics," being careful to assess how these disciplines were already (and likely would be in the future) applied to business problems. With respect to the School of Business curriculum, Clewett suggested that each course be examined to determine how math, economics and behavorial science could prove helpful in solving the problems posed in such courses. During an April 6, 1960, faculty meeting, participants also recommended that a study be conducted after each course to review the concepts and techniques used and how well the students mastered them.

In the wake of the reports, Donham's administration took action at both the undergraduate and graduate levels, forming committees to review the progress made on many of the survey recommendations.

As Gordon, Howell and Pierson prepared their findings for publication, Professor Lavengood was tasked with examining the school's success in developing its undergraduate curriculum, beginning with efforts that started in the 1954–1955 academic year. Among Lavengood's benchmarks were statements by Donham related to creating a program that offered students commercial prospects after graduation, while also educating them as citizens possessed of rich cultural knowledge.

"The curriculum purports to combine effective doses of education for living and education for making a living," wrote Lavengood in a progress report to Donham and Ira Anderson in 1958. "These are not perceived as altogether separate parts, however, but as mutually dependent elements, both of them conforming to the worthiest traditions of the modern university and to the needs of industrial society. Civilized taste, disciplined wits that can be used to measure, judge and impart, and a comprehension of responsible citizenship not only are liberal virtues; they also are requirements for modern business management."[48]

Lavengood's research also examined the relationship between the School of Business and the university's College of Liberal Arts "to discover how well the advantages of the College of Liberal Arts were being used to achieve the aims of the Business School's undergraduate program." As a result, Lavengood attended many undergraduate courses during the 1958–1959 academic year and interviewed exemplary students about their reaction to the school's efforts to bolster the business curriculum. His findings determined that the liberal arts college was interested in the business program and motivated to work with the School of Business.

Students expressed a generally favorable reaction to the curriculum changes, but they also felt that they should be exposed to business classes earlier in their academic tenure. Managing this mix of specialized and general education was of importance for students and for the faculty members on the Educational Policy Committee.[49] Both believed that "general education should occupy a conspicuous place in all four years of undergraduate study," rather than be confined largely to the first two years, before students went on to take their business courses.[50] Students also reported having mixed feelings about the case method, complaining that too much time passed between their studying cases and having experiences where insights from the cases might prove valuable.

During the early 1960s, one way in which the school tried to help students appreciate the utility of the tools they were learning in the classroom was by continuing the tradition of encouraging cross-fertilization of theory and practice. The "Enterprise and Entrepreneurship" elective—a senior-level course designed to develop awareness of the entrepreneur's role in American economic life—invited practicing entrepreneurs into the classroom as lecturers. "Course content is approached through discussions led by outstanding speakers from the business world, supplemented by appropriate cases and background readings. . . . Exposure to persons who are creators or innovators in business enterprise dramatizes for the student the spirit of adventure in capitalism," noted the course description. The historical role of the entrepreneur and the profit motive in the free enterprise system were among the topics addressed in the class.

Professor John Larson, who taught the course in the spring of 1960, stated: "Student exposures to outside speakers is absolutely essential, in my view. Most students seem to have had no such contacts; they are particularly grateful for small, informal discussions with businessmen." However, the dangers of such a course were noted as well, with Larson pointing out how the class could "degenerate into nothing more than a series of unrelated speakers, with student notions of an easy course." To avoid this, he said it was best to have the course designed logically upon a single theme, with appropriate speakers supporting that theme.[51]

An example of a course whose introduction seemed to reflect awareness of the Ford and Carnegie surveys' emphasis on the behavioral sciences was "Consumer Motivation and Behavior," taught by Steuart Henderson Britt. The class, approved at the May 4, 1960, faculty meeting, presented psychological frameworks designed to be useful in assessing consumer behavior and motivation. "After an analysis of the social-psychological foundations of consumer behavior, including cultural factors," a number of topics would be discussed, such as personality differences; social conflicts; fads and fashion; marketing factors, "including the role of the consumer in modern society"; and persuasion.

MBA Option Strengthened

Beyond the undergraduate program, the school was revamping its MBA program and creating a strategy to differentiate the school from its competitors, notably Harvard, Stanford, Chicago and Columbia, which were seen as Northwestern's main rivals. To do this in the graduate program, Donham had enlisted 26 faculty members over the 1957–1958 and 1958–1959 school years to assess the strengths and limitations of the existing MBA.[52] The dean believed the school could do more to improve the quality of its graduate offering, and he hoped to orchestrate a "significant reconstruction" and "imaginative redesigning rather than a relatively simple revision." Key changes would have to take account of the need for increased analysis and high-level quantification skills as well as a greater emphasis on scientific frameworks that could help manage increasingly global organizations.[53] First-year students pursued coursework in general management and offerings in marketing, accounting, finance and production. Second-year students took several electives, as well as a seminar and an examination of "the ideas and institutions which impinge on and influence the conduct of business enterprise."

Among the MBA courses approved in June 1960 were those presenting a balanced and comprehensive approach to qualitative and quantitative study. A first-year offering called "The Individual, Corporation and Society" applied behavioral disciplines such as sociology, psychology and anthropology to the business world. The course was described as "action oriented," and it used cases and readings to explore individual motivations, needs and wants as well as the relationships of people within organizations. It also addressed the "inevitable conflicts between individuals, the individual and groups, and between groups."

Another course, "Management of an Enterprise," used case analysis and group discussion to study the "total operation of a business enterprise, and the interrelationships which prevail within any business firm." On the quantitative side was an eight-credit-hour class called "Statistical Analysis and Analytical Tools" that promised to "build on the background of the [student's] previous work in accounting, statistics, and economics, and at the same time . . . pursue advanced work in the fields in terms of the development of new . . . ideas." This requirement was designed to integrate several disciplines to apply quantitative tools in ways that would help students manage inventory policy, forecasting, wage and compensation policy and pricing policy. It also leveraged techniques developed in linear programming and data processing. In all, 23 courses, including electives, combined to make up the two-year revised MBA curriculum.

Across all programs, Donham suggested a strategy guided by four initial goals, as articulated in faculty meetings that addressed the curriculum in detail:

1. To get students to realize that the management of an enterprise is to understand the enterprise as a whole—to begin with "whole seeing" and then pursue the pieces.
2. An attempt to focus on the individual to help him understand himself and see the relationships between himself and the corporate organizations, community organizations and greater business society.
3. To deal with quantitative aspects of business planning—use of analytical tools and figures to help analyze, understand and control business activities.
4. To deal with environment—Economics plus Business and Government and Law.[54]

Among those benefiting from the curriculum enhancements was Lawrence Revsine, who would earn three degrees from the School of Business during the 1960s and go on to join its Accounting Department faculty in 1971 after serving as a tenured associate professor at the University of Illinois–Urbana-Champaign as well as working at Arthur Andersen and the predecessor to KPMG.

Revsine recalled that when he arrived at Northwestern in 1960, the transition to a research-oriented faculty was just beginning. By the time he earned his doctorate in 1968, he said, the school's academics had grown increasingly rigorous, particularly as the Managerial Economics and Decision Sciences Department was being formed. But as an undergraduate, Revsine noted that the faculty was in transition. "There were people who were quite good, and you had faculty with higher research aspirations," he said. Yet these individuals "coexisted with some people who did not have the same aspirations."

Revsine considered the school a good one, and with tuition running about $900 a year, it also offered an affordable education—particularly for a kid who lived at home and "took the Devon Ave. bus to the Loyola El and then the El to Foster St. and walked the rest of the way." His father, Victor, had graduated from the undergraduate business program in 1940 and then became a certified public accountant, as would Revsine and his brother Bernard, who also earned a Northwestern MBA in 1965.

Revsine recalled being inspired by several faculty members, including Donald Jacobs. "Don was important to me. I never had him for finance as an undergraduate, but did during my graduate studies," he said. "Earlier I had a class with Phil Kotler, but he was virtually a rookie when I had him as a professor. You had people here who could provide the kind of excitement that, in the right atmosphere, could be successful. We were still at the verge of taking off back then, but there were people who, by demonstration of their own successes, were able to give students models about how to achieve greatness."

He also noted that the increasingly rigorous Northwestern curriculum allowed him to pursue the kind of accounting research that was only starting to emerge. "I was a hardcore accountant with a strong finance vaccination," said Revsine. "People were beginning to recognize that accounting could not be insular, that you couldn't do the kinds of things that needed to be done in terms of teaching and research if you were operating in an isolation booth, without interaction with behaviorists. The beginnings of behavioral accounting were happening at that time, though not happening widely yet outside of some of the really good schools."[55]

Revsine's studies would lead him to a fine academic career. His 1998 text, *Financial Reporting and Analysis* (now in its third edition), would prove influential in terms of going behind the financial data presented by companies to reveal how the figures—which Revsine said often reflected considerable subjectivity—could be manipulated for various ends. He pointed out that his book adopted an approach that explained how an executive had incentives and opportunities to manipulate the accounting rules to make an organization's performance appear stronger than it actually was, rewarding the executive in the process.

Revsine taught at Northwestern and Kellogg from 1971 to 2007, when he died of cancer at the age of 64.

Move toward Exclusive Graduate Business Education

Despite Donham's desire to enhance the reputation and strengths of the undergraduate business curriculum, there was at that time a broader debate under way regarding the merits of the undergraduate degree compared with graduate education. Many believed that graduate business education was the emerging trend, one rooted in a growing complexity of business that demanded higher-level training, including sophisticated analysis (such as game theory) and advanced behavioral studies.

The point arose repeatedly in faculty discussions, even as the school bolstered its undergraduate offerings. In part, the debate involved questions of resource allocation: could a school be all things to all people—that is, could it be a leader in both graduate and undergraduate education? And even if some schools could do so, could a private school, not funded by taxpayer dollars, realistically achieve this goal?

Indeed, funding had been a concern at the business school for the preceding decade, with Northwestern president J. Roscoe Miller and vice president and dean of faculties Payson S. Wild being proponents of the curriculum but forced to allocate support throughout the university. As a result, the university only modestly supported the business school's budgeted expenditures between 1954 and 1963.[56] Donham recognized that the school faced more vigorous competition at the graduate level from peers such as Harvard, Chicago and Columbia—schools that could directly solicit funds from corporate benefactors, a strategy that was unavailable to the School of Business because Miller feared the approach could detract from a university-wide effort then under way to raise $138 million. These circumstances changed somewhat by 1962, with Miller better appreciating the importance of Donham's request for corporate funding; nationally, the importance of graduate business education had grown more apparent. As a result, in July 1962, Miller authorized a limited effort called the Northwestern University School of Business Industrial Council; membership was open to corporations that contributed $2,000 to the school annually. The campaign, however, had little success, in part because Donham's poor health restricted his ability to drive the effort.[57]

Early Rankings

Then there was the matter of reputation and rankings. Although Northwestern's School of Business earned solid marks, being listed among the top 15 schools ranked by a *Chicago Tribune* survey in 1962, some observers believed that only those institutions that were willing to fully support a graduate business program would produce the caliber of education, graduates and research that warranted top-echelon status. Although no attempt was made to rank the business schools in a precise numerical order, the *Tribune* and various academic consultants rated Harvard, Stanford, Columbia, MIT, Dartmouth, Cornell, Carnegie Institute, Wharton, Purdue and Chicago as the top 10.[58] The consensus of those conducting the study was that "a liberal arts program is the best undergraduate preparation for business careers and that specialized education in business should be confined to graduate schools."[59]

Donham contacted the *Tribune* reporter to complain about methodological flaws in the study, which he believed were as apparent as they were galling to him. The dean, upon investigating, discovered that the reporter on the story had relied on the opinions of a handful of people associated with Harvard, Stanford, Columbia and the University of Chicago, without establishing any specific standards. The reporter, sympathetic to Donham's entreaties, agreed to write another article focused on the Northwestern program. In that piece,[60] which reported favorably on the many innovations the school had made since World War II, Donham explained how the curriculum "juxtaposes discussional materials which encourage exploration of general principles with case materials requiring managerial decision and action in a particular set of circumstances." A student, he said, was thereby encouraged to "experience adventures in ideas" but was simultaneously held accountable for "reconciling these ideas with the need for getting something done under conditions where the ideas . . . may be in conflict." Though the article noted that Northwestern's business program was ranked among the top 10 by a "distinguished minority of business educators, notably at Harvard," the reporter also indicated that many perceived the school's undergraduate program as a liability. "It is the overwhelming consensus of leading business educators and [distinguished] business school alumni . . . that business education should be confined to graduate schools."[61]

Keenly aware of these factors, Donham and his administrators nevertheless believed that they could create an unparalleled undergraduate program. They had, after all, demonstrated such an intent to the Ford Foundation and had produced a strategy sufficiently impressive to garner a half million dollars in funding from that organization. Still, the question of the program's future repeatedly emerged in faculty meetings as the 1960s began. Donham spoke frankly about the issue at the end of 1962, noting two questions in particular that were apparent to him. How quickly could the revised MBA program gain a reputation that would be reflected in recruiting? And would undergraduate enrollment increase in the coming few years? He believed it would take at least three and perhaps as many as five years to achieve such results. With respect to the undergraduate program, he stated that the school would have to wait to see whether enrollment figures would trend upward. He expected that within two or three years, the administration would be in a better position to determine whether Northwestern should make the transition to graduate business education exclusively.[62]

Standing before a partially demolished Memorial Hall, home to the Graduate School of Management, Northwestern University officials in 1970 display an artist's rendering of Leverone Hall, which would open in 1972. *From left:* Franklin M. Kreml, Northwestern University vice president for planning and development; Northwestern president J. Roscoe Miller; GSM dean John Barr; GSM associate dean Ralph Westfall; and William S. Kerr, Northwestern vice president and business manager.

Chapter 4

REVITALIZED:
RISKY MOVES PAY OFF
IN A BIG WAY

Dramatic changes in teaching and in the curriculum, including a transition to gradu-ate education exclusively, marked the tenure of Dean John Barr, a businessman whose Advisory Council—composed of distinguished practitioners—helped influence the modern Graduate School of Management.

Sustained focus on the undergraduate program would prove problematic, something that grew increasingly apparent early in the administration of Donham's successor, John Andrew Barr.

Barr, an attorney and former chairman of Montgomery Ward & Company who had served as a Northwestern University trustee since 1957, was nominated as dean of the School of Business on June 1, 1965. Donham had stated a desire to return to teaching after his 11-year tenure as dean, citing also "the personal toll" the deanship had taken on him.[1] Barr's tenure would be marked by significant and daring changes in the school. For instance, in the spring of 1966, the faculty would vote, by a margin of two to one, to discontinue the undergraduate program. In addition, the school would adopt a business advisory council to help guide its strategic develop-ment; it would be headed by James L. Allen, a founder of Booz Allen Hamilton and a business associate of Barr's. Although he was a businessman, Barr also would over-see a considerable expansion of the school's faculty, particularly in ways that deep-ened its research orientation in areas of quantifiable study.

Such a move was apparent in 1968 when the school created its Managerial Economics and Decision Sciences Department, headed by Professor Stanley Reiter, who arrived in 1967. In 1969, the school would also change its name to reflect its exclusive graduate orientation, now calling itself the Northwestern University Graduate School of Management. That same year, it would even stop issuing the MBA degree in favor of the more general master of management degree, designed to appeal to a broader number of students looking for careers both in business and in other fields, including government and nonprofit sectors. Barr's administration also spearheaded fund-raising for a new building to house the school. The result, Nathaniel Leverone Hall, would be erected in 1972 on the spot where Memorial Hall had stood.

These strategic moves were risky but were well studied by the school, and Barr, 57 when he assumed the deanship, had publicly expressed his desire to revitalize business education, especially in light of some studies indicating a waning student interest in business. (A Harvard survey in 1965, for example, indicated that among its graduates, only 14 percent planned a business career, down from the 39 percent reported five years earlier.)[2]

"Today's youths are seeking careers that are intellectually challenging, creative, and contribute something to society," Barr told the *Chicago Tribune*. "A career in business gives a satisfaction of these wants and we as business men have done a poor job of exciting youths and counselors as to the advantages of such a career." This process should begin at the high school level, he believed.[3]

As dean, Barr created a special committee to study the question of phasing out the undergraduate curriculum; it was chaired by Ralph Westfall, who had been promoted to associate dean for academic affairs on October 2, 1965.[4] The nine-member committee, which included Howard Bennett, Richard Clewett, and Thomas McNichols, presented its decision to the faculty on April 13, 1966, at which time Barr said that the university administration had assured its support for the school's budget "to the best of its ability" should the school decide to focus on graduate study exclusively. The dean detailed the areas in which such funds were needed: faculty salaries, research support, case development, alumni relations, library facilities, student aid and capital needs.

In tandem with this committee was another—Barr's Business Advisory Council, whose membership read like a who's who of Chicago's senior business community; it was led by James Allen.[5] Thirty-three executives from companies such as Illinois Bell, Quaker Oats, Northern Trust, American Hospital Supply, United Airlines and Inland Steel composed this board.[6] A partial list of those initially serving on the council included: Donald S. Perkins, president of the Jewel Tea Company; Leo H.

Schoenhofen Jr., president of the Container Corporation of America; Gilbert H. Scribner Jr., president of Scribner and Company; Daniel Searle, executive vice president of G. D. Searle and Company; Erwin A. Stuebner, president of Kidder Peabody and Company; R. Arthur Williams, president of Stanray Corporation; and Joseph S. Wright, president of Zenith Radio Corporation.[7]

"Jim Allen was on the board of trustees," said Westfall. "He was the one who basically recruited John Barr to come here as dean of the commerce school. He and John had been closely associated in business."[8]

The council also had begun exploring the future of business education in April 1966, determining that real-world demands called for a more sophisticated manager than the type of individual the undergraduate program was likely to produce. "Northwestern University should strive for an innovative and leadership position in management education," the council members wrote in their 1966 "Proposed Statement of Recommendation." To that end, the university was advised to create a school of management that would "encompass the development of managers, the conduct of research, and the development of teachers of management for organizations of all types—business, government, health and education."

Given the university's limited resources, the council recommended that rather than try to stretch itself too thin with mediocre results across the board, Northwestern should take a calculated risk and phase out the undergraduate curriculum even though it was successful and despite the challenges of building a sizable new graduate program.

The council members based their recommendations upon research they conducted—which included a broad survey of business and education professionals—that suggested public organizations faced similar challenges to those seen in the business world.

The academic case was presented by Westfall, who told his colleagues that there was no basis on which to collect factual data that would clearly indicate "a specific conclusion of this matter." He believed the issue was a matter of judgment. Nevertheless, the committee recommended that the undergraduate program be discontinued, despite what Westfall called its "long, successful history." Limited resources, the committee noted, meant the school should focus its energies on where the future of management education seemed to be headed and "take vigorous action to establish a position of leadership in graduate business education."[9]

On May 4, 1966, the faculty voted in a secret ballot to discontinue the undergraduate program. The motion carried by a margin of 34 to 17. Thus, at the close of the 1969–1970 academic year, the university would bestow its last bachelor of science in business degree. In addition, the school would discontinue the bachelor of business administration degree associated with the Evening Division after the 1971–1972 term.[10]

In 2005, Westfall recalled this momentous decision, including the contentious debate that had taken place among his faculty peers. "There were people on both sides of that issue and it took some time to sort through," he said. "Eliminating the undergraduate program changed the faculty to some degree, since some of them had seen their role as working with undergraduate students. We had a different [approach to] faculty recruitment afterwards. I didn't find that much [dissent] among the alumni, but among the faculty there were clearly some who thought of their role as being involved with the undergraduate program, and they felt threatened, with good reason, by the move to just being a graduate school." Westfall also noted the importance of taking this calculated risk, even though the program was "probably among the very best."

"We saw that a school like Northwestern was not going to focus on undergraduate business education," he said. "It was clear that the MBA was going to be driving business education in the future, and this is where you wanted to have your main focus," especially since limited resources precluded the school attempting to continue offering both degrees.[11]

Jacobs also recalled that, at the time, "there was a demand from some of the professions, like accounting, for undergraduate business majors, but the vast majority of the kind of people we wanted to educate would be going on to get their master's degree."[12]

Lavengood remembered this time of transition as bringing a radical change, especially given the recent efforts to bolster the undergraduate curriculum. "Having gone through a dozen years of this splendid Ford Foundation–financed development of the premier undergraduate program . . . then [we were] faced with the serious suggestion that not only should we emphasize the master's program, but doing a bit of strategic planning we soon came to realize that we didn't know if we'd have the resources to expand and pump up the MBA and continue with the undergraduate," said Lavengood. "And we'd not be able to get the kind of faculty necessary to teach MBAs if they had to teach undergraduates as well. This was a traumatic suggestion for many of us."[13] (Edmund Wilson, hired in 1972 as director of admissions and financial aid, recalled verbatim Lavengood's dramatic assessment of this key change at the school: "It was decided," said Wilson, speaking in a grave and dignified tone suggesting Lavengood's, "that in order to give strength to the weak arm [the MBA program], we cut off the good arm [the undergraduate program.]" Apparently, Lavengood's remarks made an impression on his peers, as this statement has since been cited respectfully by several faculty members.)[14]

Westfall, who noted his cordial relationship with Barr, said the dean looked to him to manage much of the academic life of the school, whereas Barr himself "tended to focus . . . more on the business or fundraising side of the university." Given these circumstances, Westfall remembered, the most challenging problem associated with this strategic realignment was how to phase out the undergraduate school and secure agreement on that. "It was not easy, but it had to take place," he said. "It took maybe three or four years [to migrate the programs]." In fact, the last full-time undergraduate class was enrolled in the fall of 1966.

Proven Leadership of Barr a Key

For many, these strategic moves, particularly the dismantling of the undergraduate program, must have seemed quite bold, but they likely were less revolutionary to Barr, coming as he had from the corporate world and a career that had placed him in the center of a brutal power struggle at Montgomery Ward in April 1955. Born in 1909 on a farm near Akron, Indiana, a town with fewer than 1,000 inhabitants, Barr was first educated in a one-room rural school, where he skipped several grades because of his good marks. He would go on to attend DePauw University and then Indiana University, where he earned a law degree, paying for tuition in part by working as a waiter in a sorority house. His career at Ward's began in 1932 when he joined its legal department. Soon, he became the company's secretary, playing a key role in annual stockholder meetings and even assuming the leadership when longtime chairman Sewell Avery requested that he do so.[15]

Barr had a competent but largely undistinguished career at Montgomery Ward, according to *Time* magazine, with "his chief claim to fame [being] that he showed a rare ability to survive the purges and resignations that cost Ward's five presidents and 30 vice presidents in 23 years. . . . Barr managed to stay by avoiding open conflict with Avery, kept quiet about things that he knew he could not change."[16] This strategy earned Barr a vice presidency at the company.

It was during an April 22, 1955, proxy battle with Louis E. Wolfson, a Florida financier, that Barr demonstrated the leadership that would enable him to rejuvenate Montgomery Ward's business. Avery, by then 81, tried to preside over an unruly group of shareholders, but his failing health made this impossible, resulting in Barr stepping forward as the presiding officer. Barr then "forced order out of the opposition's contrived disorder, and brought the stormy session thru to adjournment 6 hours and 40 minutes after it began."[17] Two weeks later, on May 9, the company's board elected him as the new chairman, replacing Avery.

Barr faced a set of "Herculean tasks," according to press reports. He had to rebuild executive and merchandising staffs and set the company on a property expansion and improvement course. He succeeded beyond expectations. In fact, Barr "dazzled the retail industry with the suddenness of his transformation," a precedent that sheds light on his subsequent ability to make several major administrative and strategic decisions at Northwestern. He would throw out most of Avery's policies and begin taking the company on "one of the biggest expansion programs in U.S. history."[18]

At Northwestern, Barr would continue this kind of leadership. Upon accepting the deanship, he noted that he was "looking forward to the challenge of helping one of the nation's great universities fulfill its mission of providing ever-better academic training for the large numbers of young people who are seeking more and better education." Northwestern president J. Roscoe Miller said the university was "singularly fortunate in obtaining the services of such a distinguished business leader, one who had deep and abiding academic interests."[19] Barr told the *New York Times* that his move from a prominent corporate role to the Northwestern post was "a matter of leaving an eminent position in business for a post equally eminent in education." The paper reported Barr as saying he "attached great importance to educating the business leaders of tomorrow, for upon them depended the health of economy and, largely, the strength of the nation."[20] Though Barr's salary was not disclosed, observers estimated it at $30,000, about $70,000 less than his salary at Ward's.

"John Barr had all the personal characteristics to help the school relate to all its many publics," said Edmund Wilson. But he also understood that leadership in the academic world meant earning trust and approval from faculty members and others, which, Wilson believed, was one reason why he created the Business Advisory Council. "He was a university trustee and also in that business community, in the country-club set. He was invited to the same parties as the head people in the Economic Club, so when he invited people to be on his board, they were rather important people."[21]

Leverone Hall and the Evanston Campus

In 1966, Dean Barr was contemplating the first year of his Northwestern tenure. In his remarks to the faculty, he reiterated his belief in the importance of the school's long-term planning, as well as the critical contributions made by both faculty and students. He also wanted to strengthen alumni relations and secure adequate financial support. Along with outlining his vision for expanding the school's management offerings, noting the need for managers in government, labor unions, hospitals and schools, he said that the School of Business should, with the exception of the evening program, be located in Evanston. However, he also noted a problem involved in doing this—"the inadequacy of the [current] physical facilities."[22] The problem was one he and his administration addressed quickly.

In May 1967, an eight-person committee, which included Ira Anderson, Howard Bennett, Frank Hartzfeld Jr. and Thomas Prince, presented Barr with a "final preliminary report" on a proposed new building to house the school in Evanston. The members outlined their understanding that the structure would be "a separate building which would become part of a complex consisting of three buildings," with the two other buildings designed to serve the School of Education and the Social Science Department in the College of Liberal Arts and Sciences. The report detailed several structural recommendations, such as the nature of office facilities (the plan called for 80 faculty offices, supported by "adequate secretarial space and teaching assistant space"), classrooms (6 that would accommodate up to 35 students and 6 more to accommodate up to 60 students), research and study areas (including 75 carrels for doctoral students) and administrative support areas (including storage, a mail room and a copying center).

In its report, the final version of which appeared in June 1968, the committee stressed the view that "the identity of the Graduate School of Business as a professional school must not be lost when the M.B.A. program is moved to Evanston where some facilities, services and resources will be shared. Specifically the concern is that there is some risk of identity loss inherent in planning which places major emphasis on the total university concept."

These fears were apparently addressed, since by October of that year, Barr and Northwestern's dean of faculties, Payson Wild, announced that the new building would indeed be located in Evanston and that the university development office was prepared to assist the school in fund-raising.[23] The graduate program, then located in downtown Chicago along with the Evening Division, would migrate to Evanston, where the doctoral program was already situated. This arrangement would, the administration hoped, provide the space needed for each program. "We didn't have much building thrust in the MBA program at this time," said Jacobs. "We did have a day program downtown, which was small for the building we had. And we had an evening program which was large for the building we had."[24]

As the demolition crew moved onto the Evanston campus in June 1970 to dismantle Memorial Hall (the Little Red Schoolhouse), onlookers may have wondered if Joseph Schumpeter's economic theories of "creative destruction" were being realized, for the old structure literally was being consumed to give birth to the new.

Within the dust, more than a building disappeared. The wrecking ball took with it the vestiges of the undergraduate program and propelled the school into a future that was uncertain but clearly promising.

By then, faculty members were ready for this exciting change, said Jacobs. He recalled:

> Nobody wanted to keep that building up. The wood was creaky and the faculty offices weren't very nice. We didn't teach very many classes in Memorial Hall. When we had undergraduates, we were teaching in the Technological Institute or in other buildings around campus. It was old but beautiful, but the beauty was lost on us because we had to put up partitions, which made things ugly. We were three and four to a room in some cases; very few people had their own offices. It was an interesting-looking building from the outside, but it probably lived 50 years beyond its real life.[25]

Faculty, he said, embraced the hopes symbolized by Leverone Hall, the newly constructed, seven-level Evanston home of the full-time graduate management program, which opened on September 11, 1972. Four years earlier, some $5 million for the $7.1 million project had been contributed by Nathaniel Leverone, the founder and president of the Chicago-based Canteen Corporation, a pioneering vending machine merchandiser. This initiative formed part of a larger $180 million effort dubbed the "First Plan for the Seventies," led by Northwestern president Miller. Leverone, who died before construction on the building began, specified that his gift should be used to strengthen private education and the training of future executives and "to help perpetuate the free enterprise system as an integral part of the American way of life."[26]

Remarking on the gift, Barr said that it "assures candidates for master's degrees and doctorates of the Midwest's finest study and laboratory facilities." Miller noted that the "splendid gift comes at a moment when rising costs and steadily increasing demands in teaching and research make this a critical period for private higher education."[27]

Professor of Management Walter Scott, whose grandfather had been president of the university from 1920 to 1939, agreed that these changes brought a new vitality to the school. "Getting out of downtown Chicago and bringing the MBA program to Evanston gave you an opportunity to create a different kind of culture," he said, adding that this kind of "constant reinvention" has been one of the "remarkable characteristics" of the business school at Northwestern. (The school did retain a downtown presence in the form of its part-time MBA curriculum, which remains vital today and is directed by Associate Dean Vennie Lyons '72. See the later discussion for additional details.)

Ed Wilson also accented the move's impact on student culture, which proved especially important as a unique hallmark for the school. With Leverone Hall opened, he stated, "students now had access in Evanston to the university library and recreational centers, the religious centers, playing fields, all of which really changed the character and quality of student life from being urban to suburban."

Still, some people retained fond memories of Memorial Hall long after its destruction. "The Little Red Schoolhouse was an affectionate name," Lavengood said in an interview more than a decade after the demolition. "But the building was not a meager one. It had generous halls and there were many large classrooms with windows you could actually open and shut. We had high ceilings for high thoughts. There were surprising nooks and crannies and sudden turns that I think preached a useful moral lesson, which was: Be sure you know where you are going."

Research Faculty Key to Graduate Program's Success

Along with this major facilities upgrade, the school also revamped its approach to research and teaching. As the 1970s began, the Northwestern University Graduate School of Management would build on the large-scale changes initiated by the early Barr administration. Quantitative and behavioral methods would both contribute to a unique culture shaped, in some respects, by necessities imposed by resource constraints. The school refined its curriculum and invited students to play an active part.

The management paradigm had shifted in the 1960s, and the Graduate School of Management adapted quickly not only to remain relevant but also to position itself in the educational vanguard. By attracting a new kind of professor and student while taking steps to develop what would prove a unique culture, the school ultimately would find its strategies widely emulated. But first, challenges confronted the school from outside and inside the organization. Overcoming each demanded leadership, as well as an entrepreneurial spirit that was increasingly evident among the administration.

Outside the university, larger cultural events were having a significant impact on business and education everywhere, including at Northwestern. The Ohio National Guard opened fire on Vietnam War protestors at Kent State in May 1970, leaving four students dead and nine others injured. That incident further tore the nation's social fabric, which had already been frayed by the ongoing Vietnam conflict as well as racial tensions that had led to riots in several U.S. cities, including Watts (in 1965) and Newark and Detroit (in 1967). The assassination of Martin Luther King Jr. in 1968, only months before Chicago erupted in clashes between police and protestors in Grant Park during the Democratic National Convention, exacerbated the social strife.

At Northwestern, racial concerns resulted in black students occupying university business offices in 1968 during an effort to force improvement in integration on campus. John Barr already had initiated a minority scholarship program with the help of the Advisory Council in 1968.[28] A dozen corporations donated funds for the effort, increasing the number of black students to 57 by 1974. (The number had been 20 in 1958.) In addition, the U.S. economy was experiencing "stagflation," with high price inflation and low output growth. In response, in August 1971, President Richard Nixon ended the convertibility of the U.S. dollar into gold, effectively collapsing the post–World War II Bretton Woods system of international monetary management and allowing the dollar's value to fall in world markets. The move increased global economic uncertainty and contributed to what would be the 1973 world oil shock.[29]

It was against this backdrop that the Graduate School of Management was reinventing itself. Indeed, such broadly important social dynamics argued in favor of the school's general management strategy and emphasis on management in the context of a larger environment.

In a speech before the Illinois Bankers Association in 1969, Barr outlined the forces reshaping the business world and the way educators were preparing students to enter that arena. Along with organizational complexity, Barr noted how technology, particularly the computer, was transforming the management landscape. In addition, he said, the changing social, economic and legal context in which businesses operated was likely "the most powerful and influential force of all." International business was expanding too, forcing leaders to understand dynamics on a global stage. "Business operations have become multinational as we have rushed overseas," said Barr. "Today, 100 of the 500 largest companies have at least 25 percent of their assets, earnings or production in foreign lands—and double this number are not far behind." As organizations expanded in size and scope, Barr believed, new communications problems would demand new management solutions.[30]

Such solutions were reflected in the school's efforts to refine its curriculum, develop its research-oriented faculty and research centers and pursue quality students for the new MBA program. The pressing challenge was achieving these goals on a limited budget and with limited staffing. The sluggish national economy was reflected in a university budget that had little room for expensive ambition: in January 1971, Northwestern's financial vice president, Arthur Schmehling, informed Barr that the university was grappling with a fiscal deficit of $1,643,000. And as a result, colleges across the university would find their budgets frozen. At the Graduate School of Management, this meant there would be no faculty hiring in 1971; in addition, all salary increases would have to come from open faculty positions.[31] Though the school had offered a graduate program for decades, its undergraduate course had largely overshadowed the smaller MBA curriculum. Now, without the BBA program, the school essentially was confronted with a new and daunting venture.

Other internal challenges existed. Clearly, by dropping the undergraduate program, the school lost revenue and reputation, and beyond that, the decision also raised concerns among some alumni of the undergraduate program, who worried that the move might have repercussions for their careers. In addition, the school lost a number of faculty members who had grown comfortable with teaching younger students and were disinclined, or unprepared, to teach at the graduate level. Though no one was forced out, some left voluntarily, recalled Jacobs, who was chairman of the Finance Department at the time.

"If you were a faculty member and didn't like what was going on, you left," he said. "And there was a massive turnover originally. After that, we were fairly stable."[32] New faculty hires would come primarily from a talented pool of junior scholars, not established professors who commanded a price beyond the school's modest means. This financial limitation, however, resulted in a fortunate by-product—a tightly knit and unique academic culture.

"We hired young people and brought them up in the Kellogg culture," said Jacobs. "They grew up in this culture and therefore lived the values of the culture afterward. Very frankly, it wasn't until later that we started hiring any senior professors. At first, it was because we couldn't afford it, but afterwards it was because we didn't want to do it. . . . We had a culture we wanted to protect."[33]

To be successful in this mission meant recruiting the best research faculty members, who would, in turn, attract the best students. "It was pretty clear that the way you build a reputation among other schools was with your research, so we went out to get research-based faculty," said Westfall. "When you're looking for good people, others are doing the same."

The school's Marketing Department already boasted impressive figures such as Kotler and Levy, as well as earlier influential scholars like Clewett, Boyd, Britt and Westfall himself. But this level of intellectual leadership would now have to suffuse the school and continue extending the boundaries of management research.

Westfall was among those responsible for bringing in key faculty members, including marketing scholar Louis Stern and organizations behavior expert Robert B. Duncan. He also helped recruit Stanley Reiter, Haskel Benishay, Morton Kamien, Nancy Schwartz, Venkatanaman Balachandran and David Baron, all of whom helped create the school's potent Managerial Economics and Decision Sciences (MEDS) Department. The rigorous analytical frameworks of this discipline would influence all areas of the school, as well as complement the important contributions of the Organization Behavior Department, which would prove instrumental in creating the famous Kellogg School collaborative learning model starting in the early 1970s. As Westfall noted:

> We made no bones about it when we talked to prospects: This was going to be a publish-or-perish situation that they would be walking into here. If that wasn't what they were looking for, then they didn't want to consider Northwestern. If they were looking [to be part of a research-oriented team], we had a good product to sell. We were very successful in recruiting good people. When we got Stan Reiter, part of the reason was that he was interested in coming to the Chicago area. He was looking for a bigger field to play in. Dave Baron we got as a new assistant professor and he turned out to be a star. We had others who didn't work out and who we had to let go afterwards, and one or two that we let go that we probably shouldn't have. But that's the way those things happen. You can't always be 100 percent.[34]

Indeed, top-caliber faculty members like Reiter soon attracted more talent in the quantitative sciences, including Kamien, Mark Satterthwaite, Ehud Kalai and others. "Stan Reiter's arrival here in 1967 was a watershed event," said Robert Magee, the Keith I. DeLashmutt Distinguished Professor of Accounting Information and Management, who arrived at Northwestern in 1976. "Over the next 15 years, he and his fellow MEDS faculty members built arguably the best economic theory department in the world."

Reiter, a University of Chicago graduate who had been teaching at Purdue (where he helped establish the Department of Economics), was attracted by the "maverick quality" of Northwestern and agreed to join the school, and he had a clear objective. "I wanted to be part of establishing the research foundations in an MBA school," he said. "The mission [at Northwestern] was to train future managers. Well, in what? Are you going to show them how to file? There was a significant development going on in economic theory, statistics and operations research. But these things were not so sharply separated or defined."

So Reiter set out to "bring in the people to create a new department out of the ashes of the old establishment." The new area drew upon a range of quantifiable sciences that were "foundational . . . to lots of things that go on—or should go on—in schools of management," he said. MEDS did that, and it did it in a wildly successful way. "It also scared the hell out of a lot of people," said Reiter, because its analytical rigor challenged everyone across the school to measure up to the lofty standards that governed the young department. In some quarters, he added, there was considerable resistance to this more analytical shift, but since the senior administration supported the effort, it went forward, though eventually, even the dean's office began expressing concerns with the theoretical bent of the department.

Mort Kamien, a graduate of Purdue's doctoral program (where he was a student of Reiter's, studying economics), arrived at Northwestern in 1970 after having been on faculty at Carnegie-Mellon University since 1963. He recalled the efforts he and his colleagues made to build the MEDS Department. When Dean Barr named him department chair in 1971,[35] Kamien said he told him, "'Look, if I'm going to be chairman I'm going to do revolutionary things. . . . You're going to get complaints from the existing senior faculty. If you reverse me, if you don't agree with me, it's over.' . . . And he did support me, and people did complain."

But by working closely with like-minded peers, including Reiter and Jacobs, who was on the Committee of Department Chairmen,[36] Kamien was among those who increased academic rigor in managerial economics and, by extension, throughout the school.

"Jacobs was an economist and he knew what we were doing," said Kamien.

What they were doing was hiring some "very theoretical people" whose appointments might have been resisted by Barr had the dean fully appreciated the subtleties of economic theory. But Barr's expertise was in law, not economics, said Kamien, who enjoyed a good relationship with the dean because Barr trusted the professor to recruit the appropriate faculty for MEDS. There came a point, however, when Barr understood just how theoretical the MEDS Department had become, as in its pursuit of game theorists in order to try to apply abstract mathematical principles within the business school. Reiter and Kamien recalled the dean attempting to stop MEDS from traveling in the direction it was, but by then, the intellectual path had been set.

"Barr became upset over MEDS," said Reiter. "He took steps to slow it down, which led to some conflicts." But the university's central administration, according to Reiter, convinced the dean to relent. In fact, university support helped establish the interdisciplinary Center for Mathematical Studies in Economics and Management Science in the spring of 1972. Directed by Reiter, the center coordinated faculty research in economics, engineering and management. "It was a hot place for economic theory," recalled Reiter.

Kamien's strategy in building the MEDS Department was to recruit faculty members based on one fundamental criterion: candidates did not have to fit into a narrow disciplinary category, but they did have to be exceptionally smart. The strategy was sound, but it was easier to achieve in theory than in practice.

"We would interview kids from all the leading schools and make them offers, but they wouldn't come," said Kamien, adding that the school's reputation at the time was insufficiently strong to attract those who were lured by brands such as Harvard, Chicago or Stanford. The school soon modified its approach. "We had to take long shots, be more aggressive and take risks," he remembered. "I had this approach of not looking for people by area—a labor economist or an international economist—because you can interview someone from another field and find out that the person is smarter than [the specialist]. You take the smarter candidate. The teaching, we could fill in. No. 1, we wanted smart people." (Kamien was among those who interviewed and hired Roger Myerson, who would earn a Nobel Prize in economics in 2007, the distinction conferred for research conducted during a 25-year tenure at Kellogg.) In fact, this strategy was not entirely unprecedented at the school, as it had built its Marketing Department along similar lines a decade earlier with the hiring of nontraditional marketing scholars like Levy and Kotler.

Coming out of Carnegie-Mellon, Kamien said he "had some ideas about how a department should be run." Carnegie had hired many young people but tried to direct their research in ways that did not appeal to Kamien, who was then a technical economist whom Carnegie was encouraging to be more policy-oriented. "I'm not sure they were wrong," he said 30 years later, "but at the time I was young and the idea of being pushed around and redirected kind of got me annoyed."[37]

So when he arrived at Northwestern, Kamien worked with the administration to cultivate an environment where young, talented faculty members could collaborate and "do whatever they wanted to do as long as it was first rate." The ambitious academic effort soon created an extraordinary and influential department. "You now had economic theorists in the least likely place, a business school," said Kamien; at the same time, however, he insisted that MEDS professors honor their commitment to provide management students with training that would prove valuable to them, rather than overwhelming them with highly technical (and possibly impractical) abstractions. "When we talked to the candidates we said—and acted on this—that you can do any kind of research that you want, but when you go into a classroom to teach MBAs, you're going to teach what the MBAs want, not want you want."

Game theory was a remarkable strength of the department and the school, leading to pioneering work in applying this discipline to business education. "We had the franchise in game theory," said Kamien. "Other schools missed the boat. Game theory started with tremendous promise as a fresh way of thinking." Today, according to Kamien, the theory has become part of mainstream economics, but at the time, the Graduate School of Management was highly influential in disseminating this approach—somewhat accidentally, as it turns out.

"To be honest, it wasn't out of foresight," said Kamien. The school hired the smartest people it could find given its limited resources, he added. "We were opportunistic at the time. The part that worked out the way I thought it would was that by putting smart young people together good things would happen."

One of those improbable hires, Ehud Kalai, would advance the frontiers of game theory and its interface with economics, social choice, operations research and computer science. His work proved instrumental in opening and expanding the understanding of bargaining, strategic learning, large games and related subjects. But when he arrived at Northwestern in 1975 from Tel Aviv University, where he was an assistant professor of statistics, he was unsure how long he would remain.

Kalai had been associated with the Math Department at Tel Aviv, and his doctorate from Cornell in 1972 had been in mathematics. Since "mathematicians hold their noses at business schools, I was coming in with very mixed feelings," he said, noting that the situation seemed convenient for his family, a fact that induced him to give the appointment a try. "I thought I would be in a business school for a year; I'd put up with it. Little did I know that when I got here it would be a first-rate academic place, despite being in a business school. That was a surprise to me."[38]

Having been working in Tel Aviv with Meier Smorodinsky, with whom he shared an office, Kalai recalled how one of their seminal papers was published. Smorodinsky was a mathematician who knew nothing about game theory, said Kalai, but his colleague had a curiosity for the subject.

"We started talking about the Nash Bargaining Problem [research from the 1950s that was considered definitive and complete], and then at the end of the afternoon we had this alternative solution. We showed that the subject was actually still open."

Smorodinsky said, "We got the new solution; write it down," which Kalai did, leaving it on his desk that Friday afternoon. On Saturday, the Yom Kippur War broke out. "And the paper is sitting on my desk," remembered Kalai. "This fellow is sitting there and while I was in the war for six months, he sent the paper in to a journal. It got accepted. It took us one afternoon the writing of this paper. The rest of the summer he and I were trying to solve this very difficult mathematical problem dealing with game theory. We did and sent it to a math journal. Both papers were published. The one that took months and months [to write], I doubt it gets a single citation from anybody. The one that took one afternoon's work has become well known."

What Kalai found especially exciting about the MEDS Department was the innovation and willingness to experiment there. He recalled his colleagues at the time being "out of the mainstream" and all discovering game theory on their own. "Not knowing it, they were also all inventing it," he said, adding that these people are today "among the most highly cited names in economic theory." Mark Satterthwaite was trying to study strategic behavior, John Roberts was interested in strategic issues in industrial organization and Theodore Groves was investigating various ways to have people behave efficiently despite selfish motives, said Kalai.

"All of these issues deal with strategic behavior, and once you deal with strategic behavior, the only tool is game theory," he added. "Satterthwaite invented what we call in game theory dominant strategy without knowing it. He was making up his own tools, so to speak. [Others similarly pursued this kind of research.] So when I got here as the first game theorist [on faculty at the school], it was heaven. It was a place to put together the theory with the application. There was a revolution here."

The influence of the MEDS Department proved sweeping and enduring, even years after its founding. Robert Magee recalled being enticed to go to Northwestern as an accounting professor in part because of the department established by Reiter, Kamien and others. "Although I wasn't in MEDS, there was the same intellectual approach in accounting when dealing with problems of information. That's what attracted me here in 1976," said Magee.[39]

Similarly, the Finance Department would undergo a transformation in the early 1980s under the leadership of MEDS professor David Baron, enlisted by Dean Jacobs to oversee the finance area. MEDS alumnus Artur Raviv, who graduated from Northwestern in 1974 and served on the faculty of Carnegie-Mellon and Tel Aviv University before returning to Northwestern in 1981, recalled the need for improvement.

"The department was in bad shape then," said Raviv. "So what Jacobs did was very clever: He appointed David Baron to do the overseeing and, in fact, the Finance Department was put into receivership. They couldn't hire; they couldn't do anything. Jacobs let Baron hire for them, and in 1981, when I arrived, Baron recruited me and Milton Harris . . . to run the Finance Department. We came in and were interviewed only by the MEDS guys."[40] According to Raviv, he and Harris "started hiring from scratch." Among the talents they recruited were scholars who remain with the school today, including: Deborah Lucas (PhD University of

Chicago), Kathleen Hagerty (PhD Stanford), Michael Fishman (PhD University of Chicago), Robert McDonald (PhD MIT) and Robert Korajczyk (PhD University of Chicago).

"Our innovation was to go more via people who were from economics [backgrounds]," said Raviv. "All of our hires, except Bob Korajczyk, came out of economics versus business schools. That way we could get the best talent. We thought at that time the best talent was coming out of econ departments."

Raviv said he was confident in his abilities to direct the Finance Department, since the research between economics and finance was converging. "Partially the economics field was moving its research into finance, particularly with respect to issues surrounding uncertainty and information," he said. "This became also synergistic with game theory. So the field of game theory started moving into finance and we were in that sense early on, building on the strength of MEDS."

Said Magee, "The Finance Department went through what would have to be called a rebirth when they hired Art Raviv and Milton Harris. Harris, Raviv and [Roger] Myerson were doing research that was really central to the questions of incentives, the sorts of things that affect corporate finance and accounting, political science and lots of other stuff."

Since then, the Finance Department has blossomed into a strength for the Kellogg School, with its faculty members consistently regarded as authorities in the field. Seven professors, for example, have earned the prestigious Smith Breeden Prize from the *Journal of Finance,* recognizing the scholars who have produced the top three papers published in the journal each year. One of those earning the prize, Robert McDonald, the Erwin P. Nemmers Distinguished Professor of Finance, also is the author of an influential 2002 textbook, *Derivatives Markets,* which is required reading at leading business schools around the world.

The department today offers two areas of concentration: the finance major provides an excellent background for a variety of careers, including investment banking, money management, venture capital, real estate, insurance and corporate control and treasury functions, whereas the analytical finance major, introduced in 2001, provides a more technical understanding of financial markets and the theory and tools that underlie modern finance practice. Offerings such as the "Entrepreneurial Finance" course focus on every aspect of the subject; the Asset Management Program, added to the curriculum in spring 2007, is designed to let students manage a portion of the school's endowment, providing experiential learning.

"Students blend academic research with practical insights from visiting practitioners and day-to-day portfolio management," said Korajczyk, the Harry G.

Guthmann Distinguished Professor of Finance, who was leading the Asset Management Program.[41]

Other earlier efforts by the school that laid the foundations for this analytical rigor included the establishment of the Banking Research Center by finance professors Jacobs and Eugene Lerner in 1969. The effort helped promote the school's research orientation among faculty and attracted new professors looking for an academic environment where they could focus on substantive business problems. The center was touted as the first of its kind in the Midwest, and it operated in coordination with 11 Chicago banks to deliver the "objective and impartial research" that Barr said was critical given changes in technology and the banking structure.[42]

Jacobs appreciated the importance of technology in banking, having researched the subject years earlier to predict the coming revolution in computer automation in the banking field.[43] He had been a director of Northwestern's Vogelback Computing Center and was familiar with the power this technology had brought to business—a perspective that would prove central to strategic decisions that Jacobs later introduced during his deanship (see chapter 5). The research center was initially codirected by Jacobs and Lerner, who oversaw a 10-person committee that studied a variety of issues related to banking, such as interest rate changes, organizational structures, yield patterns and the goals of financial organizations. The center's findings were made available to the public in articles, books and symposia, as well as in the *Journal of Financial Intermediation,* the field's leading academic periodical, published by the center itself.

In 1994, the center marked its twenty-fifth anniversary. Observers noted its academic rigor and surprising predictive abilities. "Decades before the automated teller machine made banking as convenient as fast food, Kellogg's Banking Research Center predicted that electronic fund transfers would revolutionize the industry," wrote Matt Carey in *Kellogg World.* "Years before the collapse of the savings and loan industry, the center warned of the danger in a major study for the government. . . . Since its inception . . . the center has steadily churned out visionary research in the finance and banking arenas."[44] Professor Stuart Greenbaum, who assumed the center's leadership in 1975 after Jacobs became dean, remarked on a textbook produced by the center in 1994, titled *Contemporary Financial Intermediation.* He considered it groundbreaking. "It is a new-age textbook that will change the way the subject is taught," said Greenbaum.[45] Of additional value to the school was the center's function in establishing and developing relationships with banking practitioners, a situation that resulted in ongoing dialogue among students, scholars and bankers.

During that time, "the growth and development of the management faculty and staff were reflected in a steady upward trend in annual budgeted expenditures from approximately $1.4 million in 1965 to nearly $3.4 million in 1974."[46] This research orientation was possible only because of the bold strategic choices the school administrators made.

"Dropping the undergraduate program was really an act of bravery," said Jacobs. "Had we not done this, we would have been diffused. There would have been a need for a lot of faculty members to teach undergraduates, and that clearly is a very different educational milieu. [Dismantling the undergraduate program] really allowed us a great deal of freedom in changing the faculty and programs."[47]

This research-oriented approach was one part of the school's strategy. Another was recruiting talented but often young professors, rather than more senior figures who might command a higher salary than was available at Northwestern and who would perhaps not fit easily into the culture the school was creating. "There wasn't any money," said Robert Duncan, one of those who played a key part in building the school's culture starting in the early 1970s.

A graduate of the Yale doctoral program in organizational behavior, Duncan would enjoy a long tenure at Northwestern, from 1970 until 2001, during which he served in a variety of roles, including associate dean for academic affairs, chair of the Organization Behavior Department, the Richard L. Thomas Professor of Leadership and Organizational Change and Northwestern University provost under President Arnold R. Weber from 1987 to 1991. In 2001, he became dean of the Eli Broad College of Business at Michigan State.

"What the school had done that was very smart, during those early years, 1970–1975, was going out hiring the best new young PhDs," said Duncan. "We were very good at that . . . at [assembling] a good cadre of up-and-coming faculty . . . who were brought up in our culture. The next thing was to get some money and resources coming in. There always was a research push, but we needed a development push to attract and retain talented faculty."[48] (See chapter 5 for a discussion of how Jacobs would accomplish this mission, as well as for background on Duncan's role in creating the Organization Behavior Department.)

Curriculum Revision Builds Graduate Strength

What began as an analytical force in MEDS inspired academic rigor throughout the curriculum, but that factor was not the only important element in the mix. What impelled the school's strategic direction was a shift in focus to general management. "By focusing on management as a profession in itself, rather than concentrating on describing the characteristics of one or more of the various institutions in our society, the Graduate School of Management is able to prepare students for careers in a wide variety of organizations," stated the school's promotional materials. "Graduates of the program will have the flexibility to shift from management of one type of organization to management of others."[49] An article by James Allen and Frederick Genck in 1970 also promulgated this idea: "A school of management—encompassing management education for business, government, health and education within one school—offers competence in both business and public enterprise. The inherent intellectual excitement of this concept, the advantages to students in broadening the scope of their education and their career opportunities, and the management capabilities that such graduates could provide both public and private organizations are convincing."[50]

Supporting this effort was a curriculum revision, including the development of a core set of required courses for all first-year students. Among these were offerings on the computer and accounting information systems; quantitative methods in decision making; organization behavior and the management of organizations; economic analysis; and management of the financial, marketing, and operations functions of the organization. The goal was to both familiarize students with organizational theory (e.g., the firm as an integrated system) and expose them to fundamental management concepts applicable across all kinds of enterprises, independent of a student's area of specialization. In so doing, the curriculum was intended to offer insights into systems theory, formal model building and information systems, while also addressing functional fields.[51] Second-year students were required to take a three-quarter course sequence in environment, organizations and strategy to grasp how the organization as a system functioned within a context informed by economic, political, social, legal and historical forces.

The "Management and Its Environment" class, for example, forced students to analyze particular situations and focus on the "broad effects of the total environment upon the administration of business enterprise." Students were encouraged to test their own values while developing definitions of the "appropriate relationships and responsibilities of business to its various publics."[52] Other environmental courses, such as "Planning and Management in an Urban Environment" and "Inner City Enterprise Development," introduced students to a variety of topics garnering national attention. Subjects included the growth and development of contemporary metropolitan areas, housing and transportation, poverty and racial strife and urban finance and politics. In addition, a seminar presented issues related to understanding the state of minority group involvement in U.S. business management.

In presenting the subject of environment, the "Management and Its Environment" course divided the topic into several segments, such as an introduction to the field, considerations of classical models of free enterprise, current economic goals and the roles of both public and private sectors, political power structures, the role of various interest groups in the formations of economic and social policies, demography, legal and judicial considerations and the role of technological and sociological forces. "Managers have always had to cope with an environment that provided a continuous stream of problems. Today, the manager must continue to do this, but he is also expected to take a leading part in solving social and economic problems of the U.S. and the world,"[53] said the school's marketing materials.

One indication of the administration's seriousness in developing the general management model occurred in 1973, when the school formed a partnership with Northwestern's Law School to offer a joint-degree program. This initiative offered students the chance to complete both an MBA and a JD in four years instead of five. The student's initial two years focused on both management and law, alternating courses in each area for 12 months at a time. The remaining two years were dedicated to interdisciplinary study.

A similar program, the "3-2" program, arose in 1973. A collaboration between the Graduate School of Management and the Northwestern College of Arts and Sciences, the program let students earn both bachelor's and master's degrees in five years rather than six. Under the program, students entered the Graduate School at the start of their senior year, earning credit toward their undergraduate degree requirements and receiving the bachelor's degree at the end of their senior year.[54] The program was short-lived, though, since the school soon found itself looking for students with more experience, not less

Conceptual Issues in Management and Birth of Student Culture

Part of the new curriculum was a student orientation immersion experience, begun in 1969. Called Conceptual Issues in Management (CIM), the program was designed to encourage the rapid development of camaraderie among students while exposing them to the kinds of management issues that their two years of business education would address.

The program was initially faculty-driven, and it presented an assortment of academic content, including computer simulations that refined crisis leadership skills. As CIM (pronounced *sim*) developed over the years, it became more student-directed, with a balance of team-building and social experiences as well as academic content, a trend that continues today. The original program lasted two weeks, with students arriving on campus a week prior to the start of classes. They participated in an intensive noncredit course conducted by 24 faculty members and "closely patterned after Northwestern's Executive Program,"[55] with readings, problems and cases assigned. Typically, two 100-minute class sessions were held each morning, and one session was given each afternoon. In addition, evening sessions were held three times during the week.

Each day's instruction centered on a theme, such as a global economic view, pricing strategies, the firm-as-system model, automation's impact on production, behavioral systems within a firm, economic goals and personnel planning, managerial control, technology and control and managers' social responsibilities. Model building, quantitative methods and computer tools were highlighted throughout CIM. Another component of the initiative was the way in which it created "an immediate opportunity [for students] to meet a large and representative cross section of the faculty and administration in a natural environment" as well as introducing students to their peers. The program met with immediate success and was praised by students, and it has only grown more popular in the decades since its inception.[56]

An important part of the CIM agenda involved bringing students together with each other and with professors and members of the business community. In 1973, for example, the program featured seminars taught by senior school professors and professionals such as Donald Perkins, chairman of Jewel Companies Inc.; Edward Martin, city manager for Evanston; John Gallagher, chairman of Chemetron Corporation; Bernard Lachner, president of Evanston Hospital; and James Haughton, executive director of Cook County Hospital. Associate Professor of Finance William J. Breen managed the computer simulations that formed a central part of the experience.[57]

CIM, along with the Organization Behavior Department under the leadership of Duncan and his faculty's emphasis on human interactions within groups, served as a catalyst for the collaborative culture that has become a Kellogg School hallmark. "This whole notion of learning from one another in teams emerged at Kellogg," said Jacobs, adding that prior to that time, the concept of working in groups struck some as cheating. "Bob Duncan was responsible for a lot of the team dynamics here."

Wilson noted that the school's administration thought there was great value to having many heads working toward a solution of a problem. "This may not seem so startling today," he said, "but can you imagine how much more rewarding the academic experience is when you are working with others on problem solution? It creates an interactive, participatory environment."

CIM was part of an overall philosophical change in how the school approached its mission. "Learning rather than teaching is emphasized," noted the school's catalog. "Relevant knowledge and understanding, however obtained, are not enough.

Development of skillful habits in the use of knowledge and in the application of understanding is as important for the management student as it is for those preparing for medicine, law, or other professions." Through case study, lecture, small-group discussion, independent study and action learning, students were to learn that modern administration required the development of keen perceptions and awareness of how the elements of a complex situation worked. Only "habits of orderly thinking" would serve the modern business professional, just as only "insights regarding cooperative efforts within the organization [could] accommodate . . . personal exercise of administrative leadership."[58]

These enhancements were predicated upon the work and oversight of several standing committees established in 1969 and 1970. On recommendations made by the Educational Program Committee and reported in May 1970, the school established specialized groups to develop various areas in the curriculum and culture. The Educational Policy Committee concentrated on issues of policy and long-term planning. The Section Committee examined the strength and integration of the school's five student sections of core courses, further dividing the work into subgroups for each section.[59] The Evening MBA Program Committee examined that program's operation, and the Doctoral Program Committee and Research Committee addressed developing strengths in those areas. In addition, committees oversaw executive programs and admissions. In all, each main area of the school's curriculum and administration was subject to review. Along with these areas was a committee chaired by Lavengood that concentrated on urban studies and was responsible for reviewing that portion of the school's curriculum, as well as serving as a liaison with the university's Center for Urban Affairs.[60]

Each of these committees contributed to the school's development in significant and lasting ways, but of particular note for the school's academic strength was the Educational Policy Committee. Chaired by Westfall and consisting of seven other faculty members—Kamien, William J. Breen, Alfred Rappaport, Joseph S. Moag, Prem Prakash, Richard L. Smith and Stanley Stasch—the committee was tasked with monitoring developments and trends in graduate education for management, in both in business and nonbusiness areas. The objective was to ensure the school's academics remained current and in "the forefront of educational programs for management responsibility." The committee's oversight extended to "assur[ing] that course additions, deletions and changes accord with the School's long-term plans and objectives." Its members would also serve as a curriculum committee to review any changes submitted by departments and would make recommendations with respect to such proposals. The committee would also recommend to faculty that existing courses be changed or dropped or that new courses be added.[61]

Of special importance in strengthening the curriculum's quantitative portion was a new major in Managerial Economics and Decision Sciences in 1972. Approved by faculty vote on May 24, 1972, the major was in place in September of that year. In addition, the administration approved two new MEDS courses: "Management and Resource Allocation in the Public Sector" and "Analytics of Managerial Decision Making in Non-market Environments."

In a proposal for creating the managerial economics major, faculty members noted several recent government efforts to use economic tools to check inflation, to reverse unfavorable balance of payments by devaluing the dollar and to deal with ecological problems by imposing and enforcing air and water quality standards. "In order to cope with these changes in a reasonable fashion the entities involved must comprehend their economic implications and thereby turn to economists for guidance," stated the proposal. Arguing the case for the new major, faculty members pointed out that "the high cost of providing health services and educational services, together with the continued growth of corporations, especially conglomerates, has required application of economic analysis to problems of resource allocation, planning and control in nonmarket environments. Thus a need has been created for economists capable and oriented towards solving the problems of management."

To succeed, such professionals, furthermore, would need to be versed in all areas of management, from finance and marketing to accounting and production, and they would especially require dexterity with the latest economic analysis and quantitative methods. The training recommended by the committee could not, they believed, be obtained anywhere else in the university. "The proposed major in managerial economics is designed to produce 'professional' economists conversant with the latest developments in the discipline and oriented towards problem solving in management."[62]

Such innovation was widespread in the school and included entrepreneurial offerings. "Entrepreneurship and New Venture Formulation," proposed in 1972 and formally added to the curriculum in February 1974, was taught by Samuel I. Doctors and Charles W. Hofer, both Harvard-trained management experts. The class was described as valuable for those seeking to start or become affiliated with a new venture within 10 years of graduation. "It would also be useful for the student who expects to make substantial investments in new ventures whether personally or professionally," according to the course proposal. The objectives as laid out in the initial syllabus were "to describe the entrepreneurial process, to develop an analytical framework for analyzing prospective new venture situations, to examine some of the typical problems encountered in the early life of new ventures, and to explore some potential areas for future entrepreneurial activity." The course consisted of case study and detailed readings from several books and dozens of journals and magazines. In addition, students were assigned to teams in which they developed and assessed a potential new venture. Each team would make a presentation before the class and a panel of outside experts at the term's conclusion. "The major course activity will be the preparation of a business plan for a new venture," stated the proposal. "This could involve either the formation of a new organization or the creation of a new activity in an existing organization."

The school directed considerable energy to its part-time MBA program, known as the Evening MBA Program, with a committee dedicated to examining its operation and curriculum. Chaired by Clewett and consisting of Ira Anderson, Claude Cohen, Loring C. Farwell, James T. Godfrey, Frank Hartzfeld, Erwin E. Nemmers, Francis J. Houri, Harold W. Torgerson and Richard B. Westin, the group addressed concerns posed by Barr about the curriculum's standing.

Clewett prepared a report that was noted in the faculty minutes for May 26, 1971. There, he listed several recommendations, which included "bringing this program more in line with the Day program with respect to course coverage, class size, and availability of faculty." The committee members also explored the feasibility of moving the program to Evanston from Chicago but determined that maintaining the downtown location would prove better for the program's working participants. Perhaps more notably, the committee raised concerns about the program's marketability, suggesting that the name be changed from the "Evening" MBA Program to something that would brand the offering as distinct from the University of Chicago's part-time program.

The committee addressed whether "the pattern of the Day Program was appropriate for the Evening Program, especially the nature of courses, number of courses, teaching materials, computer usage and teaching methods." The members also wondered if there was there a need to develop distinctive Evening Program courses. It was recommended that courses and teaching should remain consistent between the two programs, although the part-time students were justified in taking slightly fewer courses overall, since they earned a degree over three or four years while remaining employed and "during that time they [would] have benefited by their ongoing business experience." The committee's research highlighted a number of important points, including that the Evening Program students were more interested in "practical solutions to problems they face or will face on the job, the context of which is much clearer than is the case with the Day student." However, many Evening Program students were deemed "unable to do the intensive preparation characteristic of most Day students. Job and home pressures as well as limited time for library work undoubtedly contribute to this situation." Of special concern, Evening students reported feeling like "second-class citizens" compared with Day students.

To build the part-time program, the school made a special effort to reinforce its importance among faculty members so they would deliver the same quality teaching for the Evening Program as they did for the Day Program's students. To address concerns about marketing the program as distinctive from other offerings in the geographical area, the school changed the name to "The Managers' Program." In explaining why, Clewett and the committee reported: "The term 'Evening Program' for many people connotes 'night school' and even the programs serving deprived immigrants to this country. In general it implies a lower level program than a full-time program. . . . The committee recommends that a new name be selected. It seems wise to avoid any reference to Chicago (to avoid confusion with U.C.), location (to avoid a later move if desired) and time offered."

To reinforce the findings of this initial study, the school maintained a committee chaired by Allan R. Drebin to direct The Managers' Program from 1972 to 1973. Other committee members included Hartzfeld, Westfall, Anderson, Steuart Henderson Britt, Vennie Lyons, Leonard W. Swanson and two recent graduates of the Evening Program to be chosen at a later date.

After his graduation from the school's full-time program in 1972, Lyons was appointed director of the part-time curriculum, which he said "just didn't have any identity to it originally," with students simply taking classes but having little connection with one another or the school.

"They needed an administrator," recalled Lyons, who remains director of the rebranded Part-Time MBA Program today. The curriculum in June 2007 was also expanded to include the Saturday MBA Program to serve the needs of students who wished to earn a Kellogg School degree while continuing to work on a full-time basis.[63] As a result of its weekend scheduling, this offering has attracted a wider range of part-time students from across the United States, whereas traditional part-time programs attract only more regional participants. Such enhancements to the Kellogg part-time curriculum have helped create a legitimate student culture and an enrollment in excess of 1,200 students, more than double the number when Lyons assumed the program's leadership.

"When I was a student, I worked with the administration doing certain projects," said Lyons. "I had gotten my master's degree in engineering in an evening program [at the University of Missouri–Columbia], so they felt that I could offer some perspective to this program and appreciate what the students experience."[64]

Lyons noted that it was a challenge to build the student culture, given the program's demographics, with students arriving on campus after work and balancing professional lives, family responsibilities and academics. He also recalled the challenges from area competitors like DePaul University, Loyola and the University of Chicago's 190 Program (so named for its address at 190 East Delaware). Beating these odds required commitment from faculty and administrators, said Lyons, who praised Dean Barr and Dean Jacobs for emphasizing to professors the program's importance, despite the "logistical challenges" of traveling from Evanston to Chicago. One of the benefits the program has historically offered faculty members, said Lyons, is the ability to interact with working professionals who (similar to executive students, though younger) challenge professors to make the curriculum relevant as well as rigorous. Today, Lyons points to the quality of the students, faculty and staff as critical factors in making the Part-Time MBA Program a long-standing success.

"One of the things we're proud of is that about 85 percent of students who start the Part-Time MBA Program will eventually get their MBA degree," Lyons remarked. "They have heavy work and family commitments, social commitments. Then you add school to that. . . . It's a challenge for them, but they make it through with a very high percentage. I don't know of any other evening program with these completion rates."[65]

Doing More with Less: Students Challenged to Lead

All of the school's ambitious initiatives and strategic changes occurred while administrators contended with resource constraints, including limited staff numbers. The school boasted about 85 faculty members in the early 1970s, but its administration cadre fell to fewer than a dozen people. The catalog for 1972 listed 11 individuals as "school officers"; one of these was Myrtle Burkland, an administrative assistant, and another was M. Rosalie Kempe, a librarian at the Joseph Schaffner Library in Wieboldt Hall. The school's leadership consisted of Dean Barr, Kenneth M. "Pete" Henderson (associate dean), Westfall (associate dean), Hartzfeld (assistant dean, administrative director of the MM program), Kurt R. Stoehr (assistant dean), Philip A. Warren (director of admissions), Russell N. Cansler (director of placement), Daniel J. Cullinan (director of computer services), and Edward T. P. Watson (director of the doctoral program).

"We were one-deep. I was director of admissions and didn't have a full-time assistant," remembered Ed Wilson, who was appointed assistant dean in 1972, taking Warren's place and also overseeing financial aid. At the same time, Hartzfeld assumed responsibility for the school's new Leverone Hall facilities as well as staff personnel. Any hint of complaint from Wilson was immediately swept aside by his obvious affection for the school. "It was enormously satisfying, but I can't tell you how many hours we worked. We were happy, though, because we believed our efforts were making a noble contribution to a fine institution."

If the staff was limited, its aspirations were not limited at all. What's more, far from being a liability, the slim administration actually inspired a fruitful partnership with students that became the cornerstone of Kellogg School culture, giving rise to a host of initiatives—from student-run conferences and community outreach efforts to curriculum innovations that have created extraordinary leadership and learning opportunities since the 1980s. Initially, students' contributions were limited, but over time, the culture encouraged more and more student leadership. The CIM experience began inculcating a strong sense of identity among the students, even as its primary purpose was academic, but it soon became apparent that students were willing to be cocreators of their management education.

Students started participating on pivotal committees, such as the Master's Program Committee, which was chaired by Philip Kotler. Tasked with reviewing and monitoring the curriculum and educational policies of the master's program and making recommendations to the faculty and dean, the committee featured a dozen members of the faculty and three members of the student body. Students also played parts on committees that reviewed the objectives, operations and curriculum of the Evening MBA Program, the doctoral program and research initiatives, Urban Studies, admissions, the Public Administration Program and the Hospital and Health Services Management Program. In short, nearly every aspect of the school's operation began to welcome student input, creating a culture that offered opportunities for students to put classroom insights to work in helping run their school.

"Students were given more and more permission to take an active part in the life of the school," said Jacobs, who noted that the school had the leanest administration by far of any school in the country.[66] "For instance, students quickly made up an admissions committee. They're a part of reading the admissions applications. They start to be the backbone for the people who actually did the interviews. They quickly become a very strong part of the decision process about who is going to be here in the future.

"We weren't exploiting the students," he added. "We were giving them practical leadership experience. It broadened their education, and a lot of the *esprit* around here comes from the fact that the students are part of the culture. It has changed the way the place feels and acts."[67]

As it turned out, students suggested any number of innovations at the school, and with diligence and personal commitment, they often made them a reality. Yearbooks, clubs, theatrical reviews, a student newspaper, the weekly social event known as TG and a convocation ceremony—anything was possible if students were willing to partner with the administration to advance the initiatives. (The first convocation ceremony, in 1978, featured Karl D. Bays, chairman of American Hospital Supply Corporation and chair of the school's advisory council, who cautioned the graduates about pitfalls of competition and instead encouraged collaborative learning.)

Students even introduced lasting enhancements such as the honor code. "And they made it much more rigorous than I would have, and I told them so," said Jacobs. "But this was important to them and they brought it to the administration and it became a part of our culture."

In addition to challenging students to step forward as partners with the school, administrators also reached out to alumni. In 1973, for example, the school introduced the Dean's Council, an organization of graduates from all Northwestern business programs. Members pledged financial support and participated in a variety of programming, including continuing education opportunities through the school. Graduates pledged either $200 annually (for those who matriculated at least 10 years earlier) or $100 annually (for those who matriculated less than 10 years earlier). By 1974, the Dean's Council claimed a membership of more than 250 graduates, and it was growing thanks to an initiative by the Northwestern Management Alumni Association (NMAA) designed to encourage alumni to contribute more to the school's annual budget. (Alumni had been giving about 2 percent of the overall $3.8 million annual budget. The initiative set an alumni fund-raising goal of $110,000 and was spearheaded by William Achenbach '69, president of the NMAA.)[68]

At the same time, the school's alumni had been forming regional clubs to maintain connections with each other and with the Graduate School of Management. New chapters arose in New York City and Minneapolis/St. Paul in early 1974, adding more than 1,000 members between them to the alumni network. Existing chapters included clubs in Chicago (with more than 10,000 members) and San Francisco (nearly 550 members). Other regions, including Los Angeles, Milwaukee, Detroit and Washington, D.C., also boasted significant alumni numbers, promising additional potential clubs.[69]

Student Recruitment: Another Challenge

The opinions of the Business Advisory Council in 1966 continued to influence the direction the school would take in positioning itself in the market in 1969, with implications for recruiting students. The council had stated that the complexity and expansion of the nonbusiness arena presented an "urgent requirement for trained managers in nonprofit organizations." Moreover, the council noted the serious sociopolitical rifts of the day, including the debate over the Vietnam War, which was then dividing the country. On many campuses, students wanted little to do with the "military-industrial complex" and frequently turned to law schools, rather than business schools, in hopes of making a social contribution.

"The intellectual questioning and striving of our young people today for new answers and new directions, especially in regard to matters of public concern, argues well for the appeal of . . . a school of management [which] might help to overcome the disenchantment of some bright young people with careers in business," wrote the council in its recommendations. The council also urged that the university accept "the challenge to use this opportunity for creating a concept of education for *management*, for the development of teachers of *management*, and for the conduct of research in *management* disciplines, not necessarily limited to business management" (emphasis in source).[70]

Such a shift in perspective was slowly affecting enrollment. About 450 students were registered at the Graduate School of Management in 1972. Of these, some 15 percent were international students, 10 percent were minority students from the United States and 4 percent were women. Ninety students were in the doctoral program. Enrollment would steadily grow in number and quality of candidates by 1975, with the school recruiting to the capacity of its new Evanston facilities—630. Achieving this goal, though, took considerable effort for the fledgling program, especially as it had to compete with powerful rivals, including the University of Chicago.

The local market challenges were formidable, said Pete Henderson, recalling the early days of his tenure as associate dean of administration at the Graduate School of Management from 1971 until 1981, a post he took up after a 10-year career as a vice president at Booz Allen Hamilton. However, this situation would gradually change, vastly exceeding the Dartmouth graduate's modest expectations that Northwestern could be merely "more competitive" with Chicago.[71]

Ed Wilson, who worked under Henderson in the admissions office, recalled the challenges of having to recruit students when he went out on the road to visit colleges. "The University of Chicago was a beacon for talent, one of the premier MBA programs in the country," he said. "When I went out recruiting, I was always hearing about Harvard, Stanford and Chicago. Give me a break, I thought. I've got to go out and compete against these players? That made it harder."

But with some of the changes that Barr's administration was enacting, Wilson's job would gradually grow less difficult. The shift to a general management credential helped differentiate the Graduate School of Management, he recalled, as did other changes that logically supported the school's claims about management's broader role. The school publications highlighted the transformation:

A profession of management has emerged in recent years—a profession which is applicable to most types of organizations, including business, government and government agencies, educational institutions, hospitals, labor unions, churches, associations, and foundations. Many characteristics of these organizations differ, but the management problems are basically the same. Every manager has the problem of organizing groups of people to work together towards common goals; he must ration limited resources in a manner that will optimize the output of his organization; and he must control the activities of his organization so that waste is minimized and the objectives are achieved. These activities are accomplished through concepts and methods which can be learned.[72]

To that end, the school added a business management program in 1969. Two years later, both its Hospital and Health Services Management Program and its Public Management Program were introduced. And in 1973, a program in education management arrived. As Wilson reported:

In our [recruitment] bulletin we described these four sectors and communicated the message that students could prepare for careers in management across a variety of sectors, not just business. We thought this approach would expand our ability to attract students and also differentiate ourselves from MBA programs. The management concept said that if you had the skills of a manager, you could, over your career, move out of one area and into another because you had the basic managerial skills to do this. This was a valuable concept, because it gave us something special to recruit with.[73]

Out of necessity, the school had to pursue potential students through creative means. Because it was a young and as yet undistinguished graduate program, recruiters had to find students whom others had overlooked—good candidates whose records might not have indicated their ability at first glance.

Said Donald Jacobs: "Frankly, if you got admitted to one of the great schools back then, you weren't going to come here, so we needed to find people who weren't being admitted to the top schools, but were of the top quality. We needed to find people whose folio didn't demonstrate the true quality of who they were."

To succeed in this strategy and identify hidden talent, the school began personally interviewing every student. In the beginning, however, the Graduate School of Management simply needed to build momentum, which meant admissions were "virtually open," according to Wilson. He pointed to statistics from 1972 that indicated there were 890 applicants to the school. Of these, some 80 percent were admitted. The Graduate Management Admissions Test (GMAT) scores of those who were admitted averaged 560, Wilson said; of those enrolled, the average was 539. Similarly, grade point averages reflected the state of a program striving to attract students, build critical mass and develop its culture: the average grade point of those admitted was about 3.0. The school was taking some chances on students and "still not enrolling enough," said Wilson.

A graduate of Bates College, Wilson arrived at Northwestern after serving as director of admissions and financial aid at the Stern Graduate School of Business at New York University. He had also been director of admissions at the School of General Studies at Columbia University and assistant dean of admissions at his alma mater. From 1984 to 1999, Wilson would serve as associate dean for student affairs in the full-time program and associate dean for master's degree programs, where he helped build the Executive Master's Program applicant pool, increasing its size by nearly 80 percent. The effectiveness of his efforts is reflected in the fact that the executive program has consistently been ranked number one in its category by every U.S. ranking service.[74]

Initially, however, Wilson had his work cut out for him. He and Henderson were joined in their efforts by Mary Corbitt Clark, a student of the Graduate School of Management. Little did Clark realize that when she walked into the school, an entire decade would pass before she would leave, despite earning her degree in 1975.

"When I arrived, I also began a professional association with the school, working as the student assistant in the admissions office," said Clark, who went on to be the executive director of Winning Workplaces, an Evanston-based nonprofit whose mission is to help small and midsized organizations create productive work environments. "From the beginning, I was treated as a colleague," she remarked. She would eventually become admissions director when Wilson took a new position as associate dean for student affairs in 1977. "I accepted the full-time position in the admissions office because I believed it offered an opportunity to assume a good deal of responsibility quickly and have an impact on the school's development," said Clark. "Both of those things were true."

The three colleagues spent considerable time on the road, recruiting students anywhere they could. Interest in the new Graduate School was limited. "Initially it was the case that if we visited, say, Boston College, we might have three people signed up to see us," said Wilson, who recalled five-day junkets to the East Coast that returned little in the way of student numbers. Soon, the school was taking a more aggressive and innovative approach to recruiting, with the Admissions Office researching prospective candidates and their schools more rigorously, sending away for critical background information and also developing relationships with MBA advisers at these institutions. If a campus had a business fraternity or club, the admissions team would volunteer to present their pitch to members of that group the evening before their scheduled campus visit.

"We wrote to the chairs of the departments where business school prospects might be studying, such as economics or political science or history or industrial engineering," recalled Wilson. "We sent posters ahead, advertising that we would be on campus. These are things that had never been done by us before."

In a 1973 interview, Wilson credited improvements in the school's physical resources as one inducement to attract students to Evanston, along with an excellent placement program. "An important magnet is our new building and its special facilities," Wilson told *Printout*, the school's almuni journal, at the time. "Add to that a broad range of studies keyed to the functional concept of management."[75]

Wilson believed that with Henderson's leadership and their team's commitment, they "transformed the art of admissions" by reviewing every applicant and treating each one as a potential customer. Applications rose steadily between 1972 and 1977, with admissions trending from 458 to 702 and test scores on the GMAT increasing from an average of 540 to 605. At the same time, tuition was going up, from about $2,700 per year in 1972 to $4,260 in 1977. "This was considered a pretty good record," said Wilson. "I think this trend caught the attention of people."[76]

For Henderson, assessing the school's success in recruiting required taking a longer view. "How do you know when you've arrived? This isn't when a light bulb goes off, but more likely when you perceive a trend happening," he said. For him, one helpful metric was on-campus recruiting, particularly when firms like the Boston Consulting Group (BCG) began actively recruiting the school's graduates as the 1970s progressed. Henderson remarked:

> I thought of BCG as just a superb consulting firm. They initially had very little interest at Northwestern; they were hiring primarily at Stanford and Harvard. I called Bruce Henderson, a colorful southerner who headed BCG at the time, and told him about the business school at Northwestern, describing it as a wonderful school. There was a pause and he said, "Naw, I don't think so. I've not heard many good things about you. Call me when you're better." After a few years, I called him back and he said, "Where ya

been? I hear you're better!" They then began very actively recruiting at Kellogg. . . . That's something that isn't a particularly meaningful measure of how the school is doing for most people, but it was pretty clear to me that it captured a lot of the change in the types of students we were recruiting and the kinds of academic experiences they were having here.[77]

End of an Era, Start of Another

In May 1973, John Barr's health began to fail after he was hospitalized in Evanston with pneumonia. He announced plans to retire in the spring of 1974, as did Ira Anderson, who was concluding a 37-year tenure at Northwestern. But Barr would remain in place until the university identified a new dean, a process that took longer than anticipated; consequently, Barr continued his service into 1975.

As his deanship concluded, Barr reflected on the school's advancement over the previous decade. Enrollment was at a historical high by September 1973, and the school's relationship with the business community had been enriched significantly thanks to the Business Advisory Council and the Affiliate Program. Both the Hospital and Health Services Management Program and the Public Management Program had become established entities, with Donald Haider hired that year in Public Management; furthermore, stars like Louis Stern arrived in the Marketing Department, and Ted Groves and Bala Balachandran were among the new hires in MEDS. Even the school's budget, once a gloomy topic, assumed a brighter prospect: during a faculty meeting in the fall of 1973, Raymond W. Mack, vice president and dean of facilities for Northwestern, reported that the university's financial condition had improved thanks to the work of the Budget Resources Advisory Committee. Mack commended the leadership of Donald Jacobs, who had chaired the committed between 1972 and 1973.

As the school moved into the middle of the 1970s, it could take pride in having established its new graduate curriculum in a new facility. Its student body was becoming more diverse, with 50 women and 25 blacks among a total enrollment of 500. The school could also cite growing strength in its faculty and students, so much so that Barr cautioned the school would require more resources to safeguard the advances already made, especially with respect to retaining professors whom other schools would find attractive. Additional challenges lay ahead, Barr said, including the need to remedy a shortage of student housing on campus, perhaps by establishing a residence hall reserved for management students. Barr looked to alumni to help by suggesting improvements in continuing education and career planning initiatives and strengthening the school's connection with the Chicago business community.[78]

But Barr would not be the leader to take the school to international acclaim. Another man would do that, a person who never even sought the deanship but who would emerge from the school's faculty to utterly transform management education over more than a quarter century.

Finding him, however, would prove an adventure.

Donald P. Jacobs and students celebrate the Kellogg School
being ranked number one by *BusinessWeek* magazine.

Chapter 5

THE JACOBS ERA:

1975–2001

Entrepreneurial and innovative, Donald P. Jacobs was by his own admission an improbable dean. Yet he would do more to shape the modern Kellogg School of Management than anyone before him. With a focus on academics, executive education, student culture and international partnerships, Jacobs oversaw an administration responsible for transforming the school into an elite and unique management institution.

PART 1

"The fact of the matter," as Donald P. Jacobs is fond of saying, is that he never wanted to be dean. Instead, the role came to him more or less by default and only after the dean's search committee had stalled in its efforts to find a suitable replacement for John Barr. Though he had been an accomplished finance professor at the school since 1957, Jacobs seemed an unlikely figure to occupy the institution's chief executive office. Yet starting in 1975, that was exactly what he would do—and for longer than any other business school dean in the country.

Born the son of a baker in 1927, Jacobs grew up on Chicago's West Side, home to the city's famed Maxwell Street Market. He lived above the family's bakery at Roosevelt and St. Louis. A street-smart kid with a sense of adventure, Jacobs found excitement running with friends in the working-class neighborhood, which attracted a diverse array of immigrants. His older half sister, Celia, recognized his intellectual gifts and tried to encourage his academic focus, with some success. Still, Jacobs was enthusiastic about joining the U.S. military during World War II and so enlisted in the navy at 17, intending to serve as a navy frogman. His sister, however, traveled to Florida, where he was stationed, to convince him that the pursuit was not in his best interests. He remained in the military for a year, on a navy destroyer in the North Atlantic.

Despite the bold aspects of his personality, Jacobs also was attuned to the arts and sciences. As a teenager, he occasionally worked as an usher at the Lyric Opera of Chicago. And after the war, using the GI Bill to help fund his education, he earned his bachelor's degree in economics from Chicago's Roosevelt University in 1949, going on to receive a master's degree and a doctorate in economics from Columbia University in 1951 and 1956, respectively. Before joining the faculty at Northwestern in 1957, Jacobs taught briefly at the City College of New York. He subsequently would serve as senior economist for the Banking and Currency Commission of the U.S. House of Representatives (1963–1964) and costaff director of the Presidential Commission on Financial Structure and Regulation (1970–1971); as chair of the Finance Department at Northwestern's Graduate School of Management (GSM) (1969–1975); and as a member of several corporate boards, including Amtrak's (1975–1979), which he chaired.

Later in his career, health concerns led Jacobs to vegetarianism, and he also continued his daily exercise routine—often jumping into an Olympic swimming pool at 6:30 a.m. and doing 45 minutes of laps. "During rainstorms, he sometimes dashes without an umbrella between buildings on the Northwestern University campus here, even as the wind off Lake Michigan musses his hair," wrote David Leonhardt in a 2000 New York Times profile that tried to capture some of Jacobs's energy and casual style. "When he gives public speeches he often wears a sweatshirt. And when he finds something funny, he throws his head back, crosses his arms over his chest and guffaws."[1]

Those closer to home also took note of his style. "Don Jacobs is a street fighter. He won't be deterred," Edmund Wilson, associate dean emeritus, has said. "He saw potential in this place, things that others never even thought of dreaming. He wanted to make a difference."[2]

Wilson, who joined the school in 1972, recalled Jacobs as a natural leader. "You could see that he could lead. He was always busy. He was on the Hunt Commission.[3] He was also involved in executive education, the Institute for Management . . . furthering the school's international program. . . . That's where you saw Jacobs. If you were thinking of Jacobs as a force during the Barr years, he *was* a force: on the faculty."

Summing up the perspective of many colleagues and associates, longtime Jacobs friend Pierre Tabatoni remarked in 2000: "He's a superb strategist. He was the first to design new, strategic thinking about management education, instead of just imitating, as was done at less creative institutions."[4]

Such flattering hindsight, however, can make risky ambitions appear to have been foregone conclusions, when nothing could be further from the truth. With his vision for a state-of-the-art executive education center at Northwestern, for example, Jacobs took a substantial gamble, one that would inform his entire deanship.

Jacobs's Dream of Lifelong Learning Comes True with the Allen Center

"That was one of the coldest days I've ever experienced," said Dale Park Jr., holding a black-and-white photo of perhaps three dozen people bundled in coats and hats and sitting in what resembled a bombed-out building crouched against the freezing Lake Michigan shore. "It was just bitter, bitter cold," recalled Park, an attorney and Northwestern University life trustee. "I was there in a raincoat and shaking, actually shaking from the cold. The concrete was so cold and the cold just came at you from all sides."[5]

Despite the inhospitable weather, at least one man was glowing during the October 16, 1978, ceremony to lay the cornerstone for what would prove a monumental accomplishment in his own legendary tenure as dean of the Northwestern Graduate School of Management.

Just before noon, Donald Jacobs stood at a podium inside the shell of what was to be the James L. Allen Center, still under construction on Northwestern's Evanston campus, nearly in the shadow of Leverone Hall. He fought the wind to share his remarks with the audience of influential friends and supporters who had made his dream of an executive education center a reality. Among those present at the 30-minute occasion was university life trustee Jim Allen himself; his daughter Martha, who was married to Park;[6] Pete Henderson, a former executive in Allen's prestigious consultancy, Booz Allen Hamilton; Dean Emeritus John Barr; and Northwestern University's president, Robert Strotz.[7]

"The Allen Center is the best facility of its kind in the country," Jacobs told those gathered to mark the occasion. "It has been especially designed for executive education, drawing on the knowledge that such education takes place most rapidly and effectively when faculty and students live and work together."[8] He also noted the building's "ideal location" in the midst of an intellectually rigorous, leading university near the dynamic commercial center of Chicago. Jacobs said the Allen Center's programming would offer specialized and general management courses, in both degree and nondegree programs, and draw large numbers of managers to Evanston from around world. Among these courses, he added, would be a "large number and variety of shorter seminars and conferences, meeting for a day, three days, a week or more, covering all aspects of management within the purview of our faculty."

During the ceremony, Strotz traced Northwestern's contribution to management consulting. He referred to the practice's origins in World War I, when Walter Dill Scott, Northwestern's president at the time and an industrial psychologist, produced seminal frameworks that advanced the nascent sector. "One of his students, James L. Allen, together with his friends and fellow Northwestern alumni, Mr. Booz and Mr. Hamilton, nurtured management consulting from its Northwestern cradle to successful adulthood," said Strotz.[9]

Now, the Graduate School of Management was planning to bolster its legacy in executive education by dramatically expanding its infrastructure. The school already had dozens of corporate clients who participated in executive education programs in Evanston, such as Baxter Laboratories, Bethlehem Steel Corporation, Caterpillar Tractor Company, the city of Chicago, Gulf Oil Corporation, S. C. Johnson & Son, Inc., Kraft Corporation, Unilever and the U.S. Army. As stated in the formal proposal for the Allen Center, "The demand for executive programs is strong and growing." To meet this demand, the school required a building that "eliminates the size and seasonal restrictions of current facilities. . . . With classroom, residential, dining, and recreational areas under one roof, the Allen Center will provide an ideal year-round setting for intensive, live-in educational experiences for executives." Such facilities would also provide a home for the school's degreed executive program, launched in 1976, a year after Jacobs assumed his deanship. The resulting Executive Master's Program met with immediate success and expanded from a single cohort a year to two.[10] Within five years, some 280 students would be enrolled in the program at all times.

But Jacobs foresaw more.

As a finance scholar at Northwestern since 1957, he had long understood the value of combining theory and practice. He had taught in and helped develop the school's monthlong, Evanston-based Institute for Management and, later, its international extension, the three-week Institute for International Management (IIM) at the Bürgenstock in Switzerland, both offerings devoted to executive students. He had seen the promise of such programs; in particular, IIM, founded in 1965, brought together an exceptional group of multinational leaders from corporations such as Unilever, Chemie Grunenthal, Lufthansa, Skandia Insurance, Citibank and the Fuji Bank. International participants benefited from exposure to U.S. management experts, and in turn, the faculty members and American participants benefited from the perspectives of the international executives.[11]

By the middle of the 1970s, though, Jacobs knew that executives needed more rigorous frameworks, and he felt strongly that Northwestern could build on its existing programming to differentiate its business curriculum. He believed the Allen Center would become "a national center for the interchange of ideas and information on management between the academic community and the management community—a place where the professors and the practitioners can sit down and test theory against practice" in what he called "the total immersion" method, which encouraged intimate, informal give-and-take discussion.

Jacobs claimed that such a dynamic had long occupied his mind. Very early in his deanship, in fact, he had moved to make executive education a critical part of his administration's agenda. "The Allen Center is a dream I have had since the day I was first approached about becoming dean. . . . That same day I decided that if I did become the dean I would make executive education my top priority."[12]

The school had publicly announced the Allen Center in the fall of 1977, when several key administrators had explained the rationale for its development. Thomas J. McNichols, who was associate dean, director of executive programs and professor of management policy and environment, said: "Executive programs are most effective when classroom sessions are combined with informal, small-group discussions among live-in participants and live-in faculty." McNichols had been instrumental in earlier executive programming, including the Institute for International Management (see chapter 3). "The Allen Center is designed to facilitate this interaction."[13]

In the initiative's formal proposal, the administration noted: "Good management practices rest on the bedrock of solid and established principles, but the world in which they are applied is changing rapidly. Also changing are the tools and techniques of management." Jacobs believed such circumstances demanded that executives renew and upgrade their intellectual tools. Indeed, he contended that market pressures had rendered the MBA a critical degree but one that could no longer be considered a sufficient final credential.

"What we announced was, given the rate of technological change, you had to think of education not as a degree-granting conclusion, but rather as a beginning of a process of education for life," said Jacobs in 2005.[14] He recalled his conviction that the school would have to develop an educational system that welcomed graduates back to campus throughout their professional years. The unique program demanded a unique home, an effort that in turn required significant financial resources.

The Allen Center was that home, a facility dedicated to lifelong learning for executives who faced increased complexity and competition in a marketplace that was growing more global and technologically sophisticated each year. Beyond that, these executives valued the opportunity to earn an MBA degree without disrupting their lives. But other midcareer professionals would choose nondegree executive education in ever-growing numbers, and by 1987, Kellogg had an impressive portfolio of 32 institutes, seminars and programs scheduled throughout the year for managers wanting to hone their skills and learn the latest frameworks.[15]

The university would support the endeavor by allocating a piece of real estate, but President Strotz, a friend of Jacobs, was dubious and unwilling to provide funding for what many in the university administration would dub "Jacobs's folly."

"The university was convinced this was going to be a failure," said Jacobs, revealing only a hint of satisfaction at proving the naysayers wrong. "As a matter of fact, the central administration believed they were going to get a dormitory out of this building . . . which is why they gave us a prime location on campus."

Undaunted, Jacobs turned to prominent Chicago businessman James Allen to help raise funds for what was estimated to be a $4 million project. (Actually, total costs were between $5.5 and $6 million.) Allen's decades of success had resulted in an impressive professional network, and the financial support provided by that network proved critical for the building project. For example, the $500,000 donation from the S. C. Johnson & Son Company was undoubtedly at least partly the result of a relationship with Booz Allen Hamilton that dated to 1939.

Born on a farm in Somerset, Kentucky, on November 21, 1904, Jim Allen earned an economics degree from Northwestern in 1929. That year, he joined fellow Northwestern graduate Edwin G. Booz (class of 1914) at his business survey company. This Chicago-based consultancy, known as the Business Research Service, was founded in 1914. Allen became a partner in the company in 1936, resulting in the firm changing its name to Booz Allen Hamilton. He went on to organize an executive committee there in 1946, becoming the firm's first managing partner. In 1947, he became its chairman, a post he held until 1970, and during his years at the helm, he helped develop many of the company's management tools. In addition, early in his career, Allen had been secretary-treasurer of Ditto, Inc., and vice president and director of Hall Brothers, Inc., which became Hallmark, Inc. His efforts earned him Northwestern University's Alumni Merit Award in 1952, as well as its Alumni Medal in 1960 for outstanding achievements in the field of American business. He was elected a university trustee in 1961 and a life trustee in 1975, having served for nine years as a member of the school's Advisory Council. When Allen died of a heart attack in November 1992, he was remembered as an "extraordinary friend" of the Kellogg School—a man whose leadership and generosity would benefit the school's community "immeasurably."[16] Besides his significant personal financial contribution to the building project, Allen also exerted his considerable influence among the university trustees to pave the way for the construction, and he helped convince the university to provide the necessary land. In addition, he and Jacobs proved expert at fund-raising for the initiative.

"We were a partnership," said Jacobs, who had been introduced to Allen by Barr. "I needed him very badly because he neutralized the [doubt] among the [university] trustees." Jacobs, who recalled Allen as "very austere . . . I don't think I ever remember him laughing," said the two of them became close friends.

Dale Park recalled Allen as "always forward-thinking, planning for the future, planning ahead. A very fine man." He displayed no frivolity. "He was pretty serious and had great friends in the business community."

Despite Allen's powerful connections, Jacobs admitted that Strotz, "a friend and a good economist," had every right to be skeptical of the Allen Center venture, since no other school had produced a viable executive facility at that time. "A number had been tried and none had been successful," he recalled. "[The University of] Chicago had one that they were just closing."

If the university expressed doubts, Jacobs, for his part, was confident that executive education was where the school should build value through "two-way teaching" between executives and the school's faculty, whose research would benefit from contact with senior practitioners. The market indicators all pointed to this eventuality—for those with the ability to perceive the signs and construct a strategy to capitalize on developments. Said Jacobs:

> We knew the economy was globalizing; that was clear. Secondly, business was increasingly using the developing computer technology of the time, which we believed was going to continue developing and, in effect, change the way we do business. So we had these two very large changes acting on the economy, which we clearly believed would speed up the rate of change in the economy. If you believe the rate of change is going to speed up, then that meant the model used for business education was no longer appropriate. It was a model that, in effect, said, "Let's teach people to do what we're [already] doing." It was really dominated by case study, which said, "Here's what the best companies are doing. Do it their way."

This path, Jacobs knew, was insufficient to educate the leaders that the market was demanding. Allen shared the dean's vision and was "clearly attuned to the changes being announced," said Jacobs.

The Allen Center went quickly from vision to reality, taking only four years from conception until the doors of the world-class facility opened October 31, 1979. "We did this extraordinarily quick for a university," said Jacobs. "To fund, plan and construct a new building in only four years . . . I couldn't even get a sign up in four years later in my career."

At least some of Allen's fund-raising efforts were apparently understated. Park, when helping clear his father-in-law's office upon his retirement from Booz Allen Hamilton, discovered correspondence between Allen and several peers. "I found all these letters that he had written to his friends soliciting money for the Allen Center," said Park. "[Financial support for] the dining room and the kitchen was given by Sam Johnson [then president of S. C. Johnson], a very close friend of his, and Tom Singleton and Larry Plym. I didn't know anything about these letters that Jim had written to his friends."[17]

(The fact that the letters were unknown to Park is more understandable given that Jim Allen kept family and firm largely separate, according to his son-in-law. Allen did reveal a few details pertaining to the firm's founding. Said Park: "He told me that when he first started with Booz Allen [in 1929] . . . what people did during those times in business management was look at time studies with stop-watches, that sort of thing. Jim thought it was more important to see how people worked together, how they fit together as a group. When they started the management consulting work, he told me they were ridiculed. People thought it was the most stupid idea. But they persevered. Ultimately they proved it made a lot of sense.")[18]

The Allen Center originally was designed as a four-story, 60,100-square-foot facility boasting 5 classrooms of various sizes, 64 two-person bedrooms, a dining room seating 146 people, a study lounge, recreational areas and administrative offices. Inside, the building featured superb design and modern art, including pieces by well-known artists. "We always considered sculpture and art as integral to the design of the Allen Center," said Wilmont Vickrey, whose architectural firm, Vickrey, Ovresat, Awsumb Associates, designed the building.[19] The Chicago interior design firm of Eva Maddox Associates, Inc. was an early partner with the architects and administration.[20] A variety of touches, large and small, graced the building. For instance, one of Jim Allen's favorite quotes, from the Roman poet and philosopher Lucretius (c. 99–55 BCE), was inscribed into a plaque beneath one of the building's several sculptures, a shimmering open column of brass and bronze rods situated in the lobby:

> *No single thing abides, but all things flow.*
> *Fragment to fragment clings; the things thus grow*

Until we know and name them. By degrees
They melt, and are no more the things we know.[21]

In subsequent years, the Allen Center's art collection would grow dramatically. Today, the building is home to an impressive variety of museum-quality Inuit sculpture and painting, a particular favorite of Jacobs's.[22]

The building underwent two expansions. In 1987, the addition of the H. Wendell and Elinor Hobbs Hall nearly doubled the facility's space, adding 36 bedrooms as well as new classrooms and study areas to support the school's enhanced curriculum, which included more custom offerings for specific companies.[23]

Stephen Burnett, who arrived at Kellogg in 1981 as a visiting assistant professor of marketing, would go on to play key roles in designing the school's nondegree and custom executive education offerings as faculty director of the school's Advanced Executive Program, its oldest and most senior management program,[24] as well as the International Advanced Executive Program (IAEP).[25] He explained the rationale for the increase in programming in a 1988 interview. "In the current state of affairs, with competition on a global scale increasing, with mergers and acquisitions, with the flattening of general economic growth, and with the increasing sophistication of customers, more firms are pursuing major shifts in strategy," Burnett told *Kellogg World*.[26] And more of those firms were approaching Kellogg, he noted, seeking help as the companies tried to refine and implement new strategies. "The demand for these company programs is strong, and we are in the enviable position of being able to pick and choose the firms and groups we'll work with," Burnett said. "We're interested in making connections that promise multi-faceted, long-term relationships in such areas as . . . recruiting our graduating students, funding research, providing our faculty members with access for research purposes, or having their executives attend our other offerings in executive education."[27]

In 1994, the Allen Center grew again, adding 57,000 square feet of bedrooms, classrooms, offices and reception areas. Among these enhancements was a 200-seat amphitheater and quiet study rooms to serve the 3,500 executive students then using the facility. The expansion would allow for about a 40 percent increase in EMP enrollment and offer "the flexibility to match the amazing diversity of what goes on here," said Ed Wilson, who was the associate dean of master's degree programs and student affairs at that time.[28] Overall use of the Allen Center had risen some 40 percent by then, with a range of classes, conferences, seminars and other programming serving the needs of custom, degree and nondegree participants.

Overseeing this activity, Wilson had been assisted by colleagues such as Nancy Hartigan, a graduate of the Institute for Management. Hartigan previously had worked with Thomas McNichols to run the school's Executive Education Program prior to Meyer Feldberg's arrival in 1979 (see the later discussion), when she became assistant director of executive education. Arriving at Kellogg as a department secretary in 1974, Hartigan had a "marvelous facility for professionalizing things," according to Jacobs.[29] She gradually assumed more and more responsibility in the executive programs until she became associate dean for that curriculum in 1985, overseeing a thriving nondegree portfolio during a tenure that lasted until her death in 1994 at age 56.

Emphasizing the central part Hartigan played in developing executive education at Kellogg, Jacobs said in a 1994 tribute: "We knew where we were going, but the fact is we had 64 bedrooms and a real facility to get going and a staff to hire and all of the infrastructure to do. There's no doubt in my mind that the glue, the mortar and the real impetus was Nancy."[30]

Today, the Allen Center offers some 140 programs to more than 5,000 executives annually and features 150 bedrooms, 3 dining rooms and state-of-the-art communications and conferencing technology. Alongside Executive MBA Programs that encompass various schedules, Kellogg continues to offer many custom and shorter-term executive programs to meet the needs of its eclectic clients.

When the school added to the Allen Center in the early 1990s, it also remodeled Leverone Hall, home of the Full-Time MBA Program. Built to accommodate about 650 students and 80 professors, the facility had become stretched to its breaking point with some 1,200 full-time students and 150 professors. To ameliorate the situation, between 1994 and 1995, the school added a 3,000-square-foot, four-story atrium with capacity for 300 people; a 3,000-square-foot student lounge; 4 new classrooms, bringing the facility's total to 15 from an original 7; 15 group-study rooms; a cafeteria; and enhanced facilities for the Office of Career Development and Placement, the Office of Admissions and Financial Aid, Alumni Relations, Development and Communications. Kellogg also made significant enhancements to its computer and communications technology, adding a computer lab and increasing access to the Internet and World Wide Web with upgraded terminals on the school's ground floor, greater e-mail access and remote access via a dedicated modem number for students and faculty working from home. Also new were 3 dedicated Internet terminals in the atrium, as well as a training facility with 20 new computers running sessions on software considered critical to the business environment: Netscape, LotusNotes and Microsoft were staples. A "massive effort" was made to train incoming students in computer literacy skills, according to a *Kellogg World* feature on the initiative that detailed the still-novel Web-based technology.[31] Kellogg also launched its Web presence in 1995, creating its first online home page, which contained descriptions of Kellogg programs, press releases and announcements of upcoming news. Its purpose was both to serve the informational needs of internal and external constituents as well as to market the school to the broader world, including prospective students. "With more than 3,000 files connected to its home page, Kellogg has one of the most extensive sites of any business school on the Web," bragged *Kellogg World,* which noted that more than three months were spent designing the pages, according to Jarvis Smallfield, one of the computer programmers on the project who also was part of a team overseeing the Web site.

"There has been an explosion in society's ability to share, communicate, and analyze information," said Dean Jacobs. "This is having a huge impact on the productivity of the economy. Kellogg must be a leader in the field of information technology to remain the top management school in the country."[32]

In making these modifications, the school acquired Andersen Hall, adjacent to Leverone. Andersen had housed the university's School of Education and Social Policy as well as its Economics Department. Although the latter tenant remained in the new facility, completed in 1995, the former was relocated to Walter Annenberg Hall, a project funded by the Jacobs administration in a negotiation with Northwestern to acquire more space for the business school. Kellogg also began the renovation of Wieboldt Hall, home to its Part-Time MBA Program. The project was completed in 1998. "The best [buildings], in their form and function, reflect not just the needs, but the culture of the people who inhabit them," Jacobs wrote in a letter to alumni in 1993. "If you watch the creation of the new Andersen/Leverone complex, you'll see taking shape a home that fits our culture like a glove." The atrium, in particular, was designed as a large, skylit space where students and faculty could congregate and mingle. "It will be the hub, the locus, of the intense interaction that drives Kellogg's philosophy," said the dean.[33]

Executive Center Makes Wide Impact

The Allen Center's legacy, in addition to influencing all of management education's executive curricula, has been threefold: it has challenged faculty members to hone their teaching and research through vigorous interaction with real-world practitioners, it has enhanced the school's relationships with those practitioners, and it has served as a significant revenue stream for the school. Indeed, within a year of opening, the Allen Center was generating $400,000 in annual profits.

"It was our hidden jewel," said Jacobs. He noted that instead of just retreating into an ivory tower and talking only to each other, faculty members had the ability and the impetus to teach at the Allen Center, where they were instructing executives and would develop into outstanding teachers. "It was a very nice dialogue between faculty and management that turned out to be extraordinarily useful to Kellogg and it really, in effect, was one of our strong, strong talents."

One of those responsible for helping launch the executive facility was Meyer Feldberg, the Sanford C. Bernstein Professor of Leadership and Ethics and dean emeritus of Columbia University. Prior to his appointment to oversee executive programming at Kellogg, Feldberg had been dean of the University of Capetown, South Africa, as well as a visiting professor at Northwestern in 1968 and 1978. He recalled many tours of the Allen Center with Jacobs and members of the university's central administration, one of whom, said Feldberg, remarked, "I can see we'll have to take this over and turn it into a Holiday Inn."

That Jacobs proved them wrong, Feldberg said, is a "gross understatement."

"To put it quite bluntly, the Allen Center was a very ballsy strategy," stated Feldberg, who remained at Kellogg from 1979 until 1982 before going on to serve as dean at Tulane University, as president of the Illinois Institute of Technology and then as dean of the Columbia School of Business for 15 years. While at Kellogg, Feldberg worked with the faculty to design a variety of executive education offerings, primarily shorter-term ones—an innovation for the time, he said.

Though a few other schools had offered executive education for years, the courses nearly all ran for 12 or 14 weeks. The historical market segment for such classes was made up of large corporations that would send a few of their executives away for six or nine weeks of education. Kellogg saw an emerging opportunity and moved quickly to capture its value.

"The revolution that Don created through the Allen Center was, in some sense, the democratization of executive education," said Feldberg, who, in 1980, was instrumental in creating the Kellogg Executive Development Program (EDP), a three-week offering designed for middle-management personnel likely to become general managers with the potential for top leadership roles. The program, which featured 10 senior professors,[34] was an immediate success, with some 60 people enrolled in the course; as a result, it would be offered three times a year, rather than once. The favorable response, said Feldberg, translated into other, shorter-term programs, a week or two in duration.[35]

The trend also gave rise to innovations like the Kellogg Management Institute (KMI), a nine-month general management program designed for mid- to senior-level managers. The nondegree executive education product was launched in 1993. "It's very clear from talking to people that they've wanted the educational experience but didn't have the time [to pursue degree programs]," Associate Dean Nancy

Hartigan told *Kellogg World* in 1993. "In our marketing, we played to the notion that you shouldn't have to sacrifice your personal life for continuing education." The program's inaugural session drew hundreds of inquiries and 42 students. The program has continued uninterrupted since its inception, appealing to applicants because of its combination of academic rigor and "family-friendly" schedules that do not require on-campus residence (although periodic overnight residencies are part of the program). "In today's world it is getting increasingly difficult for people to leave their jobs and families," said Academic Director Steve Burnett when describing KMI's advantages in a 1994 interview.

Feldberg ultimately traces such innovations back to Jacobs. "Don understood that, yeah, universities and business schools in particular had the opportunity and responsibility to educate senior management of large corporations for 10, 12 weeks at a stretch," he said. "But the schools should actually be educating not hundreds, but thousands and thousands of executives across the country by running programs of a week, or two weeks or four weeks. Don understood that the market need was not one or two or four executives [from a company], but 60, 80 or 100 a year. That was a fabulous insight."[36]

It also proved a fabulous opportunity for all involved: students gained valuable insights to advance their professional lives, and faculty members benefited from having their research tested against the experience of seasoned practitioners. In addition, the programs enhanced the school's reputation and revenue. Equally important to the Kellogg executive education mission was the speed with which the administration expanded the programs.

"One of the things that everybody [that is, peer schools] learned at their cost was that you could not underestimate Jacobs," said Feldberg. "The guy had a vision and brought in top-quality people to execute the vision."

Ken Bardach agreed with this assessment. Bardach was director of the school's Executive Master's Program when it began. "Don found a vision," said Bardach, now the associate dean and the Charles and Joanne Knight Distinguished Director of Executive Programs at the John M. Olin School of Business at Washington University. "Executive education wasn't just a program; it was a vision of where he wanted to take the school. It was built on the idea of continual improvement and continually listening to the customer, designing a strategy and tweaking that strategy, and convincing the faculty of the viability of the vision."[37]

The executive center would inspire many new ideas, including a lecture series named in honor of Jim Allen. In recognition of his fiftieth anniversary with the firm, Booz Allen Hamilton made a 10-year commitment to fund the series. The first lecture, in 1981, featured Frank T. Cary, chairman and CEO of IBM. Guidelines for selecting the annual speaker called for identifying "a senior statesman of the corporate world capable of addressing the core issues of management from the perspective of a long and successful career."[38] The following year brought Charles L. Brown, chairman of American Telephone & Telegraph Company, to Evanston. Brown spoke to an audience of more than 700 people in Pick-Staiger Hall during an afternoon lecture on October 26.[39]

"In the end, Jim was extraordinarily proud of the Allen Center," said Jacobs of the building's chief benefactor. "I think if you asked him, he would have said this was one of his life's great accomplishments, one of the things he did that really helped society."[40]

The Reluctant Dean

Jacobs faced long odds when he took on the task of developing the Allen Center and making it a success. And he beat the odds in being named dean of the Graduate School of Management in 1975—a position he claims never to have sought.

"The truth is, I didn't want to be a dean," he said. "By then, I had almost 20 years committed to Northwestern's business school, so I was very interested in having a first-class dean taking the school where it should belong."

A member of the eight-person committee tasked by President Strotz with finding a replacement for the retiring John Barr,[41] Jacobs recalled there was a paucity of candidates he felt could do the job. "We ran through the applicants and got down to people for whom I didn't have a high regard."

The search committee, organized in the fall of 1973, consisted of faculty members Jacobs, Al Rappaport, Sidney Levy, James Thies and Robert Duncan, as well as three corporate executives: Karl Bays, president of American Hospital Supply Corporation; Hugh Campbell, a partner at Price Waterhouse & Co.; and John Hanigan, chairman of the board of Brunswick Corporation.

"We're really looking for God, as long as He or She is available by next September," said Rappaport, chair of the search committee. "A major and obvious criterion is the capacity for empathy with faculty, with other deans and university administrators and with foundations, government and business."[42]

Duncan, a young professor who joined Northwestern in 1971 after earning his doctorate in organizations behavior at Yale, recalled the challenge facing the committee. "It was a rocky deal," said Duncan, who would leave Kellogg in 2001 to become dean of the Eli Broad College of Business at Michigan State University. "The [corporate] outsiders said, 'Your place isn't any good. We've got to make it better.' We looked at a lot of people, but nobody would take it. This was a school somewhere in the top 20, maybe, [but] it wasn't viewed as a plum job or anything like that."[43]

Duncan said the committee made some offers to academics and businesspeople, although he and his academic counterparts had reservations about hiring someone from the corporate world despite Barr's successes in moving the school forward. "Businessmen typically don't make very good deans," Duncan said.

One desirable candidate, the French academic Pierre Tabatoni, declined the university's offer in order to remain in France, where he was a professor at Dauphine University in Paris in addition to serving in government advisory positions.[44] As the months passed, the committee grew increasingly desperate to fill the position. Discussions grew contentious, and the tension was palpable. Members of the committee had been at the mission for nearly two years.

"I can remember the final meeting like it was last night," said Duncan. "The final meeting was at the Tower Restaurant in Skokie in 1975. The businessmen said, essentially, 'This is [nonsense]. This is it; we're picking a dean tonight.' They start going around the table, and of course the only two people who could have taken the job were Rappaport and Jacobs. It was ugly, just an ugly meeting. They were just going nuts."[45]

The committee's decision, though, represented only part of the deliberation. The university president, provost and others still had to accept the formal recommendation, something that initially seemed in doubt, according to Duncan.

"The president then was Bob Strotz and he didn't want Jacobs—and Strotz was a close personal friend of Jacobs," said Duncan. "Maybe he thought he was too academic; I don't know, but he really fought it and fought it for a while." Finally, however, Strotz relented, perhaps understanding that the committee's arduous efforts had produced the best candidate from among those available.

"If you looked at the announcement, I don't think anybody was happy. Being on the committee, we were happy the search was over," said Duncan.

For his part, Jacobs said he was willing to take the job thinking it would be short-lived while he and the university continued an informal search for a suitable long-term dean.[46] Having served on the search committee, he believed that he understood the school's strategic objectives as well as anyone, but he said that academics had been and remained his primary focus—a focus that he could trace to his postgrad days in the mid-1950s. At that time, Jacobs was professionally satisfied teaching and researching in New York City after earning his doctorate. He was working at the National Bureau of Economic Research (NBER), a private nonprofit, nonpartisan organization founded in 1920 whose mission was to study the U.S. economy.[47]

It was then that Roland Robinson, a visiting NBER scholar on leave from Northwestern's Finance Department, approached Jacobs with the idea of joining him in Evanston as part of the school's business faculty. Initially, Jacobs protested. He was happy with his current work, although, he admitted, he and his wife, Mary, had just had a child and were not thrilled at the prospect of raising a family in New York. Robinson facilitated a meeting between Jacobs and Northwestern representatives. The Finance Department, they promised, would be receptive to the kinds of research he wished to pursue. Soon, Jacobs was convinced that the move to Evanston would be mutually beneficial, and he accepted an offer from Northwestern.

Early on in his career at the business school, he would take every third year off to study mathematics at Harvard and MIT, he recalled. In addition, he enjoyed a rotating stint in Washington, D.C., where he contributed his talents to public policy. "So I was having a very nice career sort of alternating between these worlds," he said, adding that, because of that arrangement, he was not initially enticed by the opportunity when the deanship offer came along. But in the end, pressure from the search committee convinced him to take on the school's leadership. He remained in that post for 26 years.

"I didn't think I would spend that much time in my career as a dean," said Jacobs. "Truthfully, if anyone had told me that I would have that kind of tenure, I would have laughed because no dean has spent that much time in the role. This wasn't one of my career targets."

Once in the job, Jacobs immediately began acting on his ideas with respect to executive education and building academic strength. Appointed dean in April, it took him only two months to establish an innovative way of running the dean's office to help execute his plans. There would be an associate dean, but the position would be rotated to ensure staff members would not get burned out and to enable them to maintain some continuity with respect to their research. Bob Duncan was the first person named to the position.

"[Jacobs] decided he needed a good associate dean to work on the academic side," said Duncan. "But if you pull somebody in there on a long-term basis, that kind of hurts their [academic] career. So he came up with this rotating plan to bring three people through: myself, [Hervey] Juris and Mort Kamien.[48] I was the first."

Duncan was only an associate professor, coming up for tenure review the following year. He said that "everyone was flabbergasted at first," but soon, people understood the logic behind the strategic move. "The three of us, certainly me, thought, 'You gotta be kidding,'" said Duncan, laughing. But the plan proved a good one. So good, in fact, that Duncan served in the position three times: from 1975 to 1976, 1980 to 1982 and 1984 to 1986.[49]

The arrangement was designed to allow the school to benefit from each administrator's expertise. "These men are outstanding members of the faculty," said Jacobs at the time. "Each will bring the insights of different disciplines and approaches."[50] Associate deans were expected to continue their teaching obligations and participate in another organizational innovation: the Dean's Planning Committee. Consisting of the three rotating associate deans, Assistant Deans Frank T. Hartzfeld and Edmund Wilson and Associate Deans Kenneth Henderson and Thomas McNichols, the committee was to exemplify the school's new organizational plan by reinforcing what Jacobs called the "special dynamics of the Graduate School of Management . . . a variety of disciplines interacting" to reach the same goal.[51] The school also created a new post, assistant to the dean, to manage some administrative details. Sondra Fargo, a former assistant professor of English at Barat College, was the first to occupy the role.[52]

This structural change was the product of a larger cultural environment in which knowledge and skills were evolving very rapidly, Jacobs has said. In such a setting, a hierarchical leader is less effective because circumstances demand many specialists whose expertise can contribute to the overall organizational mission. "You need to allow the people who have knowledge of these areas to be part of the leadership," Jacobs noted. "This [dynamic environment] results in a diffusion of leadership."[53]

With the administration in place, Jacobs said he soon came to see that the school had a good shot at becoming great. "When I became dean, this was a good school, but not a distinguished school," he remarked. "It needed some work. But what we did was we were hiring very good young people and making good decisions. We made a very strong bid on game theory, and we hired a bunch of very, very good young game theorists in the Managerial Economics Department. Bob Duncan is probably most responsible for us building a great Organization Behavior Department. And of course our Marketing Department was strong. The place was coming into focus."

Maverick Spirit

The Jacobs administration was committed to a collaborative culture. Team-oriented study and social interaction, already strong elements in the school, became hallmarks, for both students and staff. Contributing to the camaraderie was a profound belief in the school and its prospects. But some of the esprit came about by necessity and was driven by a lean organizational hierarchy, which itself was the result of limited financial resources.

Carole Cahill, today an associate dean and the director of administrative services, began working at the school in 1971 as a department assistant in finance. She recalled Jacobs as a person who did not suffer fools but also as a leader who always had enormous passion for building Kellogg into an exemplary institution.

"This family thing that we talk about at Kellogg? We *were* a family and we had many children who we cared about an awful lot," said Cahill, whose spouse, Donald, was assistant and then associate dean for administrative affairs from 1981 until 1986.[54] She recalled that her peers all understood that Jacobs felt strongly about adopting a nonbureaucratic management style and that this approach meant fewer people doing more work.

"The staff was really, really small and stretched," said Cahill, who also remembered the school being constrained in terms of space as enrollment boomed from 400 to 1,200 students over time. "I think maybe because of that, we grew really close on the staff. Vennie [Lyons] and Ed [Wilson] and I all came on board at the same time. . . . We just got the job done. . . . The dean kept his focus and kept Kellogg foremost in his mind. He made the tough decisions. People didn't like him, they did like him. Who cares? On the one side you had Dean Jacobs, this tough kind of guy; on the other side you had this guy who put his arms around the whole place and kept us going—a purposeful leader who kept us going forward."[55]

According to a story that has become Kellogg folklore among faculty and staff, Jacobs's passion for building the student-driven culture sometimes resulted in extraordinary displays. If a student expressed any doubt that he or she had made the right choice in enrolling at Kellogg, the dean was not above offering to refund the person's tuition. He might make the gesture in the most public way—for example, during a student-faculty forum or during "Day at Kellogg," an annual orientation for admitted students.

Jacobs himself confirmed the story:

I have said to people who were admitted . . . that if you are a loner and we admitted you by accident, don't come here. I was serious. Look, the truth of the matter is if we admitted a loner, he or she would be miserable here. The culture is so strong that if you try to be a loner, you are so out of the culture that it really must be a bad experience. That famous scene where I've offered to refund money? I've done that. Lots of times. If during CIM Week or early on in the interactions a student started to act up in ways that were counter to our culture, and if they did that in a big group, I've said, "Look, I don't think you're going to be happy here. Let me give you back your money. I'll refund it fully and even pay you a little for your efforts." I've even offered to call the dean at Wharton or wherever the student thought they might be happier.[56]

No one ever took Jacobs up on the deal. Some of those who expressed initial concerns even ended up making exceptional contributions to the school's culture, said Jacobs, in part because they came to understand the opportunities for real student leadership.

Jacobs has cited the influence of the "servant leader" model as informing his administration. This view, advocated by Robert Neuschel, a popular professor of management and strategy at the Kellogg School for 25 years,[57] emphasized the importance of having a leader who cared about others and was an active listener. To Neuschel, sharing power and "serving your troops first" were essential for success in any endeavor, a tenet he supported by any number of historical references, from ancient Rome to World War II, a conflict he experienced in the Philippines under General Douglas MacArthur's command.

Servant leadership, said Jacobs, "was an important development for us at the school . . . the idea of a leader listening and caring for his people. I really think this describes the dean of a good management school. There is a team here; that's very important."

Undoubtedly, the team concept has played a central part in the Kellogg School's modern incarnation, yet it is also true that Jacobs developed a reputation as a maverick spirit who shared administrative power but also remained strongly committed to his personal vision.

"Don was not and is not an administrator," said Meyer Feldberg. "Had he been, the Allen Center would not have happened. He hired good administrators, but he had a leader's mindset and an entrepreneur's mindset. One thing Don is not is tentative. When he has a passion for something, he goes for it. He doesn't have a plodding, pedestrian, administrative mind that wants to cross all the T's. He has the ability to run with the ball and bring people behind him."

Stanley Reiter agreed, adding that Jacobs is a "very forceful personality" who "scares the hell out of a lot of people" but who also supported the school's academic infrastructure, including the Managerial Economics and Decision Sciences Department. One time, however, a tenured professor in MEDS—"a very good research person [who was] very smart and very dumb," according to Reiter—was experiencing problems with the copy machines. Someone on the clerical staff failed to help the professor, so he marched into the dean's office to complain loudly. "He went down to Don's office and pounded on the desk," Reiter recalled. "Don basically kicked him out of the school. He just told him, 'Go.'"[58]

Another telling anecdote about Jacobs revealed his limited patience for business-as-usual practices. When members of the Dean's Advisory Board (DAB) pressured Duncan to present a strategic plan for the school at one of their meetings, he did so but had to improvise—rather poorly, by his own admission—since a written plan did not exist. "I remember it as if it was yesterday," said Duncan. He also remembered Robert Malott, the chairman and CEO from FMC and a DAB member, being less than impressed with the plan. Jacobs was not present at the Allen Center where the meeting was being held, and he was hardly thrilled when he discovered that his associate dean had made an unscheduled presentation before the august body. Afterwards, in his office, he told Duncan, "You want a strategic plan? Here!" And he wrote it on the back of one of the matchbooks he used to light his ubiquitous pipe.

But if Jacobs could occasionally be prickly, his prodigious leadership gifts allowed him to build consensus to drive his agenda and vision. Beyond that, his genuine interest in others and his ability to listen to them enabled him to benefit from various perspectives as he directed the school's strategic growth.

When asked to describe the secrets to his success, Jacobs was disarmingly straightforward. "First of all, I like people. And I'm a listener," he said. "Right from the beginning we assembled an extraordinarily bright group of faculty. Frankly, [much of the success] was faculty-driven after the initial changes were implemented to get us moving in the right direction. The truth is, the so-called leadership was a leadership of the team."[59]

That early success was starting to attract attention.

In 1976, the school's marketing programs were ranked the best in the United States by a Wake Forest University study titled "Peer Ratings of Programs for Business." The school was ranked number one at the executive level and number three at the MBA level. The survey included the assessment of 276 department chairs from colleges in the American Association of Schools of Business. Richard Clewett, chair of the Marketing Department at the Graduate School of Management, attributed the high ranking to the success of the school's candidates in dissertation contests. In recent years, GSM's marketing students had won more first-place awards in national competitions than peers in any other schools, he said.[60] Another survey conducted that year by *MBA Magazine,* a periodical sent to executives and business students, also indicated the school was continuing to gain broader recognition. Readers and deans of some 100 accredited graduate schools ranked the best management programs. Northwestern's Graduate School of Management placed at number seven in the standings, up from number eleven the year before, with the rise attributed in part to better publicity surrounding its initiatives. Marketing professor Philip Kotler was also rated number one in a 1975 survey of 440 marketing educators as reported by *Marketing News,* affiliated with the American Marketing Association. His colleagues Louis Stern and Steuart Henderson Britt were among 30 other scholars named "thought leaders" in the marketing field.

In a spring 1977 roundup of these and other rankings, editors of the alumni journal *Printout* wrote: "We do not believe the studies are revealed truth, but we have no illusion as to their real power to make converts and influence people. . . . There's no doubt of it—the word about us is getting around."[61]

They had no idea just how true that statement would soon prove.

A Fortune and a Face: The Kellogg Gift

Donald Jacobs's predecessor as dean, John Barr, died just two months before representatives of the John L. and Helen Kellogg Foundation, in March 1979, officially informed Thomas G. Ayers, chairman of the Northwestern University Board of Trustees, that the Graduate School of Management would receive a $10 million gift from their foundation. In his later years, Barr must have been pleased to know that Jacobs was taking the school to another level of excellence, building on the foundations established by his predecessor while making unique innovations in a culture he was defining along entrepreneurial lines.

Indeed, from the time he began his deanship, Jacobs expressed a desire to take calculated risks that could advance the school's fortunes in directions where he believed the faculty and students could go. "I've told the departments," said Jacobs in a 1975 interview, "that if one were to characterize my regime, it should be entrepreneurial."[62]

At that time, he saw himself as the steward of a "thriving enterprise that has made great strides in the last decade." Much later, he acknowledged that the enterprise he inherited required significant enhancements to assert itself among the top ranks of its peers. "When I first became dean, this was a good school but not a distinguished school," Jacobs said more recently.[63]

Although he acknowledged that innovations such as Barr's Advisory Council helped bring the school closer to practitioners and that the move to graduate education exclusively had been a wise strategy given the business world's technology-driven, shifting demands, Jacobs also knew that there was more to do.

His administration began hiring young, research-oriented faculty who would mature at Northwestern, rather than come to the school with a lifetime of opinions and habits that may not have fit the culture being created. In addition, the school was seeking talented students whose formal academic records might not have done justice to their real abilities. These strategies were necessary because of

Northwestern's modest reputation, which put it at a recruiting disadvantage relative to the competition.

Still, the school had results to show for its efforts. Hiring in 1975 and 1976 brought 51 new faculty members to the Graduate School of Management, among them Richard Sandor, vice president and chief economist at the Chicago Board of Trade; marketing professor Alice Tybout; and MEDS professor Ehud Kalai. In the Organization Behavior Department, the addition of Douglas T. Hall and W. Clay Hamner in 1975 led Duncan to declare that the school now possessed "one of the strongest—perhaps the strongest—departments of organization behavior in the country."[64] The following year saw the arrival of accounting scholar Robert Magee; MEDS professors Nancy D. Griffith, Roger B. Myerson and Eitan Zemel; industrial relations experts Myron Roomkin and Jeanne M. Brett; and finance scholar and future Olin School dean Stuart I. Greenbaum. "Addition of these outstanding scholars and teachers to the faculty carries on our long-term goals of attracting talented [new professors] and supporting present faculty," said Kamien, associate dean of academic affairs.[65]

These professors were attracted to Northwestern because its business school already had gained a reputation among its peers as a rising star, according to Roomkin. "Something that is really important to understand is that the public recognition and all the accolades that the school acquired really lagged behind the real reputation," said Roomkin, who would remain at Kellogg until 1998 in various roles, including professor of human resources and chairman of the Management and Strategy Department. He would go on to be dean of the Kogod School of Business at American University (1998–2004) and dean of the Weatherhead School of Management at Case Western Reserve University (2004–2006), where he remains as a professor of management and policy studies today.[66] Prior to his Kellogg tenure, Roomkin also was on faculty at Case Western, and he recalled that when he and his colleagues there were contemplating starting a business school in 1974, they were looking to the "fast-moving object in business education" at Northwestern. "We had a committee to decide what kind of MBA program we wanted, and I said, 'Let's not waste time [trying to create a program from scratch]. Why don't we just go out and get one that's really cool and copy it?' I said, 'Who's the best MBA program around?' And everyone said, other than Harvard and Chicago, which everyone knew about, the really hot place was Kellogg."[67]

So hot, in fact, that word spread quickly among prospective faculty members looking for an exiting place to launch or continue their careers, said Roomkin, who was among an impressive crop of untenured associate professors joining the school because of its "up-and-coming reputation."

The school's culture proved attractive, he noted, because it was apparent that its leadership valued junior faculty and wanted to nurture them:

> People want to invest in an institution that offers them a future. We had a belief that the young ate first, in terms of priorities. If you go out to other schools, even good schools, that's not necessarily true. Senior faculty get the cream. We had a belief that our job was to hire only people who we thought would get tenure, then we didn't have any disappointments. We were going to get untenured people and nurture them to grow . . . basically giving them the resources and leaving them alone. . . . It was a very exciting and heady time. We thought we were pioneering in ways that were really significant.[68]

This academic culture was attracting support that would enable it to endure. For example, the school garnered an important endowed, chaired professorship in early 1976, the Gaylord Freeman Distinguished Chair in Banking. Jacobs noted that the chair would permit the school to improve its "already strong position in this field of management study and research" while also honoring one of Chicago's financial community leaders, who commanded international respect.[69] Three years later, Jacobs himself would be awarded the chair.

By 1979, the school was on the cusp of greatness. Indeed, the January 15 edition of the *Chronicle of Higher Education* reported results from a poll of more than 4,000 college faculty members about their choice for the most distinguished schools and departments nationally. Kellogg was ranked number five, having moved up from number eleven only five years earlier. Still, a few remaining pieces needed to come together before the school's true promise could be realized.

Early that year, the air at Northwestern was charged with anticipation as the business school waited to learn whether the John L. and Helen Kellogg Foundation, planning to disburse about $40 million to deserving organizations, would send some of that money to Evanston after considering a proposal put together chiefly by attorney and university trustee Dale Park Jr.

"In those days, $40 million was a huge, huge amount of money," said Park, adding that the figure was comparable to the Wrigley estate.

The stakes were significant. This Kellogg money would provide irrefutable proof that a prestigious external foundation had noted the innovations occurring at the school: the research-based faculty, the school's commitment to executive education and its general management and collaborative learning focus. Jacobs's deft fundraising—generating about $4 million annually by 1979—and his uncanny ability to connect with business leaders were key to these successes. "The fact of the matter is, I have no ego, so people accept me," explained Jacobs.

Capturing part of the Kellogg Foundation's millions could now radically alter the playing field for the school, providing resources to redouble its efforts—maybe even affording the chance to jump past a competitor and move a notch closer to the very top ranks. But a concerted effort would be required.

Park was no stranger to leading business figures, having Jim Allen as his father-in-law. But he primarily identified himself as a lawyer, not a businessman. "I write wills and trusts for a living," he said. In fact, he landed on the Kellogg Foundation's board as vice president and secretary only after Vernon Loucks, an older colleague at his law firm, introduced him to Helen Kellogg, whom Park helped resolve an important legal matter. Vernon was a wonderful lawyer, Park recalled, and a person with a lot of friends who were prominent in Chicago's cultural world, including Kellogg. After Helen's death in 1978, Leonard Spacek, the renowned Arthur Andersen managing partner, became the foundation's president, working with a relatively small board whose members included TransUnion CEO and director Jerry Van Gorkom (the foundation's vice president); Baxter CEO Vernon Loucks Jr.; E. H. Moore (treasurer); Vincent Dole, the Rockefeller University physician who discovered methadone as a treatment for opiate addiction; and W. Keith Kellogg II, grandson of the cereal company cofounder.

"And there was me," said Park, with a self-deprecating smile.

"I was sort of in awe," he admitted. "Leonard was something else—great ethics, so smart. After some of these meetings he would say to me, 'Dale, are you OK?' Well I was exhausted from trying to take notes so I could write the minutes! Leonard was so fast with ideas."

Park said the board's decision to give away the Kellogg money was unanimous. The alternative, outlined by Spacek, was to continue the foundation for years, running up administrative bills. To avoid this and to place the funds in the best hands, each board member was to write a letter to Spacek proposing how the foundation should allocate its resources, recalled Park, who consulted with Allen about the matter, telling him, "I might be able to get you $1 million."

Allen suggested Park talk with Pete Henderson, the school's associate dean. "I had lunch with Pete and, as we were leaving, he said, 'If you give us $10 million we'll give you the name of the school,'" said Park.

After researching the origins of the Kellogg fortune, noting its connections to business, Park wrote a five-page proposal to Spacek and the board. The letter, dated July 29, 1978, and written on Gardner, Carton & Douglas letterhead, the Chicago-based law firm with which Park was affiliated, was divided into four main parts: a history of the Kellogg company; an analysis of the transfer of Kellogg shares from

John L. Kellogg to Helen L. Kellogg and her retention of those shares; an analysis of the minutes from previous Kellogg Foundation directors' meetings to explicate the guidelines established by Helen Kellogg on the use of foundation funds; and Park's personal recommendations regarding the foundation's overarching goal.

"Compared to funds disbursed annually by federal, state and local governments, by other charitable organizations, and by individuals for charitable purposes," Park wrote to the directors, "the foundation's funds are modest. We as directors need to find a way to multiply their effectiveness."[70] Articulating why Northwestern deserved consideration, Park concluded: "I can think of no way of achieving greater multiplication over a longer period of time than through support of management education."[71]

Behind his reasoning lay a belief in education's power, as well as a suspicion that many businesses and charities suffered from mismanagement. Competent managers, he believed, could make widespread and significant contributions, including in fields such as health care and medical research.

"If you want to multiply the effect of a grant, I always thought you should give it to education," noted Park, "because you don't just benefit one person; you benefit a tremendous number of people."[72]

Henderson could find no flaw in this logic. A former Booz Allen Hamilton executive who went to Northwestern seeking a new career that would offer him, a recent widower, flexibility to raise his two children, Henderson said he "tried to play every angle" to ensure the university received some Kellogg money. "I called Leonard Spacek at his home in Palm Springs," he remembered. "I told him, 'We would love to come and see you. We think we've got a wonderful school here, one that would be an appropriate place for you to designate funds.'"

This zeal hardly moved the famously circumspect accountant.

"He told me, 'Let me describe the scene here, Mr. Henderson. There are 12 nuns in my backyard, five priests in the front yard. None of *them* has broken through my defenses. You too are welcome to come out and stand with those priests and nuns, Mr. Henderson, but none of you will get into my house.'"

It did not take a religious conversion for Northwestern insiders to appreciate how far the business school had come. They knew that daring changes to its curriculum and scope, begun during the 1965–1975 Barr era, had flowered under the entrepreneurial Jacobs. But for those outside this community, the school's merits had to be spelled out—which they were, in an 83-page formal proposal delivered to the Kellogg Foundation on January 12, 1979, along with a letter from Park praising the school.[73]

The school was among the top management institutions in the United States, Park noted, and it aspired to be better, "to be the absolute best."[74] His research into the school had impressed him, and he believed it had all the fundamentals in place to earn an elite reputation: a brilliant young faculty, a select and highly motivated student body and outstanding classroom facilities. "The school is probably even better than its current rating," said Park, reiterating that he believed the foundation's grant could achieve no better use than at Northwestern. "What . . . I have seen at the GSM is an organization that has undergone remarkable development in the past 10–12 years. Its balanced programs of management education and research are already very strong. Its leadership is excellent and their plans for moving the school to a position of preeminence appear to be attainable."[75]

The school could achieve this lofty goal with sufficient resources to pursue four primary goals, in three main categories: faculty support, research support and facilities support. With the funds, the school would establish three faculty chairs—the John L. and Helen Kellogg Distinguished Professorships—endowed at $1 million each. "Such chairs will enable us to attract to Northwestern three distinguished management scholars," the administration wrote in the proposal to the foundation. Initial occupants would come from the areas of finance, public/nonprofit management and management policy.[76] The proposal noted that the school was "close to an overall position of preeminence" in the area of finance but that "a new revolution is taking place in finance theory," bringing with it sophisticated, dynamic models of financial processes. "Addition to the finance faculty of a distinguished theorist working in this pioneering area would give the School a complete portfolio of research capabilities in this field."[77] Similarly, the school's recently established Public Management Program would benefit by the addition of an outstanding scholar in that area, as would the area of management policy.

Furthermore, the school would leverage the funds to support research, notably by establishing two major interdisciplinary research centers, each endowed by $1 million of the foundation grant. The centers, to be known as the Institute for Advanced Study in Managerial Economics and Decisions Sciences and the Center for the Advancement of Marketing, were already being planned, according to the proposal. They would "provide a focal point for existing research capabilities" and also "stimulate and support new groupings of faculty members and . . . enable the School to draw in visiting scholars to participate in research projects of substantial promise."[78] Even more heft would be added through the establishment of four John L. and Helen Kellogg Research Professorships, endowed for $250,000 each. The school would award these chairs annually to professors whose research records or proposed research "suggest findings of unusual significance to management." The income from each research chair would be used for the faculty member's summer support, research assistance, and a partial release from other duties.

It would be difficult to overstate the value of research afforded by a John L. and Helen Kellogg Foundation gift, the proposal's authors noted. "Quality research serves to improve management practice, provide new insights which could lead to resolution of major public policy issues, and enrich teaching in both degree programs and executive education. In all of these ways, the free enterprise system is strengthened."[79]

These objectives were ambitious and the rationale for them sound. But would the foundation really give the money to an institution that, though indeed promising, lacked the historical pedigree of the Ivy League schools that had dominated the field for decades?

"We had an office pool in sealed envelopes wagering what we would receive from them," said Pete Henderson. "The answers ranged from zero to $10 million. Don's vote was $10 million; mine wasn't. I was not that hopeful."

"A lot of people bet zero," said Jacobs. "I felt good about it." And soon, his optimism about the school's chances was rewarded, thanks to Park's efforts to articulate the administration's plan to bolster its academic reputation and create a new student residence. When the letter Park wrote on behalf of the Kellogg Foundation, dated March 12, 1979, arrived on the desk of Thomas G. Ayers, chairman of the Board of Trustees at Northwestern, the school had its answer.

"We are impressed by the quality of the faculty that has been assembled at the school, their productivity, and the importance of their research," wrote Park. "We have learned of the accomplishments of the school's students, and have toured the new facilities, under construction, for continuing executive education.

"*We understand that the goal of the Graduate School of Management is to attain preeminence in the field of management education and research. To assist toward that goal, the John L. and Helen Kellogg Foundation hereby confirms the following grants—* (emphasis in source)."[80]

The school would receive its $10 million request and be renamed the J. L. Kellogg School of Management. In effect, the bestowal of the gift announced that a major new force in management education had arrived.[81]

Carole Cahill recalled the day the award was made public. "It was Friday and the student TG [weekly social event] was going on," she said. "The university president [Robert Strotz] gave us a call with the news. The provost came over and played the drums with the student band in the lounge. It was really a great celebration."[82]

Jacobs wryly observed his reaction to the news of the gift: "I told Leonard Spacek this was the worst day of my life. Leonard said, 'What are you talking about? We just gave you $10 million!' 'Yes, but for the rest of my life I'm not going to sleep at night, thinking I should have asked for more.' I told them they should have given us nine-point-nine or nine-point-nine five—anything but the exact figure we requested," said Jacobs, laughing. "But Leonard was a straight shooter and he assured me they wouldn't have given us another dime."

With the foundation's gift, one of the largest of its kind at the time, the stage was set for the Kellogg School's meteoric ascent into the top echelon of management leaders.

The school allocated the funds in all the ways outlined in its proposal to the Kellogg Foundation. Of special note, given the school's student-driven, collaborative culture, was the $4 million renovation of Evanston Apartments, a seven-story residence complex located at 1725 Orrington Avenue that was "in really bad shape," according to Jacobs. It had housed 650 Northwestern undergraduates but would now be home to some 300 graduate business students and their families. The university had opened the facility in 1947 to accommodate faculty and married students in response to a postwar enrollment boom. The original building cost $3 million to erect and contained 208 living units and a 110-car garage. It was one of the first buildings on campus to feature a "garden roof," a grass lawn atop the garage. Kellogg purchased the facility from Northwestern in March 1979 and began remodeling it. Once completed, the Living-Learning Center opened in September 1981.[83]

"[The center] will add an important dimension to the Kellogg School," said Edmund Wilson, dean of students, who chaired the faculty-student conversion committee associated with the building renovation. "For the first time we will be able to offer a substantial number of our students housing that is ideally located—just three blocks from Leverone Hall—and study facilities made to order for them and our program."[84]

The building subsequently would be named after James R. McManus '56, chairman of Marketing Corporation of America, a member of the school's Advisory Council and, later, part of the executive committee in a major fundraising effort at Northwestern. McManus expressed gratitude to Kellogg for providing him with the education that underpinned his professional success. He noted the importance of financial support in advancing institutional goals, but he also credited "the contribution of . . . time and energy [as being] just as important." Support for education, he said, was the best investment for society. "True, it's not a low-cost investment," McManus added. "But if you think education is expensive, consider the cost of ignorance."[85]

Jacobs credited Park with being a catalyst in helping bring the $10 million Kellogg gift to the school. "Dale was a very, very important person in the whole thing," said the dean emeritus. "He has done more for Kellogg than almost anybody, and he won't take any credit. But he deserves a lot of credit."[86]

For his part, Park has remained modest about his role in helping the Kellogg School achieve its contemporary reputation, preferring to credit Jacobs and others. Fortunately, he has retained all the correspondence associated with the efforts to win the Kellogg Foundation gift, calling the letters "my personal treasures."[87]

Rankings Climb Brings National Attention

The Kellogg gift, coming on the heels of innovations in executive education made possible by the Allen Center, caught people's attention and resulted in the school gaining a national reputation, as well as additional academic resources. A January 1981 article in the *Wall Street Journal*, for example, took notice of the Midwest business school in a flattering profile that would prove important to elevating its national visibility.

NORTHWESTERN'S SCHOOL OF BUSINESS SCRAMBLES ONTO THE FAST TRACK, the headline announced. "It scales the academic ranks with eclectic curriculum and ties to 'real world,'" wrote staff reporter Frederick C. Klein. In addition to the school's academic strengths, the article noted the administrators' skill at fund-raising.

Jacobs unabashedly admitted his goal: "We want to be No. 1 in our field! What's wrong with that? We're teaching people to be managers in a competitive world, so it's only fitting that we be competitive too."[88]

"That Northwestern could even pretend to vie for preeminence among graduate schools of business or management would have seemed outlandish little more than a dozen years ago," wrote Klein. But starting in 1970, the school began climbing into the top 15 U.S. business schools. In 1979, the *Chronicle of Higher Education* placed it in the number five position, Klein noted, just behind Stanford, Harvard, Chicago and Wharton.

Even rival Chicago's dean, Richard N. Rosett, remarked: "While I find it hard to say anything about Northwestern that would make it look good in print, I must say I envy and admire its rare good fortune in landing the Kellogg money."

"Northwestern's climb is especially notable for a number of reasons," Klein wrote. "One is that it comes at a time when booming enrollments have swelled the number of such schools and intensified their competition for faculty members."

Associate Dean Bob Duncan considered the *Wall Street Journal* article a "big breakthrough" that signaled how serious the school was about achieving its goals. "[The article told people] 'Wait a minute. They're really doing interesting things there—We'd better pay attention,'" said Duncan. "We just kept grinding away and raising money. Crank, crank, crank and the rest is history. Once the Allen Center got going . . . we were continually able to get good faculty and keep them."[89] Duncan also noted the importance of other administrators, including Donald Cahill and Pete Henderson, in helping raise funds during the early 1980s. In addition, he said, there were certain members of the Advisory Council—"we used to call them the Gang of Four," Duncan recalled—who helped "push the school and who were really instrumental in getting Jacobs plugged into New York and other places."[90]

In fact, by the 1979–1980 academic year, the school was generating $4 million in philanthropy annually, which was attributed to a partnership between administrators and Advisory Council members.[91] This relationship began to flourish during the Jacobs deanship: in April 1978, for instance, Jacobs convened a meeting of the group to outline a more active role for its members, a role that included fundraising, evaluation of the school's programs and planning.[92]

The school's lack of affiliation with any particular pedagogical approach served to distinguish it from peers such as Chicago, whose "free market" economic views positioned it clearly in the minds of prospective students much as the "case study" model did for Harvard. At Kellogg, the positioning was different.

"We offer an educational cafeteria and make no apologies for it," Jacobs told the *Wall Street Journal.* Taking a friendly swipe at rivals who sniffed about the school's nondoctrinaire style, Jacobs said, "We're a business school, you know, not a religion."

Klein outlined the way Kellogg distinguished itself from its rivals: "By its own account and others, Northwestern has made its mark by excelling in the difficult art of fund raising, by recruiting and retaining bright, young faculty members from a wide variety of academic disciplines, and by adding what it considers a vital dose of contact with the 'real world' of business through an active program of executive education."

The media exposure continued. In October 1985, Kellogg topped a survey conducted by Brecker & Merryman, Inc., a New York–based management consulting firm, as the best of the nation's more than 600 graduate business programs. The survey polled 134 leading companies that recruited and hired holders of MBA degrees. Previous surveys, which usually polled business school deans, rated Kellogg no higher than fifth place. The Brecker & Merryman survey found that Kellogg graduates were ranked the best in 4 of 15 areas: marketing knowledge, ability to work in teams, being most likely to remain with a company over the long term and offering the "best value" to employers.

"For the first time someone thought to ask the customers about the product, and the result was a reshuffling of the business school lineup," reported *Kellogg World.*

The school received 206 points and first place overall in the survey, with the Wharton School placing second (with 192 points), followed by Harvard (172 points), Columbia (121) and Chicago (100).[93] Some schools, such as Harvard and Chicago, groused about the survey's metrics, but there was no denying that the ranking had begun to bring increased national attention to Northwestern's business program, including to the Marketing Department, which continued to earn distinction for its research and teaching.[94] Indeed, the publicity was expected to increase enrollment at the school by up to 25 percent, said Steven DeKrey, admissions director. Professor Lawrence Lavengood even expressed concern about a possible flood of applicants causing the school to swell its ranks from 390 to 450, stretching resources and facilities. "Our success could be modified by our success," he said.[95]

The worries proved unfounded, as the school would consolidate its strengths over the next couple of years, earning corporate respect and support for its efforts. Carole Cahill does admit that the staff "added another 100 student mailboxes each year" and that the school's gathering popularity was making it clear it would require more resources.[96] Fortunately, the publicity about the school rankings resulted in increased support for Kellogg scholarships and research.

In 1986, General Motors Foundation awarded Kellogg a $500,000 grant to establish the General Motors Research Center for Strategy in Management. The center was to "support the study of ways in which business can develop and implement strategies for competition in national and international markets," and it would be headed by Associate Dean Duncan. By that time, several hundred GM managers had participated in strategic business management programs at the Kellogg School's Allen Center. These were developed jointly by the school's faculty and GM's corporate strategic planning group. In addition, some 2,000 GM managers had attended other executive education courses at Kellogg.[97]

That year also saw a significant award from the William and Flora Hewlett Foundation to support the Dispute Resolution Research Center. Led by Jeanne Brett, the J. L. Kellogg Distinguished Professor of Organizations and Dispute Resolution, the center supported research and teaching in multidisciplinary approaches to conflict resolution. The center was one of three launched between 1986 and 1987. In addition a gift from alumnus Gary A. Rosenberg '63 established the Rosenberg Chair in Real Estate Management and led to the creation of the Real Estate Research Center. Today, the center is one part of the school's strong real estate program.

In 1987, a $1 million gift from the PepsiCo Foundation endowed a fellowship program at Kellogg. Robert H. Beeby '59, the president and CEO of Pepsi-Cola International, as well as a member of the Kellogg Advisory Council, confirmed the gift. "PepsiCo hires Kellogg grads for two reasons," said Beeby in announcing the gift. "The school has a terrific marketing curriculum and we are a market-driven company. And Northwestern has a Midwestern, sod-buster work-ethic reputation that is well deserved. . . . Kellogg graduates . . . get things done, and [are performance-driven]."[98] A succession of exceptional management students were to be supported by the endowment, with the gift providing financial backing to five recipients annually for the two-year program.

That year, Quaker Oats also gave the school $250,000 to endow a scholarship fund. William D. Smithburg '62, the company's chairman and CEO, called the gift "the largest in the Foundation's history, but fully merited given the Kellogg School's achievements and the fine relationship between Northwestern and Quaker Oats."[99] Smithburg was a Northwestern trustee and vice chairman of the Kellogg Advisory Council. The year 1987 also brought a gift from General Foods, which funded a professorship in marketing; Brian Sternthal, who had been with the school since 1972, was made the General Foods Professor of Marketing.

At the same time, the school continued to build its faculty strengths too. The young research professors were challenged to go beyond their own disciplines— math, the social sciences, and so on—to pursue cross-disciplinary studies that resulted in innovative discoveries. "This place was hungry," recalled Duncan. "We were a young faculty, excited about the place, and we thought it was a lot better than its reputation. People were committed to making it better."[100]

Creation of the Management and Strategy Department

Even those who had long been part of the school's establishment sought ways to reinvent themselves in light of new market conditions. A prime example was the way in which the Policy and Environment Department took steps to re-create itself as the Management and Strategy Department in the early 1980s. The process was challenging according to some of the central decision makers involved in the transition, such as Professors Roomkin, Juris and Satterthwaite, but most of the faculty recognized a need to change what had largely been a department filled with talented teachers— including Lavengood, McNichols, Edward T. P. Watson and Leon Bosch—rather than researchers oriented toward quantitative methods.

Policy and Environment had formed in the early 1970s during another time of change at Northwestern. Course content such as business history, ethics, environment and labor relations were among the subjects incorporated in the department.

"You had several people in that department who were senior professors who came out of different functions—a couple of finance people, economics people," said Al Isenman, professor of management and strategy and director of custom programs in executive education. Isenman earned his MBA (1976) and doctorate (1984) from Northwestern and was a student in the Policy and Environment Department. "[The department] was part of the conscious repositioning, a new direction away from the traditional schools of commerce where the job of the school was essentially to fill the toolkit with the technical skills." With the creation of Policy and Environment, said Isenman, Northwestern began adding a series of general management and strategy courses, a move that was "integral to the changing of direction of the school."[101]

A decade later, however, even those in the department were unclear about its raison d'être.

"By 1980, when I was chairman, the question was: What was the department?" said Juris, who arrived at the school in 1970 after serving as assistant dean of students at the University of Chicago, working under its president, George P. Schultz. "Policy and Environment had great teachers . . . but pretty much qualitative people." The department was also a "polyglot," he recalled, with subjects that now included entrepreneurship, small business administration and a rather nascent international business module.[102]

In fact, some considered the department a kind of "catchall," an arrangement that had its benefits. But the area would gain more strength as the school focused its resources on refining the department's content and mission.

"Every school needs a 'not-otherwise-classified' grouping," said Roomkin. "Hervey and I were labor economists and taught human resources. . . . We were struggling to figure out what the department should be. . . . One of the things that happened during my time here was the breaking out of what were non-priority areas into priority areas and standing them up as important parts of the Kellogg organization. The most prominent of those was international business."

Roomkin and his peers would develop the area of international business first through seminars and other curriculum innovations, among them the Global Initiatives in Management Program, which was one of a small number of offerings at that time with an overtly "international" perspective. He admits the progress was halting at first, since some believed Kellogg should remain a clearly defined "American" program, rather than take steps to develop a full portfolio of international business courses. Soon, however, the international move gained steam, in part because of the strong support of others, including marketing professor Kotler, who wanted to broaden the school's global curriculum.

"I remember regarding the international issue that one question was whether our largely U.S. students wanted to know that much about other countries and exporting and investing in them," Kotler recalled. "The world moved slower at the time, outsourcing was less pronounced and the world wasn't as flat." Another related issue, he said, was whether the school would invest sufficient resources to attract the best talent to teach international business or indeed whether the existing faculty had enough international background to impart that thinking to their courses. "I was highly in favor of going strong on international and was concerned that other schools were moving faster than we were," said Kotler, whose publications include texts such as *The Marketing of Nations: A Strategic Approach to Building National Wealth* (1997), *Marketing Places: Europe* (1999) and *Rethinking Marketing: Sustainable Marketing Enterprise in Asia* (2003).[103] Ultimately, the school elected to pursue a rigorous international business program and would hire faculty to teach it (see the fuller discussion later in this chapter).

Other aspects of the Policy and Environment Department also improved once the faculty applied the same kind of quantitative rigor there as the MEDS Department had ushered in elsewhere in the school.

To respond to what the dean wanted from a revamped department, Roomkin and Juris asked faculty members in MEDS for help. Juris recalled the situation: "Even though I'm more of an institutional economist, I appreciate quantitative research and the importance of it. It wasn't what I did, but that was immaterial. If you were going to build a strong department, it was important to bring in these kinds of people. I got together with Mort Kamien and Mark Satterthwaite and said, 'You guys do strategy research. Why don't you take joint appointments in our department and start pushing us in this direction?'"[104]

Both were interested. Satterthwaite, who was MEDS chairman from 1978 to 1983, joined Policy and Environment in 1985 and would become its chairman in 1990, the year it changed its name to the Management and Strategy Department. "When I came up here the department was full of very nice, intelligent people who took cases and were very skilled in making a classroom period go by," he said, noting that among the "distinguished and important members of the department" were Lavengood, McNichols and Bosch. Yet when students were asked what specifically they learned from a case, "they had a hard time expressing it."

Consequentially, Satterthwaite said, even though traditional Policy and Environment faculty members were "wise people," passing along this wisdom proved difficult, as did hiring people and getting them through the tenure process successfully. "This was a huge problem for the school," he said, yet Kellogg was unwilling to let the department disappear because of the importance of general management to the school's overall portfolio.

What he and his colleagues did was essentially import into this area the analytical approach that had served MEDS so well. Satterthwaite asked Juris to cross-list a course that the younger professor had been teaching in MEDS, called "Competitive Strategy and Industrial Structure," which still exists today and was originally taught by renowned game theorists John Roberts and then Paul Milgrom.

"We were downstairs developing these ideas of strategic behavior, game theory. Looking at problems from a rational perspective," said Satterthwaite. "We were using the word 'strategy.' We thought it must be important for the firm in thinking about its strategic decisions." The idea, he said, was to bring some of these ideas—"the so-called new industrial organization"—into the curriculum. The course, which studies the determinants of competitive strategy and how a firm's industry affects its choices and performance, garnered a very good response almost immediately, said Satterthwaite.

David Besanko, senior associate dean for planning and external relations, recalled the impact that Satterthwaite's course had for the department. "When Mark started to teach it, he really reinvented it. He started to use Michael Porter's book on competitive strategy and use cases to add material that made this subject come alive for MBA students. He figured out how to do this. He was so successful at this, that people around the school were taking notice: Here's how strategy could be taught, using the principles of economics in the background."[105]

At the same time, the department began recruiting quantitative professors, including figures like Raphael Amit, a former student of Kamien's who graduated from the MEDS doctoral program in 1977 and was on the Kellogg faculty from 1983 to 1990. Other hires at that time were Cynthia A. Montgomery and Birger Wernerfelt. Montgomery, who won the school's Professor of the Year Award in 1988, was considered "a brilliant teacher," said Satterthwaite.[106] The department then hired Pierre Regibeau and Katharine Rockett, "first-class industrial organization economists," as Satterthwaite described them.

"These were all young people who had good or excellent training," he said. "They started developing the department. They brought in these ideas. I think they were instrumental in helping get me into the department."[107] (Later, as associate dean for academic affairs from 1990 to 1992, Satterthwaite would also prove instrumental in developing the school's body of clinical professors and providing a rigorous framework for assessing their performance. "We put in a policy that . . . appointments have to be reviewed periodically," he said. "Now there are clinicals in every department, and I think they enrich the school very substantially. I'm rather proud of that innovation.")[108]

This foundation attracted other scholars to the department, such as Daniel Spulber, the Elinor Hobbs Distinguished Professor of International Business, who arrived in 1990 and is considered by Besanko a catalyst who helped subsequent hiring and enabled the department to gain "critical mass." The author of 11 books, including *The Theory of the Firm, Global Competitive Strategy* and *Management Strategy,* Spulber is also the founding editor of the Kellogg-based *Journal of Economics and Management Strategy (JEMS),* published by Blackwell Publishing, and founder of the Kellogg International Business and Markets Program, created in 2001 as part of the school's high-profile effort to expand its academic leadership globally. The program's centerpiece is the international business major, which is complemented by resources such as the International Business and Markets Research Center. In 1991, the school hired the Stanford-trained economist David Dranove, who is currently the Walter J. McNerney Distinguished Professor of Health Industry Management and coauthor of *The Economics of Strategy,* an influential and widely used textbook, as well as author or coauthor of three other texts and dozens of journal articles.

Besanko also joined Kellogg in 1991, having received his doctorate in managerial economics and decision sciences from the school in 1982. Today the Alvin J. Huss Distinguished Professor of Management and Strategy, Besanko chaired the Management and Strategy Department from 1992 to 1996 and has published more than 40 articles in various peer-reviewed journals. In addition, he is coauthor of *The Economics of Strategy,* a textbook that has broadly influenced MBA courses that focus on competitive strategy. The book, he said, "gave some visibility to what we were doing here," in a department that had no real rivals at the time. "This department really became, and still is, a leading example of a strategy group that's built around economics," said Besanko,[109] who is also coauthor of another text, *Intermediate Microeconomics.*

Shane Greenstein, the Elinor and H. Wendell Hobbs Professor of Management and Strategy, joined Kellogg in 1997. A graduate of Stanford University's doctoral program in economics, Greenstein has published five books, including *The Industrial Economics of Computing; Diamonds Are Forever, Computers Are Not: Economic and Strategic Management in Computing Markets;* and *Communications Policy in Transition: The Internet and Beyond.* His recent research includes investigations into competition and innovation in computing as well as Internet infrastructure and Internet service provider (ISP) pricing. He served as the Management and Strategy Department's chairman from 2002 to 2005.

Other key faculty hires in Management and Strategy have included Scott Schaefer, who was on staff from 1995 to 2005, and James Dana and Kathryn Spier, both of whom arrived in 1994 and departed in 2007. Among the more recent hires is Stanford-trained economist Michael Mazzeo, who joined Kellogg in 1998. His varied research interests have included product choice and oligopoly market structure and investment strategies and market structure. Another graduate of the Stanford economics doctoral program, Scott Stern, joined the Kellogg faculty in 2001. Stern is an innovation expert, and his research is devoted in part to exploring the differences between producing and distributing ideas as opposed to more traditional economic goods, as well as the implications of these differences for business and public policy. Alberto Salvo joined Kellogg in 2005, having earned his doctorate from the London School of Economics. His research interests include empirical industrial organization, international economics and antitrust policy. Therese McGuire, the current department chair, came to the school in 1988, having earned her doctorate in economics from Princeton University. An expert on state and local public finance, fiscal decentralization and tax incentives, McGuire also is director of the Kellogg Real Estate Management Program and the Guthrie Center for Real Estate Research.

Today, Management and Strategy has evolved into what Juris called a "cross between Organization Behavior and MEDS," with faculty members researching both behavioral and economics aspects. "You don't want silos," he said, adding that the old Policy and Environment Department essentially evolved into Management and Strategy and Organization Behavior. "One has to do with strategy formulation, the other has to do with strategy implementation," he noted.

Rigorous Tenure Process Builds Top Faculty

The school would demand much from this faculty and all faculty members across the school, but it also worked to nurture the new professors in order to acclimatize them to the Kellogg culture and the "Kellogg way" of doing things. Junior faculty members were teamed with more senior mentors, and they were exempt from administrative duties so that they could focus on their teaching and research, which was encouraged to be collaborative. Teaching loads during the first three years also were reduced. After this initial orientation period, professors were asked to do more. "The bar is set not pretty high, but very high," said Jacobs. "And then the day you get tenure, the dean calls you into the office and says, 'You made it. Now it's your turn to start doing the administrative duties. You've been allowed some leeway to focus on your research and teaching, and now you've got to do a little of the overhead because younger people are going to get the leeway now.'" Even those who do not get tenure after the six-year review process,[110] said Jacobs, are still in "a great position to go out and get another job, because [they have] done more than most people have, just not the quantity and quality that Kellogg requires."[111]

Indeed, Jacobs raised the promotion standards significantly, said marketing professor Louis Stern. "People around campus would look at us and say, 'There's no one who reviews its faculty more rigorously. If someone at Kellogg gets tenure, you know they've made it. You know they are one of the top two or three people in their cohort."[112]

This tenure process had its roots in the Barr administration, but it flowered under Jacobs and, today, Jain. "It's very important to the school's history . . . fundamental," said Besanko. The process has been imitated by other schools at Northwestern and elsewhere, he indicated, adding that such meticulous personnel selection is one pivotal ways in which Kellogg has built its outstanding faculty.[113] Colleague Robert Magee, the Keith I. DeLashmutt Distinguished Professor of Accounting Information and Management, agreed.

"Most of the people who don't get tenure here get other academic jobs at schools that are a notch down from Kellogg, on average, though we've had people go to other very good schools too," said Magee, who has been a part of the school's Personnel Committee for more than a decade and who served as senior associate dean for faculty and research from 2001 to 2005. "They have good prospects, but we don't grant tenure on the basis of prospects. We grant it based on accomplishments."[114]

Magee described the Personnel Committee as the centerpiece of the school's tenure and promotion process. Consisting of six full professors, one from each of the school's six academic departments, the committee also is composed of the Kellogg dean and the senior associate deans. When considering a tenure candidate, the committee also forms an ad hoc committee consisting of three people, one from the candidate's department, another from a second department and a third person (the ad hoc chair) from the Personnel Committee, who is also from outside the candidate's department. "You want a variety of perspectives," said Magee. "You try to find a committee that's going to be able to read the work and evaluate it. That's the objective."

During the process, which includes rigorous internal and external reviews of the candidate's teaching and research, the committee members solicit outside letters for evaluating the candidate's work. The candidate and the Ad Hoc Committee both choose the sources for these letters, said Magee.

The Ad Hoc Committee then takes the internal and external evaluations, plus its own evaluation, and creates a report for the Personnel Committee to review along with all the other supporting materials, such as the candidate's research portfolio and teaching evaluations. The Ad Hoc Committee presents the case to the Personnel Committee, after which the two Ad Hoc members who are not also members of the Personnel Committee are excused. What follows is a discussion and vote among members of the Personnel Committee.

That vote is a recommendation to the dean, said Magee. The dean then takes that recommendation, as well as his own hearing of the case, and makes a recommendation to the university provost, who in turn makes his own recommendation to the Board of Trustees. The review at central administration is "not a rubber stamp," Magee noted, but by the time the process reaches the trustees, they tend to trust the committee's assessment.

Most professional services firms—such as accounting and law firms—have an up-or-out policy, said Magee. "You either get admitted to the partnership or not. Tenure effectively means we're making a career-long commitment to you. That's something that's not given lightly. We have a limited size of faculty. We don't need a thousand faculty members here, so you want to make sure you are getting the people who will contribute intellectually, both in their research and in the classroom, to contribute to the continued vitality of the school."[115]

Schwartz Memorial Lecture and Oh Be Joyful Build Community

Those who work under the rigors of the tenure process and the high standards to which Kellogg holds its faculty members are rewarded in any number of ways, including with a culture that offers a rich research life and social engagement. These opportunities are exemplified by long-standing traditions such as the Nancy L. Schwartz Memorial Lecture series and the annual Oh Be Joyful event, a ceremony and dinner recognizing the school's staff and faculty.

Established in 1983 by family, friends and colleagues in honor of the late Nancy Schwartz,[116] who joined Kellogg in 1970 and was the first woman to be appointed to an endowed chair at the school, the lecture series attracts extraordinary scholars in the field of economics. The inaugural lecturer was Hugo Sonnenschein, then a Princeton University economics professor who would later serve as president of the University of Chicago (1993–2000). Other speakers have included Nobel Laureates Robert C. Merton, Daniel Kahneman, Joseph E. Stiglitz, Kenneth J. Arrow and Robert J. Aumann. In all, nine Nobel Prize winners have delivered papers at the lecture series, most of them having earned the honor after speaking at Kellogg.

"This shows we pick serious people doing good work who later end up winning the prize," said Ehud Kalai, the James J. O'Connor Distinguished Professor of Decision and Game Sciences and the director of the Center for Game Theory and Economic Behavior at Kellogg.[117]

Besanko, a former student of Schwartz's, recalled her as "a wonderful person" and dedicated teacher always looking out for her pupils:

> I remember applying for a Sloan Fellowship at the end of my third year. I had to write a 15-page proposal and gave it to all my advisers. I gave this to Nancy and within two hours it was back on my desk completely marked up

in red. She really cared about her students, about all the PhD students. . . . She was totally on top of things. She was a great mentor and a wonderful scholar. We used her book written with Mort [Kamien] in our class. Truly pathbreaking work. No one at that time [early and mid-1970s] was using the tools of dynamic optimization to explain problems. Economic theory, for the most part, was fairly static. Mort and Nancy were pushing a huge frontier forward in the work that they did, particularly on R&D, and other topics as well.[118]

Equally important for the school's inclusive community is the annual Oh Be Joyful celebration. Held each summer, the event features a detailed recognition ceremony for faculty and staff, followed by a formal dinner reception. Established in 1984 by Dean Jacobs after he became aware of a similar event at Unilever Corporation, Oh Be Joyful is a chance for the school's leadership to report on the year's academic and other highlights and recognize members of its community for their accomplishments, which range from research production and teaching excellence to administrative service. Among the honors bestowed at the event are awards such as the L. G. Lavengood Professor of the Year Award (see chapter 6 for additional details on research and teaching awards and their importance to the school's academic life). Another tradition, the Annual Dean's Brunch, is held near the start of each academic year, bringing together faculty and staff.

Campaign for Kellogg

All the academic advances that began in the 1970s represented the vanguard of an effort to consolidate gains in research and teaching that became public in 1987—the Campaign for Kellogg. The two-year fund-raising push was designed to position Kellogg for a leadership position over the next decade. The campaign's initial target was $25 million, a figure subsequently raised to $35 million due to many early successes, according to Jacobs, who shared the news with the graduating class of 1986. The campaign's broad goals included funding faculty and research, providing student assistance and curriculum renewal and supporting executive education. More specifically, the effort sought to fund at least seven new endowed professorships in a range of fields, at $1 million each. Another dozen endowed research professorships were also included in the target, as were several research centers, to be endowed with at least $3 million. Scholarships and loan support were also part of the school's agenda, with some $5 million targeted to expand these recruiting tools. With respect to curriculum enhancement, Kellogg sought funds to enable the faculty to create, test and implement new courses and programs. Finally, the growing demand for executive education at the Allen Center inspired an effort to fund a major addition to the building—the H. Wendell and Elinor Hobbs Hall—which would expand existing capacity by 50 percent.[119] Hobbs Hall would feature a glass-enclosed octagonal atrium for dining and meetings, a classroom that could accommodate up to 120 executives, 18 breakout rooms, 36 bedrooms and new lounges and recreational areas. Construction began in February 1986 and was completed in the fall of 1987.[120]

The Campaign for Kellogg effort was led by a group of business leaders and alumni, including William Smithburg, who chaired the executive committee. Among the two dozen committee members were: Robert H. Beeby '59, president and CEO of Pepsi-Cola International; James F. Beré '52, chairman of Borg-Warner Corporation; Raymond F. Farley '51, president and chief operating officer (COO) of S. C. Johnson & Son, Inc.; Michael Miles, president and COO of Kraft Foods Inc.; James J. O'Connor, chairman, CEO and president of Commonwealth Edison Company; Patrick G. Ryan '59, CEO and president of Combined International Corporation; and Walter D. Scott '53, chairman of GrandMet USA, Inc.

"Kellogg has become the standard-bearer for management education," said Smithburg. "The pioneering research conducted at Kellogg is of enormous value to management, in both the short and long run. In executive education, Kellogg is the role model for other leading schools of business."[121]

By the time the campaign officially closed on May 4, 1989, it had raised a total of $40,176,068, far outdistancing original and even revised expectations. Put to work, the funds created 18 endowed chairs, 9 research professorships, 4 research centers and 38 scholarship funds, and with the addition of Hobbs Hall, it doubled the Allen Center's capacity to deliver executive education programming.[122] "Simply put, the intellectual thrust that Kellogg has achieved through the Campaign will imprint for decades the field of business education," said Smithburg.[123]

Northwestern president Arnold Weber (1985–1994) recalled the campaign's impressive results, as well as Jacobs's talent for fund-raising. Weber's administration had been tasked with returning fiscal strength to the university, which had suffered some financial setbacks in the years prior to his tenure. Like Kellogg leaders, Weber sought to "raise [university] expectations and advance academics," leveraging good fiscal planning to achieve the objective. He said, with a laugh, that Jacobs, though never actually articulating it, communicated to the central administration that "I'm better [at fund-raising] than the rest of you klutzes."[124]

"Don really deserves 98 percent of the credit; the rest I'll give to the climate and the gods," said Weber, who, prior to serving at Northwestern, had been on the faculty at the University of Chicago for 14 years, as well as assistant secretary of labor in the Nixon administration. "Don was building the brand equity. You get better students, you attract better faculty, and you also build a constituency for the university. Don also built a cadre of supporters from the business community. He did that with his advisory committee. He was sweeping the board as they say in billiards: He was raising the quality of the students, raising the quality of the faculty and research, and building the external cohort."

PART 2

King Kellogg: 1988, a Year of Renown

In the middle of the campaign, another boon occurred, one that would help shape the Kellogg School's fortunes significantly afterward. A high-profile cover story in *BusinessWeek* proclaimed Kellogg the nation's best business school. "A dark horse wins—and some prestigious rivals stumble," noted the article.[125]

Although earlier surveys had boosted the school's prominence, the 1988 ranking in *BusinessWeek* proved most influential. The magazine's inaugural survey shook the management world with news that a formerly middling midwestern business institution was providing the best management education in the United States. What differentiated this investigation from other previous efforts was that *BusinessWeek* turned to "customers"—recruiters, students—who actually used the schools' services, rather than soliciting responses from business school deans or faculty, as had typically been done in the past. Previous surveys also had placed much emphasis on professors' reputations and their published research. "There's no disputing that research is vital both to a school and to American business," the *BusinessWeek* writer stated. "But traditional surveys may not fully reflect a school's teaching excellence, its curriculum, or the value of its graduates to Corporate America."[126] (Indeed, Kellogg was pursuing both academic rigor and a customer focus: in 1988, for instance, Professor Ehud Kalai founded the prestigious journal *Games and Economic Behavior,* consolidating the school's trailblazing approach to using game theory in a business context. In 1990, finance professor Stuart Greenbaum founded the *Journal of Financial Intermediation,* and the following year saw Professor Daniel Spulber launch the *Journal of Economics and Management Strategy* at Kellogg.)[127]

The survey asked recent graduates to assess their schools according to 35 characteristics, ranging from the quality of courses to the overall environment to the efficacy of the school's placement offices. A total of 1,245 graduates and 112 corporate recruiters responded. Kellogg placed first overall, followed by Harvard, Dartmouth, Wharton and Cornell. The school earned top marks with recruiters, especially in marketing and general management. The curriculum and the placement office were among the elements more highly regarded by class of 1988 graduates, followed by teaching quality. *BusinessWeek* noted the efforts Kellogg expended to discover the best students: "Northwestern is the only major school that interviews all its applicants—4,000 of them in one-hour sessions in places as far-flung as Tokyo and Kuala Lumpur."[128] The reasons for this extraordinary recruiting were tied to Jacobs's belief that "it's not possible to assess a person's composure, articulateness, or leadership ability from test scores or past grades," wrote the article's author. (Jacobs later elaborated on the practice: "We went about increasing the number of students, and since we weren't a high-ranked school, the way we would get students of quality was by interviewing everybody, something nobody else was doing. We were looking for the students that everyone else was missing.")[129] In addition, the article noted the Kellogg School's ability to raise funds for its efforts: "Jacobs has adeptly raised the cash to accomplish his goals."

Some students complained about inconsistent teaching quality despite giving excellent overall ratings to the school, but the administration pointed to the learning curve associated with hiring very talented, but young, professors—some 10 percent of the total faculty each year. These teachers generally became accomplished leaders in the classroom after a couple years of experience and mentorship from more senior Kellogg colleagues. In addition, Jacobs noted, students evaluated the professors, with the results posted publicly. "If you have a big ego," he told *BusinessWeek*, "you don't want to be at the bottom of any list."[130]

Included in the magazine's coverage was a selection of criticisms being leveled at business schools. Complaints ranged from Wharton and Stanford students' bemoaning poor teaching quality and limited curriculum variety to corporate recruiters' lamenting the absence of leadership and "people skills" in the average B-school program. Unlike most peers, Kellogg distinguished itself by having a prescient approach to teamwork, delivering exactly the kind of collaborative experience coupled with rigorous academic frameworks that recruiters were demanding.

Comments by Kellogg students participating in the survey were given to the school by *BusinessWeek*. One student remarked, "Kellogg did a great job of providing personal attention prior to enrolling, as well as throughout the two years of school. You felt wanted, appreciated and well cared for." Another student wrote: "The Kellogg program provided me with a balanced education that I do not feel I could have found elsewhere." Others noted the strength of the school's general management model and its overall curriculum, as well as its commitment to team-oriented learning—a quality that particularly distinguished Kellogg, according to the students.[131]

Carole Cahill recalled the atmosphere at the school when the rankings were announced. Physically, the Kellogg building was considerably smaller than it would become over time, and the school community was on edge, eagerly anticipating the results, which were not revealed to anyone in advance.

"This was huge. Huge," she said. "It was the first time we were No. 1 [in *BusinessWeek*][132] and it came out of nowhere." At that time, the school had one fax machine, located in Cahill's office. "Back then, they used rolled paper [Canon had introduced the first plain-paper fax machine only a year earlier], and when the rankings started coming in there was all this paper everywhere."[133] Cahill and her colleagues watched as sheet after sheet was transmitted with results: number twenty—University of Rochester; number nineteen—Yale; number eighteen—New York University. Tension mounted as the final 10 schools were counted down. Then the final 5. Still no mention of Northwestern. Either the Kellogg School had somehow been entirely left out of the rankings, which seemed unlikely, or it would be among the top three.

Number three—Dartmouth. Number two—Harvard.

It had happened. Kellogg was at the top of the management world. Jacobs's vision had taken the school from nowhere to everywhere.

"Everyone was hugging each other," Cahill remembered. "We grabbed up all the paper we could to start making copies and passing them out . . . to students gathered in O. L. Coon Forum, where Dean Jacobs addressed them."

People were ecstatic. Somebody made an oversized reproduction of the *BusinessWeek* cover that announced the rankings. The school had scheduled an Advisory Council meeting that day, directly after the rankings were announced. "There was a planeload of advisory members flying in on one of the corporate jets," said Jacobs. "When they heard the news, they started to celebrate."[134] Upon arriving in Evanston, the group convened in the Orrington Hotel for a party, since the school's quarters were too cramped at the time.

Advisory Council member James McManus recalled that the excitement surrounding the rankings news spread beyond the students and into the alumni community. "I think we'd been suffering from something of an inferiority complex until then, especially with regard to some of the East Coast schools."[135]

President Weber remembered that "everyone was on a big high" that day, since the rankings were a confirmation of the administration's hard work. Jacobs in particular had "taken Kellogg from an also-ran to one of the best schools in the country."[136] Seeking to put the matter in sober perspective, the president emeritus added: "In Weber's Law, all these rankings are specious, misleading and erroneous . . . except when you're No. 1. Then you say about the rankings, 'What brilliant insight!'"[137]

What impressed current Northwestern president Henry Bienen about the Kellogg School's rise to international fame was how it happened. "It was done on a financial base that was slimmer in terms of endowment than a lot of competing business schools," said Bienen, who assumed his role in 1995 after serving as dean of Princeton's Woodrow Wilson School of Public and International Affairs. "It had this very excellent executive education program, which gave it a lot of cash flow." What's more, he noted, Kellogg proved to be an inspiration for the entire university.

"When I came here, I did see Kellogg as a kind of model of how to succeed. Not necessarily that you would replicate how Kellogg did it, because in some ways how it did it was peculiar to a business school," said Bienen. "But that you could be that good, that Northwestern could have the best business school in the country. The university could do it and make big strides. I saw Kellogg as really having a special place by virtue of being so strong. It was a kind of beacon that said Northwestern could be really successful."[138]

Jacobs had always noted that faculty members create an institution's reputation, but he also appreciated the ranking's importance in publicizing the school to a large external audience—and he understood well the role that publicity played in boosting recruitment. Positive PR was especially important to a school like Northwestern, he said, since it lacked the "halo effect" enjoyed by schools that were part of "brand name" universities with long histories, such as Harvard and Stanford. "We were a different class of school at that time," said Jacobs. Indeed, the rankings resulted in a flurry of applications and inquiries, with more than 50 new companies asking to participate in on-campus interviewing.[139] Steven DeKrey '84, director of admissions and financial aid at the time, had to add two telephone lines and hire several temporary workers to handle the unprecedented volume of interest in the school after the rankings were released. He anticipated receiving 4,000 applicants for enrollment in 1989, up by nearly 400 from the previous year. Similarly, the school's Part-Time MBA Program experienced an increase in the percentage of applicants who were admitted and enrolled: the yield following the rankings release was 92 percent, compared with 75 percent for the year before.[140]

The Kellogg School's administration attributed its rankings success to a combination of academic rigor, business relevance and attention to students. This "customer focus" did not always meet with approval from peer schools that believed the administration always knew best and that students, though of course the institution's raison d'être, occupied a secondary role in the school hierarchy. At Kellogg, the students had long been embraced as cocontributors to the school's culture. Now, that approach was paying off with publicity far beyond the school itself.

With the rankings win, Jacobs, not content to rest on any laurels, was already looking ahead. He and his administration were posing questions about where to take the school next. The questions were easier to devise than the answers, he admitted, but he recounted the importance of academic research and teaching and anticipated that these would continue to guide the school's progress, especially as complex challenges, such as government-business relationships, seemed likely to persist. (In particular, he noted the challenges of deregulation.)

"How far can we stretch our curriculum? I am often asked, shouldn't we open a special center for ethics studies?" said Jacobs. "Or one for international business? Should there be a separate focus on Europe? Or Asia? Or the new capital markets? Or the communist turn to capitalism? As the list grows, our challenge is to continue to teach the core principles that will serve the manager and his or her organization best, over time, against a background of change."[141]

Alongside the questions were some certainties about what the school had already accomplished. In particular, the Kellogg model of collaboration was producing major benefits, said Jacobs, which was demonstrated in the school's willingness to "embrace and produce change in the classroom, where students are radiating a new spirit of cooperation." This model, the school leaders believed, was suited to contemporary management practice, just as the general management focus provided "a framework for decision-making that will stand up over time and across fields," he said. The school's collaborative culture eschewed "cutthroat competition, because we believe team players are better managers of modern organizations than are single combat warriors."[142]

Many of the points raised by Jacobs would be among the initiatives subsequently addressed by the school. In particular, international business and regional focuses in Asia, Europe and the Middle East would, by the middle of the 1990s, result in academic partnerships that advanced the school's global presence.

The Kellogg School's success in continuing to build its academic strengths would become apparent with subsequent rankings surveys. The school once again earned the number one spot from *BusinessWeek* in 1990 and 1992. It would remain in the top three continuously, again landing at number one in 2002 and 2004, as well as earning number one marks from the Economist Intelligence Unit, the parent of the *Economist* magazine, each year from 2002 to 2004. In 1990, *US News & World Report* and *BusinessWeek* began ranking executive MBA programs, and both named Kellogg number one that year,[143] and the school's EMBA program has retained that distinction ever since. "The balance between an in-depth academic experience and a welcoming culture is what once again put Kellogg at the top," said *BusinessWeek* in announcing that Kellogg was the top school in 2004.

"We've done what we said we were going to do. I'm very proud of that," said Jacobs.

Management Crisis, but Kellogg Stays ahead of the Pack

During much of the 1980s, business school graduates enjoyed plentiful and secure professional opportunities, particularly those who ventured into the financial sector. So pervasive were these lucrative opportunities that the stories of certain banking and investment moguls gave rise to dramatic Hollywood treatments; films such as Oliver Stone's *Wall Street* (1987) portrayed the archetypal 1980s excess as seen through the characters of ambitious stockbrokers and unscrupulous corporate raiders. The film's Gordon Gekko was said to be based loosely on Carl Icahn and Ivan Boesky, whose well-known speech on greed, delivered at the University of California in 1986, became modified as Gekko's "greed is good" argument in *Wall Street*.[144]

The 1990s began with an economic recession that some believe was at least a partial result of slowdowns in the finance industry and the real estate market in the wake of a wave of savings and loan association failures in the 1980s. In response to these failures, estimated to total some $160 billion, the U.S. government subsidized the majority of the cost required to rescue the Federal Savings and Loan Insurance Corporation, which in turn resulted in large government budget deficits.[145]

Not surprisingly, along with this larger economic crisis came doubts about the ethics of those graduating from management programs. Questions arose about the value of hiring these people. Did they deserve the high salaries they demanded? Was it worth putting up with the sense of entitlement that some graduates displayed? Did they even have the skills necessary to contribute meaningfully in the contemporary business world?

Such hand-wringing was expressed in articles in numerous mainstream and industry journals, from the *Economist, Fortune* and *BusinessWeek* to *Management Review* and *Incentive*. Making matters worse, the lure of Wall Street had apparently produced a glut of MBA graduates in the early 1990s. Some 70,000 were produced in 1992 alone, and half of them were not bothering to look for work because of the recession and the fallout from the banking crisis.[146]

"In the past 10 years, business schools have focused mainly on finance, but now everyone recognizes that as too one-dimensional," said Ambar G. Rao, operations research professor at the Stern School of Business. "With bank failures and the problems on Wall Street, there's going to be more of a demand for people who can go into other industries."[147] "The heady days are over for business schools," claimed *BusinessWeek* in 1993, noting that experimentation and innovation were the new order of the day as schools—particularly those outside the top 20—fought to remain relevant.[148] The *Chicago Tribune* ran a story headlined BUSINESS BACKLASH SNARES

MBA's IN CATCH-22. The article traced some of the changes affecting business graduates in the early 1990s and compared the situation to that just a few years earlier. "In the late 1980s a booming economy turned the ivory towers of business schools to gold. Their graduates were received like royalty, showered with huge salaries, penthouse offices and stretch limos. They swelled corporate bureaucracies—and expenses. Now the boom has gone bust." The *Tribune* noted a "seismic shift" in the economy had resulted in tens of thousands of white-collar workers losing their jobs as firms cut budgets and realigned their organizations to become leaner.[149]

In an article titled "Shaking Up the MBA," the *Chronicle of Higher Education* highlighted the changes that business schools were proclaiming, though some skeptics called them modest or superficial. Among the recurring themes in these reports was the need for MBA graduates who possessed so-called people skills—the ability to communicate and lead in teams. "Confronted by a steep decline in student demand, as well as by corporate complaints that MBA programs have failed to keep up with a rapidly changing world, the schools have become caught up in a high-profile struggle for status and market share."[150]

Some critics suggested that management education needed radical change and a massive overhaul of its curricula. "These days, the business of business schools is change. Not tinkering, tweaking alterations, but radical, revolutionary experimentation," noted *BusinessWeek* in a 1992 profile of the best U.S. business schools.[151]

But one dean was not rushing to dramatically alter his school's curriculum. "If a business school's curriculum was that far out of date, why did it push so many students through it?" Donald Jacobs asked *BusinessWeek*. "I find it terribly embarrassing."

The Kellogg School could afford to adopt such a view. For one thing, it had just garnered the number one ranking for the third consecutive time in *BusinessWeek*'s list of the best graduate schools of business.

"The award is a reaffirmation of what we all know," Jacobs told the *Daily Northwestern*. "Kellogg is a place with wonderful students, a remarkable, world-class faculty, great programs—and we're housed in a fantastically wonderful university."[152]

"The award is even better than the last time because it demonstrates that we haven't rested on our laurels," said Marc Landsberg '89, assistant to the dean and Graduate Management Association president in 1988. "We've continued to do what we do well even better."[153]

Indeed, the school was ahead of the curve compared to most of its peers. It had long made a point of connecting theory and practice to produce graduates with an understanding of and ability to solve real-world problems. It also, for more than a decade, had emphasized the collaborative, team-oriented skills that were starting to grab mainstream headlines in the early 1990s. "Group work fosters a team feeling and brings out the best in people," said Luke Parker '93, president of the Kellogg Graduate Management Association. "We really learn from each other."[154]

And even earlier, the school had broadened its management focus to train people for a variety of careers—whether in public policy and government, in for-profit corporations or in nonprofit organizations. That change began in the early 1970s.

So Kellogg was perfectly prepared to answer the complaints of some, such as the editors of the *Economist* who wondered in 1991, "Have business schools lost touch with business?" Although admitting the impact of the economic recession on hiring, the *Economist* editorial claimed that "an increasing number of employers are starting to ask what they are getting for the premium they pay to MBA graduates . . . [and] firms do not want the sort of academic specialists that business schools tend to produce; they want graduates with a broad range of management skills who know how to apply them to real business problems."[155]

The Kellogg dean was quick to point out how management education finally had caught up with the direction the school had traveled since 1975. "Imitation is the best form of flattery, and they are all coming in my direction," Jacobs told *BusinessWeek.*[156]

Despite its many strengths, the school was continuously aware of opportunities to enhance its curriculum, paying close attention to its student "customers" and recruiters. For example, in 1992, Kellogg formed an innovative partnership with Northwestern's McCormick School of Engineering and Applied Science, launching a joint-degree program to leverage the strengths of the MBA with product design and technology skills. The Master of Management and Manufacturing (MMM) Program has a unique focus that attracts a range of students interested in working alongside faculty to turn technological breakthroughs into sound business proposals, while gaining the skills needed to lead product-driven businesses. The majority of applicants to the program have an engineering background, although students with business backgrounds who have worked in manufacturing are also accepted. The curriculum includes both a manufacturing core and a management core, teaching students leadership, accounting, business strategy and logistics, as well as technology and manufacturing. Among the highlights is a capstone course, "The Integration Project," which requires second-year students to take an entrepreneurial approach to problem solving by serving as consultants to leading manufacturing companies or by developing a business venture based on a new product. Classroom experience is complemented by visits to domestic and overseas manufacturing facilities, conferences and extracurricular activities and clubs. Originally, MMM emphasized quality management, but market emphasis near the turn of the twenty-first century would guide modifications to the curriculum, including a new focus on supply chain management. (The school would also continue developing its curriculum in entrepreneurship—see chapter 6.)

The school had already begun taking steps to export its leadership with initiatives such as its Sasin partnership in Thailand, as well as through efforts spearheaded by Bala Balachandran, the J. L. Kellogg Distinguished Professor of Accounting Information and Management. Chairman of the Accounting Department at Kellogg from 1979 to 1983, Balachandran began his teaching career in 1960 while a graduate student at Annamalai University in India, where he earned a master's degree in mathematics/statistics; he earned his doctorate in industrial administration from Carnegie Mellon University in 1973 before joining Northwestern's business school that year. In addition to helping organize and lead the inaugural Indian Business Conference at Kellogg in 1992, he was successful in securing more than $500,000 in funding from the United Nations Development Programme to support the establishment of the Management Development Institute in Gurgaon, India, between 1991 and 1992. There, his leadership was instrumental in producing the "Train the Trainer" module. Similarly, he later would be critical in founding the Chennai-based Great Lakes Institute of Management (2004) and the Indian School of Business (ISB) in Hyderabad (1999).

By the middle of the 1990s, Kellogg would bolster its international focus with joint-degree executive MBA offerings established with partners in the Middle East, Europe and Asia. The school set up programs with the Leon Recanati Graduate School of Business at Tel Aviv University (1996), the Otto Beisheim School of Management at Koblenz School of Corporate Management in Vallendar, Germany (1997) and the Business School at the Hong Kong University of Science and Technology (1998). A subsequent partnership arose in 2002 with the Schulich School of Business in Toronto, Canada. Alliances with schools in Thailand, Japan, China and India further expanded this global reach.

The program, said Jacobs at the time, "promised very important advantages to us. It meant working with a group of institutions around the world where we had long relationships, but we were able to solidify those relationships in a segment of the market where we have a great deal of expertise."[157]

These partnerships, based on the school's Executive MBA Program format, have created an integrated global portfolio that has allowed the school to build an international network of MBA students, all fluent in the common Kellogg language of academic excellence, team leadership and the power of diversity. The partnerships have resulted in a unique relationship between Kellogg and the alliance schools, said Steve DeKrey, associate dean and director of the Hong Kong program. "This [arrangement] has created a network of partners who all hold the Kellogg values and aspire to the Kellogg culture," he noted. "Yet partners have the freedom to adapt to cultures away from the 'mother school,' providing the best of two worlds. . . . The freedom to adapt our curriculums and administrative approaches to our regional markets is key, as is the inspiration and . . . high standards set by Kellogg faculty and administration."[158]

Israel Zang, academic director for the Kellogg-Recanati program, agreed, saying the partnership model made sense from both curricular and cultural standpoints, as well as from a strategic or operational perspective. "It allows mixing of Kellogg expertise, experience and culture with those of the partners," he said. "By teaming up with leading schools worldwide, Kellogg can better leverage its resources and influence more people, enhancing an international network of executive alumni."[159]

Erica Kantor, assistant dean of executive education, was associate director of the Executive MBA Program when the Recanati partnership was created. She recalled the way the administration of the two schools sought to address obvious political concerns that surrounded the Middle East program. The Kellogg-Recanati program "was an attempt to create a place and a classroom where different groups from all over the Middle East could come together and have one common goal—to learn about doing business," said Kantor, who went on to serve as the EMBA director from 1999 to 2003. "Don Jacobs and Recanati Dean Israel Zang created an environment that required students to leave their political beliefs at the door and work together in the classroom," she added. "Teamwork took on a whole new meaning."[160]

By pursuing these partnerships, Kellogg has transformed itself, in a mere three decades, from a local enterprise in Evanston to a globe-spanning network that offers top-ranked leadership education on several continents.

Before this portfolio even developed, however, Kellogg had enjoyed a decade of success in its partnership with the Sasin Graduate Institute of Business at Chulalongkorn University in Bangkok, established in 1982 as the Graduate Institute of Business Administration.[161] The venture, a partnership with the Wharton School at the University of Pennsylvania, has flourished despite an inauspicious start: Khun Bancha Lamsan, of the Thai Farmers Bank, and Toemsakdi Krishnamra, former dean of Chulalongkorn, had traveled 8,500 miles to visit Jacobs and pitch their idea for a partnership. Jacobs was interested, but he knew that other schools had failed at similar ventures. Undeterred, the Thai representatives arranged a meeting with the dean to discuss the proposal in more detail. But after their night in an aging downtown hotel, the two men were lucky to arrive on campus.

"That night there was a snowstorm," said Jacobs. "Toemsakdi walked in the next morning and there was Khun Bancha—this very handsome, elderly Thai gentleman—[who had been] in bed covered with about two inches of snow that had come in through a window that was stuck open." The persistence of the Thai men won Jacobs over, and a handshake that day began a formal partnership.[162]

More recently, Toemsakdi has remarked: "It would not be wrong to say that the Sasin program is in fact 'Dean Jacobs' program' in Thailand. We in Thailand certainly had no experience running an MBA school, so he had to hold our hand and guide us all the way through. We are thankful that he did so with grace and vigor."[163]

Jacobs and Duncan flew to Bangkok to consult with administrators there regarding the curriculum and faculty, and Thai administrators also visited Evanston. The plans included 5-week modules taught by Kellogg professors whose instruction would form part of a portfolio that also incorporated the work of Wharton and Chulalongkorn faculty members. The curriculum would resemble that of Kellogg and of Wharton but feature modifications that added special value for students seeking knowledge about management practice in Southeast Asia. All courses would also be conducted in English, with an emphasis on students developing proficiency in the language. The venture enjoyed the financial backing of Thai businesses, financial institutions and public organizations, with the additional support of foundations and businesses outside the country. The initial class had 35 students, selected from a total of 128 prospects who were screened by a Kellogg admissions team that included Ed Wilson and Dianne Dardes.[164]

By the turn of the twenty-first century, Jacobs was proud to note that "the sun never sets on Kellogg," since at any time of the day "someone, somewhere is working on a Kellogg degree in one of our programs."

Student-Centric Culture Takes Kellogg Places

An academic innovation launched in 1989 exemplified both the Kellogg School's student-centric culture as well as its desire to expand its international business and leadership offerings, as many in the press and corporate world had been suggesting business schools should do.

What has become a cornerstone of the Kellogg School's international curriculum, the Global Initiatives in Management (GIM, pronounced *jim*) Program began in the 1989–1990 academic year when a group of students organized a course and a 2-week trip to what was then the Soviet Union. Since that time, the program has expanded greatly. Today, more than 400 students—about two-thirds of each Kellogg class—participate annually in the program, as do the students in the school's Part-Time and Executive MBA Programs.

The GIM Program is an intensive global business leadership offering designed by students. Teams of classmates plan and facilitate a challenging 10-week curriculum with a faculty adviser and coordinate a 2-week international field experience. GIM students and their faculty advisers work in teams on research projects in a country and industry of their choice, developing analyses through lectures from country and industry experts, extensive background studies and firsthand field research. By participating in GIM, students gain valuable leadership skills and enhance their awareness of the global business environment.

"We put the first class together with no great vision of what it would grow into," said Sandy Haviland '90, who was among the student leaders who helped create GIM. "Our objective was simply to get us into places where things were happening, to go beyond the academics and theory and really interact. We're incredibly proud and excited to see how the program has grown," said Haviland, now president of Haviland & Company, a financial services firm in Connecticut.[165]

Jacobs recalled the importance of student leadership in developing the course and in helping inspire the school's faculty members to learn more about Eastern Europe, an area that the school had little exposure to at the time. "GIM was a student idea," said Jacobs. "We wanted to create a permission-granting culture that demonstrates respect for the students, that demonstrates collegiality. We feel they are our colleagues."[166]

The dean expressed some initial concerns, despite being intrigued. "Sandy came into my office and said, 'The Berlin Wall has come down and there's all this happening in Eastern Europe and we want to be part of it,'" Jacobs recalled. "He wanted a student-driven, student-organized trip. We said 'OK, but there ought to be some faculty who go along with you.' We were worried about the volatility in Russia at the time, and we wanted to be able to guarantee the students' safety."[167]

Myron Roomkin, then chair of the Policy and Environment Department, where the international business major was housed, recalled Haviland making initial contact with him to assess the viability of this sort of field research. At the time, said Roomkin, the school's curriculum had a modest focus on international business, with much room to develop the subject area. "Haviland came to see me and said 'The Soviet Union is falling apart and we should have a class on that.' And I said, 'Sure, let's have one,'" Roomkin recalled. Haviland pushed for a student visit to the country, he continued, "and I said, 'Sure! You go find a professor who is willing to teach the class and we'll have a class.' This is what the Kellogg curriculum is all about: flexibility and being able to go after the current issues."[168]

Haviland, along with peers (including Dennis Valdes '90, president-elect of the student government), refined their initial proposal and sought faculty assistance; accordingly, he approached Katharine Rockett, an economist in the Policy and Environment Department. "Turns out she had a master's degree in soviet studies and spoke Russian fluently," said Roomkin. However, personal reasons prohibited Rockett (now on the faculty of the University of Essex) from traveling. Stepping into the leadership role instead was Walter D. Scott, professor of management, who embraced the program's idea and, according to Roomkin, leveraged his contacts at

American Express to help finance the inaugural trip. In fact, Scott recalled traveling to Russia about a week before the students arrived, "to set up some meetings and ensure the success of the program."[169]

Scott became the program's first faculty coordinator, outlining the objectives and noting that the course helped expand student perspectives. "They . . . gain an understanding of the need to listen and not apply pat American solutions to business issues in other countries," Scott said in 1991. Students also benefited by gaining a "sensitivity to local cultures and market characteristics" and learned the need for "patience and persistence, because it may take years to succeed in some markets," he added.[170]

The success of the initial excursion quickly generated enthusiasm among the students, remembered Roomkin:

> The next year, other groups coalesced and wanted to go to two other countries. The dean calls me in and says, "What the hell's going on? . . . Do me a favor and take over this thing and regularize it." Out of this came the GIM Program, and the dean got behind it big time because he realized that this was the way that Kellogg could create some defining distinctiveness in international business. No one else had these things. . . . We were literally the first ones to do this on the scale we did. It very quickly became virtually a required elective for the first-year students.[171]

Indeed, the course was soon running smoothly and proved an immediate success with students: participation jumped eightfold from an initial 30 students to nearly a quarter of the class by 1992. "The program is quintessential Kellogg," Jacobs said at the time.[172] Students expressed excitement at the hands-on learning opportunities. "You can read about international business in a magazine, but you actually have to do business in another country to know what it's all about," said Dan Vinh, a student organizer for a 1992 excursion to Thailand.[173] GIM offered a chance to meld classroom insights with real-world situations. It also afforded some unexpected leadership opportunities. David Bardach '91 was among those on the first GIM trip when he suddenly found himself standing before 150 Soviet physicians who wanted to know all about Kellogg and why the students were visiting the Soviet Union. Bardach had been attending a family-planning conference there, researching his project on the nation's contraceptive market. He and a fellow student ended up giving an impromptu lecture, through an interpreter.[174]

Anthologies compiling student research from the GIM Program have been produced in recent years. *Kellogg on Global Issues in Management: Building Competitive*

Advantage in Global Markets (2002) explores the managerial challenges of operating in an evolving global market, animating the discussion by examining the innovative approaches some firms have developed. The text, edited by Kellogg School associate professor Anuradha Dayal-Gulati, comprises some of the best reports written by MBA students in the GIM course. The resulting anthology focuses on strategic business issues related to China and Latin America but also includes studies of the European Union, Russia and Africa. A second text, *Kellogg on China: Strategies for Success* (2004), continues the student-faculty collaboration by presenting GIM-related research that seeks to understand the complexities and implications of contemporary sociopolitical change in China. The text was coedited by Gulati and marketing professor Angela Y. Lee. Another text, *Kellogg on Biotechnology: Thriving through Integration* (2005), pursues a similar collaborative strategy between faculty and students, leveraging insights garnered from the experiential course known as "TechVenture," which took students on field excursions to high-tech companies in the Bay Area (see chapter 6). *Kellogg on Biotechnology* was edited by Professor Alicia Löffler. Earlier collaborative texts include *Kellogg on Innovation and Technology* (2002) and *TechVenture: New Rules on Value and Profit from Silicon Valley* (2001). Both texts were edited by Professors Ranjay Gulati, Mohanbir Sawhney and Anthony Paoni.

The GIM Program's recent director, Mark Finn, has said that the projects associated with the course impart real and lasting insights for students. "Students in GIM gain the ability to focus on an important business problem and analyze it," stated Finn, clinical professor of accounting information and management. "It's an extremely fascinating thing to do. You meet top-level people and interview them on a topic that's relevant to you personally and to your professional trajectory. It's something every Kellogg student ought to do at least once."[175]

The legacy of GIM has included more recent academic field research, including the Global Health Initiatives (GHI) Program, introduced in 2004 as a collaboration between Kellogg and the McCormick School of Engineering and Applied Science at Northwestern under the leadership of Professors David Kelso and Daniel Diermeier. Funded by a four-year, $4.9 million grant from the Bill and Melinda Gates Foundation in 2006, GHI has pursued the research and development of affordable diagnostic devices for testing and treating HIV in developing countries, including throughout Africa.

Kara Palamountain '04 and Aparna Saha '04 developed the Kellogg portion of the grant application for the program while earning their MBA degrees. Palamountain subsequently returned to the school as executive director of GHI, which she said focuses on solving critical problems in some of the world's poorest places.

"Not only are we developing processes and best practices for discovering what healthcare providers and people in developing countries need," she said, "but we are exposing future business leaders to issues facing the developing world."

Professor Diermeier observed that "there are unique problems in designing products for these markets because there is no existing market structure or understanding of the market."[176] To meet the challenge, GHI has built partnerships with industry and academic experts and nonprofit donors to research market dynamics, government issues and distribution channels to help develop diagnostic innovations for use in countries that have limited health care infrastructures. In addition, the goal is to help the citizens who cannot afford diagnostic devices as currently configured. For example, Palamountain noted, "existing HIV diagnostics often require a central lab with electricity, refrigeration, trained phlebotomists and lab technicians." GHI seeks to adjust these technologies for success in developing countries.

Kellogg students also have orchestrated a dozen or more annual academic conferences, addressing issues ranging from marketing to private equity to technology. In addition, they run some 130 student clubs, dedicated to any number of topics, from scholarly pursuits, such as the Investment Management Club, to leisure activities, such as skiing.

Special K Revue: B-school Broadway
Offers Lighthearted Leadership

Equally important to the students' contributions to the school's academic life have been their contributions to its social life. Of particular note is a 1980 innovation dubbed Special K Revue. A student-produced song-and-dance review involving dozens of talented students (and a few faculty and staff members) has grown into an annual extravaganza that is especially popular with alumni, which is why the sold-out performances have typically coincided with Reunion Weekend each spring. The show has even gone on the road, offering select performances for Kellogg alumni in New York City and San Francisco.

Poking fun at B-school life and ambitions, Special K is more than an amateur hour. Although the students in any given production may or may not have formal training or experience in theater, the show has, year in and year out, reflected the eclectic and ambitious abilities of those involved with it.

The origins of the initiative date to a 1979 comedy skit called "100 Animals" performed by Kellogg students William A. Jerome '80 and Frank McGann '80 at Northwestern's annual talent night, the long-running Waa-Mu Show. The skit, which suggested a novel way to use wildlife to improve the fortunes of the

Northwestern football team, was a hit—including with Ed Wilson, dean of students, who sent a memo to Jerome and McGann telling them that, in his view, "the entire audience found that number to be one of the best in the entire show."[177] Wilson's enthusiasm led to the students collaborating with him on adapting Waa-Mu so that its spirit could be imported as a Kellogg-specific performance. Jerome, who had written sketch comedy while a student at Princeton, credited Wilson with helping "create a . . . culture that stimulated and allowed students to pursue their passions and to consider new endeavors."[178]

To solicit talent from among their Kellogg peers, Jerome and his colleagues, including coproducer Betsy Stolte Youngdahl '81, simply placed an announcement in student mailboxes: "People ever mistake you for Charlton Heston?" the memo asked. "Well, if you can part the Red Sea or if you have trouble parting your hair, we want *you* to perform in the upcoming revue, UP FOR SALE."[179] Some 100 volunteers responded to write, direct, produce music, create costumes—anything and everything associated with the grassroots production.

On May 9 and 10, 1980, the students offered *Up for Sale*, a two-act performance with a scheduled running time of 120 minutes; it was similar in format to *Saturday Night Live*. The title was a lighthearted reference to the fact that the school had recently been renamed in honor of a $10 million gift. "Can a small school in a big city find happiness with a landfill on a big lake?" was the alternate title of Act 1, making a jibe about the Evanston campus, which had previously created a lakefill expansion to accommodate burgeoning enrollment in the 1970s.

One number, "Bummertime," recounted the efforts of the administration to raise the school's reputation against the competition:

> Bummer time—'cause our image is sinking
> Stanford's climbing and ol' Harvard is high
> Well, we don't publish those cases and we don't have nice weather
> So hey there Dean Jacobs, what should we try?[180]

At that point, Wilson recalled, Brian Curtis '80 went on stage pushing a wheelbarrow and holding a miniature version of Leverone Hall. "He was calling, 'School! School for sale!' It was just terrific. It brought the house down," said Wilson.[181]

The inaugural performance "surprised a lot of people with the quality of its material, the talents of its amateur cast, and the sheer improbability of getting it together at all given an academic load and severe time constraints," observed Lisa Weirich in a May 22, 1980, edition of the *Merger,* the Kellogg School's student newspaper.[182]

Other skits included parodies of group work, job searches, interviews, operations management and widgets. In one skit, "Good Morning," the CIM Week orientation experience was transformed into a quasi-military address performed by Associate Dean Pete Henderson, dressed as General George S. Patton. "Be seated," intoned Henderson, addressing an unseen audience from a podium. "Now, I want you to remember, no member of a marketing group ever got an 'A' by crunching all the numbers and doing all the work. He got it by making the OTHER poor dumb members crunch all the numbers and do all the work." The skit went on to describe all the ways a manager is an individual, rather than a member of a team—such as paying income taxes and playing golf.[183]

"It doesn't take much to start something new," wrote Jerome and Stolte in the program notes for *Up for Sale*. "You simply need initiative, drive, imagination, direction, and somebody else's idea." The codirectors took a moment to be somewhat more serious in outlining the initiative's intent: it was not meant to insult, nor necessarily entertain (though they hoped it would) or make money ("which we pray it might!") but simply to provide participants and the audience with a "slight diversion from the oft-time too serious approach to business and school. . . . Should the Revue become an annual event, we hope this will remain its prime emphasis—the development of friendships, fun and fantasy."[184]

Indeed, Special K did become a tradition, one that continues to this day. Subsequent efforts included appearances by faculty and staff. Lawrence Lavengood made a cameo appearance as "Yoplait," a Yoda look-alike, complete with robe and pointed ears, in a 1981 Special K parody of *Star Wars*. In the 1984 production, Wilson and Morton Kamien appeared as stage-hungry comics attempting to impress the show's producer. Wearing sunglasses, the duo performed a soft-shoe dance, saying, "You want clowns, we got clowns; you want deans, we got deans; you want fancy-schmancy economic theory—"[185]

More recently, Jerome expressed his delight that the tradition he helped create has continued to be an annual Kellogg event for more than a quarter century, bringing students together to share their talents while creating another kind of leadership opportunity at the school.

"We now have a tradition that lets students explore their talents and be the renaissance people we know they can be," said Jerome. "It's exciting, and it's also humbling to see where Special K is today. . . . It truly embodied the Kellogg spirit of teamwork."[186]

Passing the Baton: The "Dean of Deans" Steps Down

In 2000, Jacobs entered his twenty-fifth year as dean, an impressive feat so far unequaled in management education. His accomplishments had earned him widespread respect, as well as the sobriquet "the dean of deans."[187] Jacobs was quick to share credit for the school's success with others, citing the institution's team-oriented leadership model. That team, he said, included all the students, alumni, faculty, benefactors, Advisory Board members, Northwestern administrators, staff and various friends in the business world and academia.

"Kellogg is about people and the culture in which we work, study, teach and live," said the dean. "Kellogg is about innovative people who challenge each other to focus beyond the status quo—not as individuals, but as partners and colleagues."[188]

That year also saw yet another major expansion of the Kellogg School's facilities, as a new north wing was added to the Andersen/Leverone structure, creating a 240,000-square-foot edifice. Alumni and friends of the school raised more than $8 million for the addition, which benefited from student input regarding the design. Completed in 2001 as part of a $25 million project, the complex of three buildings was named the Donald P. Jacobs Center in 2000 to honor the dean's contributions over nearly a half century at the school. The Jacobs Center is equipped with 17 classrooms, more than 50 group-study rooms, conference rooms, quiet study areas and a student lounge, in addition to 2 cafés and the large central atrium, named in 2001 for Joseph Levy Jr. '47 and his spouse, Carole, longtime benefactors.[189]

The school would again renovate the building in the 2003–2004 academic year, at a cost of $3 million. Enhancements included expanding the Levy Atrium to accommodate about 80 more people. Seven classrooms were refurbished to include wood paneling or acoustic fabric panels, as well as new seating and enhanced audio-visual technology. Electronically controlled shades replaced window blinds. The school's café was also expanded, and its menu was augmented to include a range of quality food, including more fresh fare, such as fresh bread, paninis, grilled chicken and sushi, and 2 full-service gourmet coffee bars were added. These amenities were again revamped in 2007 to enhance quality and service. Most striking was the 2003–2004 renovation of a large student lounge on the main floor. This room would undergo further redesign in 2005 to create a "solarium" featuring an entire wall of glass overlooking Deering Meadow to the south.

In 2001, Jacobs was feted with a special celebration on May 6. A gala dinner in Northwestern's McGaw Memorial Hall brought together business leaders, associates, family and friends—more than 700 of them. People traveled from as far away as Japan, France, Germany, Israel, Hong Kong, Bangkok and the United Arab Emirates to honor Jacobs, who would retire as dean on July 1, 2001. He would remain a professor at Kellogg and would serve as director of the Zell Center for Risk Research at the school.

Jacobs said he had contemplated the decision to leave the deanship for nearly a year. The time had come for him to return to the faculty on a full-time basis, teaching and spending more time with students. "I feel I have devoted my full energies to this position," said Jacobs. "The time has come to step down from this leadership position."[190]

Praised for his intelligence, tenacity and vision in transforming Kellogg into one of the world's premier management education brands, Jacobs was honored by friends and colleagues throughout an evening that culminated in a video tribute produced by the Leo Burnett Company.

Each guest received a 112-page, hardbound book filled with hundreds of congratulatory letters and photographs highlighting the dean's career. Many of the notes recalled not only Jacobs's academic initiatives but also his warm personal attributes—especially his ability to leave an indelible impression on colleagues and their families.

When asked about the secret of his success in bringing Kellogg to the top of the management education world, Jacobs was typically frank and pithy. "The school was built with the belief in the way the world was going to be shaped, and it turned out to be correct. . . . The Allen Center was the core around which a lot of our accomplishments centered."[191]

Patrick Ryan '59, chairman and CEO of Aon Corporation and president of the Northwestern University Board of Trustees, served as master of ceremonies for the evening as eight esteemed guests recalled their memories of Jacobs's deanship and celebrated the man behind those professional achievements. Among the evening's testimonials to Jacobs were the remarks of Lawrence Lavengood, emeritus professor of business history:

> Don Jacobs is not only the remarkable head of the Kellogg family, but probably the senior dean in the world. While there's a staggering array of publicly observed effects associated with his deanship, there is also a less conspicuous side of Don Jacobs. Early in his tenure, Don took to speaking of the school's faculty and staff as family. He called us other things too, but his favorite reference was to family. He wanted to think of us as bound together, not only in a common enterprise, but in a kind of kinship that presumes mutual care. He created a community that regards itself and everyone in it with true affection.

Quipped Northwestern University president Henry Bienen, "I've worked for Don Jacobs for six years and he's one of the best bosses I've ever had." Alumni offered their perspectives as well, as in this remark by Wade Fetzer '61: "Don Jacobs is a risk-taker who doesn't believe in red tape. He can see around corners and moves quickly to address lacks. . . . Don has also been the architect of the school's open culture."[192]

Longtime colleague Stuart Greenbaum spoke of the professional influence Jacobs had on his own career. "Working with Don Jacobs was what gave me an appetite to be a dean," said Greenbaum, former dean of the John M. Olin School of Business at Washington University and emeritus Kellogg professor of finance. "I saw what you could accomplish, what value you could create. He's been a role model for me, and a mentor."[193]

Perhaps the one colleague who had worked most closely with Jacobs in the recent years was marketing professor Dipak C. Jain, who joined the school in 1987 and had served as associate dean since 1996. Jain, an indefatigable advocate for the school, said it had been a "wonderful experience" to work with Jacobs. He praised Jacobs's contributions to faculty development and intellectual growth at Kellogg. "Don has always emphasized that learning is a lifelong activity, and not only for business executives, but for faculty as well," said Jain. "I have learned a lot. He can discover the hidden skills of a faculty member to broaden that person and offer encouragement, pushing us in the right direction, away from the silos we work in." Jain concluded by saying: "Don's intuition is always right."

Very soon, Jain himself would have the chance to prove this claim. The day after the gala, it was announced that Jain would be the new dean of the Kellogg School. Said Northwestern provost Lawrence B. Dumas: "We had an extremely strong field of candidates for this position as a result of an exhaustive national search and Dipak Jain was the most outstanding of that group. The combination of his breadth of experience, his exceptional academic achievements and his strong management skills will enable Kellogg to continue its leadership in graduate business education."[194]

On July 1, Jain would be cast into the spotlight officially to follow perhaps the toughest act in all of academia.

The Kellogg School's eleventh dean, Dipak C. Jain,
is a marketing scholar and innovation expert.

Chapter 6

THE JOURNEY AHEAD:
DIPAK JAIN AND
THE FUTURE OF KELLOGG

A new century brought new challenges and a new leader for the Kellogg School: Dipak C. Jain. Consolidating the advances made by Donald Jacobs while delivering his own innovations, Jain would undertake the most ambitious global branding effort in the school's history, reaffirm the centrality of academics and dramatically enhance the alumni experience. He also found that a national crisis would mark his deanship and test his leadership almost immediately upon assuming his new office.

The young Indian mathematics scholar could have calculated the odds himself, and they weren't good.

It's a long way from Assam to Evanston, thought Dipak Jain. More than 8,000 miles, in fact, from the northeastern state in his home country of India. The distance must have seemed even greater when the 43-year-old recalled that his early education featured lessons in a small schoolhouse with a rough-hewn floor, where the children scratched words and numbers onto personal slates.[1] His grandfather had been a teacher and headmaster, so education was important to his family,[2] but material wealth and the opportunities that accompanied it were as intangible for him as the scent of the famous tea that wafted over the sloping fields of his hometown, Tezpur, India, whose 30,000 citizens knew few details of the larger world. "People would hear there is something called America and Europe," Jain has said. "But not many people know about it."[3]

Now, Northwestern president Henry Bienen was telling the mathematician-turned-marketing professor that the university trustees had named him the Kellogg School's new dean. His tenure would begin on July 1, 2001, just two months from the formal announcement on May 7.

This development was improbable for several reasons, including Jain's early quantitative, rather than commercial, focus.

Dipak Chan Jain had earned his bachelor's degree in 1976 from Darrang College, a small school in Tezpur notable for its academics and for being the site of His Holiness the Dalai Lama Tenzin Gyatso's first public appearance in 1959 after fleeing Tibet in the aftermath of a failed uprising against the Chinese government.[4] In 1978, Jain added to his credentials a master's degree in mathematical statistics from India's Gauhati University, a respected institution whose milewide campus was built in 1948 and is surrounded by hills on one side and water on the other. There, he embraced the spirit declared in Gauhati's motto, which, translated from the Sanskrit, means "Achievement through learning." University administrators were not unaware that the *Sri Isopanisad*, a text by a noted Indian philosopher, went so far as to declare that knowledge provided a vehicle through which immortality and personal perfection might arise. Such a background puts Jain's subsequent comments about education into perspective: he has called teaching a "religious devotion" and proclaimed that "at every stage in life you should have a learning mindset."[5]

Proving this thesis, Jain turned his mind to marketing during his doctoral training at the University of Texas–Dallas (UTD) in 1986, after having taught statistics, operations research and business administration at Gauhati for five years. He retains a letter dated April 1982 from UTD computer science professor R. Chandrasekaran inviting him to pursue graduate studies in the United States.[6] At UTD, Jain worked with prominent marketing scholar Frank M. Bass, known for his efforts to bring quantitative science to bear on the discipline. The Bass Diffusion Model, for instance, describes dynamics associated with new product adoption and has assumed an important role in forecasting.[7] Jain, who earned his management science degree from UTD in 1987, has called Bass a significant influence, a person who attracted him to marketing and away from operations research, which Jain said was becoming "very saturated" at the time.

That Jain made the journey from humble beginnings half a world away is remarkable enough. That he would go on to distinguish himself in the United States as a professor and leader of one of the world's most prestigious business schools—well, even those who recognized his prodigious talents, including his sharp, analytical mind and exceptional memory, might have placed other bets.

"I could never have imagined this," Jain said shortly after assuming the Kellogg deanship, the eleventh in the school's history.[8] "It is as if someone handed me a wonderful, thriving plant with the highest level of responsibility to care for it. Now we must strengthen the roots and grow the branches wider."[9]

The *Chicago Tribune* noted that Northwestern University "played to its strength in marketing" by tapping a "well-liked" insider as the new dean. University provost Larry Dumas praised Jain as a scholar with international standing, a person with a proven record of success in graduate and executive education. "Dipak brings to the position a keen appreciation for the distinctive Kellogg culture as well as an intimate familiarity with the operations of the school," said Dumas.[10] Jain noted the importance of maintaining the school's key attributes—teamwork and an entrepreneurial approach—while preparing students for the challenges of an uncertain market.[11]

"No matter what you do, you have to cope with complexity and uncertainty, which includes risk," he said in a *Tribune* interview. "Management schools have to make sure that we are giving students the skills, tools and concepts to manage in an uncertain environment. I honestly believe that's why we have a good future, because things are going to get more uncertain, and that's why an MBA is good training for management."[12]

But some uncertainty appeared to hang over the Kellogg School as it changed leadership. How could Jain—or indeed anyone—fill the shoes of Jacobs, a living legend, the "dean of deans"? The question was on the minds of nearly everyone associated with the school, and comparisons with Jacobs, who had spent an unprecedented 26 years in office, were inevitable. In fact, his shadow fell over fully half the school's history, for he had arrived at Northwestern in 1957. The concern about who would take the school's reins occupied those with the unenviable task of selecting the new dean.

David Besanko, a management and strategy professor who joined Kellogg in 1991 after receiving his doctorate in managerial economics and decision sciences from the school nearly a decade earlier and then teaching at Indiana University's business school, recalled chairing the 12-member dean's search committee, assigned the job by Provost Dumas. The selection process proved rigorous, he said, lasting from October 2000 until April 2001, with some of the school's most senior faculty and staff helping to make the choice, in conjunction with student, alumni and university input.

"This was a very tough crowd," said Besanko of those who participated, "and there was a lot of speculation about who would be dean. The legacy of Don Jacobs did weigh on us."[13]

The university, along with recruiting firm Spencer Stuart, had targeted some 120 candidates, including prominent corporate executives, in the exhaustive search.[14] Jain was considered among the top prospects, although he initially contemplated returning to India to take a leadership role at Hyderabad's Indian School of Business, a joint venture launched by Kellogg and the Wharton School that opened in 2001.[15] Others, though, encouraged him to pursue the Kellogg deanship, pointing to his eminent qualifications—including his outstanding scholarship and teaching,[16] as well as a five-year stint (1996–2001) as associate dean, working indefatigably alongside Jacobs in a role that sought "balanced excellence" between "rigor and relevance."[17]

"I learned a lot from him [Jacobs]," said Jain, recounting the unexpected circumstances leading to his own appointment as associate dean. In June 1996, he had traveled to New York City to participate in a Columbia University conference that attracted leading marketing scholars from around the country. He was awakened in the dead of night by the ringing of a phone; fearing the worst, the father of three picked up the receiver with trepidation.

"What's wrong with the children?" asked Jain, thinking his wife, Sushant, had placed the call from their Evanston home. The voice at the other end said: "This is not Sushant. This is Dean Jacobs. I want to make an announcement tomorrow at the 'Oh Be Joyful' dinner and I felt that I should inform you first since I understand you will not be there."[18] After a pause, Jacobs continued, "I want to announce that you will be my associate dean for academic affairs. Now go back to sleep." Said Jain in 2001, referring to the job's many responsibilities, "I haven't slept in five years!"[19]

Making the appointment more extraordinary was the inauspicious beginning to Jain's relationship with Jacobs. One of his first encounters with the dean was a brusque exchange in 1988, a year after the marketing professor had joined the school. Wanting both to make a good impression and to learn the Northwestern culture, Jain immersed himself in the academic and social life of Kellogg. "My very first year here there was an alumni reunion weekend," he recalled. "Don saw me at the Allen Center during one of the activities and got very angry. He was mad! He said that this is not the place for us [as junior faculty members]. He knew I was on the faculty but he didn't know my name since I was hired while he was out of town. I always believed that was why I got the job."[20]

Jain's enthusiasm and dedication eventually would win Jacobs over. It turned out that the two "D. J.'s" shared a passion for Thailand, and they found themselves collaborating on the Kellogg partnership with the Sasin Graduate Institute of Business Administration at Bangkok's Chulalongkorn University. With Jacobs, Jain also played a supporting role in the partnership Kellogg launched in 1997 with the Guanghua School of Management at Peking University in Beijing, China.[21] Starting in 1996, he helped establish a series of joint-degree programs between Kellogg and its partner schools, including the Leon Recanati Graduate School of Business in Tel Aviv, Israel; the Otto Beisheim School of Management in Vallendar, Germany; and the Business School at the Hong Kong University of Science and Technology that opened in 1998 (see chapter 5).[22] As Jain and Jacobs further developed the curriculum of the young Sasin school—it had opened in 1982—the colleagues came to respect and trust each other more and more. In addition, Jain was willing to take on many responsibilities in the Marketing Department, often appearing at events to support the school and his colleagues. Jacobs noticed.

"Dipak was always working," said the dean emeritus, explaining why he selected his younger colleague for the role of associate dean. "Whenever I needed something done, I could turn to him and he would make it happen."[23]

The Modern Kellogg Teaching Culture

Jain's immediate predecessor as associate dean was Mark Satterthwaite, professor of management and strategy. Satterthwaite, today the A. C. Buehler Professor in Hospital and Health Services Management, held that role from 1992 until 1996, making curriculum enhancement one of the central parts of his responsibilities, although neither he nor Jacobs endorsed the kind of radical overhaul adopted by some schools. Instead, they preferred to make continuous adjustments to offerings and programs, shaping the academic experience in "real time" to what the market demanded. Jacobs had long recognized that the school was situated in a rapidly changing society, and so he advocated "a moving curriculum of continuous change."[24] His associate dean agreed with the philosophy of modest enhancements and experimentation, saying that the "overhaul style of change imposes large costs" and can prove disruptive to a school's overall educational mission.[25]

"A lot of the trick with a good business school is giving the students what they want, so they feel they are getting a good education," said Satterthwaite in a 1994 interview, "but at the same time teaching them and giving them brand new things they've never thought about."[26]

As associate dean, Jain would strive to continue these efforts and build a culture that supported both faculty research and teaching. "I need to create the right research environment for the faculty members so that they have all the resources they need to do their research," he said in an interview upon joining the dean's office. "At the same time, I need to work with them to make sure there is good teaching here." Of primary importance for him would be enabling faculty and students to draw connections between theory and practice.[27]

Jain also credits another colleague, Stuart Greenbaum, associate dean for academic affairs from 1988 to 1992, with helping invigorate the school's teaching culture. "Stuart was focused on the role of teaching. He really felt strongly about this," said Jain, adding that not everyone shared this enthusiasm, particularly those whose work was more research-oriented, rather than classroom-oriented.[28]

Greenbaum, who holds a doctorate in economics from Johns Hopkins University and served as dean of the Olin School of Business from 1995 to 2005, recalled the circumstances: "The truth is, all of that happened long before I entered the dean's office. I would say I was a bit of a cheerleader. This goes back to Donald Jacobs taking over as dean." (This was in 1975, the year Greenbaum arrived as a finance professor at Northwestern at the invitation of Jacobs, whom he originally met in the late 1950s at an academic conference.) "He [Jacobs] tried very hard to shift the culture and make the school more student-centered. At that time, most of the leading business schools were very faculty-centered in terms of their culture, and this gives rise to a primacy of research, often to the disdain of teaching."[29]

Not only was such a customer-centric move "the right thing" to do, according to Greenbaum, it was also the strategically smart thing to do, he said. "It was a way to distinguish the Kellogg School as a place with its own unique priorities and culture." With this change, which he called a top-down decision from the dean,[30] came a more blended approach to research and teaching, and faculty members were encouraged to view both as critical to their success at the school. Calling himself "a champion" of this approach throughout his tenure at Kellogg, Greenbaum, once in the dean's office, said "[I] did all I could to foster this student-centered culture and advance it." Doing so, however, did not mean discarding research. Indeed, Greenbaum himself founded the *Journal of Financial Intermediation* and served as director of the school's Banking Research Center for years.[31] "We accepted the importance of research at all times," he said, but the administration recognized that Kellogg was "first and foremost a professional school, and this set us apart from programs in the social sciences, for example."

The genius of the school, said Greenbaum, has been its ability to bring theory and practice together in powerful ways. "I never took the two to be separate. We saw them as complementary." Although other schools have tried to emulate the approach, Greenbaum pointed out that Kellogg was "an early innovator" that won acclaim for being "a change agent."[32]

Being able to merge research and teaching has become a hallmark of Kellogg faculty, said Sunil Chopra, the IBM Distinguished Professor of Operations

Management and Information Systems. A supply chain expert who has published widely, including the influential volume *Supply Chain Management: Strategy, Planning and Operation*, Chopra is also senior associate dean for curriculum and teaching. "Our faculty has done a great job converting their research into pedagogy, into textbooks and paradigms," he said. "These are texts used by other top business schools. As a result, they have defined how courses are taught."

Kellogg professors' teaching notes often form the foundation for these books, he said, citing examples such as David Besanko and David Dranove's *Economics of Strategy* and Robert McDonald's *Derivatives Markets*. "A number of texts have come out of Kellogg, especially within the last 10 years," added Chopra in a 2007 interview. "There are books related to negotiations and leadership, a whole collection related to derivatives and operations. A lot of material—textbooks, cases—comes from our Dispute Resolution Research Center. If you look at operations and supply chain, we were one of the first groups that put out textbooks that are being used in other places." The school's perspective is that research and teaching form a continuum, said Chopra, a view that goes back decades. "[MEDS professor] Mort Kamien, for instance, has always been a researcher at heart, but he focused on taking the research and applying it."[33]

At the root of the Kellogg School's teaching and research excellence is its collaborative academic culture. Greenbaum traced the roots of this culture to the 1970s, saying the school was "cooperative within and competitive without," demonstrating a pronounced desire to distinguish itself among other top schools. Since then, senior professors routinely have shared their ideas and lesson plans with their junior peers, said Chopra.

"The supportive atmosphere at Kellogg gives a huge advantage to junior faculty," he said, adding that the school supports new colleagues in a variety of ways, including teaching workshops and mentorships. "It is not enough just to start a mentor program, but what does the mentor program do? Here, it is in our culture for any mentor to share their notes, their overheads, everything they have in regard to a course. And then they share their time explaining what they have."

Jain himself recalled being the beneficiary of this kind of mentorship. New to marketing when he arrived at Kellogg, he was helped by his colleagues in making the transition to the role of marketing professor upon his arrival in Evanston. In particular, Lakshman Krishnamurthi, the A. Montgomery Ward Professor of Marketing and chair of the Marketing Department from 1993 to 2005, provided the junior professor with several lecture plans to help him begin teaching his marketing research class. At the conclusion of the term, Jain's students gave him glowing marks on the school's Teacher Course Evaluation (TCE) system (see the discussion later in the chapter for details on this assessment tool).

"He took my materials and he taught them better than I do," Krishnamurthi told the *Daily Northwestern* in 2002. "There's magic that transpires in the classroom. There's no question that people leave a session [with Jain] quite inspired. . . . It's not just verbal communication. [He has] a tremendous sense of respect for the material he's teaching and respect for the students."[34] Indeed, Jain has been honored widely and won various awards for his teaching and research, including the Pravasi Bharatiya Samman Award for leadership in education, bestowed by the prime minister of India in 2004.[35]

Krishnamurthi, a marketing strategy expert who joined Kellogg in 1980 and has earned distinctions for his research,[36] said that he learned the importance of sharing ideas while he was a student in the Stanford doctoral program. Because doctoral students did not teach in the MBA program there, he recalled, he had no experience in front of a classroom. Fortunately, a faculty member offered him a chance to observe his class. "I knew him pretty well and told him that I was going to be teaching a course on marketing research at Kellogg [after graduation]," said Krishnamurthi. "He invited me into his class and said, 'Use all my notes.' That was unusual. He was a unique guy and willing to share his stuff. He was very confident about his own teaching, and it didn't matter to him if someone was teaching [from his notes] because you can't teach it the same way."[37]

With that experience, as well as his own views about the importance of sharing knowledge, Krishnamurthi carried these values into his role at Kellogg. He said he believes that an academic institution, unlike a corporate entity, should encourage the free exchange of ideas. "Here, we're in the business of creating knowledge, disseminating knowledge and sharing that knowledge—including with each other. I absolutely believe that," he affirmed.

What began as more of an ad hoc practice became formally enshrined in the school about 1990 when the faculty mentor program took shape, Krishnamurthi recalled. Under the program, each incoming faculty member is assigned a senior peer. During the first quarter of their tenure, the young professors do not teach but instead observe their mentors' teaching. The mentors are responsible for sharing teaching insights and helping introduce their new colleagues to the school's culture. Examples of this mentoring appear throughout the school, said Krishnamurthi, but he is most familiar with how the Marketing Department has approached the practice. Besides himself, many other professors have understood the importance of their roles as mentors, among them Brian Sternthal and Gregory Carpenter.

Carpenter, who arrived at Kellogg in 1990, is the James Farley/Booz Allen Hamilton Professor of Marketing Strategy and has been chair of the Marketing Department since 2005. His research and teaching have been widely recognized.[38]

Sternthal joined Kellogg in 1972 and is the Kraft Foods Chair in Marketing and a past chair of the Marketing Department. He is also widely recognized as an expert in consumer information processing and advertising.

"Greg Carpenter helped me a lot with the strategy course," said Krishnamurthi, "and Brian Sternthal has been extremely helpful in sharing his advertising materials, letting everyone who teaches the advertising class use all his videos, all his examples. If you think about what Brian is doing, this is the accumulated knowledge over 25, 30 years. He can give you an historical record of advertising going back. It's impossible for a new faculty member to put that together."[39]

Metrics for Teaching Contribute to Classroom Excellence

Alongside this collegial atmosphere, other elements have encouraged superior teaching. Two in particular are noteworthy: the Teacher Course Evaluations and the Dean's Exit Survey. Both tools attempt to assess the "voice of the customer" in ways that enable Kellogg to refine and enhance its curriculum and culture. Dating to the early 1970s and gradually developing in influence and scope throughout that decade and continuing today, TCEs have been one way for students to critique faculty members' classroom performance. At the end of each course, students make their assessments. The students remain anonymous, but their ranking of the teachers is made public. "No one wanted to have their name highlighted at the bottom of that list," said Jacobs.[40]

Satterthwaite remembered his introduction to TCEs and the effect they had on the school's culture. "Inevitably we started competing against one another," he said. "It's been a powerful thing, at times too powerful. But it's just remade the quality of teaching here." By the 1980s, this teaching culture was fairly well established, he said. "There's enormous peer support now, not like when I arrived [in 1972]! I had three days to hand in a one-page syllabus and head to the classroom. There were TCEs back in 1973, and I remember one comment I received: 'Boy, did you improve over the quarter!'"[41]

The public nature of the TCE is an important part of the teaching culture at Kellogg. "Those of us who teach take pride in what we do," said Besanko. "The fact that the results of our efforts are made public is a factor, if we didn't need it already, that motivates us to do well in this dimension." Chopra agreed: "Performance visibility makes a huge difference."[42]

TCEs are calculated on a 10-point scale, with 10 representing the most outstanding performance. The evaluations take into account overall difficulty, workload, learning, group interaction, clarity of lessons and other factors.

In the 2006–2007 academic year, Kellogg faculty scored an average of about 8.4 on the TCEs, as compared with about 8.0 in the 1999–2000 year, according to data tabulated by Robert Korajczyk, the Harry G. Guthmann Distinguished Professor of Finance and former senior associate dean for curriculum and teaching.[43] The Kellogg Student Association, with the support of the school's administration, officially runs the TCE initiative, providing valuable feedback to the faculty and school, said Chopra, who added that he and his peers also meet weekly with student government leaders to assess and address any issues. The collegial relationships among faculty members, he stressed, are also evident among faculty, staff and students—translating into a strategic and operational boon.

"All the feedback we get is very useful," said Chopra. "The advantage of having good relationships is that you shorten the feedback loop. You get information back to where it is supposed to go before things really mess up." Almost all issues can be resolved easily, he added: it is simply a question of when they are noticed. "In operations we talk about defects. The most expensive defect is the one that reaches the customer, so the quicker you catch it, the better the situation is. It's the same thing with most issues," Chopra concluded.[44]

Another valuable tool and metric is the Dean's Exit Survey, which was begun in 1992. An idea that originated with Associate Dean for Student Affairs Edmund Wilson and accounting professor Lawrence Revsine, the survey was intended to obtain a holistic and very detailed assessment of the school's culture and curriculum from students about to graduate. The feedback was then analyzed and disseminated to all department chairs. In an effort to strengthen the initial methodology, Jain and marketing colleague James Anderson refined the instrument to ensure that the data were reflective of the actual student experience across the school. "The statistical issue that came up was, did you really get a representative sample?" recalled Jain, citing "nonresponse bias" as one of the challenges they worked to overcome. "Nonresponse bias is seen when people do not respond to a survey either because they are too happy or too angry," he said. "We thought the idea of the surveys was good, but the methodology had some issues, so we wanted to do a more statistically representative sample . . . a stratified sample where we thought we would obtain representation of international students and American students. That was important."[45]

Anderson and Jain also conducted a major study of TCEs worldwide in 1994 in an effort to refine that tool. "A year after we created the exit survey we thought about the TCEs and wondered, 'Are we using the right TCEs?' We modified those too."[46]

The particular importance of the Dean's Exit Survey, said Jain, is that it captures student impressions that should reflect the entire MBA experience, unlike TCEs, which offer a snapshot (albeit a valuable one) at the end of a single course. "Teacher Course Evaluations give you short-term ratings—I taught the class, 10 weeks later you evaluate me," said Jain. "But it's important to find what students say after two years here, how they find your teaching and coursework in the larger context." And the Exit Surveys are designed to go beyond the academic quality of the school too, assessing the students' overall feelings about the facilities, the culture and a wide variety of opportunities that form the Kellogg MBA experience. The survey effort has proven very helpful to leadership in the Office of the Dean, generating innovations and enhancements throughout the school.

"Our customers are evaluating the school nonstop, every year," said Besanko.

Teaching and Research Honors Reward Top Performers

Other initiatives have played a part in building the Kellogg teaching and research culture. Among these are the various public acknowledgments that take the form of awards, such as the Lawrence G. Lavengood Professor of the Year Award and the Stanley Reiter Best Paper Award. These annual honors recognize top faculty members for their achievements inside and outside the classroom. The Lavengood Award, renamed in 1994 in honor of the longtime and beloved Kellogg professor,[47] began as the Professor of the Year Award in 1975 and is bestowed by members of the graduating class. The initial recipient was Ram Charan, today a well-known management and leadership consultant. Lavengood himself won the award in 1976. In 2007, for the first time, the award was jointly given to two outstanding faculty members: clinical professor in marketing Julie Hennessy and Sergio Rebelo, the Tokai Bank Distinguished Professor of Finance. Indicating the depth of teaching excellence at Kellogg today, students had nominated 87 professors for the honor. Upon receiving the award, Hennessy told an audience of students, faculty and staff, "Our award comes every day we step into the classroom with you."[48] The only person to win the Lavengood Award more than once has been Steven Rogers, the Llura and Gordon Gund Family Professor of Entrepreneurship and director of the Levy Institute for Entrepreneurial Practice; he received the honor in 1997 and 2005. Winners of the Lavengood Award have included younger faculty members, such as Karl Schmedders from the MEDS Department in 2002, as well as more senior ones, such as Daniel Diermeier, also from MEDS, in 2001. Recipients have come from all Kellogg departments, including Mitchell Petersen from Finance in 2000; Louis Stern and Brian Sternthal from Marketing in 1992 and 1982, respectively; Robert Duncan from Organizational Behavior in 1984; and Lawrence Revsine from Accounting in 1983.

Other awards to honor exemplary teaching at Kellogg include: the Chairs Core Teaching Award, established in 1997 and bestowed by department and program chairs for teaching excellence in the school's nine core classes; the Sidney J. Levy Teaching Award, established in 1992 and bestowed by department and program chairs to recognize teaching excellence in elective courses; the Alumni Professor of the Year Award, created in 1988 and bestowed by the school's alumni at reunion each year upon the faculty member deemed most influential on the graduates' professional life; and the Executive MBA Program Outstanding Teaching Awards, established in 1992 and bestowed upon two professors each year who are chosen by executive students for excellence in both core and elective courses.

Since 2001, Kellogg and its students have been increasing the focus on these teaching awards, said Besanko, who won the Lavengood honor in 1995. "We asked the students to make the award announcement more dramatic. The Professor of the Year had always given the remarks at our Convocation, going back to the 1970s, but we wanted to add some drama to the announcement." Students started making short films that profiled the five finalists for the Lavengood Award, and the announcement is now made during the faculty-student TG in the spring quarter. "The Lavengood Award is something that really attracts a lot of interest from the students," said Besanko.[49]

To highlight faculty scholarship each year, the school established the Reiter Award in 2001. Named after the professor who was instrumental in bringing a more rigorous, research-focused approach to the school and founding the MEDS Department in the late 1960s, the award highlights the faculty research article judged to be the best among those published in the preceding four calendar years. A selection committee accepts nominations from Kellogg faculty and makes a single choice based on the article's creativity, craftsmanship and disciplinary impact.

"A lot of people view Stanley Reiter as the intellectual godfather of the research culture at the Kellogg School," said Robert Magee, the Keith I. DeLashmutt Distinguished Professor of Accounting Information and Management, in announcing the award's establishment. Winning the first Reiter Award in 2002 was Timothy Feddersen, the Wendell Hobbs Professor of Managerial Economics. Subsequent winners have been Alvaro Sandroni, the Mechthild Esser Nemmers Professor of Managerial Economics and Decision Sciences (2003); J. Peter Murmann (2004); David Dranove, the Walter J. McNerney Distinguished Professor of Health Industry Management, and Mark Satterthwaite, the A. C. Buehler Professor in Hospital and Health Services Management (2005); and Angela Lee, the PepsiCo Professor of International Marketing (2006).

All these awards are meaningful for faculty members, of course, but beyond that, they are the manifestations of an underlying excellence that flows throughout

Kellogg, said Chopra. "You can always provide motivation [including teaching awards], but that only takes you so far. It's really the support, the collegiality, the flow of information back and forth, along with the motivation. All of these things are the keys. The motivation part is easy for any institution to replicate; the other cultural and organizational parts are not easy for others to replicate."[50]

Increasing the Research Culture

Beginning in 1996, the administration instituted several innovations to spur research. One of these involved taking an entrepreneurial approach to how the school managed research funding. Rather than have professors request money ad hoc each time they wanted support, the dean's office streamlined the process and created incentives that better engaged faculty while reducing bureaucratic requirements that detracted from the research focus. "Asking for money takes time away from you," said Jain. "We said let's just give faculty members a research budget and have them act like entrepreneurs to manage their budget most effectively for their needs." By giving them a budget and making them responsible for it, the dean's office created more flexibility while increasing faculty "ownership" of their research, said Jain.[51]

Another development involved working closely with the faculty to find ways to reduce initial teaching loads so that junior professors would have additional opportunities to pursue research. Although all faculty members were expected to teach, the school used innovations such as the endowed Donald P. Jacobs Chair to "buy down" courses for young professors, thereby reducing the classes that recently hired faculty taught and freeing them to do more research. The deans also collaborated with Northwestern University to ensure that the central administration understood "that teaching matters in business school," said Jain.[52] The tangible outcome of this communication was the procuring of extra time for the tenure process—extending it to seven years instead of six. As a result, faculty members have the chance to cultivate teaching and research excellence, each of which is deemed critical to securing tenure. The agreement was formalized after Jain became dean in 2001.

"We wanted to create a culture of giving faculty support and helping them to develop," said Jain, adding that Greenbaum had previously initiated a faculty mentorship program, an effort that Jain, Satterthwaite and Jacobs deepened. "You have to have the talent [to teach], but good mentors are like a compass that help point you in the right direction" for true professional development, added Jain, citing Jacobs as one of his own mentors in addition to Frank Bass and several members of the marketing faculty who provided support early in his career at the school.

Research Centers "Dig Deeper" to Deliver Knowledge, Bridge Theory and Practice

Other academic boons involved the launching of various research centers. The school had begun developing such bridges between the academic and professional worlds decades earlier (see chapter 1 for details about the Northwestern Bureau of Business Research, founded in 1919), with some key additions coming in the 1970s, including centers devoted to banking and mathematics, and others in the 1980s, such as those focused on dispute resolution or game theory. Today, Kellogg boasts more than 20 research centers where academics and practitioners pursue interdisciplinary scholarship on a range of subjects, from accounting and operations to strategy, teams, technology, risk and entrepreneurship.

Created in 1971, the Center for Mathematical Studies in Economics and Management Science (CMS-EMS) brings together economists, mathematicians and social scientists at Northwestern who use mathematical methods and models in their research. One significant focus of the center has been to use game theory in the analysis and design of systems, organizations and institutions for managing and regulating economic and political activities. The center, housed at Kellogg, closely collaborates with the Northwestern Institute of Complex Systems, as well as the university's Economic Theory Center, in producing seminars, theory workshops and a large number of working papers (some 1,500 papers were available on the center's Web site in 2007, with more being added continuously). Professor Stanley Reiter was the center's founding director, a position he retained until 2007, when Rakesh Vohra, the J. L. and Helen Kellogg Professor of Managerial Economics and Decision Sciences, assumed the leadership. Vohra, who joined Kellogg in 1998, is formally trained in mathematics and operational research and has taught Kellogg courses in pricing theory, game theory and managerial economics. His text, *Advanced Mathematical Economics,* is based on lecture notes for a doctoral course Vohra has taught.

The Accounting Research Center (ARC) was founded in 1978 with the mission of supporting research conducted by the school's accounting faculty. Through frequent seminars, symposia and workshops as well as occasional conferences and publications, the center plays an important role in disseminating accounting information. Directed initially by Professor Alfred Rappaport, the center's leadership passed to Bala Balachandran, the J. L. Kellogg Distinguished Professor of Accounting Information and Management, from 1985 to 2006. Today, Professor Robert Magee directs the center, which is seeking to build additional relationships with accounting firms through center-sponsored activities. In 2007, for instance, ARC continued its long-standing relationship with Ernst & Young, whose philanthropy is supporting the leadership and innovation research at Kellogg. Specific areas being supported by

Earl S. Enzer '86 shows his pride after Kellogg was named the number one business school in 1985 by the *Wall Street Journal*. This was the first high-profile national exposure the school enjoyed and would help catapult it to increasing prominence afterward.

Robert B. Duncan was the Richard L. Thomas Professor of Leadership and Change at Kellogg from 1972 until 2001, when he was named dean of the Eli Broad College of Business. Duncan made significant contributions during his Kellogg tenure, including helping build a world-class Organization Behavior Department (today known as Management and Organizations). As department chairman, associate dean and university provost, Duncan encouraged a collegial and scholarly culture at Kellogg.

Collaborative learning is a Kellogg School hallmark dating back decades. Students interact inside and outside of class to create a rich academic experience.

Alice Tybout, the Harold T. Martin Professor of Marketing, teaches a class in 1986. Tybout, an expert in branding and consumer information processing, joined Kellogg in 1975.

Marketing professor Andris Zoltners teaches a class in 1983. Zoltners, cofounder of ZS Associates and an expert in sales force productivity, bestowed a $1 million gift upon Kellogg in honor of marketing professor Richard Clewett, who died in 2006.

From left: Northwestern University president Arnold R. Weber, James R. McManus '56, Dean Donald P. Jacobs and William D. Smithburg '62 admire the outcome of "Campaign Kellogg," a three-year fund-raising effort that concluded in 1989 and brought more than $40 million to the school. Smithburg, CEO of Quaker Oats Company, was chairman of the Campaign for Kellogg effort. McManus, chairman of Marketing Corporation of America, was a member of the campaign's Executive Committee.

Students collaborate in the Institute for Management, an intensive summer residential program for executives begun in 1951.

Kenneth Bardach *(left)* served as the first director of the Kellogg School's Executive MBA Program, which began in 1976. He would become associate dean for executive education, overseeing programming that would grow to serve more than 5,000 people each year with more than 120 academic offerings.

Stephen Burnett, associate dean of executive education and professor of strategic management, joined the Kellogg faculty in 1981. Since then, he has played an active role in developing and popularizing executive programs at the school, including many custom programs for dozens of prominent corporate clients. Burnett also serves as faculty director of the Advanced Executive Program, the Kellogg School's oldest and most senior management program. In addition, he founded the Kellogg Management Institute, a nine-month-long program that provides a thorough understanding of business functions for professionals working in general management positions. Today, Burnett also oversees the James L. Allen Center, where more than 6,000 executives and other professionals visited in 2007.

On its completion in 1972, Leverone Hall provided a much-needed facilities upgrade for the burgeoning Graduate School of Management. The structure rises seven stories, including an underground level, and was built at the same time as the adjacent Arthur Andersen Hall. Andersen Hall, originally home to the Northwestern School of Education, would later become a Kellogg facility as the business school continued growing.

Jeanne Brett, professor of management and organizations, leads a seminar at the James L. Allen Center in 1986. Today, Brett is the DeWitt W. Buchanan Jr. Professor of Dispute Resolution and Organizations and director of the Kellogg Dispute Resolution Research Center.

Mark Satterthwaite, the A. C. Buehler Professor in Hospital and Health Services Management, during CIM Week in 1982. Satterthwaite joined Northwestern's Graduate School of Management in 1972 and was a key figure in creating its Management and Strategy Department.

Accounting professor Lawrence Revsine circa 1980s. With texts such as *Financial Reporting and Analysis,* Revsine provided a sophisticated way to examine the financial markers for corporate performance—and warned about how the numbers could be manipulated for various ends. Revsine, who was the John and Norma Darling Distinguished Professor of Financial Accounting, died in May 2007.

Home of the Kellogg School's Executive MBA Programs, the James L. Allen Center is a state-of-the-art facility that opened in 1979. Since then, it has set the standard for quality throughout the management education world.

Dean Donald P. Jacobs and Assistant Director of Executive Education Nancy Hartigan (wearing hats) prepare a meal for executive students at the James L. Allen Center, circa 1992.

(Top) The Leon Recanati Graduate School of Business Administration in Tel Aviv. The Kellogg-Recanati Executive MBA Program is a joint-degree venture that began in 1996.

(Left) The Vallendar, Germany, home of the Kellogg-WHU Executive MBA Program, a joint-degree curriculum developed in 1997 and part of the Kellogg School's integrated global portfolio of programs.

(Above) The Business School at the Hong Kong University of Science and Technology, a member of the Kellogg global portfolio of joint-degree executive MBA offerings. The Kellogg-HKUST program began in 1997.

(Left) Toronto is home to the Kellogg-Schulich Executive MBA Program, a joint-degree venture founded in 2002.

Dean Emeritus Donald P. Jacobs *(right)* with Adolfo Autrey '70, who donated the stained-glass window that has become iconic at Kellogg. The artwork is installed on the first floor of the Jacobs Center in Evanston, with a replica downtown in Wieboldt Hall, home of the Part-Time MBA Program.

Bill Gates, Microsoft founder, is among the many leaders from the business, government and nonprofit sectors who have visited Kellogg. Gates participated in an April 1997 Technology Series Conference at the school.

Bringing theory and practice together, Kellogg has invited select practitioners to serve as adjunct faculty members at the school. During 1999 and 2000, media executive and talk show host Oprah Winfrey taught a course on the dynamics of leadership. She also delivered the Kellogg School's Convocation address in June 2001. *From left:* Northwestern president Henry Bienen; Winfrey; and Kellogg then-dean Donald P. Jacobs.

Donald P. Jacobs, the tenth dean of the Kellogg School, with longtime colleagues Carole Cahill, associate dean for facilities and human resources, and Naomi Schapira, the dean's administrative assistant. Schapira *(right)* retired from Kellogg in 1999 and died in 2004.

In May 2001, Northwestern University president Henry Bienen *(center)* introduced Dipak C. Jain *(right)* as the eleventh dean of the Kellogg School of Management. Joining in the celebration were *(from left)* Kellogg Graduate Management Association president Brian Poger '01; Northwestern provost Lawrence Dumas; and Kellogg professor David Besanko '82, who headed the search committee to identify the new dean.

After being introduced by Henry Bienen, new Kellogg dean Dipak C. Jain turned to address an audience of Kellogg students, faculty and staff in the Levy Atrium, one of the school's social centers.

Sergio Rebelo, the Tokai Bank Professor of Finance, brings his insights about macroeconomics and international business to Kellogg students. Rebelo has taught at Kellogg since 1988.

Kellogg School faculty and administrators join Executive MBA Program students in 2001 to celebrate the school being ranked number one by *BusinessWeek* magazine. The Kellogg EMBA program has perennially earned top marks in national rankings—including garnering the top spot from *BusinessWeek* and *US News & World Report* each year since their surveys began in 1991.

Kellogg students gain an intimate understanding of business in Vietnam during a 1999 research excursion known as Global Initiatives in Management (GIM), a course that has remained very popular since its inception in 1990. Today, some 500 students participate in GIM each spring, spending 10 weeks preparing in class for an intensive 2-week trip to one of more than a dozen countries where they meet top business and government leaders.

Kellogg students prepare to take over Wall Street in a Special K Revue performance from 2001. An annual Reunion tradition, Special K spoofs B-school life while also celebrating the many talents of the Kellogg community.

Students perform in Special K Revue in May 2007.

Professor Robert Magee, Dean Dipak C. Jain and Professor Robert Korajczyk applaud faculty and staff during a 2002 Oh Be Joyful celebration, an annual event that recognizes the school's community and its accomplishments. In the background, note the books and binders full of articles that faculty published in the preceding year.

Each May, Kellogg graduates return to Evanston for Reunion. Since the first reunion in 1977, which attracted about 100 graduates, the annual event has grown to include more academic and social programming. Today, more than 1,600 alumni and guests participate in Reunion.

Dean Dipak C. Jain and members of the Kellogg School celebrate being ranked the number one business school in 2002 by *BusinessWeek* and by the Economist Intelligence Unit (affiliated with the *Economist* magazine).

Students in the Master of Management and Manufacturing Program (MMM) on a field visit to Toyota. The MMM Program is a dual-degree offering between Kellogg and Northwestern's McCormick School of Engineering and Applied Science.

Professor Stanley Reiter *(left)* with Professor Robert Magee in 2001 when the Kellogg School announced the Stanley Reiter Best Paper Award in honor of the longtime professor of managerial economics and decision sciences. Reiter's arrival at Northwestern in 1967 has been called a "watershed event" by Magee, who said that Reiter's strong research orientation soon exerted a powerful influence throughout the school, including in the recruitment of faculty members trained in the analytical sciences.

The Kellogg School and Northwestern University offer a robust doctoral program for students seeking advanced degrees in management-related disciplines. More than 700 doctoral students have matriculated from the program over the school's history, including those working here with Katherine Phillips, associate professor of management and organizations.

In 2000, Amazon.com founder and CEO Jeff Bezos *(right)* was among the keynote speakers at the Kellogg Digital Frontier Conference, an enormously popular gathering of industry leaders, academics and students. Today known as the Technology Conference, the student-led initiative continues to attract business luminaries who are focused on innovation.

NATHAN MANDELL

The first day of CIM Week 2001 fell on September 11. Assistant dean and chief marketing officer Richard Honack '94 interrupted the morning's proceedings to inform students that the United States had been attacked. This crisis, and the economic fallout from the dot com bust, would mark the early deanship of Dipak C. Jain, who was welcoming the new class when word of the terrorist attacks arrived.

EVANSTON PHOTOGRAPHIC STUDIOS

The Donald P. Jacobs Center, home of the Kellogg School's Full-Time MBA Program in Evanston.

© MATTHEW GILSON

The Kellogg School's entrepreneurship program has been significantly enhanced through the support of Larry Levy '67 and his spouse Carol. The Larry and Carol Levy Institute for Entrepreneurial Practice was established in 2003; it serves as an umbrella for dozens of initiatives, including conferences, case studies, speakers and internship programs related to entrepreneurship at Kellogg.

NATHAN MANDELL

Kellogg students show their spirit and determination during CIM Week 2002.

Finance professor Vidhan Goyal teaches students in the Kellogg-HKUST MBA Program, a joint-degree partnership between Kellogg and the Business School at the Hong Kong University of Science and Technology. This EMBA program was ranked number one in the world in 2007 by the *Financial Times*.

Billionaire real estate entrepreneur Samuel Zell has been a friend to the Kellogg School. His support has created the Zell Center for Risk Research, which studies how people perceive risk, while exploring the implications these perceptions have for risk management across various enterprises.

Senator Barack Obama, D-Ill., delivered a keynote address at the Kellogg School's 18th Annual Black Management Association Conference in 2005.

Carly Fiorina, former HP chief executive, visited Kellogg in October 2006.

Visiting Kellogg in May 2006 for a forum on health care sponsored by Huron Consulting Group, former U.S. president William J. Clinton delivered a keynote address about the health-care crisis in America.

Patrick Ryan '59 at podium during graduation: Founder and executive chairman of Aon Corporation, Ryan delivers the Kellogg School executive MBA convocation address June 9, 2006, in Evanston. In addition to his service as a Northwestern University trustee, Ryan has been a great supporter of Kellogg, including previously chairing the school's advisory board.

Entrepreneurship has been central to the way the Kellogg School has approached management education, and the school's entrepreneurship curriculum has been ranked among the top three in the United States. Among those who have played leadership roles in entrepreneurship at Kellogg are, *from left:* Morton Kamien, emeritus professor of managerial economics and decision sciences; Donald P. Jacobs, dean emeritus; Joseph Levy '47; and Steven Rogers, the Gordon and Llura Gund Family Professor of Entrepreneurship and director of the Larry and Carol Levy Institute for Entrepreneurial Practice.

Wieboldt Hall, home of the Kellogg School's Part-Time MBA Program.

Collaborative learning is a Kellogg hallmark. Here, students in the school's Part-Time MBA Program work on a group project in Wieboldt Hall, located in downtown Chicago.

International Live-In Week students at the James L. Allen Center in 2007. Each summer, students from all the Kellogg School's joint-degree executive MBA programs converge on Evanston for an intensive residential program that allows them to interact with peers from around the world, all of whom are united by the school's unique "Kellogg culture."

Team culture suffuses every aspect of the Kellogg School experience, beginning with the annual CIM Week orientation. Renamed "Complete Immersion in Management" in 2007, the program began in 1969 as "Conceptual Issues in Management" and introduces new students to the Kellogg way of learning, inside and outside the classroom.

Steven Rogers, the Gordon and Llura Gund Family Professor of Entrepreneurship, shares his knowledge of entrepreneurial finance. He also is director of the Larry and Carol Levy Institute for Entrepreneurial Practice.

Dean Dipak C. Jain, the Sandy and Morton Goldman Professor of Entrepreneurial Studies. Jain is the eleventh dean of the Kellogg School of Management since its inception in 1908, assuming the role in 2001.

From left: Professors Mark Satterthwaite, Ehud Kalai and David Baron were among those instrumental in developing the Kellogg School's Managerial Economics and Decision Sciences Department, an area that drew upon mathematical analysis, decision theory, statistics and microeconomics. World renowned, MEDS was credited with bringing more academic rigor to the school's overall curriculum.

Dean Dipak C. Jain celebrates with Scott and Margee Filstrup and Northwestern provost Larry Dumas *(far right)* at the naming of the Filstrup Quiet Study Lounge in the Jacobs Center in October 2001. The Filstrups are generous supporters of the Kellogg School, and Scott, a 1967 graduate of the business school, has previously served on the Northwestern board of trustees and as president of the university's 150,000-member alumni association. Since 1994, he also has been a member of the Kellogg Alumni Advisory Board.

On the campus of the Kellogg-Miami Executive MBA Program in Coral Gables, Florida, professor of management and organizations J. Keith Murnighan, the Harold H. Hines Jr. Professor of Risk Management, consults with a study group as its members work on an assignment. The Kellogg-Miami Program launched in January 2006, featuring a custom-designed classroom and study facilities.

RICH FOREMAN PHOTO

In 2007, Kellogg and Northwestern University launched an undergraduate certificate program designed to provide younger students with an advanced analytical education. The program is a collaboration among Kellogg, the Weinberg College of Arts and Sciences and the McCormick School of Engineering. At an open house in November, Northwestern students joined senior associate dean Kathleen Hagerty (*center,* in scarf), finance professor Janice Eberly, program director Carol Henes, and Kellogg School dean Dipak C. Jain.

EVANSTON PHOTOGRAPHIC STUDIOS

Kellogg School Office of the Dean, 2007-2008. *From left:* David Besanko, senior associate dean, planning and external relations; Dipak C. Jain, dean; Sunil Chopra, senior associate dean, curriculum and teaching; Kathleen Hagerty, senior associate dean, faculty and research.

One hundred years ago, Northwestern's School of Commerce began educating students to help them achieve professional success. Today, that mission remains alive and, as always, students are at the center of the Kellogg School's efforts to create a new generation of exceptional leaders. These students, however, are far more diverse in every way — race, creed, gender, sexual orientation, educational background and work experience — reflecting the Kellogg goal of producing leaders prepared for the fast-changing global economy. Some of those recent graduates, pictured here with Dipak C. Jain, the school's Centennial dean (*second from left*), are: Michael Ginal, Saqib Nadeem, Liliahn Johnson, Ricardo Cilloniz, Hui Sha and Shannon Taylor (all '05).

the $1 million total gift are internal reporting and its effect on decision making, governance and management control systems. Magee stressed that accounting practice is as important as it has ever been and that fallout from the Enron scandal will continue to occupy the accountancy world. "It will be another 10 years before we're 'post-Enron,'" he said in an interview in 2007. "The litigation continues." Magee also noted that the "excesses that we have experienced in the last seven or eight years" have historical precedents. "It's not the first time stuff like this has happened," he said. "Some of the things that we are worried about in the current financial crisis are the same things we worried about in the savings and loan crisis in the 1980s. Then there was the Foreign Corrupt Practices Act that arose from corrupt practices in the 1970s." One goal of research and practice in accounting today, he added, is to determine which limits and regulations are necessary to prevent widespread economic damage and which rules can be relaxed somewhat.[53]

One important outgrowth of the Kellogg focus on teamwork and negotiations was the Dispute Resolution Resource Center (DRRC), directed by Professor Jeanne Brett, an expert in cross-cultural negotiations. The center was founded in 1986 to research competitive decision making, negotiations and conflict resolution, and it has become a recognized leader in this area of study, while also enhancing the Kellogg curriculum for students. "The DRRC has generated research that has kept Kellogg's management and organizations classes at the forefront of knowledge," Brett has said. "We've studied how biases affect negotiators' decisions, how negotiators learn and how culture affects negotiators' preferences and strategies."[54]

Kellogg created many new research initiatives during the 1990s and into the new century. Building on the school's historical strengths in collaborative learning, the Kellogg Team and Group (KTAG) Research Center was launched in 1997 under the leadership of Leigh Thompson, the J. Jay Gerber Distinguished Professor of Dispute Resolution and Organizations. The center began in conjunction with a new executive education course on teams, recalled Thompson. "We needed to have an excellent team of instructors at the Allen Center to make sure the launch was successful," she said. "It just made sense to try to create a mecca for research on teams at the same time."[55] She has said that the "heart and soul" of the KTAG Research Center is its postdoctoral program, which brings in "fresh, exciting research" continuously. Graduates of the KTAG program, said Thompson, go on to "great academic jobs" and continue spreading the center's reputation. With a mission that involves being a nationally recognized resource for research on teams and groups, the center also hosts occasional conferences—such as a 2005 event focused on conflict and a 2003 forum on creativity—that result in book-length monographs.

Other research institutions also appeared at Kellogg, including the Center for Family Enterprises, launched in 1998. Codirectors John Ward and Lloyd Shefsky are leading authorities in family business and entrepreneurship. "With family business-es, you have manager relationships that last a lifetime," said Ward, an international expert on the subject and author of five prominent books and more than a dozen substantial booklets on family business.[56] Center research has shown that "the char-acteristics of the family more profoundly affect the outcome of an enterprise than [do] the classical business issues," according to Ward. The center, which Jacobs called "an important move for Kellogg" given that families control more than half of the world's largest corporations,[57] studies every aspect of family business, including governance issues, succession challenges and product life cycles. When the center opened, Shefsky noted that it would prove beneficial to all Kellogg students: "As a professor of entrepreneurship, I have watched the percentage of students who say they will be entrepreneurs continually increase, and witnessed a staggering increase in the number of students who launch businesses earlier in their careers. Many of them will prove to be the founders of family businesses. And who knows how many of our students will work for, finance, represent, sell to, buy from, align with or oth-erwise deal with family businesses?"[58] Each year, the center hosts a popular, invitation-only conference that attracts family business leaders from around the world to participate in a daylong exchange; in addition, an award is bestowed on the family business deemed most distinguished.

Adding to the Kellogg School's research strengths in early 2001 was the Ford Motor Company Center for Global Citizenship. Founded with a $3 million gift from Ford, the center "explores strategies to achieve global competitive advantage through environmental stewardship and socially responsible business practices."[59] The center merged the school's existing Center for the Study of Ethical Issues in Business and the Kellogg Environmental Research Center,[60] both of which began in 1994; at that time, they were led, respectively, by David Messick, the Morris and Alice Kaplan Professor of Ethics and Decision in Management, and Max Bazerman, the J. Jay Gerber Distinguished Professor of Dispute Resolution and Organizations. Messick initially directed the Center for Global Citizenship, which brought togeth-er the disciplines of management and organizations, accounting, strategic change and leadership. "Companies are becoming more important while government becomes less important," observed Messick in 2001.[61] "Those companies that first accept global leadership responsibilities will become global leaders."[62] The Ford Center has become a central part of a broader Kellogg curriculum dedicated to socially responsible global leadership, including the school's Social EnterprisE at Kellogg (SEEK) Program, details of which will be discussed later.

Equally important was the Center for Executive Women, started in 2001 and directed by Victoria Husted Medvec, the Adeline Barry Davee Professor of

Management and Organizations. Its mission is to research the dynamics associated with women executives, particularly the hurdles confronting them as they strive to obtain senior leadership roles in companies and on their boards of directors. The center's goals are to increase opportunities for women to serve on the boards of Fortune 500 companies by providing training and awareness to women and to corporate boards. Cofounded by Kellogg professors Walter Scott and Lloyd Shefsky, along with Sheli Z. Rosenberg, vice chairman and former CEO of Chicago-based Equity Group Investments Inc., the center boasts a steering committee that features many of the most powerful advocates of women in business, including Brenda C. Barnes, chairman and CEO of Sara Lee and former president and CEO of PepsiCola N.A.; Ginger Graham, adviser to the president of Guidant Corporation; Betsy Holden '78, former Kraft Foods president and co-CEO; Nell Minow, editor of the Corporate Library; and Penelope L. Peterson, dean of Northwestern's School of Education and Public Policy.

With its three-day Director Development Program, the school's first executive education program exclusively for women, the center has addressed challenges facing female professionals, including stereotyping and exclusion from formal networks. The program helps women obtain the skills needed to join the corporate board network, while also offering networking and mentorship opportunities. The program articulates the responsibilities of board membership and emphasizes analytical skills and decision-making abilities. "Our goal is to help women make the leap onto nominating committee radar screens, and we're already doing that," Medvec said in a 2003 interview. "We feel we have truly surfaced some new candidates, and that is very gratifying."[63]

The Center for Biotechnology was launched in 2001 to bring two seemingly divergent worlds together. Headed by Professor Alicia Löffler, the center has as its mission helping scholars and students understand the leadership models required for success in the business of science, which encompasses a broad variety of endeavors from agribusiness to medicine. "Biotech is all about making products," Löffler has said. "It's an industry that's highly entrepreneurial and moving extremely fast. When you move that fast, traditional business models break down, so you need to develop new ones."[64] The center helps managers understand the technical and commercial details associated with the biotechnology industry, as well as the capital demands of a business that can take half a billion dollars and 15 years to bring a product to market successfully. "It took us a long time to realize that biotechnology is an information science," said Löffler.

The Center for Research on Strategic Alliances was another scholarly institute that opened in 2002. Led by Ed Zajac, the James F. Beré Professor of Management and Organizations, the center is the only academic research center in the United States focused solely on the impact of strategic alliances, which can be fraught with hurdles. "There can be enormous cultural impediments when creating mergers," said Zajac, who has consulted for numerous organizations on this matter, including the U.S. Department of Homeland Security. With government agencies seeking to merge, there are special challenges, he noted. "Even details as seemingly trivial as uniform insignias can present challenges. Whose badge will survive the merger? These things matter to the people wearing the uniforms."[65] The center's mission involves furthering the understanding of such alliances by promoting and support-ing research, seminars and workshops.

Today, the Kellogg School faculty includes experts who have contributed land-mark research in a wide array of areas, including marketing, finance, health care, negotiation, teams and leadership. Scholars such as Ranjay Gulati, the Michael Ludwig Nemmers Distinguished Professor of Strategy and Organizations, investi-gate the power of strategic alliances and other relationships. Gulati has created a framework called network resources to explore this subject, and his work has earned him wide recognition, including being ranked among the 10 most-cited researchers in economics and business by ISI-Incite. Kellogg thought leaders in crisis manage-ment include Daniel Diermeier, the IBM Distinguished Professor of Regulation and Competitive Practice. Among his recent work is research on strategic markets and nonmarket strategy coauthored with former Stanford and Kellogg professor David Baron, in which they evaluate tactics that nongovernmental organizations (NGOs) employ to pressure firms to change business practices. A brief sampling of other influential Kellogg faculty members follows:

- Sergio Rebelo, the Tokai Bank Distinguished Professor of Finance, whose research in macroeconomics and international business has investigated the impact of economic policy on economic growth, as well as the effects of exchange rate–based stabilizations. He also has pursued a theoretical framework to understand international currency crises. Rebelo has said that most currency crises stem from the inability or unwillingness of governments to collect sufficient tax revenues to support their spending. "When this happens, the government, sooner or later, has to resort to printing money or using other financing strategies that tend to destabilize the exchange rate," he explained.[66] A fellow of the Econometric Society, the National Bureau of Economic Research and the Center for Economic Policy Research, Rebelo also has served as a consultant to the World Bank, the International Monetary Fund, the

Board of Governors of the Federal Reserve System and the European Central Bank.

- Ravi Jagannathan, the Chicago Mercantile Exchange/John F. Sandner Distinguished Professor of Finance, whose research interests include asset pricing, capital markets, financial institutions and portfolio performance evaluation. His articles have appeared in many leading academic journals, including the *Journal of Political Economy,* the *Journal of Financial Economics* and the *Journal of Finance.* In addition to serving on the editorial boards of top journals, he is a member of the board of directors of the American Finance Association and a research associate at the National Bureau of Economics Research, as well as president of the Society of Financial Studies. He also serves as codirector of the Kellogg Financial Institutions and Markets Research Center. Some of Jagannathan's recent research involves developing a theoretical framework to improve the way in which initial public offerings (IPOs) are structured, such as changing the book-building system to suit the needs of companies going public. He has commented on the weaknesses of standard IPO auctions, saying that their main problem is "that they do not adequately reward those who devote time and effort to serious evaluation of an unlisted company." Furthermore, when investors who are uninformed try to ride on the coattails of more savvy investors, he has said, the sophisticated investors begin avoiding IPO auctions.[67]

- Robert McDonald, the Erwin P. Nemmers Distinguished Professor of Finance, researches corporate finance, taxation, derivatives and applications of option pricing theory to corporate investments. Several of his papers have won research awards, including the Graham and Dodd Scroll from the Financial Analyst's Federation, the Iddo Sarnat Prize from the *Journal of Banking and Finance,* the Smith Breeden Prize from the *Journal of Finance* and the Review of Financial Studies Prize from the *Review of Financial Studies,* where he is coeditor. His text titled *Derivatives Markets* (now in its second edition) is widely used at leading business schools. McDonald has said he wrote the text out of dissatisfaction with existing books on the subject. In his version, he has included more useful examples and illustrations, he added. Colleague Robert Korajczyk has called McDonald "a pioneer in developing option pricing theory" in situations that vary from those applicable to exchange-traded options. "The problems that Bob's research addresses require a greater grounding in economic analysis than do standard problems," said Korajczyk. "This grounding in economics carries over to *Derivatives Markets* in that the book does a wonderful job of teaching the reader the economic intuition of derivatives markets in addition to the mathematics of derivative pricing."[68]

- Angela Lee, PepsiCo Professor of International Marketing, whose research into consumer learning, product evaluation and brand choice, as well as cross-cultural studies of the similarities and differences in information processing, have earned her distinction, including the Kellogg School's Reiter Award for Best Paper. Among her research works are publications that demonstrate how context influences marketing's effectiveness. For instance, she has reported that consumers are more likely to evaluate a product favorably after having seen an advertisement for a similar product that, in effect, "primes" the consumer, making him or her more receptive to subsequent ads. Her work in this area includes the investigation of ideas such as perceptual fluency, "liking without conscious awareness" that develops through sensory exposure, and conceptual fluency, a preference that occurs when the mind can more easily process it. Professor Alice Tybout, former chair of the Marketing Department, has praised her colleague's research: "[Lee's] depth of understanding . . . how memory operates provides the foundation for unique strategic insights about how to develop more effective persuasive messages."[69]

- David Dranove, the Walter J. McNerney Distinguished Professor of Health Industry Management, whose research into the U.S. health care market includes his books *How Hospitals Survived; The Economic Evolution of American Health Care: From Marcus Welby to Managed Care; What's Your Life Worth?* and *Code Red: Reviving the American Healthcare System.* He is also coauthor (with David Besanko and Mark Shanley) of *Economics of Strategy.* His work (with Mark Satterthwaite) on the ramifications of public disclosure of individual doctors or hospitals earned him the Stanley Reiter Award for Best Paper from Kellogg in 2005 (see the previous discussion of this award). "Is More Information Better? The Effects of 'Report Cards' on Health Care Providers" was published in the June 2003 *Journal of Political Economy.* "The success of report cards is a necessary condition for the success of free market healthcare," Dranove has said. "Otherwise, cost will become the dominant [consideration] over quality, and markets are supposed to do better than that."[70]

- Philip Kotler, the S. C. Johnson and Son Distinguished Professor of International Marketing, has helped redefine modern marketing practice.

Through nearly 50 books and some 140 articles over four decades, Kotler has remained at the pinnacle of marketing thought. He has been ranked by *Financial Times* as among the most influential business thinkers, and his seminal textbook, *Marketing Management,* is appearing in a thirteenth edition. For more details about Kotler's considerable influence, see chapters 2 and 5.

- Alice M. Tybout, the Harold T. Martin Professor of Marketing, whose research explores consumer information processing, categorization processes and the philosophy and methods of theory testing. A 1975 graduate of the Northwestern University doctoral program in marketing, Tybout joined the school that year as an assistant professor. She was made a full professor in 1985 and was named the Harold T. Martin Professor in 1988. She served as chair of the Marketing Department from 2004 to 2006. Tybout has earned numerous teaching and research distinctions, including the American Marketing Association's first prize for her doctoral dissertation, the Sidney J. Levy Teaching Award, the Chairs Core Teaching Award, and the Kellogg Alumni Professor of the Year Award. She has served on the editorial boards of several leading journals, including the *Journal of Marketing,* the *Journal of Marketing Research* and the *Journal of Consumer Research.* Tybout's publication credits include three books she coedited, including *Kellogg on Branding* and *Perspectives on the Affective and Cognitive Effects of Advertising.* Her book chapters and journal articles have focused on branding and segmentation, among other subjects.

- David Austen-Smith, the Peter G. Peterson Chair in Corporate Ethics and professor of political economy, whose research and teaching has been centered, in part, on political theory, political economy, social choice and game theory. A charter member of the Game Theory Society and a fellow of the American Academy of Arts and Sciences, Austen-Smith also has earned the Sidney J. Levy Teaching Award and numerous grants from the National Science Foundation to support such research as investigations into deliberation and voting in committees, redistribution in divided societies, strategic information transmission via experiments and information aggregation and the Condorcet Jury Theorem. Recent publications have included "Deliberation, Preference Uncertainty and Voting Rules" (coauthored with Timothy Feddersen) and "Redistribution and Affirmative Action" (coauthored with Michael Wallerstein). Among more than 50 articles and several books he has coauthored or edited are: *Positive Political Theory I: Collective Preference, Positive Political Theory II:*

Strategy and Structure and *Social Choice and Strategic Decisions: Essays in Honor of Jeffrey S. Banks.* Recently, he has studied how incentives to share or suppress information arise in small-group deliberations, such as corporate committees, juries and congressional hearings. Austen-Smith has summarized the application of his findings: "You had better be very careful designing your committees because doing so will affect how decisions are made. The rules under which people vote influence the way they speak and what they say."[71]

The school's research tradition is continued among more junior faculty, such as Brian Rogers, senior lecturer and the Donald P. Jacobs Scholar in Managerial Economics and Decision Sciences, and Camelia M. Kuhnen, senior lecturer and Donald P. Jacobs Scholar in Finance. Rogers's research, some conducted in collaboration with Stanford professor Matthew O. Jackson, has focused on social networks, game theory and microeconomics. Rogers has noted that social networks are diverse, encompassing personal friendships, electronic correspondences, online chat rooms and scientific collaborations. "Though they come from really different settings, the structures of these networks are found empirically to have quite a lot in common," he has said. "We wanted to write a model that can be seen as a reasonable description of how networks form in all these different applications."[72]

In her research on neurofinance, Kuhnen has been one of a small number of people who have made important contributions to understanding the roles that neurochemistry and brain structure play in financial decisions. In the emerging field of neurofinance, Kuhnen's work has helped articulate how primitive areas in the brain, largely ignored by earlier economists when devising theories, actually seem connected to higher-level cerebral processing, such as decisions related to risk and reward.

Another young faculty member whose work is proving influential is Adam Galinsky, the Morris and Alice Kaplan Professor of Management and Organizations, whose research focuses on such areas as workplace ethics, power dynamics and mimicry. Susan E. Perkins, senior lecturer and Donald P. Jacobs Scholar in Management and Organizations, has pursued research that helps explain institutional variation between nations, identifying potential risks inherent to multinational corporations. Her research focuses on the international business implications of industry regulation, corporate governance and ownership structure, experiential learning and firm-level nonmarket strategy.

These and many other Kellogg scholars have contributed—and continue to do so—in vital ways to the school and to their various disciplines. Indeed, during the tenure of Dean Jain, research and teaching have flourished at Kellogg.

"An Honorable Burden"

When Jain was formally installed as dean in 2001, the school held a tribute to him at the weekly student social gathering known as TG. During the search to fill the position, David Besanko and the committee repeatedly heard that whoever was chosen to replace Jacobs would have to establish a direction for the school very quickly. "The new dean would have to hit the ground running," said Besanko in 2007. "That's all we heard on the search committee."[73]

To ensure that Jain understood the urgency of maintaining the school's preeminence while also imparting his own leadership stamp, Besanko and the students presented the dean with an oversize pair of running shoes at the TG. "You have some big shoes to fill," Besanko said, "but we are convinced and confident that you can hit the ground running."

In fact, Jain did establish early priorities for his deanship and the school. First and foremost, he wanted to maintain the overall excellence and reputation that Kellogg enjoyed, making decisions that bolstered existing strengths while seeking new opportunities. The overarching framework would have three parts: leadership, scholarship and partnership. These were the foundations of what the dean called the Kellogg School's "culture of innovation and excellence."[74] "We are dedicated to creating path-breaking knowledge that defines and shapes the business and management fields," Jain said.[75] Faculty members were immersed in a culture that valued research and teaching, sending a powerful message to professors hoping to advance their careers in an environment that simultaneously nurtured them and challenged them to excel. In addition to scholarship, Kellogg placed renewed emphasis on partnership with all members of its community—from faculty, staff and students to alumni and corporate friends. More resources would flow to alumni relations (see the later discussion) and help build the network. Jain himself would fulfill a pledge to network more intensely with the school's alumni, traveling from Asia to Europe and throughout the United States beginning in July 2001. Leadership, the third part of the plan, was important at all levels of the school, in the classroom as well as throughout the administration. The administration would undergo key organizational changes; so, too, would the curriculum, which would offer more leadership courses and tools, such as a 360-degree leadership assessment and TeaMBAnk, a repository of team and leadership resources created exclusively for Kellogg students.

Taking this blueprint and building with it would require vision, innovation and actual execution. Jain called the challenge of succeeding Jacobs "an honorable burden" and said: "It is difficult to follow him, but I also got my training under him. The last five years working with him have been very valuable for me."[76] Yet he knew he "still had a lot to learn" because he "was not involved in all aspects [of the school]," including admissions.[77] In addition, he expressed a desire to take the school from "individual to institution," believing that Kellogg would build strength by adopting a model of distributed leadership and making a shift to perpetuate the best elements of curriculum, teaching, research and culture in ways that were largely independent of any one person, no matter how brilliant a leader.

Kellogg had traditionally operated with a lean staff, but its continuous growth argued for organizational changes inside the dean's office and in other areas as well, including Student Affairs, Development and Alumni Relations. Rather than having one associate dean, as had been the case, Jain would split the one role into two and create the Office of the Dean. One senior associate dean would address teaching and curriculum, and the other would manage faculty and research. (In 2007, Jain added a third senior associate dean position to oversee planning and external relations. Besanko filled that role.) The new Office of the Dean would distribute the school's leadership to move toward "institutionalizing" the administration, but the move would also enable the dean to pursue objectives away from Evanston that would strengthen the school. Achieving these goals (detailed later in this chapter) as well as delivering on his "partnership" promise to alumni would demand extensive travel on Jain's part. "I am eager to engage in a dialogue with our alumni to determine how Kellogg can continue to deliver meaningful programs and services that enhance the careers, and the lives, of our graduates," he said in 2001. "We always emphasize that Kellogg is a lifelong experience. I want to be sure to communicate the school's renewed commitment to this ideal, and benefit from the recommendations of our alumni."[78]

Admirable objectives, to be sure, but the need to make important decisions at the school would not stop while the dean was traveling. To enable Kellogg to continue functioning effectively while Jain pursued these critical partnership objectives, the senior associate deans, working closely with him, would have the authority to take action in his absence.

Appointed to the dual roles in 2001 were Besanko and Magee. Magee would oversee faculty and research, and Besanko would manage curriculum and teaching. One of their first tasks was to help Kellogg rate itself against the competition in terms of academics and alumni relations, among other things.[79] Challenges facing the school included the perennial one of recruiting and retaining top faculty and students. Retaining faculty was expected to be a significant focus, said Magee. "It's not easy to do, so we must ensure that Kellogg remains competitive in the packages we offer," he noted. "Those packages are multidimensional, involving compensation, but also the resources available to a faculty member, including the quality of the colleagues here." Kellogg would also work to increase its intellectual product—for example, publications, including discipline-shaping textbooks, such as McDonald's *Derivatives Markets* (2002) and Kotler's *Marketing Management: Analysis, Planning, Implementation and Control* (thirteenth edition, forthcoming 2008). "Textbooks enable your teaching to have a kind of legacy as you make a real contribution to your field," said Besanko.

The senior associate deans also shared Jain's philosophy of leadership, including the objective of institutionalizing the culture and operations that had for so long distinguished Kellogg. For instance, Besanko noted that his research into the links between corporate strategy, organizational structure and incentives had revealed the realities of how communication and leadership functioned within a modern organization. "One of the things we learned is how important it is to clearly communicate to everyone in the organization," he said in an interview shortly after assuming the role in the dean's office. "At the end of the day, it's not Dean Jain and Bob and David making all the decisions around here. The decisions that impact this school are made every day by hundreds of people: teachers who are teaching their classes, administrators who are making decisions about running their areas."[80]

Associate Dean Carole Cahill noted Jain's "boundless ability to do and do and do every day," but she also pointed out that running a school such as Kellogg has become impossible to do without a committed team working together. "Today, we're bigger and things move faster. Dean Jain has said to us, 'I trust you to do the right thing. We need to gather and be collective about things.' He didn't add any layers. He's handed off some of that responsibility. Big picture, strategy—that's what he does. But by and large, day to day, the staff can talk to each other and make decisions, because he needs to be focused in other places."[81]

Other changes included reorganizing the Student Affairs Office in early 2002, after Edmund Wilson announced his retirement. Similar to the dual role of the senior associate deans, Student Affairs would now have two codirectors, one for academics and another for student life and experiences. Assuming the former post was Michele Rogers, a graduate of the Harvard Business School who had worked in consulting and as admissions director for Northwestern University's Medill School of Journalism prior to joining Kellogg in 1990. She would now manage the annual class schedule, course bidding and registration, the academic calendar, the Kellogg Honor Code, major field meetings and general academic and classroom policies. Fran Brasfield Langewisch, a 1995 graduate of Kellogg who joined the Student Affairs Office that year as assistant director, would oversee student life, including student governance, student services, housing, CIM Week, conferences, speakers and club activities. Together, they were expected to constitute a leadership team dedicated to making the student experience at Kellogg second to none, including helping to enhance the diversity and range of activities that had already distinguished the student culture.

(More recently, this structure was revised. In 2007, Langewisch was promoted to assistant dean of academic affairs and student life, and Rogers became assistant dean for integrated programs and experiential learning, responsible for interacting with other schools at Northwestern University on joint-degree programs, such as the JD-MBA and the master of management and manufacturing. Other changes in 2007 included the promotion of Theresa Parker from assistant dean to associate dean for finance and budget planning and Carole Cahill from assistant dean to associate dean of facilities and human resources.)

Jain has repeatedly emphasized the importance of creating an inclusive, collaborative environment where all members of the school work toward a common objective. "My main message . . . is that we are only able to achieve these successes by treating this business like a family," he said in a 2004 interview. "Every person is important in the organization. I have found it very useful to always acknowledge everyone's efforts . . . I personally ignore all levels of hierarchy. You should never consider anyone to be beneath you or be too difficult to approach. My door is always open and any student or member of staff can come in here to see me at any time."[82] He has also brought a quiet philosophical air to his work at the Kellogg School: "You cannot control what people say, so the only ornament that one must wear is that of forgiveness. I believe that a moment of silence [resisting the urge to say something in anger] can save you years of grief."[83]

This quiet confidence and collaborative leadership approach may in part derive from the dean's Jainist religious beliefs, which emphasize respect for others and an appreciation for deep listening and multiple perspectives on any subject or situation. Undoubtedly, his upbringing in Assam, a state located in northeastern India and connected to the mainland by a narrow stretch of terrain called the Siliguri Corridor (or, more colloquially, "the chicken's neck"), also has influenced his contemplative views and willingness to engage others, regardless of their rank or social status. Home to diverse races who settled the land over time, Assam (the name is derived from the Sanskrit word meaning "peerless") developed a unique composite culture. Tezpur, an ancient town on the banks of the Brahmaputra River, is the largest of the region's north bank towns. Tezpur's many temples and ruins date back to the eighth century; the land's myths and legends seem timeless.[84]

With respect to new objectives at Kellogg, Dean Jain was clear: he preferred taking a systematic approach, "start[ing] slow and small" before scaling up, since "our currency is our reputation and we have to be very careful in our approach."[85] The school didn't need to make radical changes, he told the *Chicago Tribune.* "We have started so many initiatives that need to be institutionalized."[86] His scaffolding would be the concepts of leadership, scholarship and partnership, identifying the three keys to the school's success. His administration would continue enhancing rigor and relevance, ensuring that both teaching and research remained strong and balanced. At the same time, the school would reach out to its growing alumni network to create value for graduates while also strengthening the school through their reengagement with it. In addition, Kellogg would expand its leadership offerings, particularly those with an experiential component, in an effort to differentiate itself and meet marketplace demands, as administrators also took steps to enhance the school's global reputation, including by building a presence in key markets such as Asia, Europe and Latin America.[87] One important way the school would advance this goal was by launching the Kellogg-Miami Executive MBA Program in Coral Gables, Florida, in January 2006, although the idea for the program dated to about 1996. Modeled closely after the Evanston-based EMBA Program, the Kellogg-Miami Program represents a tangible example of the school's ongoing commitment to global business and brand extension. The inaugural class of 42 executives came from throughout Central and South America, as well as the southeastern United States. "Today, we see a dream coming true," said Jain at the program's launch on February 13 at the Hyatt Regency Coral Gables, the luxury hotel adjacent to the dedicated Kellogg classroom where the program is conducted. "With this piece we continue our mission to bring the Kellogg School's leadership to executives worldwide through our global centers of knowledge that unite all Kellogg students and alumni."

These global centers would be critical components of Jain's vision for expanding the Kellogg footprint internationally. Of particular value, he believed, was the uniformly rigorous and integrated curriculum that afforded students the flexibility to complete their Kellogg degree at any of the school's locations, whether in Asia, Europe, the Middle East or North America. Jain also spoke of the school's "moral imperative" to bring its leadership to Latin America, where adverse economic and political conditions have historically caused privation. "This objective is consistent with the Kellogg School mission to create responsible global leaders who contribute to the community in important ways," said Jain during the Kellogg-Miami Program's launch.[88]

Julie Cisek-Jones, assistant dean and director of the Executive MBA Program, noted the importance of the school's mission in this area. "What's exciting is that we're seeing the realization of a long-term vision," she said.[89] "Our students are no longer based solely in North America. They're doing coursework on several continents. They're interacting with each other and taking those Kellogg skills and relationships into the world." What is more, the Kellogg EMBA curriculum has repeatedly been ranked number one in surveys such as those conducted by *BusinessWeek* and *U.S. News & World Report*.

The focus on global brand building was not surprising, given Jain's marketing background, but more was driving this issue than mere personal preference. Brand perception was increasingly important in the competitive management education space. In 2002, Kellogg had once again earned the number one place in the national rankings, but remaining in the top tier was getting more challenging, as more schools were fighting for the scarce resources of excellent faculty and students while enhancing their physical facilities with ever more glamorous, state-of-the-art buildings. Clearly, a multifaceted effort was required if Kellogg was to remain a top-level management leader.

Most fundamentally, Jain would spend the first year of his administration listening to the various constituents involved with the school: students, faculty and staff, alumni, recruiters, corporate partners and the external media. In a whirl of seemingly constant travel between 2001 and 2002, Jain and members of his administration, including Assistant Dean Roxanne Hori, director of the Kellogg Career Management Center, circled the globe, visiting with alumni and recruiters to learn how the school could better meet the needs of companies.[90] The information they gathered allowed the school to anticipate and modify its curriculum as needed. "I believe that in this role [of dean] there is no such thing as forecasting; the real word is anticipation," said Jain in 2004. "You anticipate what the trends are going to be and you prepare action plans. That's all you can do. Nobody knows exactly what's going to happen. You need to combine the data that you get with your intuition and come up with a plan."[91]

The message recruiters sent the school was that Kellogg students had an outstanding reputation as team leaders and the Kellogg curriculum was legendary for its marketing prowess, but other aspects of the school, such as its finance strengths, were less known externally. In addition, Kellogg graduates did not enjoy a strong external reputation as people who could handle advanced quantitative, analytical tasks, and they were perceived by some as lacking in detailed knowledge. Even though some of these complaints were more the result of perception than a reflection of reality, the school moved quickly to address any legitimate concerns. In 2002, for the first time since the 1970s, Kellogg would launch a major, comprehensive curriculum review. Previous efforts had addressed smaller-scale needs with more modest changes.[92] Now, a curriculum task force would focus on the first-year curriculum to ensure content and sequencing were optimal, particularly with respect to preparing students for summer internships—key to procuring postgraduation jobs—between their first and second years in the MBA program.

The 11-member task force, led by Besanko and including senior faculty and staff, with student input as well, discovered that the school's curriculum was both rigorous and relevant, matching up well against its peers and offering an abundance of opportunities for students to master team and leadership skills. However, the group recommended one primary enhancement, a change in how the school presented a core Management and Organizations (MORS) course. By including the class in an intensive, 10-day "preterm" program associated with the traditional CIM orientation activities, Kellogg would enable students to take either core finance or marketing courses earlier in their MBA careers, in the fall quarter, which would strengthen their academic portfolios and their performance in summer internships.[93]

"We were seeing that internships were becoming an ever-more important factor in landing job offers after graduation on a full-time basis," recalled Besanko, who cited the fact as one of three prime drivers influencing the Curriculum Task Force's decisions. Other factors included a desire to strengthen the school's emphasis on leadership and ethics, which included rethinking the Management and Organizations course. This resulted in the preterm MORS offering for first-year students. "For the same reasons, we developed the pre-term SEEK offering for second-year students," he said.[94] Several other enhancements included adjustments to the school's class schedule, which created more opportunities for students to gather between classes for club meetings, presentations, seminars and study groups. The school also changed the pass/no pass requirements to make them more rigorous, while simultaneously developing new processes to review experiential courses.

With respect to engaging alumni, Kellogg took several major steps, most notably adding staff and other resources to the Office of Alumni Relations in the 2002–2003 school year; the same was done in the Office of Development, where a new position was created to deal with planned and major gifts, filled by Stephanie Blackburn Freeth '02. This arrangement resulted in a dual approach to engaging the school's graduates and building mutually beneficial relationships with them. In addition, the school merged the two departments in May 2004. In 2002, Megan Byrne Krueger '90, who had joined Kellogg in 1988 and had been assistant dean and director of alumni relations, took her expertise to the school's Part-Time MBA Program on the Chicago campus; there, as assistant dean and director of student affairs, she would help build its student culture in much the same way her colleagues had developed the full-time program in Evanston, increasing student activities along both social and professional dimensions. The school would bring several new staff members into the department to oversee the ambitious efforts devoted to expanding alumni services and building a deeper connection between alumni and Kellogg.

When Liz Livingston Howard '93 became associate director of the Center for Nonprofit Management in 2004 after serving as assistant dean and director of development from 1994 to 2003, Kellogg recruited Roger W. Shepard to assume the leadership of the school's development and alumni efforts. Bringing nearly two decades of experience in fund-raising from his former roles as associate chancellor for development and vice president at the University of Illinois Foundation and his tenure as associate dean for external affairs at the Graduate School of Business at the University of Chicago, Shepard spoke enthusiastically about engaging Kellogg alumni, whom he called "the bedrock" of the school's development initiatives.

Early in his Kellogg tenure, Shepard noted the need to engage alumni with exciting and ambitious goals for the school. "We cannot go to our alumni and say, 'We need money for what Kellogg is now and has been,'" he said in 2004. "That's not good enough. We have to provide 'the lift of a driving dream.' This is a plan that identifies the future of Kellogg, one that is exciting, believable and easy to understand."[95] Shepard and Dean Jain both emphasized the lifelong opportunities for alumni to remain engaged with Kellogg but noted that the benefits—a powerful network, access to ongoing intellectual capital—came with a price: alumni would have to "give back" to the school to help maintain its brand strength and intellectual resources. Indeed, doing so created a win-win situation for both the graduates and Kellogg, said Jain.

"The more our alumni invest in Kellogg, the more value is produced both for them and for our school," he said, adding that "now is not the time to stop our efforts," given the fierce competition for premium resources among top business schools. He viewed philanthropy as a "two-way street," a bargain made between Kellogg and its graduates. "We cannot just ask them for resources," said Jain. "We also have to give back to them. That's why we continuously look for ways to replenish our alumni's knowledge base." If alumni felt that they were being renewed by their connections with Kellogg, they would be more apt to commit resources—not only financial but also relational, in terms of their networking connections, their experience and ideas—to the school.[96]

Kellogg had already begun increasing alumni engagement and philanthropy, setting a record for fund-raising in the 2000–2001 academic year when its efforts produced nearly $18 million in cash and $10 million in additional pledges. The figures reflected a 61 percent increase over totals for the previous year.[97] In addition, graduating students in the full-time program in 2001 raised nearly $250,000 with a 90 percent participation rate, and graduates of the part-time program raised $62,000 with half of the class participating.

The synergy gained by streamlining two offices to create the Office of Development and Alumni Relations began paying off. Attendance at Reunion

Weekend in May has steadily increased since 2001—growing by 20 percent year over year from 2002 to 2005 and with nearly 1,300 people participating in 2006 and 1,600 alumni and friends returning to Evanston in 2007. The annual event began in 1977 with a modest 100 alumni returning to campus for what was termed the Alumni Alert and Management Update, a two-day affair that included walking tours of the campus, a national Frisbee-hurling contest and Waa-Mu Show rehearsals. More than a dozen faculty members gave a series of seminars. Alumni also enjoyed a wine and cheese reception and a picnic on Deering Meadow, where a Dixieland jazz band entertained them. The event was considered an instant success, and the school made plans to make reunion an annual highlight, with administrators announcing early details of the 1978 gathering. Alumni could expect three new seminars: an introduction to computers, another on personal finance and a session on hospital and health service management.[98] Northwestern University provost Raymond Mack greeted alumni in the Norris University Center in 1978, informing them: "The state of the Graduate School of Management is excellent. GSM's faculty continues to gain prominence, its academic reputation is growing, and the school is acquiring increasing national, public recognition. You can be proud of your school."[99]

Since its inception, the scale and scope of the reunion has consistently expanded. Besides offering the traditional variety of social opportunities, reunion planners also began adding significant intellectual and professional development components starting in 2002, with faculty members conducting more rigorous, intensive class sessions and other programs during the action-packed weekend. In addition, class gifts have reflected an increase in student engagement. In 2006, members of the full-time class gave a record $812,407 with a 91 percent participation rate, the money going to renovate more than three dozen group-study rooms and to further fund the school's SEEK Program, which focuses on social enterprise. The year before, the full-time class had broken a previous record, generating more than $500,000, the funds going to convert Room 102 into a solarium overlooking Deering Meadow. Meanwhile, students in the part-time program contributed $163,635 during a record-breaking campaign in 2004. Most recently, students have shattered even these records: the full-time class of 2007 raised a total of $1 million,[100] earmarked for major facilities enhancements. In terms of alumni engagement, Kellogg boasts more than 80 active regional and 19 special interest alumni clubs on every continent except Antarctica. (Actually, Kellogg alumni have traversed even that icy region: Robert "Bo" Parfet '06 traveled to Vinson Massif in Antarctica between 2004 and 2005 as part of a philanthropic effort to climb the world's seven highest mountains. See "Taking Leadership at Kellogg to New Heights" in the spring 2005 edition of *Kellogg World*.)

The school has also introduced several major alumni-oriented initiatives, most notably a program of lifelong learning that incorporates offerings like the "MBA Update"; under that program, senior professors deliver abbreviated but highly informative courses designed to let graduates enhance their business knowledge with the latest research from Kellogg thought leaders. The effort, which was begun in 2000, initially included professors traveling to various locales around the world to deliver the update to alumni clubs, an approach that was especially valuable for those who had been out of school for several years. The daylong offering would present a variety of topics, from financial analysis and strategic value creation to entrepreneurship and family enterprise. Each MBA update would focus on a different subject in detail and would allow participants to learn about current research and teaching at Kellogg. The initiative was designed both to provide a tangible academic benefit to graduates and to reengage them with the school.

Equally ambitious was a move to bolster the Kellogg Alumni Network—some 50,000 members strong—by enhancing the online communications tools available to them. The effort, dubbed "Power Up" and launched on January 14, 2004, significantly improved the ease and range of networking options that Kellogg graduates could use to remain connected with the school and each other. Almost immediately, more than 10,000 alumni became increasingly active in the network, including more than 1,300 new users. Nearly 7,500 graduates took advantage of the communications tools to update their contact information—a simple move but one that is critical for the school and its graduates to remain connected with one another in order to facilitate effective interaction. As part of a promotion to encourage alumni to use the system, Kellogg sponsored a number of contests that engaged alumni clubs. One event featured the 20-millionth laptop computer manufactured by IBM being given to an alum randomly selected from all those logging onto the Web site.[101]

Among the benefits afforded by the enhanced site was faster, easier access to Kellogg career services, the alumni directory, reunion information, alumni club activities and discussion groups. Graduates were also granted easier access to purchase Kellogg School–branded items and faculty publications. Catherine Grimsted, then associate dean of finance and administration and COO, noted that the portal was "truly alumni-centric." "At one glance, they will be able to find everything at Kellogg that's applicable to them."[102]

In conjunction with the outreach efforts via the Internet, the school redoubled its commitment to other ways of reaching alumni, the business media and the public to keep them apprised of Kellogg initiatives. The school's Web site was continually upgraded, with more staff being added to manage the ever-increasing number of pages on the site. By 2007, the site had some 30,000 pages and was attracting more than 900,000 visits per month.

Kellogg World magazine, the school's alumni periodical, also underwent a transformation in the latter part of the 1990s and into the new century. The Marketing and Communications Department grew under the leadership of Assistant Dean and Chief Marketing Officer Richard P. Honack '94, who arrived at the school in 1995 as its director of media relations and communications after a 15-year career developing and executing promotion strategies for the *Chicago Tribune* and *Chicago Sun-Times*. Prior to that, he worked in the industry for a decade as a reporter and editor. Upon assuming his Kellogg role, Honack noted his objective was "to create one voice for Kellogg, be it full-time, part-time or executive [MBA] programs. We want to deliver this message worldwide as we continue our international strategic initiatives."[103] Working with Honack were several staff members trained as writers or graphic designers. With support from the Office of the Dean, the staff revitalized the alumni magazine by incorporating more sophisticated content that blended the institution's public relations agenda with a journalistic approach designed to engage its readership, which had grown to nearly 50,000 subscribers, both alumni and others. In particular, the magazine began building more value into the "Class News" section—the heart of the book for readers seeking to network with peers. By 2006, the magazine's four-color design, which had previously been confined to the front 40 pages, was expanded to include the entire magazine, which often totaled 120 pages or more, indicating the success of the department's efforts to enhance the alumni experience through print and digital media.

In addition to the framework of leadership, scholarship and partnership announced in 2001, the Kellogg School administration would employ an approach that accentuated leadership in three main dimensions: thought leadership (academics and research), team leadership (collaborative learning, with students viewed as "cocreators" of their MBA experience) and civic leadership (community-oriented perspectives and initiatives that carried Kellogg knowledge into the world). The groundwork for this agenda had been laid at various times throughout the school's history, although the efforts would now be redoubled and articulated more overtly, with the full resources of the Office of the Dean driving the process.

Among the leadership offerings are formal classroom instruction and student-driven initiatives. Courses such as "Leadership in Organizations" provide an intensive opportunity that prepares students for decision making and effective team building. Students also benefit from exploring ethical issues in the "Values and Crisis Decision Making" course, which culminates in a 24-hour crisis-management simulation.

Other offerings include TeaMBAnk, encompassing "the Kellogg School resources for team development and excellence." Developed in collaboration with the Business Leadership Club and the Kellogg Team and Group Research Center, the TeaMBAnk initiative was intended to support team leadership and provide development tools to help students become extraordinary leaders. The TeaMBAnk Leadership Development Series was established to help leaders understand who they are and how they can draw out the best from themselves and those they lead. It also enhances their ability to develop professional relationships, cultivate unique attributes and map out a developmental plan to benefit from strengths while remedying weaknesses.

Another tool, the mandatory 360 Degree Leadership Assessment, also identifies strengths and weaknesses in students' leadership skills based on their work experiences. By learning what areas needed improvement, students can tailor their courses and activities to accelerate their leadership development. The Leadership Speaker Series, meanwhile, has brought people such as Jack Welch, former CEO of General Electric, and Lovie Smith, Chicago Bears coach, to campus for interactions with students and professors. Leadership also is highlighted each year through the Kellogg Award for Distinguished Leadership, sponsored by the Business Leadership Club and the Office of the Dean. Created in 2002 in honor of Dean Emeritus Jacobs, the award recognizes outstanding leaders and brings them to campus to address the school community. Recent winners have included real estate entrepreneur Sam Zell, Berkshire Hathaway CEO Warren Buffett, former Honeywell CEO Larry Bossidy and Women's World Banking president Nancy Barry. Under the Executive Leader in Residence Series, Kellogg brings senior-level executives to the school for extended visits with students and faculty in an informal setting—an exceptional opportunity for participants to learn firsthand about executive responsibilities and gain insights directly from top executives.

The abundance of leadership opportunities, formal and informal, at Kellogg necessitated the appointment of a faculty member to oversee the extensive portfolio. In 2006, Kellogg named Michelle Buck, clinical associate professor of management and organizations and associate director of executive education, to be director of leadership initiatives. The decision was the result of a larger, two-year effort, in which a leadership task force, composed of students, faculty and administrators, sought ways to leverage existing leadership offerings and generate new ones. Today, the director of leadership initiatives integrates and coordinates existing leadership-related offerings. These range widely from leadership positions in clubs, associations and committees to roles in student government or as organizers of academic conferences and community outreach initiatives, such as those associated with Business with a Heart. The Kellogg Student Association (KSA, formerly the Graduate

Management Association) works with faculty and administrators in areas such as curriculum and technology, offering suggestions for how to improve the MBA experience at Kellogg.

Assistant Dean Langewisch told the Kellogg student newspaper, the *Merger,* in 2005: "There has been a huge proliferation in the number of clubs and student professional conferences over the years. The array of extracurricular activities has mushroomed.... There has always been a large diversity of clubs at Kellogg and as the number of clubs grew, the mix between professional, social, sports, volunteer, and personal development clubs has not changed. The numbers of each tend to grow in proportion with each other. Even during bad economic times, students have started new philanthropic and volunteer clubs." Among these, she noted, were such initiatives as the Business Leadership Club, the Leadership Conference and Leadership Development Exercises, as well as the 360 Degree Leadership Survey. "In the past, there was a lot of informal and experiential leadership, which still exists today, . . . but now there is definitely a much more formalized and academic approach to leadership from the students' viewpoint."

Students would perhaps gain their most important leadership lesson—understanding the need for action under uncertainty—while watching how the school responded to national tragedy in 2001.

Under Attack

The news was unexpected and devastating, and it shattered the clear, bright day for the 540 new MBA students who filled the Jacobs Center on the morning of September 11, 2001. The terrorist attacks that struck at the economic and political heart of the United States, killing three Kellogg School alumni in the process,[104] also dramatically altered the way in which the school and its community would manage the uncertain times ahead.

The 2001–2002 Kellogg academic year was just beginning; indeed, students had arrived filled with enthusiasm for the annual orientation event, CIM Week.[105] Dean Emeritus Jacobs had already greeted the students, delivering a brief introduction from the podium in the Owen L. Coon Forum, before Dean Jain began addressing the congregation. Then, the tragic news arrived. Within minutes of each other, two planes had crashed into the World Trade Center towers in Manhattan. Initially, word spread slowly: someone told section leader John Thee '02, who was positioned near the back of the auditorium. Thee expressed disbelief and ran to confirm the information by checking the television in the student lounge. By the time he returned to the auditorium, the news had begun to spread among the administrators seated in the front row, but many of the 540 new students still remained uninformed.

Assistant Dean Honack told Jon Neuhaus '02, the CIM Week master of cere-monies, what had happened, advising him to stall for time while the administration quickly figured out how best to tell all the students about the tragedy. Neuhaus wait-ed until Jain had concluded his remarks and then improvised his own presentation, saying that since some speakers had been delayed, he would be willing to take ques-tions from audience members about what they could expect from their next two years at Kellogg.

Within minutes, Honack stepped to the podium with the awful news. "As I am speaking, the United States is under what appears to be a terrorist attack," he said. At first, some students believed this might be either a strange joke or else part of the orientation—a "crisis leadership" simulation, perhaps. Honack assured them it was not.

After an initial silence, some 100 students jumped up and left the room, cell phones in hand as they desperately tried contacting family and friends who could have been directly affected by the attack. The remainder of the audience sat stunned. The school brought televisions in so that the community could remain informed as events unfolded. Phones and counselors were available throughout the building. Further complicating matters, the Allen Center was hosting the annual Executive MBA Live-In Week, and some 150 students had traveled to Kellogg from partner schools in Hong Kong, Israel and Germany to study negotiations with their Evanston peers. "Everywhere you saw the same stare, the same shock," said EMBA student Roger Mason at the time. People tried contacting relatives back home over telephone lines that were jammed and overtaxed.[106]

"It was just absolutely shocking," said Besanko, who was scheduled to address the students later that morning. "This was not the way we expected to start the aca-demic year."

The CIM Committee decided to suspend activities for the day, although stu-dents wanted to "try to salvage as much of CIM Week as possible in an appropriate and tasteful way," said Besanko.[107] As the week progressed, students pulled together to find ways to honor the spirit and purpose of CIM while also keeping a perspec-tive on the tragic development in the larger world.

"CIM Week is a vehicle for passing on the Kellogg culture, and the culture is what makes this such a great school," said Jeff Zeunik '02, chairman of the CIM Week executive committee. "If we didn't have CIM Week for this class, in theory we could have lost [the culture] forever. It was a tough decision, but we had to carry on."[108] Although keynote speaker and Mattel CEO Bob Eckert '77 was forced to cancel a live presentation on Saturday because airline travel had been stopped nationwide, he delivered his address twice via live video transmission on Friday and Saturday from his location in California. Meanwhile, students canceled a

Friday night diversity talent show, since it coincided with a candlelight vigil in Evanston; they rescheduled it for Sunday evening, when the event became a mixture of "joy, sadness, fresh starts, uneasiness and anticipation," according to Nancy Rosen '03. Some participants delivered poems or songs in honor of the victims of September 11. Also among the CIM events that week was a fund-raiser featuring student musicians that garnered more than $12,000. Those funds were sent to the families of the three Kellogg alumni who died in the attacks, one inside the World Trade Center in New York City, one at the Pentagon and one aboard American Airlines flight 11.

Dean Reaches Out to Alumni for Recruiting Assistance

The enormity of September 11 compounded other grim, if less tragic, developments that the school had begun dealing with months earlier. In the wake of the dot-com crash and subsequent recession starting in March 2001, companies began delaying projects and postponing hiring. Consulting firms and investment banks, among the biggest employers of the class of 2001, announced that new jobs would be deferred anywhere from two months to one year. The Office of the Dean took the unprecedented and controversial step of aggressively seeking ways to help students find jobs.

"I turned to our alumni from 1995 and earlier to find temporary work for the affected graduates," said Jain. Some feared that the move, which included an e-mail appeal in August as well as in-person contacts, would appear too much like "begging," but the school's leadership believed the most important thing was to support its students in any way possible.

"The response was extraordinary and overwhelmingly positive," said Jain.[109] More than 100 offers came into the Office of the Dean from around the world, with nearly 2,000 alumni responding. And the effort paid off, for 91 percent of the students received job offers within 30 days of graduation, even as other schools were striving to hit their numbers.[110]

Besanko remembered that the administration expressed concern about how the strategy would appear to the public. "We weren't sure if this was a good move or bad," he said, adding that some 45 or 50 students were affected. Would the media pick up the story and turn it into something embarrassing for Kellogg? No one knew. In fact, Lou Dobbs, the CNN reporter, did do a story on the school's efforts to find employment for its students, calling the piece "Dean Jain's Plea." But Kellogg and the dean eventually came out looking strong and proactive. Despite some criticism, Jain forged ahead with his attempt to engage alumni and find jobs for the class of 2001, keeping in his mind the image of a certain student with a pregnant wife and no medical insurance and another student with a mortgage but no job.

"Soon after I took over I realized that this was not a good time to be dean as things were very bad," Jain told the *Economic Times* (India) in 2002. "And I told . . . my wife that I will feel bad if I let them (team Kellogg) down."[111]

Besanko considered the effort exceptionally effective, noting that Kellogg had previously tried to work through back channels to engage other top business schools who were experiencing similar recruiting woes. Perhaps by working together, the schools could pursue collective action to benefit their students, he thought. No one else seemed interested.

But Kellogg did not stop with an e-mail appeal. Jain and members of his administration also traveled continuously to meet with recruiters and alumni in person, reengaging graduates with the school in ways that could help stimulate employment for recent alums while benefiting everyone in the Kellogg community by strengthening the school's overall network. "Recruiter Roundtables" in cities throughout the world allowed Jain and Roxanne Hori, director of the Kellogg Career Management Center, to understand specific corporate needs and obtain a firsthand assessment of what the school could expect for the coming hiring season. The administration also met with corporate advisers and major donors to gain their insights. In addition, Kellogg hosted top business leaders, such as John Chambers, CEO of Cisco Systems; Jack Welch, retired CEO of GE; and A. G. Lafley, CEO of Procter & Gamble. These and other leaders met with the school's faculty and students, providing fresh perspectives on the market and suggesting strategies to help secure success. In general, Kellogg also appealed to alumni repeatedly to reengage with the school, bringing their ideas and enthusiasm to bear on the future direction of Kellogg and helping shape the school's course with financial and intellectual support.

"It was a brilliant vision that Dipak had to do all this," said Besanko, who, along with Bob Magee, offered his personal contacts to students seeking employment. "No other business school dean was doing it. . . . It was a huge amount of work. I really am convinced that this set of things that we did in the dean's office were instrumental in bringing us back into the No. 1 position in *BusinessWeek* in 2002,"[112] since student satisfaction with the school's leadership played a part in the rankings for that year.

What's more, Besanko believed that these crises—September 11, as well as the recession and the accounting scandals associated with Enron and other firms that gave business a black eye—enabled the school's post-Jacobs leadership to establish itself in ways that might otherwise have been more difficult.

"We were somewhat naïve," reflected Besanko. "Had we been a little more experienced we might not have tried all the things that we tried.[113] Times of crisis help facilitate management innovation and make you more willing to try things that you might not have tried in times of stability. Crisis led the dean to very quickly become his own person, with the situation testing his administration. He was not judged by, 'What would Don [Jacobs] have done?' I think he was able to step out of the shadow of Don readily, because of how skillfully he responded to crisis."[114]

The job market did not bounce back immediately, of course, but Kellogg administrators remained dedicated to learning the needs of the market and determining how the school could best position itself and its curriculum to meet those needs. Kellogg also increased its online resources to help alumni and students find jobs, and it boosted the number of its career coaches from one to five. One of them, Ann Browning, explained the services the coaches provided: "We're here to help alumni with self assessment, developing a strong résumé, refining their interviewing skills and improving their job search tactics and networking skills. We can also help with negotiating job offers and making job-related decisions."[115] The service, costly on the open market, was offered free to Kellogg alumni. Online leadership assessment tools and tutorials also provided support for graduates. Perhaps most valuable for alumni, however, was an ongoing engagement with the school's network.

In a 2003 interview with *BusinessWeek,* Hori said that the outreach to alumni and other partners was critical for identifying employment opportunities for Kellogg graduates. When asked how she, a veteran recruiting expert, would characterize the 2002–2003 recruiting season, Hori replied: "Exhausting. It has been a challenging year for employers, students and career-service folks. But it has also been a time for people to reflect on what they really want to do, because job opportunities are limited."[116] Hori, who was herself spending 50 percent of her time in one-on-one counseling with students, noted that uncertainty in the market meant recruiters were proceeding cautiously, "making sure that they don't make any missteps." Even though she characterized the situation at the time as a "buyer's market," she said that smart buyers still wanted to do their due diligence and identify the best of the best from among a robust talent pool.

During this difficult time, applications to the school remained strong. In 1999, nearly 6,100 people applied for admission to the Kellogg Full-Time MBA Program, a figure that dipped only slightly the following year (to 5,802) before again breaching the 6,000 mark. Not surprisingly, the economic downturn of 2001 resulted in a jump in applications for the class of 2002, when 7,631 students applied. Three years earlier, consulting had garnered the largest number of graduates from the class of 1999 (some 40 percent went into the field), but by 2002, that figure had fallen to 26 percent, and there was instead a more balanced distribution among the fields: general management and strategic planning (16 percent), marketing (21 percent), finance (28 percent), business development (5 percent) and other areas (4 percent). Only four years earlier, general management had represented only 6 percent of the job market for Kellogg graduates, and other fields accounted for just 13 percent of the total.[117]

By 2005, Professor Robert Korajczyk observed the trend that appeared to be settling in. "Compared to 10-to-15 years back, there seems to be an overall shift from finance, which used to be the most popular major, toward a more balanced mix of finance, marketing, and management and strategy," he told the *Merger*. "These major preferences do fluctuate in the short term, however, as the business cycle dictates which industry is the most attractive at the time."

It was clear to the Kellogg School's leadership and students that the world had indeed changed radically from the recent days of the Internet boom. The class of 2003 arrived on campus for the first time on September 11, 2001. "That set a tone that was very different than what their predecessors experienced," said Hori. "They are much more tempered in their approach to things. They don't expect to make megabucks right out of the gate. People are thinking harder about their priorities. And students are being more realistic about the realities of the market place."[118]

Digital Flameout and a Stark Reassessment

It seemed as if the attacks of September 11 ushered in a whole new era for many Americans. Certainly, the business world felt the impact: as the U.S. economy, already in recession, contracted, companies cut back on capital expenditures, including nonessential travel and development perks such as executive education.[119] Revenues from custom and open enrollment programs at the Allen Center fell 32 percent in the 2001–2002 academic year, and there were 29 percent fewer participants in these programs, according to Stephen Burnett, associate dean of executive education. Burnett, a professor of management and strategy who arrived at Kellogg in 1981, was named to his administrative position in early 2003 during a reorganization of the school's Executive Education Program. The move put him in charge of the nondegree offerings, and, at the same time, Erica Kantor was appointed to the new position of assistant dean of administration for the program. Kantor had previously been assistant dean and director of the Kellogg Executive MBA Program, a position that was now filled by Julie Cisek Jones, formerly the program's director of admissions and planning.[120] After September 11, Burnett said that the school ran 21 percent fewer programs and the average class size fell by 10 percent.[121]

"The impact on EMBA applications was identical in magnitude but with a significant lag—applications dropped 31 percent from calendar year 2002 to 2003," said Burnett, noting that "this was a very deep hole indeed"; he added that enrollment has recovered in recent years to more normal levels. "As for academic year 2006, we are officially out of the 9/11 pit with record nondegree revenues, record number of programs conducted and number of participants (more than 5,000)."[122]

Shortly before this transformation affected all MBA programs at Kellogg—and indeed all other peer schools—another research center had been launched at the Kellogg School to consolidate its considerable technology offerings, since the Internet boom seemed to promise if not necessarily another Industrial Revolution, then certainly a pivotal moment that would continue developing in fascinating ways.

In June 2001, the Center for Research in Technology and Innovation opened its doors, headed by Mohanbir Sawhney, the McCormick Tribune Professor of Technology. With a focus on understanding, solving and forecasting challenges facing innovation managers, the center studies technology's role in "improving business performance, promoting organizational effectiveness, driving innovation and creating competitive advantage."[123] The center assumes a leadership role in the extensive Kellogg technology curriculum, which seeks to bring together professional and academic experts skilled in a wide range of areas such as marketing, invention, engineering, strategy and law. Faculty members lead students on experiential academic excursions—in the "TechVentures" course—to Silicon Valley companies to learn firsthand the challenges and strategies leaders in technology employ for market advantage. The opportunities to study innovation are diverse.

"Technology is drugs, bugs and plugs," Sawhney has quipped,[124] adding, "We went to Google when Google was 100 employees." He also has dated the proliferation of information technology to about 1995 and Netscape's initial public offering, a time when "the Web really hit people's radar screens."[125]

But managing this array of technological marvels demands skill, vision and leadership. "Technology is a marvelous enabler but we must keep our eyes on it to ensure we direct the innovation in ways that maximize excellence," Jain has said. "You need talented, creative leaders to manage this innovation."[126] Providing the necessary training for the task, Kellogg and the research center have attempted to remain close to emerging technologies by cultivating key relationships with companies such as Microsoft, Boeing, Motorola and others. In so doing, the school and its faculty have brought customized executive education offerings to corporate clients seeking solutions to thorny problems. In return, Kellogg professors gain a more profound understanding of contemporary market challenges, which enables them to better prepare students to develop the skills required for market leadership.[127]

During the Internet boom, Kellogg provided students with a wealth of course offerings designed to help them understand and manage technology and change in the extraordinary—and unprecedented—business environment of the time. The school offered some 16 courses in its technology and e-commerce major, ranging from "Fundamentals of Technology and E-Commerce" to "Technology Marketing" and "Frontiers of Intellectual Property Management."[128] Kellogg listened both to the marketplace and to students who were demanding a more structured approach to mastering technology management; as a result, a number of courses were added to the curriculum. Some endured, others were experimental, Sawhney recalled. "Not all of them survived," he said, "but the courses that have lasted have become viable franchises."[129]

Because of the great interest in technology courses, Jacobs appointed a curriculum committee to review Kellogg offerings in the tech area in the spring of 1999. The dean also awarded Sawhney, then a junior professor (albeit one who had been attracting attention for his research on Internet marketing and strategy), the McCormick Tribune Chair of Electronic Commerce and Technology. Jacobs also tasked him and a team of colleagues with creating a program to house all of these courses logically. The group reviewed existing offerings, performed benchmark studies and surveyed students, alumni and faculty members for their insights. Their conclusion was that although Kellogg was positioned well to be a leader in new economy management, it needed overarching guidelines for students wishing to major in technology. In addition, some new courses would have to be added to the curriculum to strengthen it. Within a week, Sawhney, Jacobs and Jain created the new major.[130]

"In this area, you just can't wait," Jain said at the time. "There's a very brief window of opportunity. If you delay, it's for a whole year. It's not just a month or two months."[131] Sawhney noted the "rather cruel paradox" of a rapidly changing world where "intellectual frameworks are outdated," providing great opportunities to younger people "who aren't hampered by preexisting ideas."[132] The comment raised some eyebrows among faculty members.

Still, the excitement of the time was fueled by what Sawhney called interesting parallel developments in the world of startups and what was happening in business schools. With Internet activity, "you saw a mushrooming of new ideas, new business models, new technologies," he said. Companies and schools attempted to engage each other to mutual advantage. In this environment, the Kellogg School's technology curriculum would have to keep its ideas fresh in a way that other courses typically did not. Clinical professor Anthony Paoni said the offerings would have to be updated quarterly to keep pace with actual market practice. "The idea of keeping the subject matter fresh is critical," he said. "But it means a lot more pressure on the faculty."[133]

Numerous innovation luminaries have visited the school, including Amazon CEO Jeff Bezos and Sun Microsystems founder Vinod Khosla. Perhaps few guests, however, could top the star power of Microsoft founder Bill Gates, who visited Kellogg in April 1997 as part of the Technology Series Conference.[134]

Some faculty members, among them marketing pioneer Philip Kotler, were quick to address the challenges that technology and the online marketplace posed for traditional businesses. "If your company is not turning into an e-business, it may not be in business," Kotler wrote in 1999, predicting that the Internet would lead to lower prices and margins for sellers and lower purchasing costs for buyers.[135]

Although it is possible to look back at the Internet boom with wry amusement—how could so many people, including business students who dropped out of school to launch ventures without benefit of sufficient due diligence, think they were going to become overnight millionaires?—Sawhney said he and his colleagues understood that technology would keep shaping business in ways that quickly turned the latest innovation into yesterday's news. "When we set up the program, it was called Technology and E-Commerce," he recalled. "At that time, I fully knew that the e-commerce part was going to become obsolete eventually. Nevertheless, it was important at that time to call it e-commerce because we wanted a point of view, and we wanted focus on the area that was emerging. But for the same reasons, when e-commerce became mainstream, my favorite tagline was 'Business is just business. The e is for "enabling."'" As Internet technology became more mainstream, he added, the school repositioned the program as Technology Industry Management. "E-commerce," he said, was the "frothy part" of the Internet revolution, and the school responded to student demand for courses in this area, but at the same time, Kellogg also was focusing on underlying technological frameworks that would endure beyond the hype of the dot-com era.

"Technology has always been with us. What varies is what is hot," said Sawhney in 2006.[136]

If students were eager to drive aspects of the e-commerce curriculum, they also wanted to play leadership roles outside the classroom. One highlight of their efforts was the Digital Frontier Conference (DFC), an annual meeting that began in 1995. Wildly popular at the height of the dot-com boom—tickets to the sold-out 2000 event reportedly fetched as much as $1,500 on eBay—Digital Frontier attracted new-economy leaders such as Mark Walsh, vice president of America On Line; George Shaheen, CEO of Webvan; and Tom Siebel, CEO of Siebel Systems. Since 2005, the event has been known as the Technology Conference, and it still attracts senior leaders from top companies, including Google, Microsoft, eBay and Adobe.

Some attendees at the 2000 conference, in particular, seemed dismissive of traditional business models and strategies. Michael Wolf, founder of Booz Allen's media and entertainment practice, proclaimed, "It's so difficult to make anything happen in a large corporation." Meanwhile, Flip Filipowski, CEO of divine interVentures, said, "No one wants to slave seven years so that some idiot partner makes all the money." Keynote speaker George Shaheen charged up the capacity crowd with his enthusiasm for the ways in which "retail industries as fundamental as food service are undergoing radical restructuring" because of the Internet.[137]

Others cautioned of an imminent market correction and ventures that were grossly overvalued. However, these views seemed a minority perspective and were largely lost in the overheated rhetoric about the promise of online models of commerce that looked ready to transform everything anyone had considered fundamental about business. The contrarians were soon proved right.

By the spring of 2001, the conference theme was "Surviving the Digital Storm." In his remarks at the event, Sawhney attempted to take stock of the rapid ascent and decline of a market that was supposed to represent an advance the magnitude of which was only equaled by the Industrial Revolution. "The truth is always in the middle," Sawhney told some 900 attendees who had gathered to glean information from 28 eclectic panel discussions and several keynote speeches. There was no dichotomy separating the new economy from the old, he said, but simply a hybrid "enhanced economy" that drew on both models.[138] Attendees heard Mark Goldston, chairman and CEO of Netzero, then the largest free Internet service provider, declare: "The Internet is not a fad. It is an evolutionary revolution." The recent tech downturn, he believed, was in part due to impatient investors who failed to give ventures sufficient time to mature. "Asking certain startups why they had not made a profit yet was like asking a sophomore in high school why she had not graduated yet," Goldston said.[139]

At the 2002 DFC event, Tom Siebel told attendees to keep a broad perspective on the recent tech market swoon. "Twenty years from now we'll look back and see that we were at the beginning of the greatest economic expansion in history," he said.[140] But some Kellogg students had begun to return to more traditional businesses a year earlier, pursuing careers in sectors like packaged goods or investment banking that could demonstrate a positive revenue stream or a tangible product. Kellogg professor Barry Merkin recalled the "euphoria" that existed just a couple of years earlier, when technology and entrepreneurship classes were oversubscribed and students were throwing business plans at professors for what they hoped might be the next eBay. "Many students and even older people were saying, 'It looks like a crazy time, but why don't I jump in and take advantage of all the craziness? We know it's a bubble and bubbles always burst, but this bubble doesn't seem to be bursting,'" Merkin recalled.[141]

Sawhney remembered that "when the NASDAQ was hitting 5,000, we were hitting 1,453, that's the number of bid points for the course in 2000," the year the class proved even more popular than one taught by Adjunct Professor (and media mogul) Oprah Winfrey. Some 400 students bid for the course, said Sawhney, and because of the school's customer service model, he said Jacobs encouraged him to accept them all. Sawhney explained that he could not do that because the teaching model did not scale up. "We are working intensely with students on these projects and papers, I said. I can't do that. But we were forced to take 163 students that year," he stated.

Although students were pleading for admittance to the course during the Internet boom, both Sawhney and Paoni recalled that once the bloom was off the digital rose, student interest waned and professors found themselves asking students to enroll in the technology offerings. Paoni tried explaining to them that the role of information technology in the corporate world represented a huge opportunity, one where technology had gone on uninterrupted. "But I think they were focused on the start-up world," he said.

Sawhney remembered: "Students detected that there was a short road to riches, and it led to Silicon Valley. When we had 163 students in class I told them, 'You are in this class for the wrong reasons.' Then when we had no one in the class, I said, 'You're not in this class for the wrong reasons.'"[142]

Sonia Marciano, former clinical professor of management and strategy, noted the change in student interest in technology relative to traditional core courses. "During the boom times, there was a sense that students were less inclined to pay much attention to subjects like finance," she recalled. "The attitude was you don't really need to know this stuff to do well; you just need to get out there and get going. After the Internet bust, there's been a reengagement with academics."[143]

Daniel Spulber, the Elinor Hobbs Distinguished Professor of International Business, also was not surprised by this trend. "What makes a successful manager is the ability to rise above the crowd and gain a broader strategic perspective. That's something we've always emphasized at Kellogg. . . . We haven't abolished the business cycle, all the New Economy rhetoric notwithstanding."[144]

In fact, the school has actually enhanced its longtime strengths in traditional areas such as finance. In 2007, Kellogg introduced the Asset Management Practicum, an experiential program designed to meet important student needs and strengthen their analytical abilities. Directed by Professor Korajczyk and drawing on the financial and intellectual support of notable alumni working in the investment and banking industry,[145] the yearlong practicum gives students exposure to cutting-edge practitioners and experience and lets them manage an actual and sizable portfolio under the guidance of a finance professor. The course, which was awarded a $1 million grant from the Chicago Mercantile Exchange Trust, has limited enrollment and requires students to register for prescribed courses throughout the practicum.

"Students will blend academic research with practical insights from visiting practitioners and day-to-day portfolio management," said Korajczyk. "In addition, students will learn how to execute trades to minimize costs and have invaluable exposure to investment styles, factors of client servicing and risk minimization." The practicum also has helped strengthen the Kellogg School's connection with investment practitioners, thereby broadening placement opportunities for graduates.

"This is clearly action learning, and experiential learning is one of the Kellogg cornerstones," said Korajczyk.[146]

Ethics, Entrepreneurship and Social Enterprise

Regardless of transient market dynamics, Kellogg's enduring strengths have continued to influence the school's overall direction. The volatility that wracked Internet companies in the early years of the twenty-first century was not altogether dissimilar to the uncertainty that roiled the economy as the 1990s began and traced its origins to "Black Monday," October 19, 1987, when the Dow Jones plunged more than 500 points, setting off a financial panic.[147]

Because Kellogg never overreacted to the dot-com enthusiasm in a way that altered the school's core curriculum, it could easily retain the tech courses with enduring value—such as "TechVenture"—and introduce new offerings like "Managerial Challenges in the Pharmaceutical, Biotech and Medical Device Industries," while still shifting the emphasis back to its perennial academic offerings as students' interests moved away from the volatile tech sector. In fact, Kellogg experts noted the opportunity for leaders to understand the hybrid model of old and new economies and how to capitalize on tough times.

"The companies that profit most from bad times are those that don't resort to massive layoffs and indiscriminate cost cutting, but remain disciplined in pursuing growth guided by a coherent strategy," said Besanko in the aftermath of the Internet crash. "Recessions offer a great opportunity for companies in leadership positions to solidify existing sources of competitive advantage and build new ones."[148]

Indeed, Kellogg faculty members provided insights into understanding the hidden advantages of a tough market, as long as organizations pursued the correct strategies to consolidate their competitive advantage. Management innovations such as information technology, marketing, supply chains and human resources all were powerful tools to mitigate economic crisis, they said. Among the keys to success, Jain noted, was leveraging resources effectively—especially staff.

"Your people are always your most important strategic resource, and during difficult times their value increases," he said. "Kellogg's collaborative culture really prepares managers to lead internal teams to drive a firm's success." That success also depended on learning from mistakes, he added, especially since "customers form perceptions about a company not when things go right, but when they go wrong."[149]

Things certainly went wrong for some major American businesses over the course of 2001 and 2002—and not merely because of the economic recession. In the wake of serious accounting scandals involving Enron, WorldCom, Tyco and Arthur Andersen, major media attention focused the public on the importance of business ethics.[150] The subject was soon revisited by many management educators, including Kellogg. However, ethics and a values-based leadership that put people first had been central to the school's culture and curriculum for years. (One of those thinking deeply on the subject was Professor Lawrence Lavengood, who delivered an address titled "Ethics in Professional Life" as the Taylor Educator-in-Residence Centennial Lecture in 1990.)[151]

In fact, even before news of the scandals hit the airwaves, Kellogg had been refining its courses in preparation for a new major in business and its social environment (or BASE). The administration designed the program in the spring of 2001, offering it for the first time in the fall of 2002. Its focus was on how corporations could "do well by doing good."

"This major is going to be driven by faculty research," said Dean Jain. "We do not view it as a flavor-of-the-day curriculum. We earned a reputation because we anticipated the market's needs better and faster than our competitors. BASE represents another example of our efforts to remain ahead of the curve in leadership education."[152]

The major, in part generated by student enthusiasm for the subject of social entrepreneurship, took a rigorous approach to teaching issues such as strategic leadership when faced with nonmarket as well as market forces. For instance, the rise of activism placed companies at greater risk. That, coupled with new technology that enabled greater communications and information symmetry between companies and the public, meant "firms need[ed] to think strategically about how to respond to activist action and to recognize opportunities to work with activist groups,"[153] said Timothy Feddersen, the Wendell Hobbs Professor of Managerial Economics, who, along with Daniel Diermeier, the IBM Distinguished Professor of Regulation and Competitive Practice, taught the BASE major's "Strategic Management in Nonmarket Environments" course. Factors giving rise to the new curriculum included shifts in the global market that increasingly put more power in the hands of corporate entities relative to the traditional political power broker, the government.

Although Kellogg faculty members did not expect the typical graduate to join a company's corporate social responsibility department, they did believe most professionals would need to demonstrate greater awareness of emerging nonmarket issues. "These are all issues that somebody who's going to be a successful executive has to be conversant in," said David Messick, a faculty member who had long incorporated case studies on ethics and leadership in his courses. "This major is going to be more important in the coming century as fewer things are done by government agencies," he noted. "People, through a political process, are going to require business to accept responsibilities that they hadn't previously thought of as their responsibilities."[154]

To advance this leadership agenda, BASE brought together existing courses, including "Strategic Management in Nonmarket Environments," as well as new ones, such as "Environmental Management," "Making Ethical Decisions" and "The Socially Responsible Business." In a CNBC News interview after Kellogg had again earned number one rankings from *BusinessWeek* and the Economist Intelligence Unit (the parent company of the *Economist* magazine) in 2002, Jain noted that ethics had been a central part of the Kellogg management approach for years and was not something new. "We always had a course on ethics and decision making," he told Ron Insana. "But what we try to do in the classroom is look at all the ethical implications of business decisions that our students are going to make in the future, and we try to integrate ethics into our curriculum across as many courses as possible. . . . Ethics is embedded in everything we do, whether it is classroom, extracurricular activities or dealing with people."[155]

In fact, student-driven initiatives and clubs, including the Social Impact Club, one of the largest at Kellogg, have been effective in shaping activities addressing ethics and values-based leadership inside and outside the classroom. Due to their interrelated missions, leadership and membership, two long-standing clubs, the Public/Nonprofit Club and the Socially Responsible Business Club, were merged in 2001 to create the Social Impact Club. Nearly half of all Kellogg students subscribe to the club's listserv and take an active part in the club mission, which is to support and inspire students interested in leveraging their business skills for advancing social good through organizations in the nonprofit, public and private sectors. The club, which earned distinction as the Net Impact Chapter of the Year in 2003 and placed second in 2004, hosts the annual Innovating Social Change Conference, launched in 2001, as well as various speaker events and career-related programs for students interested in jobs in the nonprofit, public management and socially responsible business sectors. The club represents the student arm of the Center for Nonprofit Management and the Ford Center for Global Citizenship (see the earlier discussion in this chapter).

Student enthusiasm for socially responsible business, in conjunction with the Kellogg mission to create knowledge and encourage responsible business practices, has seen the BASE major develop as part of an even more comprehensive offering called the Social EnterprisE at Kellogg Program. Launched in 2005, SEEK's mission reflects the converging challenges that managers face as they try to be socially responsible global leaders. The leadership program, which draws on faculty from a variety of disciplines, including economics, political science and public policy, psychology and management, provides a rigorous, relevant experience for students interested in the intersection between management and society across all organizations and industries.

"The traditional way the business community has thought about business management is inappropriate now. It was divided by tax status: nonprofit, for-profit and government," explained Diermeier, who was SEEK's director at the outset (Feddersen assumed the directorship in 2006). "Our research reveals a blending in these fields. Global corporations now have to solve problems traditionally held by nonprofits, while nonprofits are more and more adopting management techniques from corporations. Leaders are not in one 'world' exclusively."[156]

SEEK grew out of an effort by Magee and Besanko to review all the school's academic programs in the 2002–2003 academic year. The first two programs reviewed were the Public/Nonprofit Program and the Health Industry Management Program. Besanko recalled that the nonprofit review revealed some "significant problems and opportunities." As he exited the Office of the Dean in 2003, he advocated that the school address the concerns, perhaps even creating a department of social enterprise or something similar.[157]

As a result, the school appointed a small task force to investigate the possibilities, consisting of Besanko, Feddersen, Diermeier, Donald Haider and Lawrence Rothenberg, then co-chair of the Ford Center for Global Citizenship and the Max McGraw Distinguished Professor of Management and Environment. (Rothenberg has since joined the faculty of the University of Rochester.) The group deliberated for a year, said Besanko, before "hammering out a program that resembled the basic outline of what is now SEEK." The task force presented its recommendations to the entire faculty in September 2004, eliciting vigorous debate and additional suggestions. The proposal was tabled until later that year, at which time it became a reality after another committee worked to refine the program's details.

Courses in the SEEK major include "Values and Crisis Decision Making," which describes how firms must be prepared to handle rapidly changing environments and anticipate potential threats that can arise from finding themselves the targets of aggressive legal action, media coverage and social pressure. The class helps students gain a deep understanding of the strategic complexities involved in managing various stakeholders and constituencies. "Values-Based Leadership" focuses on the challenges of incorporating a variety of value perspectives into decision making, taking the disparate value propositions of various stakeholders and integrating them into a coherent vision. "Socially Responsible Business Practices" imparts an understanding of how nonprofit organizations are governed. The course is designed for students who will serve as board members, volunteers or staff of nonprofit organizations.

Student passion for social entrepreneurship seems likely only to grow, especially as the next generation of business leaders arrives on campus. The so-called millennials, or members of Generation Y, make up a demographic group born between about 1980 and 1997. Tech-savvy, exceptionally bright and often socially engaged, members of this group are expected to put their ethical and cultural principles into action, seeking solutions for any number of social and political challenges, from poverty to environmental damages.

Already, many students are indicating their interest in using management skills to effect greater social change. In 2006, the Kellogg School hosted the national Net Impact Conference, a three-day event presented annually by an organization founded by MBA students in 1993. Claiming a membership of some 10,000 "new generation leaders committed to using the power of business to improve the world," the group partnered with members of the Kellogg Social Impact Club to attract more than 1,200 students from 37 countries to Evanston. Among the keynote speakers and panelists were notable Kellogg alumni such as John Wood '89, founder and CEO of San Francisco–based Room to Read, a nonprofit that builds schools and libraries across the developing world. Andrew Youn '06 was among those demonstrating "How to Start a Social Enterprise: A Case Study on the One Acre Fund." The Kellogg graduate has earned multiple awards and distinctions for the One Acre Fund, a venture that works to eradicate chronic hunger in Africa.[158] Youn designed the business model while still a student at Kellogg, refining the plan during a course taught by Barry Merkin, "Entrepreneurship and New Venture Formulation." So impressed was the Kellogg professor that he called Youn's effort "the most classic example of what we teach a business plan should be." Merkin—and indeed his Kellogg School colleagues in the Entrepreneurship and Innovation Program—should know: they are award-winning experts in the subject who have personal experience running their own ventures. The program itself has been ranked among the top three of its type in the United States.

The Kellogg entrepreneurship program received its first significant support in 1988, when Edgar F. Heizer Jr. and his wife endowed the Heizer Center for

Entrepreneurial Studies. Since then, entrepreneurship has remained a prime focus of the Kellogg School's MBA program, receiving increased attention during and after the Internet boom when the school's leadership looked to entrepreneurship—which it defined as including family businesses—as one way to create broader professional opportunities for graduates, especially those hit by the economic downturn. With business schools struggling to place MBA graduates in good jobs, Dean Jain was asking a central question: were there enough high-paying corporate positions available for graduates? He doubted it.

"Our challenge today is to create new markets that will be attractive to MBAs," he wrote in an editorial for the Association to Advance Collegiate Schools of Business in 2003. "I believe it is very important to turn our attention once more to the entrepreneurial arena, redefining it in ways that include not only high-tech initiatives, but also small businesses and family businesses."

These were sectors that infrequently recruited MBAs in significant numbers, said Jain. He believed such businesses should consider developing summer internship programs with schools to familiarize themselves with the skills that MBAs could bring to an organization. At the same time, schools should adopt a more targeted approach to cultivating relationships with family and small businesses, in part through custom executive education courses for leaders in those spaces and also through creating projects in which MBA students could engage with these entrepreneurial firms. "Such projects would reemphasize the importance of designing business plans and thus help students appreciate once more the true building blocks of entrepreneurship," wrote the dean.[159]

He also underscored the need to reach out to alumni entrepreneurs for their support and expertise—which is precisely what Kellogg did in 2003 when it engaged entrepreneur Larry Levy '67, the cofounder, chairman and CEO of Levy Restaurants and the Levy Organization. The Kellogg graduate had spent decades building a restaurant and real estate business that became extraordinarily successful. Now, he and his spouse were providing the capital to establish the Larry and Carol Levy Entrepreneurial Institute at Kellogg. Their significant gift would spearhead an effort for increased investment in an important area of the curriculum by expanding the program's activities and enabling the school to advance into executive education for entrepreneurs, extend its entrepreneurship summer internship program, develop additional courses and identify new faculty members in this arena. (Other alumni entrepreneurs, such as Joseph Levy Jr. '47, had also contributed greatly to the school's development over the decades. See "Alumni Profile: Joe Levy" in the winter 2004 edition of *Kellogg World*, as well as a profile on Joe Levy in the spring 2007 edition of the alumni magazine.)

"This important gift will reinvigorate our program in entrepreneurship," said Dean Jain in regard to Larry and Carol Levy's gift.[160] And indeed it did. With some 30 courses that qualify for the entrepreneurship major and about 50 programs and projects managed through the Levy Institute, this curriculum continues to grow in ways that create value for students and alumni alike. And it has attracted outside attention too: the Princeton Review and *Entrepreneur* magazine ranked Kellogg number three nationally in a 2006 study of top entrepreneurship curricula.

"Entrepreneurs are the future of our economy," Jain has said. "As their numbers have grown, so has the Kellogg School's Entrepreneurship and Innovation Program."

The reasons for this success include an experiential curriculum that blends theory and practice; exceptional professors with real-world track records as entrepreneurs; creative partnerships between Kellogg and Northwestern University that push the boundaries of design innovation; and the contributions of notable alumni, such as the Levys as well as Gordon Segal '60 and Carole Browe Segal (NU '60), the cofounders of Crate and Barrel, who have provided generous support for teaching and research. In 2007, Larry and Carol Levy once again strengthened the Kellogg entrepreneurship curriculum with a new gift, inspired by the social entrepreneurship of alumni such as John Wood and Andrew Youn.

"We're doing amazing things in the entrepreneurship program at Kellogg, and we need role models, we need mentors and we need more great success stories," said Larry Levy. "The reason I think that entrepreneurship should be supported is that entrepreneurs create most of the new jobs in the world. If we can teach people how to be good entrepreneurs, we can have more people earning a good living and having a better life."[161]

Steven Rogers, the Gordon and Llura Gund Family Professor of Entrepreneurship and director of the Levy Institute, has also noted the importance of entrepreneurship to the overall economy. In his 2002 book, *The Entrepreneur's Guide to Finance and Business,* the 1985 graduate of the Harvard Business School wrote that the 1990s created an enormous number of new businesses: more than 600,000 were started at the beginning of the decade, and by 1997, Rogers reported, "entrepreneurs were starting a record 885,000 new businesses a year"—nearly 2,400 a day, or four times the number of firms created in the 1960s. According to recent statistics from the U.S. Small Business Association, small businesses (defined as firms of 500 employees or less) represent 99.7 percent of all employees and provide 60 to 80 percent of net new jobs annually. These businesses, numbering nearly 26 million, accounted for about $6 trillion of the U.S. gross domestic product (GDP). Many of these enterprises are characterized as "entrepreneurial."

Kellogg alumni have made significant contributions to these numbers. In fact, some 85 percent of graduates who majored in entrepreneurship at Kellogg went on to become entrepreneurs at some time in their lives.[162] As of 2006, these individuals were employing more than 7,000 people and generating an estimated $1 billion in revenue.[163]

Behind these numbers stand Kellogg School faculty members who deliver the insights to help their students create this wealth. Besides Merkin and Rogers, Kellogg experts in entrepreneurship include Professors John Ward, a preeminent family business scholar, and Lloyd Shefsky, clinical professor of managerial economics. Colleagues James Shein, clinical professor of management and strategy, Derrick Collins, clinical assistant professor of finance, and Robert Wolcott, adjunct assistant professor in the Levy Institute, lend their experience and insights to the program, as does Scott Whitaker '97, associate director of the Levy Institute.

The curriculum offers comprehensive courses that address every aspect of entrepreneurship and innovation. For example, "Entrepreneurship and New Venture Formation" focuses on business plan development; "Corporate Innovation and New Ventures" explores how to build entrepreneurial capabilities within an existing firm; "Managing Innovation" teaches how to manage research and development for organizations pursuing breakthrough industry innovations; "Entrepreneurial Finance" is designed to teach students how to become adept at managing all aspects of valuation, cash flow analysis and raising capital; and "Venture Capital and Private Equity Investing" provides an understanding of key issues related to funding ventures. "Strategic Management of Technology and Innovation," "Small Business Management," "Family Business: Issues and Solutions," "Intellectual Capital Management" and "Social Entrepreneurship" are also part of the Kellogg School's innovation portfolio, which boasts dozens of formal courses and other structured learning opportunities.

Among the latter, the Entrepreneur in Residence Program brings students face to face with successful entrepreneurs to glean practitioner insights. The Entrepreneurship Internship Program allows a student to hold a summer role in an entrepreneurial setting, such as at Smith Whiley & Company, where Venita Fields '88 is senior managing director. "[Students] get firsthand, hands-on experience," said Fields. "They don't just stay in a closet and run numbers all day. We get them involved in client meetings. They actually go out in the field and visit the company and kick the tires like we do."[164]

With business competitions such as the Kellogg Cup, students have a chance to hone their ideas, testing and strengthening them against the critiques of real-world experts. Tour de KAE offers an opportunity for Kellogg alumni entrepreneurs to showcase their achievements to members of their alma mater. At the same time, they get to offer strategic and operational insights to current Kellogg students who join faculty members for an on-site visit to the alum's company. At the annual Alumni Entrepreneur Conference in May, students also have a chance to learn from Kellogg peers who have proven skills in entrepreneurship. Similarly, the Distinguished Entrepreneur Speaker Series brings leading practitioners to Kellogg to share their experiences with students.

"We try to create environments where our students and alums can network with one another," said Rogers, who has cited his mother as an early inspiration for his own entrepreneurship.[165] "We want to teach students in the classroom in the traditional way about entrepreneurship. First and foremost they are coming to Kellogg to receive a premier education from a premier faculty. We've had more faculty recipients of Ernst & Young's Entrepreneur of the Year Award than any other school in the country." (Rogers himself has won the award.)

Rogers's mantra, which is backed by empirical evidence, is that those who attend Kellogg and major in entrepreneurship are destined to become entrepreneurs at some point in their professional lives. But he also stresses that entrepreneurship is a lifelong journey, one that Kellogg is always ready to support.

"The reality is, the entrepreneur who stops learning is the entrepreneur who dies," said Rogers. "Graduates from our program are and will always be members of the Kellogg entrepreneurship family. We expect you to come back and continue your education. We want to always be a part of your life."[166]

The Journey Ahead: The Kellogg Framework for Maintaining the MBA's Value

Lifelong education is a value shared by each of the two most recent Kellogg School deans. For Donald Jacobs, the ideal was epitomized by the Allen Center's creation, which brought executive education to a much wider audience than had previously enjoyed the opportunity. For Dipak Jain, the relentlessly challenging twenty-first-century business world demands leadership and vision refined continuously by the latest research and teaching.

Looking to the future of the Kellogg School of Management as it celebrates its first 100 years, it is clear that the school's leadership has constructed a framework designed to create an enduring institution. Built on rigorous academic inquiry, the school's foundation emphasizes intellectual depth, experiential learning, a global perspective and ethical values and leadership skills. These four factors, importantly, are found in the school's overall culture of innovation and collaboration. Taken together, they create a unique management school whose mission involves the dissemination of knowledge and the creation of responsible global leaders.

Individually, the qualities that make up this framework are valuable tools that can take students part of the way to becoming leaders, but only in concert can they provide the full complement of skills necessary to meet the goal, according to Kellogg faculty and administrators.

• *Intellectual depth* (or thought leadership) requires students to pursue their studies rigorously in order to develop the analytical and critical thinking that will make their investment in an MBA education hold value over a 30- to 35-year career in a world of accelerating and discontinuous change. Intellectual depth allows students to develop the ability to anticipate significant changes in the economic, social and business landscapes. To achieve this objective, according to Dean Jain, it is vital to take students outside their comfort zones with respect to performance standards. In so doing, professors help inspire students and liberate them from the constraints of routine thought—an ability that is critical for leaders who hope to drive success through innovation. One important and recent public manifestation of intellectual depth and thought leadership at the school is *Kellogg Insight,* a Web-based research digest that showcases research by Kellogg professors in a sophisticated yet accessible manner. The digest was developed under the leadership of Kathleen Hagerty, senior associate dean for academic affairs (faculty and research) and the First Chicago Professor of Finance. The knowledge product serves the needs of all visitors to the site seeking the latest Kellogg research across all disciplines. With its premise that "great leaders have great insight," *Kellogg Insight* is designed to share knowledge and establish ongoing connections with its readers.

Dean Hagerty was also responsible for overseeing the development of a new academic initiative in 2007, one designed to provide a small group of exceptional Northwestern undergraduates with exposure to Kellogg professors and coursework. With the introduction of two elite undergraduate certificate programs—in financial economics and managerial analytics—Kellogg partnered with Northwestern's Weinberg College of Arts and Sciences and the McCormick School of Engineering and Applied Sciences to offer talented junior and senior students greater advanced quantitative training. The two programs were each built around four courses and were developed by Kellogg faculty members under the direction of Hagerty.

About 50 students began the Kellogg Financial Economics Certificate Program in September 2007. Directed by Janice Eberly, the John L. and Helen Kellogg Professor of Finance, this program focused on corporate finance, capital markets and securities pricing and was developed for those undergraduates with a strong foundation in analytics, mathematics and economics.

Set to launch in September 2008, the Managerial Analytics Certificate Program was intended to accommodate another 50 top students interested in applying their analytical skills to guide strategic and tactical business decisions in the context of finance, marketing, operations and strategy. Operations expert Sunil Chopra served as the program's director.

The undergraduate certificate programs—supported in part by a grant from the Chicago Mercantile Exchange Trust—were a response to what Dean Jain cited as increased recruiter interest in college graduates who possessed a strong quantitative background rooted in liberal arts and infused with business acumen.

Hagerty also noted the immediate interest that the programs garnered. "Financial services and consulting firms are increasingly looking to hire and retain talented undergraduates both as interns and full-time employees. . . . There is already a lot of interest in these kids from recruiters," she said, adding that the programs provide strong academic tools for undergraduates hoping to pursue careers in financial services, consulting, investment banking or the hedge fund industry.

Said Dean Jain during a November 2007 open house for the certificate programs: "This initiative represents a completely new chapter for Kellogg and for management schools in general. We wanted to determine the optimal way to serve the Northwestern community with an analytically rigorous curriculum while also attracting the best talent from among undergraduates who might not know much about the MBA degree and its value. This is our way of expanding the Kellogg family."

• *Experiential learning* (which includes team leadership, that is, collaborative strategies to solve problems) provides real opportunities to test classroom insights, giving students the chance to sharpen their leadership skills within contexts that approximate actual management situations, a circumstance analogous to medical residencies. Some of these opportunities may involve leadership simulations, internships and field excursions, as well as orchestrating professional academic conferences and similar events that bring practitioners, professors and students together in ways that advance leadership discourse.

By working closely with faculty members as colleagues to make discoveries that bridge theory and practice while affording ample opportunity to learn by doing in experiential contexts (e.g., the practicum, internship and initiatives such as student-run conferences and clubs with a leadership component), students are invited to be "cocreators" of knowledge, not bystanders. As valuable as classroom lessons are in establishing intellectual perspective, it is crucial to augment this knowledge with actual "frontline" encounters that force students to synthesize and apply their academic insights. This is especially so in a hypercompetitive global economy in which high-performance organizations expect their MBA hires to produce immediate results and assume greater responsibilities earlier in their careers.

• *Global perspectives* (including market leadership, the wisdom to see how business influences the community) are developed when schools provide students a chance to appreciate and understand the complexity of international commerce, thereby gaining an ability to perform in a diverse context. This global focus should be part of every course, since one cannot discuss business in provincial terms today. Classroom experiences should be augmented with actual excursions that put students face to face with business in the real world. Among the Kellogg offerings that achieve this is the Global Initiatives in Management practicum, which combines 10 weeks of intensive classroom preparation and research with a 2-week field excursion to one of several countries. Students meet with leaders from business and government, going behind the scenes for a unique look at how commerce works. Other globally focused courses include such options as "Cross-cultural Negotiation," "International Finance," "International Marketing" and "International Business Strategy."

Given the importance of training managers for the global marketplace, Kellogg announced in July 2007 that a global course requirement would be added to the curriculum for all students across all programs. Officially taking effect in June 2008, this curriculum enhancement underscores the school's commitment to developing global leaders who can solve business challenges and build consensus across diverse groups.

Equally important to cultivating this global mind-set is the expansive network of Kellogg School faculty and students, reflecting the cultural diversity of a global business community. In 2007, nearly a third of the Kellogg student body came from outside the United States.

• *Leadership and social responsibility* (an area where civic leadership exerts itself) are competencies easily misunderstood or overlooked as ancillary to the primary function of business schools. In truth, this Kellogg framework is as critical as the others. It does not displace the important analytical skills required to run an enterprise; rather, it complements them. Fundamentally, the Kellogg School management philosophy is that business leaders must act ethically if they are to regain and maintain public confidence in the aftermath of the corporate accounting scandals that erupted in the opening years of the twenty-first century. These abuses sent a powerful, negative signal to the public about business. "While introducing ethical and social concerns to the curriculum helps offset an undesirable public image for business schools, the most important reason to include this discussion is that doing so helps safeguard the trust that is the bedrock of our financial markets," says Dean Jain. MBA programs are positioned to make critical contributions to society by advancing this discourse and inculcating the proper values in their graduates.

This fourfold framework is vital in guiding the Kellogg School, said Sunil Chopra. "I think it can guide every aspect of what we do, guide both the students and the school," he said. Chopra views the framework as marking a clear way for students to understand how their experience prepares them for the next step in their careers while at the same time identifying areas in which their skills require strengthening. "They can think in terms of where they need to build intellectual depth, where they need to build global perspectives," said Chopra. "What we do, both in terms of the curricular and extracurricular activities, is try to structure those in a way that can support this. And we always include some component of experiential learning. We have put a lot of effort into this in the classroom to enhance the experiential part."[167]

Experiential learning, he said, helps students find a bridge from their existing abilities and roles to where they want their professional lives to go. As one example, he cites the hands-on Kellogg Asset Management Practicum (see the discussion earlier in this chapter). "If you come from an asset management background [prior to Kellogg], you can continue to do that. But if you don't come from that background, then the coursework along with the Asset Management Practicum makes a huge difference. . . . Coursework alone will only take you so far. You need an experiential opportunity, which gives you credibility—both to yourself, because you have tested it out, and also to your potential employer."[168]

The framework has been especially important given the changes in recruiting practices since the mid-1990s, said Chopra. Previously, nearly all recruitment was conducted through the Kellogg Career Management Center, but more recently, significant numbers of students have been offered jobs through other channels, particularly in areas such as real estate. "Real estate companies tend to be small; they're not recruiting 10 people [at a time]," said Chopra. "They don't have ongoing relationships with a school. Take private equity: A group is seven people. So in those cases, it's a very different [recruitment] cycle . . . which makes this experiential learning piece even more important."

MBA Life Cycle

When designing its curricula and portfolio of offerings across all degree and nondegree programs, the Kellogg School adopts a long-range strategy. The school's leaders do not view the MBA career in monolithic terms—the same thing always and for everyone—but as a multistage cycle extending over a person's life.

"Rather than seeing management education as a one-size-fits-all proposition, we see the MBA experience as *lifelong*, possessing various dimensions over time," says Dean Jain. Just as there are different skills and objectives associated with different career steps, there are, the Kellogg leaders believe, different academic offerings to meet individual needs at different times. With the "MBA life cycle," Kellogg charts three distinct phases associated with most professional journeys.

Early in the typical career, during the *initial stage* of the MBA life cycle, graduates are called upon to *manage projects*. Doing so requires them to use many of the skills, tools and concepts taught in a conventional MBA program; key functional disciplines, such as finance and marketing, are especially important, as are statistics and economics offerings that appear in the core curriculum at many schools. This stage may last 5 to 6 years after graduation.

The life cycle's *second stage* begins when the graduate is called upon to *manage people*. This period can last until years 10 to 12 postgraduation. In addition to functional skills, this stage draws upon the person's leadership abilities to create teams and an environment conducive to achieving the organization's mission. Kellogg School courses that address subjects such as organizations behavior, leadership in organizations, managing a diverse workforce and human resources management are among the offerings of particular value for this career stage.

Finally, the life cycle's *third stage* finds the Kellogg graduate involved in *designing policy*. In addition to functional skills and leadership abilities, this advanced stage demands superior leadership and strategic vision, as the person must drive higher-level organizational change and, in many cases, change within a larger community. "This stage calls for reflection and renewal, commodities often in short supply in the busy professional career, yet essential for full development," says Jain. Here, Kellogg offers graduates special value through executive education programs that refine and update their skills to bring them in line with current market demands. In addition, Kellogg designs and delivers various custom programs to meet *specific client needs*, alongside other offerings providing insights in areas such as creating and managing strategic alliances, driving strategic results through IT portfolio management or governance. Kellogg can tailor its programs to the needs of executives whose MBA degrees were earned 10 or 12 years earlier and now require fresh frameworks to foster continued success.

To be sure, from the perspective of Kellogg School faculty and administrators, the ability to manage teams is valuable throughout one's career, and there will be crossover among these three categories in the MBA life cycle. Nevertheless, as a framework that identifies the general trajectory of most graduates, the life cycle shows how schools should address their clientele's evolving needs in a way that reflects a commitment to *lifelong learning*.

"The principle goal of management education is teaching students how to impart a structure upon unstructured business problems," says Dean Jain. Kellogg achieves this, he adds, by bringing science and philosophy together in a way that enables students to make well-founded arguments, developed by data and facts, which result in *actionable processes.*

High Stakes and Global Complexity Demand MBAs
Who Aspire to Be More and Give More

Over the next several decades, humanity will confront enormous challenges: issues of poverty, longevity and population, disease and environmental crises all loom large. Energy, prosperity and national security are linked, presenting CEOs and heads of state alike with thorny problems of vast consequence. AIDS and avian flu or other emerging threats will intrude upon global corporate strategy as surely as these blights will influence the decisions of politicians and NGOs. Hypercompetitive global markets make even traditional management roles complex and daunting.

Clearly, management leadership matters more than ever, and the job is going to grow more difficult. Consequently, those at the helm of the Kellogg School know that the MBA curriculum must remain innovative and in the educational vanguard as it prepares the next generation for success. They know that leaders must marshal diverse talents and knowledge, bringing these resources to bear in an arena that blurs the lines among business, government and broader social actors, such as consumer activists. What's more, leaders must operate from a position of unimpeachable ethical integrity; anything less will erode the collective trust at the core of market-based enterprise.

Modern challenges across all fields will see Kellogg faculty and students aspiring to achieve more and, indeed, to *be* more. "Make no little plans; they have no magic to strike man's blood." The words attributed to architect and urban planner Daniel Burnham might today also capture the imagination of those seeking to expand management education's scope. Participants in this journey will be a diverse and multifaceted group—players touching many domains and disciplines.

Perhaps most fundamentally, as Dean Jain has noted, today's researchers must not shrink from taking risks and asking "big questions." Faculty members should focus on problems that are pertinent to corporations (e.g., growth), as well as on issues confronting public/social policy makers (e.g., Social Security or health care). In so doing, management education can recalibrate itself along another essential front—the aspirational and imaginative. Such research will have a direct impact on the business world, while also benefiting society at large. Beyond the intrinsic importance of this work, one additional benefit is that the reputations of business schools will be greatly enhanced.

"Kellogg students pursuing the MBA degree should aspire to make significant social contributions," said Jain. Their focus should be on learning as much as possible to achieve this goal, not expending inordinate energy pursuing an astronomical salary. "Earnings are important," he added, "but too often they eclipse the more crucial mission that should occupy a leader: daring to make the world a better and safer place."

Surmounting major social hurdles and stimulating prosperity using intellectual tools at the intersection of many disciplines should inspire all members of the management profession, Jain stated. Reason and creativity each have parts to play in this effort, and MBA training should engage a person's whole spirit.

To achieve this goal, management training at Kellogg will continue to engage students fully through a commitment to experiential learning coupled with a rigorous curriculum that delivers business fundamentals, including analytical skills. Kellogg will reinforce its rich culture, providing opportunities for students to learn inside and outside the classroom, enjoying vigorous, two-directional interactions with faculty members to extend the boundaries of management research that produces innovative solutions to real problems. The goal, always, is combining intellectual rigor with business relevance. Indeed, the Kellogg School was founded on such a principle a century ago.

Said Sunil Chopra: "If you look at what globalization is doing, I think it is potentially going to be very good for business schools, if handled correctly." In the "flat world" model described by Thomas Friedman, global commerce is fundamentally about "taking a process and breaking it into pieces, which are farmed out, and then brought back together—seamlessly, as far as the customer is concerned," Chopra noted, adding that this scenario is happening at an accelerated pace now and demands the ability to integrate and understand customer value while also understanding the competitive advantage associated with each "piece" of the overall production process. "This does require people who have enough depth in each area, but, more importantly, who can integrate," he stated. "Of all the degrees out there, this is precisely the role of the MBA."[169]

Kellogg is pursuing new ways of keeping its curriculum relevant for the new century, including through interdisciplinary partnerships with other schools at Northwestern and elsewhere. For example, recently created executive education offerings in the Kellogg biotechnology program include "Business for Scientists and Engineers" and "Biotechnology: Science for Managers." The latter, a collaboration with Johns Hopkins Medical School, is designed to provide executives and managers with a practical understanding of the scientific and development foundations in the life sciences, learning the science behind the industry to more effectively communicate and perform in this complex environment. With "Business for Scientists and Engineers," Kellogg has formed a partnership with Northwestern's Weinberg College of Arts and Sciences, the Feinberg School of Medicine and the McCormick School of Engineering to introduce scientists and engineers to the basics of accounting, strategy, finance, marketing and the management of organizations. The program's goal is to enable participants to obtain clear frameworks about how innovation happens "from bench to market." Several additional executive education offerings in the biotechnology area complete a portfolio that seeks not only to bridge theory and practice but also to span various disciplines to create value for practitioners in the arts and sciences, as well as professional schools.

It is perhaps only a slight exaggeration to say that twenty-first-century leaders will find the strength and insight to go forward by looking back at earlier examples of "the best and brightest," at ideas and strategies that have proven enduring. And indeed, the Kellogg curriculum will make room for such broad-minded discoveries, the faculty members assert, even as it prepares leaders to master discipline-based standards such as finance, operations and marketing.

The Renaissance ideal of the polymath—the person who continuously learns, acquiring knowledge in many subjects—would surely serve contemporary leaders well as they negotiate today's multicultural, challenging global culture. Leaders might also benefit by referring to an even earlier model, the "philosopher king" in Plato's *Republic*. Plato described the proper education for the model leader:

> And when they are 50 years old, those who have lasted the whole [educational] course and are in every way best at everything, both in practice and in theory, must at last be led to the final goal, and must be compelled to lift up the eyes of their psyches towards that which provides light for everything, the Good itself. And taking it as their model, they must put in good order both the polis [city-state] and themselves for the remainder of their lives.[170]

In addition to making a rather respectable argument for executive education and lifelong learning, Plato emphasized key elements that today's MBA training must provide: *knowledge rooted in theory and practice and informed by ethical virtue that respects and cultivates the larger community.*

These are the tools that Kellogg School leaders say will transform lives by alerting students to their real calling and responsibility. And these are ideals to inform the Kellogg curriculum that will remain vital by creating not merely the means to nudge the Dow Jones up three points but also leaders who transform the world and themselves in remarkable ways.

Surely, these developments would astonish former Northwestern president Edmund James, whose complaint about the ignorance, inefficiency and cowardice of businessmen in 1902 served as the catalyst to establish what would become one of the world's most prestigious management schools.

NOTES

Introduction

1. Taylor (1856–1915) was an American engineer who sought to enhance industrial efficiency. Among his most famous contributions were time and motion studies that segmented tasks into their constituent parts, seeking ways to improve the overall process. Earlier advocates of what would be called scientific management included Josiah Wedgwood (1730–1795), the English potter credited with industrializing his practice, and Robert Owen (1771–1858), the Welsh social reformer and textile manufacturer. Taylor's quest for mechanical precision also sparked controversy for those who saw him as advocating tactics that were dehumanizing. Cf. Thorstein Veblen's *The Instinct of Workmanship* (1922).

2. *Atlantic Monthly,* Vol. 85, No. 512 (June 1900), p. 47.

3. *Higher Education and Business Standards,* Willard E. Hotchkiss (Houghton Mifflin, 1918), p. 106.

4. Ibid., p. 81.

5. Ibid., p. 103.

6. The legislation was created in 1890 but used extensively after 1900, particularly by Theodore Roosevelt in his pursuit of monopolies.

7. Debate about the efficacy and value of the Sarbanes-Oxley Act continues, with some arguing that its costs outweigh its benefits while others claim that restoring public trust in the markets should remain the priority of business and government in order to forestall a potential economic downturn of widespread and dangerous proportions.

Chapter 1

1. Many books document the advent of large commercial ventures in the United States. Two helpful sources are Glenn Porter's *The Rise of Big Business, 1860–1910* and David O. Whitten's *The Emergence of Giant Enterprise, 1860–1914.* The railroad figures are found in "Rise of Industrial America, 1876–1900," produced by the Library of Congress and available at http://memory.loc.gov/learn/features/timeline/riseind/riseof.html.

2. Not all scholars accept a facile notion of American individualism. In *The Myth of American Individualism: The Protestant Origins of American Political Thought* (Princeton University Press, 1994), Barry Alan Shain argued that eighteenth-century Americans framed and practiced individualism in accordance with reformed Protestant communalism, in which biblical ethical codes and rational frameworks informed the notion of individual liberties—a view that contrasted with most twentieth-century conceptions of liberal individualism, according to Shain. Community concern appeared in the thought of

individuals who were associated with Northwestern University's School of Commerce early on, including President Abram Winegardner Harris and Professor Earl Dean Howard. Harris expressed his views about solving social problems in the essay "On the Social Evil in Chicago," published in the *Journal of the American Institute of Criminal Law and Criminology*, Vol. 3, No. 5 (January 1913). There, he argued for a community-wide response to crime rather than a strategy that merely segregated parts of the city where vice ran rampant. "Segregation is unfair to innocent and conscientious owners of property in the segregated district," he wrote, adding that the practice was also "outrageously unfair to those poor helpless people who must live in the immediate presence of the congregated vicious element." Howard would contribute to resolving disputes as a labor manager and vice president and director of Hart, Schaffner & Marx, the prominent Chicago men's clothing firm.

3. The public came to regard these giant enterprises with suspicion, believing them too powerful. Over time, the government pursued legislation to restrain the conglomerates that had sought ways to limit individual liability as they grew. Starting in the 1880s, many firms created trusts, composed of several companies that only appeared to be competing with one another and were essentially governed by one board of trustees. Government responded by passing the Sherman Antitrust Act of 1890, an effort to enhance legitimate competition. Additional tools, such as the creation of the Interstate Commerce Commission in 1887, also were employed to protect the public against corporate consolidation. This uneasy balance between stimulating commercial development and halting its unfettered growth continued into the twentieth century, with Republican presidential nominee William H. Taft running on a platform favoring conservation and opposition to business trusts, details he unveiled on June 16, 1908, at the GOP's convention in Chicago.

4. Walton contributed his talents as an accounting lecturer. The roots of the Illinois CPA society may be traced to a predecessor organization founded in 1897. "Chicago's emergence as a major center of professional accounting began during the 1890s," wrote Paul J. Miranti Jr. in *The Encyclopedia of Chicago*. "Initially, Chicago businesses relied on semiprofessional bookkeepers who were usually ill-prepared to develop innovative responses to the bewildering measurement problems associated with new technologies, legal contracts, transactions, management practices, or organizational forms." Another Northwestern professor, Arthur Andersen, would become influential in developing the accounting profession. Andersen and Walton would also help establish the school's accounting program, particularly based on the needs of practitioners like themselves.

5. James was a "scholar with a keen interest in practical affairs," according to Frank C. Pierson's account in *The Education of American Businessmen* (p. 37). In particular, James was focused on finance and public administration. During his Wharton tenure, he oversaw a curriculum largely consisting of courses in history, government and economics, with a smaller selection from among accounting, business law and business organization, noted Pierson.

6. The Wharton School was the first collegiate business school in the United States. Founded in 1881, Wharton was followed by the University of Chicago's Graduate School of Business and the University of California–Berkeley's College of Commerce, which both opened in 1898, and Dartmouth's Amos Tuck School of Business, opened in 1900. In Europe, the Ecole Supérieure de Commerce of Paris, founded in 1819, had the distinction of being the first business school. Canada's HEC Montréal was that nation's first business school,

founded in 1907. The oldest educational institution, Germany's University of Leipzig, dates back more than 600 years to 1409, although its Graduate School of Management (HHL) was established in 1898.

7. Carnegie spent much of his later life giving away money, particularly to fund education and public libraries. In March 1901, for example, a $5.2 million gift from Carnegie established New York City's public library system. His comparatively more modest philanthropic contributions began in the 1880s.

8. *Northwestern University: A History, 1850–1975,* Harold F. Williamson, p. 105.

9. *The Evolution of Management Education,* Michael W. Sedlak and Harold F. Williamson, p. 12.

10. Only a few decades had passed since California's admission to the Union in 1850. Seven other states had been part of the Union for eleven years or less in 1900. At the turn of the century, Oklahoma, Arizona, New Mexico, Alaska and Hawaii remained territories.

11. "Business of Chicago," Peter A. Coclanis, in *The Encyclopedia of Chicago* (2004). Charles Dickens, traveling in America during 1842, presented this picture of the burgeoning but young railroad system and the society that created it in his *American Notes* (pp. 84–85): "The train calls at stations in the woods, where the wild impossibility of anybody having the smallest reason to get out, is only to be equaled by the apparently desperate hopelessness of there being anybody to get in. It rushes across the turnpike road, where there is no gate, no policeman, no signal: nothing but a rough wooden arch, on which is painted 'When The Bell Rings, Look Out For The Locomotive.' On it whirls headlong, dives through the woods again, emerges in the light, clatters over frail arches, rumbles upon the heavy ground, shoots beneath a wooden bridge which intercepts the light for a second like a wink, suddenly awakens all the slumbering echoes in the main street of a large town, and dashes on haphazard, pell-mell, neck-or-nothing, down the middle of the road. There—with mechanics working at their trades, and people leaning from their doors and windows, and boys flying kites and playing marbles, and men smoking, and women talking, and children crawling, and pigs burrowing, and unaccustomed horses plunging and rearing, close to the very rails—there—on, on, on—tears the mad dragon of an engine with its train of cars; scattering in all directions a shower of burning sparks from its wood fire; screeching, hissing, yelling, panting; until at last the thirsty monster stops beneath a covered way to drink, the people cluster round, and you have time to breathe again."

12. "Chicago," in *Chicago Poems,* Robert Frost (1916).

13. The book would spark a national controversy, attracting the attention of President Theodore Roosevelt and resulting in passage of the Meat Inspection Act and the Pure Food and Drug Act as well as the establishment of the Food and Drug Administration. (The book's 2006 expanded edition included a third more text—previously unpublished material that detailed working conditions in the steel industry and dynamics in the criminal underground.) Ironically, Sinclair, a socialist, intended for his grotesque narrative to improve conditions for the men and women laboring in the stockyards; what he accomplished actually did more to advance legislation to improve hygiene, if not exactly animal rights. "I aimed for America's heart," said Sinclair later, "and hit its stomach."

14. The enterprise even gave rise to a popular fictional character, Rudolph the Red-Nosed Reindeer, courtesy of staff copywriter Robert L. May, who created the story as part of a 1939 company promotion.

15. Some contend that the city's name derives from a Potawatomi word whose translation means "wild onion" or "skunk cabbage" or, more charitably, "strong" or "great." See http://en.wikipedia.org/wiki/Chicago#Origin_of_name and http://www.chipublib.org/004chicago/timeline/originame.html.

16. The city's population would exceed 1 million by 1890, according to U.S. Bureau of the Census records. About the time of the commerce school's founding, Chicago was home to some 2 million inhabitants, making it the nation's second-largest metropolis.

17. *City of the Century: The Epic of Chicago and the Making of America,* Donald L. Miller, p. 49.

18. Ibid., p. 77.

19. Ibid., pp. 434–435.

20. "The Rise of New Immigrant Gateways," Audrey Singer (Brookings Institution, Living Cities Census Series, 2004).

21. An unflattering contemporary opinion on the labor movement, one indicating the deep-seated class conflicts of the time, is found in George Frederick Parsons's essay entitled "The Labor Question," in the July 1886 *Atlantic Monthly,* pp. 97–113.

22. The police investigation supported Shippy's claims of self-defense, but others, including Jane Addams and attorney Harold Ickes, discerned inconsistencies in Shippy's narrative. Some of Chicago's leading Jewish figures, including Julius Rosenwald of Sears, Roebuck, helped fund an alternative inquiry to that of the law enforcement officials. Chicago newspapers in 1908 were also filled with reports of a spectacular murder mystery in LaPorte, Indiana, at the farm of Belle Gunness.

23. *Northwestern University School of Commerce Bulletin,* Vol. 8, No. 2 (July 1908).

24. "Special Report II," 1907, School of Commerce Records, Northwestern University Archives.

25. Howard originally had gone to Chicago with his family after 1893, working as a salesman in his father's lumber company, a situation that enabled him to travel through the Midwest selling the products and periodically writing articles for the *Chicago Tribune.*

26. "The Present State of Part-Time Business Education," Willard Hotchkiss, in *Northwestern University Conference on Business Education,* p. 96. Hotchkiss recalled: "I did not personally come in very close contact with the Wharton School evening courses, but merely looking on while men employed all day down town flocked out to West Philadelphia into the classrooms of Logan Hall was enough to stir the imagination."

27. "In Memoriam: Frederick Shipp Deibler, 1876–1961," *American Economic Review,* Vol. 52, No. 2 (May 1962).

28. There, as an undergraduate in 1900, he founded the *Daily Maroon,* the first daily newspaper at the university.

29. In Berlin, Howard would have studied within the context of the Historical school of thought, a model that argued against the traditional laissez-faire economics of the nineteenth century and favored a more socially progressive role for the discipline. This framework undoubtedly contributed to Howard lending his expertise to practical issues of labor management.

30. It is tempting to think that modern business leaders and their academic counterparts have been the first to grapple with ethics to combat the effects of scandals such as the Enron affair. But the dialogue was enjoined a century ago, with Chicago being one of the

nation's hot spots for labor disputes and ethical concerns surrounding the meatpacking industry.

31. Howard and Hillman would develop a lifelong friendship, even taking trips to Europe and the Soviet Union in 1922, where they met with Soviet labor leaders and the minister of trade. The multifaceted Howard also kept detailed journals and saved his correspondence with Margaret Allen, the woman he would marry in June 1907. A fan of music and the theater, Howard participated in professional theatrical efforts, at one time even working with the famous actress Dame Ellen Alice Terry. Details available in the Earl Dean Howard Papers, Northwestern University Archives.

32. In addition to labor unrest, race riots occurred repeatedly during the first decade of the twentieth century, including those in Springfield, Illinois, in August 1908, a situation that resulted in Governor Charles Deneen taking aggressive steps to restore order after at least seven people died. Barber Scott Burton was lynched by a mob during the melee; the tree used for the purpose was soon chopped up by townspeople for souvenirs, according to reports in the August 18 *Chicago Daily Tribune*, p. 2. The riot contributed to increased concern about civil rights and led to the creation of the National Association for the Advancement of Colored People (NAACP) in February 1909.

33. "Clothing and Garment Manufacturing," *Encyclopedia of Chicago,* available at www.encyclopedia.chicagohistory.org/pages/300.html.

34. "Dr. Earl Dean Howard of N.U. Is Pioneer Labor Manager and Socratic Institute Originator," *Evanston News-Index,* April 20, 1924.

35. Northwestern University President's Office document, collected in the Earl Dean Howard Papers, Northwestern University Archives.

36. "Northwestern University Chapel Address, April 4, 1918." The title of the address was "What Is the Meaning of Democracy in Industry?" Collected in the Earl Dean Howard Papers, Northwestern University Archives.

37. "Labor in a Constitutionalized Industry: As a Labor Manager Sees It," in *American Labor Dynamics in the Light of Post-war Developments: An Inquiry by Thirty-two Labor Men, Teachers, Editors, and Technicians,* J. B. S. Hardman, ed. (New York: Harcourt Brace, 1928), pp. 329–332.

38. *Northwestern University Bulletin: School of Commerce,* September 24, 1921.

39. "Training for Business Leadership," *Evanston Review,* June 28, 1951.

40. *The National Cyclopedia* (1917), p. 139.

41. *Higher Education and Business Standards,* Willard E. Hotchkiss (Houghton Mifflin, 1918), p. 103.

42. The first article appeared in *Annals of the American Academy of Political and Social Science,* Vol. 28 (November 1906), pp. 27–46; the transportation title appeared in the same journal, Vol. 31 (May 1908), pp. 85–95; the publication on trusts appeared in *American Economic Review,* Vol. 4, No. 1 (March 1914), pp. 158–172.

43. *American Economic Review,* Vol. 4, No. 1 (March 1914), p. 172.

44. With respect to financial support for the venture, Harris, like James, pursued Carnegie philanthropy, also unsuccessfully. He was, however, more fortunate in securing support from other quarters, resulting in significant improvements at Northwestern. He would help increase the Northwestern endowment by more than $1 million, creating a total endowment of more than $9 million by 1917. In addition to the School of Commerce, the

Harris administration oversaw the reestablishment of a school of engineering at Northwestern as well as the Patten Gymnasium and a complex of male dormitories arranged in quadrangles, a much-needed expansion to cope with a crowded campus. The gymnasium included a club room for men, offices for student organizations, a large dirt track and a room that was large enough to hold a baseball diamond.

45. Hotchkiss, in fact, "unofficially" dated the commerce school's opening to the fall of 1907, citing courses delivered by Howard and Seymour Walton as the academic catalyst for the school. See "The Present State of Part-Time Business Education," p. 96.

46. "Training for Business Leadership."

47. "The Present State of Part-Time Business Education," p. 97.

48. In addition to Earl Dean Howard, other early recipients of Schaffner's largesse included Will Alwin Forward in the 1908–1909 school year and Joseph Henry Gilby and Fred Norman Vanderwalker in the 1910–1911 school year. These awardees earned the distinction for having the "best record in examinations," rather than for a dissertation.

49. Mather (1867–1930) was president and owner of the Thorkildsen-Mather Borax Company, a concern that made him a millionaire. He was a champion of conservation and sought to create an agency to protect the nation's parks. In addition to being recognized by name throughout the National Park System—bronze markers note that he "laid the foundation of the National Park Service. . . . There will never come an end to the good he has done"—Mather had a Chicago high school named in his honor. See www.cr.nps.gov/history.

50. Schaffner's love of books and education led his family to make significant material and financial contributions to Northwestern; as a result, the school named the library in its downtown Chicago facility after him in 1927, upon the completion of a new building for the commerce school in Wieboldt Hall. The library remains on the second floor of Wieboldt Hall on Chicago Avenue.

51. The formal resolution of sympathy appears in the "Minutes of the Faculty of the School of Commerce," dated May 7, 1918. (This material is currently located in unofficial Kellogg archives.)

52. *Chicago and Its Resources Twenty Years After, 1871–1891,* Royal L. LaTouche (Chicago Times, 1892), p. 179.

53. "The Northwestern University School of Commerce," *Journal of Political Economy,* Vol. 21, No. 3 (March 1913), pp. 196–208.

54. Ibid., p. 196.

55. "Minutes of the Faculty of the School of Commerce."

56. *Northwestern University School of Commerce Bulletin,* July 1908, p. 13.

57. Among 1,900 in attendance for the popular holiday musical *Mr. Blue Beard Jr.,* some 600 perished in the tragedy. See www.chipublib.org/004chicago/disasters/iroquois_fire.html.

58. The event attracted more than 20 million people to the city, showcasing the impressive civic accomplishments that had taken place since the great fire of 1871. Chicago businessmen, including Charles T. Yerkes, Marshall Field, Cyrus McCormick, Augustus Swift and Lyman Gage, bested their New York peers in raising more than $15 million in advance of the fair, convincing Congress to designate Chicago as the event's host. After efforts to secure a central location became bogged down in legal issues, these businessmen would help trans-

form Jackson Park, an undesirable location some seven miles south of the Loop, into the famous "White City."

59. "That Windy City: Some of the Freaks of the Last Chicago Tornado," *Cincinnati Enquirer*, May 9, 1876, p. 2., col. 4.

60. *Chicago Tribune*, September 11, 1886. Other references include those in the baseball magazine *Sporting Life* in 1885 and 1886, calling Chicago the "City of Winds" and the "Windy City."

61. The "Burnt District" was approximately four miles long by three-quarters of a mile wide—some 2,000 acres. An estimated 18,000 buildings were destroyed, resulting in $2 million worth of property damage. Between 200 and 300 people perished. Although much of the city's heavy industry sector escaped harm, including the stockyards, the fire produced "total desolation" and an "utter blankness of what had a few hours before been so full of life, of associations, of aspirations." (The reference appears in Elias Colbert and Everett Chamberlain's contemporary narrative *Chicago and the Great Conflagration* [1871].) Indicative of the city's spirit and resolve, the *Tribune*'s first lead editorial after the fire read: "CHEER UP. In the midst of a calamity without parallel in the world's history, looking upon the ashes of thirty years' accumulations, the people of this once beautiful city have resolved that CHICAGO SHALL RISE AGAIN."

62. Bonbright was a professor of Latin at Northwestern, having been on the faculty since 1856. During his tenure as president (1900–1902), Bonbright primarily focused on the affairs of the College of Liberal Arts, although he did bring up another concern to university trustees in 1901: the rise of women students on the Evanston campus. He feared that the increased percentage of female students, growing from 36 percent in 1891 to 50 percent in 1900, would create a "feminine image" for Northwestern, discouraging male applicants. Cited in *Northwestern University: A History*, p. 102.

63. Contemporary photos reveal a room with nearly 90 dental chairs equipped with foot-operated drills.

64. This part-time approach remains an important Kellogg School component today, with the Part-Time MBA Program meeting the needs of working students from the Chicago area community. The program was formally launched in 1972, though the rationale for its curriculum was an impetus from the commerce school's beginning in 1908.

65. Some 60 percent of the initial class held such positions; another 15 percent were employed by banks or brokerages, 6 percent were in sales or advertising and 4 percent were teachers, lawyers or architects. The remainder worked in clerical roles. Detailed student demographics appear as part of the commerce school faculty's minutes of May 1911.

66. "Minutes of the Faculty of the School of Commerce," September 3, 1915.

67. Canada and Germany also provided nearly a dozen students in 1915. Other countries represented in the school's enrollment records included Australia, Bohemia, England, Norway and Turkey, among others; foreign students made up more than 15 percent of the school's student body of 855 by 1915.

68. *Evolution of Management Education*, p. 21.

69. "Minutes of the Faculty of the School of Commerce."

70. Among these candidates was David Himmelblau, who would go on to earn the bachelor in business administration degree in 1914, becoming the first person to do so at the

commerce school. In 1911, Himmelblau also distinguished himself by earning the Illinois Society of Certified Public Accountants Prize, which included an award of $100. He would later become a faculty member at the School of Commerce. The commencement bulletin for 1911 noted that "the color of the tassel on the cap indicates the school from which the wearer is graduating." Perhaps suggesting a no-nonsense approach to the seriousness of business study, commerce graduates were identified by "drab" tassels, distinguishing them from the green tassels of the medical school, the purple tassels of the law school and the white tassels of the College of Liberal Arts.

71. The Northwestern University catalogs for 1909 to 1919 indicated that a total of 90 diplomas were granted over the school's first decade. During that same time, four bachelor's degrees in business administration were conferred.

72. Voorhees also distinguished herself for having formed "the Lydians" organization at Northwestern in 1913, which took its name from a suggestion by a Northwestern University professor who noted that Lydia was a New Testament figure, a "dealer in purple." The student group's purpose was "to promote sociability and good feeling" among the female students who composed its membership. Commerce students predominated in the club, although membership was open to all Northwestern students. The club sponsored a variety of social events, including dinners, dances, parties and lectures by business and academic leaders.

73. Another member of the Board of Guarantors, Richard C. Hall, served as the chamber's chairman for 1908. Hall was a representative of the United States Rubber Company.

74. James B. Forgan, president of the First National Bank of Chicago and later a director of the Chicago Reserve Bank, wrote: "Money is scarce all over . . . the pressure on us has been so extraordinary . . . I am in daily terror of something giving way under the strain" (quoted in *The Growth of Chicago Banks*, James F. Cyril [New York: Harper & Brothers, 1938]). Such financial crises would eventually lead to the creation of a central banking system, the Federal Reserve, by congressional act on December 23, 1913. The Chicago Federal Reserve Bank, along with 11 other banks, opened for business on November 16, 1914.

75. Taussig, an expert on tariffs and international trade, was highly influential in American economics, producing a well-known, two-volume text, *Principles of Economics*, in 1911.

76. During the 1911–1912 school year and at the request of Harvard Business School dean Edwin F. Gay, Shaw would create a business policy course; the curriculum included outside lecturers who would introduce actual business problems for students to consider and report on. These details, as well as praise for Shaw as a "pioneer in proposing a systematic approach to the study of marketing," are found in "Arch W. Shaw," Melvin T. Copeland, *Journal of Marketing*, Vol. 22, No. 3 (January 1958), pp. 313–315.

77. *Evolution of Management Education*, p. 24.

78. "Influences on the Development of Marketing Thought, 1900–1923," Robert Bartels, *Journal of Marketing*, Vol. 16, No. 1 (July 1951), p. 9.

79. "Arch W. Shaw," p. 313.

80. "Influences on the Development of Marketing Thought," p. 109. Shaw was also instrumental in helping shape Harvard's case study method as part of a business policy course he taught there.

81. Registration statistics presented in "Minutes of the Faculty of the School of Commerce," September 1917.

82. "The Northwestern University School of Commerce," *Journal of Political Economy,* Vol. 21, No. 3 (1913), pp. 196–208.

83. *Evolution of Management Education,* p. 29. To this end, the school formed the Student Organization in 1908, which was renamed the Commerce Club in 1913.

84. Scott served as university president from 1920 until 1939, years of great development at the university sparked by the institution's endowment growing from about $5.6 million to nearly $27 million; in addition, 57 new buildings were erected both in Evanston and on the Chicago campus, which underwent impressive construction in the 1920s. During this expansion, the School of Journalism was opened in 1921, as was the Charles Deering Library in 1932 and the School of Education in 1934. Scott also oversaw, in 1926, the creation of the university's Chicago campus, which produced new facilities for the schools of law, medicine, dentistry and commerce. Details about the commerce facilities will be discussed later.

85. Scott's academic reputation was established by a number of his seminal texts, including *The Theory of Advertising* (1903), *The Psychology of Advertising* (1908), *Influencing Men in Business* (1911) and *Increasing Human Efficiency in Business* (1911). He also distinguished himself by establishing, in 1916, the Bureau of Salesmanship Research at Carnegie Institute of Technology. In addition, Scott served as a colonel in the U.S. Army between 1917 and 1918; in that capacity, he directed a committee on personnel, an area of expertise built on his psychological insights. For this contribution, Scott received the Distinguished Service Medal of the United States in 1919. Later, in 1933, he was awarded a cross from the French Legion of Honor, and in 1938, he was made a chevalier in the legion (established by Napoléon in 1802).

86. "Part-Time University Training in Business," p. 97.

87. *Psychology of Advertising,* pp. 1–2. Scott, tellingly, dedicated this text to the "American business men who successfully apply Science where their predecessors were confined to Custom," a clear indication of his desire to bridge theory and practice.

88. *Contribution to the Psychology of Business,* pp. 4–7.

89. Ibid., pp. 395–396.

90. In 1915, Clark was a cofounder of what would become the National Association of Marketing Teachers (NAMT), a precursor to the American Marketing Association (AMA), which was founded in 1937 by combining NAMT and another organization, the American Marketing Society (AMS). Clark would serve as AMA chairman in 1938. His *Principles of Marketing* (1922) and *Readings in Marketing* (1924) would prove influential. Chapter 2 traces the rise of marketing as a discipline at Northwestern University.

91. Departments in the School of Commerce by 1915 included: accounting, business law, economics, finance, psychology, business English, domestic and foreign trade, organization and management, transportation, statistics, public speaking and foreign languages.

92. *Higher Education and Business Standards,* p. 68.

93. "Minutes of the Faculty of the School of Commerce," special report, Fall 1915, p. 8.

94. *City of the Century: The Epic of Chicago and the Making of America,* Donald L. Miller (1997), p. 24. The text offers a compelling history of Chicago from its founding through 1900.

95. Andersen was awarded a bachelor of business administration degree in 1917 by Northwestern. The faculty minutes for September 29 of that year indicate that a special committee chaired by Professor Frederick Deibler had reviewed his abilities favorably: "While Mr. Andersen has not complied strictly with all of the formal requirements for the degree in question, the committee is unanimous in the opinion that he has met in spirit and in substance the requirements set by this faculty for the degree . . . and is duly qualified for that degree."

96. "The Final Accounting: The Fall of Andersen," *Chicago Tribune*, September 1, 2002.

97. Vanderblue earned a bachelor's degree from Northwestern in 1911 and a master's degree in 1912.

98. *Evolution of Management Education*, p. 20.

99. "Minutes of the Faculty of the School of Commerce," March 6, 1920. Also noted that day was Secrist's intention to send survey questionnaires to some 6,000 retail dealers throughout the United States.

100. Ibid., p. 54

101. "Horace Secrist, 1881–1943," Frederick S. Deibler, *Journal of the American Statistical Association*, Vol. 38, No. 223 (September 1943), pp. 365–366. Deibler also noted that Secrist's statistical acumen was always turned on problems in a way that considered their "social and economic implications" and, further, that his efforts included research into government problems, among them mechanisms to determine how to adjust pricing to output during wartime.

102. "Research in Collegiate Schools of Business," *Journal of Political Economy*, Vol. 28, No. 5 (May 1920), pp. 353–374.

103. Marketing scholar Paul D. Converse observed that real-world problems had previously been used at Northwestern in accounting and commercial law courses but that Swanson said "he used 30 or more problems which he gathered from three sources: his work as a market consultant; the members and the programs of the Chicago Sales Managers' Association; and direct from different firms in the Chicago area." Converse detailed the early history of the field in "The Development of the Science of Marketing—An Exploratory Survey," *Journal of Marketing*, Vol. 10, No. 1 (July 1945), p. 20.

104. *Evolution of Management Education*, p. 20.

105. The first AACBS meeting occurred on June 16, 1916, in Chicago. Swanson was one of six administrators elected to a committee entrusted with drafting a plan for the organization. Other committee members included faculty from Harvard, Tulane, the University of Illinois, Dartmouth and the University of Chicago.

106. "Review," R. S. Alexander, *Annals of the American Academy of Political and Social Science*, Vol. 124 (March 1926), pp. 205–206. A review by the *University Journal of Business* in its April 1926 edition similarly noted that "the attempt to deal in a general yet balanced and well-rounded fashion with such a large subject is most commendable and the author has succeeded in a difficult task."

107. "Economics and the Science of Business," *Journal of Political Economy*, Vol. 25, No. 1 (January 1917), pp. 106–110.

108. The sentiment would be echoed during World War II and by the scientists who worked on the Manhattan Project, including J. Robert Oppenheimer, the "father of the

atomic bomb," who claimed to have been so aloof from mundane politics that he only learned of the stock market crash of 1929 much later.

109. *Men Who Sell Things,* Walter D. Moody (1907), p. 14.

110. Ibid., pp. 16–17.

111. Brief selections carry titles such as "Why Slang Is Harmful," "Training the Will," "Habits of Health" and "Bathing."

112. *Daily Northwestern,* October 25, 1909, p. 1.

113. *Evolution of Management Education,* p. 30.

114. By 1917, tuition receipts totaled some $55,000, a figure that covered all operating costs.

115. *Higher Education and Business Standards,* p. 108.

116. Ibid., p. 106.

117. Ibid., p. 81.

118. Ibid., p. 103.

119. "Business in the New Era," Willard Hotchkiss, in *Man and His World: Northwestern University Essays in Contemporary Thought,* Vol. 5, *Society Today,* p. 108.

120. "Minutes of the Faculty of the School of Commerce," September 25, 1915, addendum "How to Study."

121. "Praises Modern Business Study. Franklin MacVeagh Speaks before Northwestern School of Commerce. Urges Public Service," *Chicago Tribune,* May 10, 1914, p. 8. During his visit, MacVeagh also expressed his hope that commerce would resolve political challenges, including tensions between North and South America. "Nothing else will break down the barriers and bring spiritual understanding," he said.

122. Hotchkiss returned briefly to Northwestern in 1921 to deliver a course in industrial relations with Earl Dean Howard, as noted in the *Chicago Tribune* of April 16, 1921.

123. *Northwestern University Bulletin: School of Commerce Public Lectures on Business Organization,* Vol. 18, No. 20 (January 19, 1918).

124. *Evolution of Management Education,* p. 32.

125. "Personal Qualities Requisite for Success in Business and the Role of the School of Business in Their Development," Ralph Heilman, *Journal of Business of the University of Chicago,* Vol. 4, No. 3 (July 1931), pp. 11–22.

126. Details recounted in "Memoranda Concerning Specific Requirements for Degree of Bachelor of Science in Commerce," in "Minutes of the Board of Trustees," June 15, 1930, p. 33. (This material is currently located in unofficial Kellogg archives.)

127. *Bulletin* (1921–1922), pp. 14–15, Northwestern University Archives.

128. Correspondence in the Frederick Shipp Deibler Papers, Northwestern University Archives, indicates there was an "antagonistic relationship" between Flickinger and Heilman.

129. "Memoranda Concerning Specific Requirements." The notes went on to parse curricular predicates related to the existing precommerce course, comparing them with facts stated by Dean Heilman.

130. *Evolution of Management Education,* p. 36.

131. "Minutes of the Faculty of the School of Commerce, Special Meeting," May 20, 1919.

132. "Minutes of the Faculty of the School of Commerce," May 27, 1922.

133. *Evolution of Management Education,* p. 41.

134. At this time, by comparison, a host of trade and technical schools flourished to teach everything from commercial art to fashion and photography to electrical wiring. Advertisements for these schools routinely filled newspaper classified pages, promising good positions for graduates. The Illinois School of Filing, for instance, offered a booklet promising to reveal how one could "rise from a clerk's position to that of executive"—one simply phoned Miss Lavender for details. See, e.g., *Chicago Daily Tribune,* April 12, 1925, p. D8.

135. *Evolution of Management Education,* p. 43.

136. The building was named for Norman Wait Harris, a prominent Chicago banker, philanthropist and trustee and a benefactor to Northwestern. Built as a home for the social sciences, Harris Hall also contained the commerce school, although the quarters were not ideally suited to the needs of the school and its increasing enrollment.

137. "President's Report for Northwestern University," 1921–1922, p. 62, located in the main Northwestern library.

138. In 1920, Northwestern had purchased about 8.5 acres for $1.5 million at Chicago Avenue and Lake Shore Drive in Streeterville. George McKinlock, a Chicago businessman, pledged his financial support for the campus in honor of his son, Alexander, who died during World War I. However, when McKinlock lost his money during the Great Depression, he was unable to honor his pledge to the university. Northwestern elected to forgive the debt, changing the name of the site in 1937 to the Chicago Campus.

139. Gary, born in Wheaton, Illinois, graduated from the Union College of Law, which became the Northwestern University School of Law, in 1868. In 1901 and with the encouragement of J. P. Morgan, he founded the United States Steel Corporation. He died in 1927.

140. Overall, Northwestern had raised some $8 million in 1924 and 1925, most of the funds going toward expansion of its Chicago campus.

141. *The Encyclopedia of Chicago,* Janice L. Reiff, Ann Durkin Keating and James R. Grossman, eds. (University of Chicago Press, 2004).

142. "The Relationship between Colleges of Arts and Colleges of Commerce," *Proceedings of the Northwestern University Conference on Business Education* (1927), p. 5.

143. Ibid., p. 75.

144. *Journal of Business of the University of Chicago,* Vol. 5, No. 2, Pt. 2: "Proceedings of the Fourteenth Annual Meeting of the Association of Collegiate Schools of Business" (October 1932), pp. 8–10.

145. This notion is one that, even today, can stimulate controversy. In fact, one of the commerce school's graduates, James C. Worthy '33, remarked in a 1954 address before the School of Business at the University of Chicago that "the relationship of the schools of business to business is quite different from the relationship of the schools of medicine and law to their respective professions."

146. *Proceedings of the Northwestern University Conference on Business Education,* p. 33.

147. Ibid., p. 45.

148. Ibid., pp. 65–66.

149. "Northwestern University Institute of Business," draft dated February 1922, in the Earl Dean Howard Papers, Northwestern University Archives.

150. *Evolution of Management Education,* p. 65.

151. Austin's foundation was established to provide scholarships for "male persons of the Caucasian race, without reference to nationality, religion or wealth."

152. Gross rentals amounted to $304,000 in 1928, according to James C. Worthy's *The Austin Scholarships: A History*, p. 31.

153. Ibid., p. 8.

154. "A Brief History of the Austin Scholars," James C. Worthy, *Kellogg World* (Summer 1988), pp. 24–27.

155. *Austin Scholarships*, p. 7.

156. Ibid., p. 1.

157. Worthy noted that this arrangement was short-lived as the Depression curtailed the program, resulting in the dorm being renamed Goodrich House in 1933 and the remaining scholars being relocated to another facility, Haven House.

158. *Austin Scholarships*, p. 15.

159. "Can Business Be Taught?" Ralph Heilman, *Journal of Business of the University of Chicago*, Vol. 5, No. 4, Pt. 2 (October 1932), pp. 8–10. Heilman also considered the value in introducing biographical surveys of leaders such as Napoléon Bonaparte, Abraham Lincoln, Henry Ford, Louis Pasteur and the Wright brothers.

160. *Austin Scholarships*, p. 16.

161. Ibid., p. 31.

162. Ibid., p. 33. Austin died in 1932, at which time the entire cost of the program passed to the university.

163. See chapter 3. The Austin Scholars remain a presence at the Kellogg School today, as a graduate-level program.

164. Wild and President Roscoe Miller made "two important modifications" to the business school's earlier proposal: the final approval of Austin Scholarship awards would rest with the University Scholarship Committee and housing for freshmen scholars would continue to be arranged in accordance with existing university policy, meaning these students would "live in the same dormitory with other freshmen and . . . not . . . housed with upperclassmen." The university did, however, express its willingness to assign scholars to the same dormitory floor whenever possible.

165. "Can Business Be Taught?" pp. 4–5.

166. *Evolution of Management Education*, p. 171.

167. "The Deal That Almost Was: 'The Universities of Chicago,'" Northwestern University Historic Moments, available at www.northwestern.edu/features/historic_moments/04_05_01_merger.html.

168. "Call Merger Rockefeller Plan to Wipe Out N.U.," *Evanston Review*, January 18, 1934.

169. *Northwestern University: A History*, p. 186.

170. Ibid., pp. 60–61.

171. "Part-Time University Training in Business," pp. 102–103.

172. *Evolution of Management Education*, p. 68.

173. Ibid., p. 71.

174. Heilman did, however, express his general support of collegiate business schools adopting a broader educational focus, including introducing subjects such as political

science and business and government regulation. "I believe that all schools of commerce should require at least a one-year course in the fundamentals of American government, national, state and local," Heilman told Earl W. Crecraft, who included the observation in "Political Science Instruction in Teacher-Training Institutions, Colleges of Engineering, and Colleges of Commerce." The dean admitted it was "ridiculous that in democracy we require courses in mathematics, French, German, etc., but do not require a course in government." Yet, he also reported, "we do not do this at Northwestern because our School of Commerce does not admit students until they have finished the first two years of college." See *American Political Science Review*, Vol. 24, No. 1 (February 1930), pp. 162–163.

175. See chapter 3.

176. "The Place of Economics in the Curriculum of a School of Business: Discussion," J. C. Bonbright et al., *Journal of Political Economy*, Vol. 34, No. 2 (April 1926), pp. 227–243, quote on p. 238.

177. "Mistakes of the 'New Deal,'" Earl Dean Howard, *Christian Science Monitor* (weekly magazine section), June 26, 1935, p. 5.

178. "Education for Business Leadership," James C. Worthy, *Journal of Business*, Vol. 28, No. 1 (January 1955), pp. 76–82, quote on p. 76.

179. *Big Business and Free Men*, James C. Worthy (New York: Harper & Brothers, 1959), p. 15.

180. "Review," James C. Worthy, *Journal of Business of the University of Chicago*, Vol. 22, No. 3 (July 1949), p. 204.

Chapter 2

1. "Influences on the Development of Marketing Thought, 1900–1923," Robert Bartels, *Journal of Marketing*, Vol. 16, No. 1 (July 1951), p. 16. Bartels traced marketing's birth to the United States between 1906 and 1911, but others, such as Donald F. Dixon, have suggested an earlier origin, based in part on the *Oxford English Dictionary*'s reference to the word *marketing* appearing in the sixteenth century. See Dixon's "Emerging Macromarketing Concepts: From Socrates to Alfred Marshall," *Journal of Business Research*, Vol. 55 (2002), pp. 87–95, where he highlighted the complex relationships between the market and other social institutions over time.

2. *The History of Marketing Thought*, Robert Bartels, p. 14.

3. "The Functional Approach to the Study of Marketing," Homer B. Vanderblue, *Journal of Political Economy*, Vol. 29, No. 8 (October 1921), pp. 680–682.

4. *History of Marketing Thought*, pp. 16–17.

5. Herrold "contributed to the understanding of copy writing through explanation and illustration of logical steps involved in the function, rather than through the study of examples of finished ads," noted Bartels in *History of Marketing Thought*, p. 42.

6. The initiative ran from 1936 until 1947. Anderson, a 1930 graduate of Northwestern's School of Commerce, formally joined the school as an assistant professor in marketing in 1937, after serving as assistant chief of retail trade for the U.S. Bureau of the Census for the previous two years. He would earn a doctorate in commerce from Northwestern in 1944.

7. Both of Duncan's texts would be issued in multiple editions and serve as a "major influence on the teaching and practice of retailing," according to John S. Wright's biography of Duncan in the *Journal of Marketing*, Vol. 32 (April 1968). Wright noted that Duncan's career-long orientation was to determine the underlying dynamics of marketing practice. Even after his retirement in 1965, Duncan continued publishing important monographs, including *Some Basic Determinants of Behavior in Industrial Purchasing* and *Top Management Attitudes toward Personal Salesmanship*.

8. Interview with author, 2006.

9. The book sold more than a million copies and appeared on national best-seller lists. Packard's subsequent publications followed a similar pattern. With titles like *Status Seekers* (1959) and *Pyramid Climbers* (1962), the works appealed to a mass audience looking for popularized psychological interpretations of complex social phenomena. Professional sociologists and public intellectuals, however, tended to disparage these works, often noting the author's lack of academic credentials in the subjects he addressed. Still, with jacket blurbs promising the books would reveal the world of "psychology professors turned merchandisers" and answer questions like "why men's clothes are becoming feminized," "why automobiles get longer and longer" and "what makes us buy, believe—even vote—the way we do," Packard's works proved popular and influential.

10. *Scott of Northwestern: The Life Story of a Pioneer in Psychology and Education*, J. Z. Jacobson (Chicago: L. Mariano, 1951), p. 31.

11. In 1875, Wundt established one of the world's first two psychological laboratories. Two years later, he founded the psychological journal *Philosophical Studies*. During his tenure, he supervised nearly 200 doctoral dissertations.

12. "Walter Dill Scott: Pioneer Industrial Psychologist," Edmund C. Lynch, *Business History Review*, Vol. 42, No. 2 (Summer 1968), pp. 149–170. The public's interest in this advertising was evidenced by articles such as Scott's January 1904 essay in the *Atlantic Monthly*, where he wrote: "Advertisements are sometimes spoken of as the nervous system of the business world. . . . As our nervous system is constructed to give us all the possible sensations from objects, so the advertisement which is comparable to the nervous system must awaken in the reader as many different kinds of images as the object itself can excite." Reflecting on the earliest form of advertising (word of mouth, used by the ancient merchant hawking goods at the city gates), Scott stated that advertising's evolution has been gradual but "as great as that from the anthropoid ape to P. T. Barnum himself." He traced the first English-language advertisement to March 1648, in the *Imperial Intelligencer*, but magazine ads were a recent invention: the first to appear in *Harper's* is dated to 1864. "Indeed, advertising may be said to have been in its swaddling clothes until about the year 1887," after which the practice boomed. He cited contemporary print advertising expenses estimated at $600 million, including some $600,000 spent by C. W. Post, one of those in the vanguard of advertising, to market his breakfast cereals. That advertising was widespread and had desirable results could not be questioned, indicated Scott. Yet "leaders of the profession . . . have been successful, and hardly know how it has all come about. . . . They believe that there should be some underlying principles which could help them in analyzing what they have already accomplished, and assist them in their further efforts."

13. Gale also studied at Leipzig, some 10 years before Scott. A maverick, Gale introduced the topic of sexual psychology in his course, a decision that ultimately led to confrontation with the university president and Gale being let go in 1903 due to budgetary cuts. See www.alumni.umn.edu/Sex_and_the_Psych_Professor.html. During the Agate speech, Scott referenced Gale's research into the effects of printer's ink and font type on readers' attention.

14. *Scott of Northwestern,* pp. 69–70.

15. *History of Marketing Thought,* p. 36.

16. "The Changing Nature of Innovation in Marketing: A Study of Selected Business Leaders, 1852–1958," Alvin J. Silk and Louis William Stern, *Business History Review,* Vol. 37, No. 3 (Autumn 1963), p. 188. The authors wrote that marketing innovation evolved from a "classic" period, "where men frequently innovated boldly on the basis of limited knowledge, to a version where men, as a part of a more complex system, innovate more deliberately, measuring, and where possible, reducing the risks involved." At the time of this article's publication, Stern was on the marketing faculty of Ohio State University. He would join Northwestern's Graduate School of Business in 1973, bringing with him a penetrating insight into marketing channels and antitrust issues.

17. Ibid., p. 37.

18. "'The Science of Publicity': An American Advertising Theory, 1900–1920," Ellen Mazur Thomson, *Journal of Design History,* Vol. 9, No. 4 (1996), p. 253.

19. John W. Hartman Center for Sales, Advertising & Marketing History, available at http://scriptorium.lib.duke.edu/eaa/timeline.html.

20. *The Psychology of Advertising in Theory and Practice,* Walter Dill Scott, p. 2.

21. Ibid., p. 5.

22. "Walter Dill Scott: Pioneer Industrial Psychologist," p. 152.

23. *A Contribution to the Psychology of Business,* Walter Dill Scott (1923), p. 7.

24. Ibid., p. 8.

25. Ibid., p. 175.

26. Ibid.

27. Ibid., p. 6.

28. Ibid., p. 398.

29. Ibid., p. 400.

30. "The Development of the Philosophy of Marketing Thought," D. G. Brian Jones and David D. Monieson, *Journal of Marketing,* Vol. 54, No. 1 (January 1990), p. 103. Interestingly, study at the Kellogg School today continues the experiential, "hands-on" approach to management and economics, with students pursuing courses such as "Global Initiatives in Management," a popular offering that culminates in two weeks of intensive field research in which students and faculty advisers interact with top business and government officials in several countries.

31. At the University of Wisconsin, Richard T. Ely was a "vocal and enduring disciple of the Historical school," according to Jones and Monieson, in "Development of the Philosophy of Marketing Thought," p. 103. Among his pupils was David Kinley, who would eventually lead the Economics Department at the University of Illinois, where future School of Commerce professors Clark and Ivey both earned economics doctorates in 1916 and were influenced by him. "Professor Kinley . . . was very active in the graduate work of the Department of Economics when I was there," Clark recalled in a 1940 correspondence with

Bartels. "He was a man with a particularly keen mind, very able as a theoretical economist, but also greatly interested in business and business problems. He had as fine a combination of the practical and theoretical understanding of economic problems as anyone I have ever known." In addition, Clark would teach at the University of Michigan the year before he moved to Northwestern. At Michigan, Henry C. Adams was chair of the Economics Department and had also studied in Germany in the 1870s.

32. Scott's publications on personnel and efficiency matters include *Increasing Human Efficiency in Business: A Contribution to the Psychology of Business* (1911), *Science and Common Sense in Working with Men* (1921) and *Personnel Management: Principles, Practices, and Point of View* (1923).

33. The AMA was officially formed in 1937 from a merger of NATA and another group, the American Marketing Society, created in 1931 to bring marketing and marketing research practitioners together.

34. "The History of the American Marketing Association," Hugh E. Agnew, *Journal of Marketing*, Vol. 5, No. 4 (April 1941), pp. 374–379. Members at the inaugural meeting elected Scott as the organization's first president, a role he filled for one year. Among those present at the initial meeting were Ralph Starr Butler, George Burton Hotchkiss, E. E. Troxell, Nat W. Barnes and Agnew.

35. "Dictionary of Marketing Terms," available at the American Marketing Association's site marketingpower.com. The AMA's formation and the role played by Northwestern University School of Commerce faculty in bringing it about are discussed later.

36. "N.A.M.T.—A Survey," Hugh E. Agnew, *Journal of Marketing*, Vol. 1, No. 4 (April 1937), pp. 305–309.

37. Ibid., p. 306.

38. *History of Marketing Thought*, p. 27.

39. Ibid., pp. 30–31.

40. Ibid., p. 29.

41. "The Identity Crisis in Marketing," Robert Bartels, *Journal of Marketing*, Vol. 38, No. 4 (October 1974), pp. 73–76.

42. The manuscript first appeared in mimeographed form in 1918 and was used by Clark in support of his teaching at the University of Michigan.

43. "An Appraisal of Certain Criticisms of Advertising," Fred E. Clark, *American Economic Review*, Vol. 15, No. 1, Supplement: Papers and Proceedings of the Thirty-seventh Annual Meeting (March 1925), p. 9.

44. The subject informed another of his books, *The Purposes of the Indebtedness of American Cities (1880–1912)*, published in 1916.

45. *History of Marketing Thought*, p. 150.

46. "Criteria of Marketing Efficiency," Fred E. Clark, *American Economic Review*, Vol. 11, No. 2 (June 1921), pp. 214–220.

47. "Appraisal of Certain Criticisms of Advertising," p. 5.

48. Ibid., p. 8.

49. Ibid., p. 12.

50. "Fred Clark's Bibliography as of the Early 1920's," Paul D. Converse, *Journal of Marketing*, Vol. 10, No. 1 (July 1945), p. 57. Weld, like Clark, had to rely a great deal on direct observation of marketing processes, as few texts or other materials existed. This was

especially true for Weld, who recalled the paucity of marketing literature when he began teaching in 1913. "I personally followed shipments of butter and eggs and other commodities from the country shipper in Minnesota through the wholesalers, jobbers, and retailers to New York, Chicago, and other cities," he said. "I analyzed each item of expense involved in this passage through the channels of trade." See "Early Experience in Teaching Courses in Marketing," L. D. H. Weld, *Journal of Marketing*, Vol. 5, No. 4 (April 1941), p. 380.

51. "Fred Emerson Clark," Richard M. Clewett, *Journal of Marketing*, Vol. 22, No. 1 (July 1957), p. 1.

52. Ibid. Clewett praised his colleague, who had died in 1948, for being "a wise and skillful discussion leader who stimulated and encouraged independent thinking; a lecturer whose well-organized presentations of theory were influenced by the practical wisdom of one in touch with the realities of business and government." Clewett called Clark "a man of high ethical standards, a careful scholar, an outstanding teacher, and a developer of men" who made efforts to mentor junior faculty, a practice that Clewett himself would emulate for years afterward.

53. Among other encouragements to pursue marketing, Clark recalled his youthful entrepreneurship as a door-to-door salesman of Rand McNally atlases, Wearever aluminum ware and ironing boards. See Bartels's article "Influences on the Development of Marketing Thought," p. 12.

54. Prentice-Hall published the study. An additional volume was planned but does not appear to have been completed. "Selling Expense and Expenditure Ratios" was noted in the faculty minutes for October 6, 1921, as the potential seventh volume in the series. Royalties to the university from the existing volumes totaled $324.67 as of June 30, 1921. The study's entire cost was reported as $50,000.

55. *Principles of Marketing*, pp. 13–14.

56. Clark noted two people in particular who encouraged him to publish his *Principles of Marketing*: Henry C. Adams, head of the Economics Department at the University of Michigan, and Dean Heilman at Northwestern's School of Commerce.

57. *History of Marketing Thought*, p. 73.

58. "Changing Nature of Innovation in Marketing," pp. 183–184.

59. *Northwestern University Bulletin: Training for Retailing, Day and Evening Courses*, Vol. 37, No. 33 (April 26, 1937), p. 3.

60. Anderson served as AMA secretary from 1951 to 1954, vice president between 1954 and 1955 and president from 1955 to 1956. By the end of the 1950s, he also was bringing his leadership to several "foreign assignments," including teaching an advanced management program at the Universidad Central de Venezuela in Caracas (spring 1958) and serving as an American consultant to the Special Committee for Commerce Education in Delhi, India (summer 1959). In the fall of 1956, he also helped establish graduate business programs in France. Other members of the school's Marketing Department also focused their attention abroad. Of note, Harper Boyd Jr., Richard M. Clewett and Ralph L. Westfall published "The Marketing Structure of Venezuela" in the *Journal of Marketing*, Vol. 22, No. 4 (1958). There, the authors stressed the importance of Venezuela in Latin America as a market for U.S. goods, although they cited challenges with that market's limitations due to restricted competition. "The [Venezuelan] middle class is too small to afford a mass market, and thus products are made for the upper-class market," they wrote. "There is little incentive to reduce

prices because the upper-class is ready to buy at virtually any price, the potential middle-class market is small, and the price cut necessary to bring the lower class into the market is too large to be considered. Therefore, there is little opportunity to expand markets through price reductions" (p. 397).

61. *Principles of Retailing*, Ira D. Anderson and Clare W. Barker, p. 11.

62. Ibid., p. 2.

63. Ibid., pp. 7–9.

64. "Discussion [of Current Trends in Retail Distribution]," James R. Hawkinson, *Journal of Marketing*, Vol. 5, No. 4 (April 1941), pp. 418–419.

65. Retailing itself, particularly in the form of department stores, was a major economic force beginning about 1850, giving "birth to the culture of consumption and even the modern shopping center with everything under one roof." See "The Wonderful World of the Department Store in Historical Perspective: A Comprehensive International Bibliography Partially Annotated," Robert D. Tamilia (2005), available at www.marketingpower.com/content/Tamilia_Dept_Store_Ref_2005_June.pdf. Some have said that the department store's rise was "nothing short of a major revolution, not only for business but for all of society . . . as dramatic and as far reaching as any other major innovation the world has ever known"; see ibid. Tamilia noted that this entrepreneurial innovation "affected every facet of social and economic life" and contributed directly and indirectly to the adoption of many technological innovations. In particular, he cited the department store's channel impact within the distribution chain as revolutionary, altering the shopping experience, promotional techniques and managerial and inventory frameworks, among other things. He also contended that the department store was "one of society's most democratic institutions and . . . a major force toward a more egalitarian society, especially for women," who found employment there in great numbers. Others, however, noted that women were often paid very low wages for their services. See Susan Porter Benson's *Counter Culture: Saleswomen, Managers, and Customers in American Department Stores, 1890–1940* (University of Illinois Press, 1986). Of special note is the way these stores "democratized" shopping, with their eclectic inventory assuring that nearly everyone, regardless of social background, would find something they wanted (although window shopping was also a part of the department store experience and customers could browse without obligation to buy, another innovation). In general concept, the department store arguably can be traced back to the Hudson's Bay Company founding in 1670 and, later, to the Gostinyi Dvor of St. Petersburg, Russia, that opened in 1785, boasting some 100 stores under one roof. Though impressive and indeed consisting of "departments," these entities, by virtue of the kind of inventory they stocked, varied substantially from the modern idea of the retail outlet. Many scholars consider the first true department store as having its roots in a modest Paris stall in 1838. (Although generally accepted, the point is arguable: Harry Resseguie contended that A. T. Stewart's "Marble Palace" of 1846 deserved credit as the first real department store, a claim supported by a September 18, 1846, *New York Herald* article.) A decade later, Aristide Boucicaut, son of a hat maker, would buy the small shop. With the help of his wife, Marguerite, he would build his store, Le Bon Marché (meaning "the good market" or "the good deal"), into an influential success. Upon the store's expansion in 1869, novelist Emile Zola described it as "a cathedral of commerce," a term that would attach itself to later stores, particularly as they opened in New York City and Chicago.

66. *Principles of Retailing*, p. 9.

67. Other advisory committee members included Justin W. Dart, general manager of the Walgreen Company; J. Espovich, general manager of the Boston Store; John D. Finch, vice president and general manager of Lord's, Inc.; Raymond H. Fogler, vice president of Montgomery Ward & Company; Frederick Kasch, vice president of Jewel Tea Company; D. F. Kelly, president and general manager of The Fair; Leon Mandel, vice president and general manager of Mandel Brothers; Donald M. Nelson, vice president of Sears, Roebuck & Co.; Elmer Stevens, president and general manager of Chas. A. Stevens and Company; Gordon L. Pirie, general manager of Carson, Pirie, Scott & Co.; and Mason Smith, director of personnel for Marshall Field and Company.

68. Along with John D. Rockefeller, Andrew MacLeish was cofounder of the University of Chicago in 1890. About the time of his participation at the School of Commerce, MacLeish was described as "the master of an exceptionally wide range of poetic vocabularies, both verbal and rhythmic . . . modern, almost journalistically contemporary in his interests." See "Archibald MacLeish: A Modern Metaphysical," *English Journal,* Vol. 24, No. 6 (June 1935), p. 442.

69. Field himself was influential beyond his commercial ventures. For example, in 1893, he donated $1 million for a natural history museum at the World's Columbian Exposition. He then donated an additional $8 million after the fair to establish a permanent building: the Field Museum of Natural History. When he died in 1906, his estate's value was estimated at $125 million, making him "the richest man in [Chicago] and one of the richest in the country." See http://illinoisreview.typepad.com/illinoisreview/2006/08/illinois_hall_o_15.html and http://chicago.urban-history.org/ven/dss/fields.shtml.

70. "Department Stores," *The Encyclopedia of Chicago,* available at http://www.encyclopedia.chicagohistory.org/pages/373.html.

71. See http://chicago.urban-history.org/ven/dss/fields.shtml for more details. Details on the Evanston store may be found at http://www.winthropproperties.com/evanston galleria/history.htm.

72. "Advisory Committee for the Retail Program," minutes for the meeting of June 3, 1937. In the Ira D. Anderson Papers, Northwestern University Archives.

73. The guinea pigs also instituted an annual newsletter "roundup" to remain in contact with each other, particularly as some members found employment in California. Most, however, continued to work in the Chicago area. A handwritten greeting on the "Christmas Bulletin" of 1941 suggests the news was being compiled by Betty A. Henke '40, Ira Anderson and Delbert Duncan. The newsletter for 1940 indicated a number of changes to the program; for instance, the program was moved from Evanston to Chicago's Wieboldt Hall, and the written thesis was made optional. The number of scholars in the program was reported as being the largest to date—31, with an additional 4 graduate students majoring in retailing and doing "substantially the same work as the Service Scholars, including part time [*sic*] store work." The men in the program were then living in Abbott Hall, a 17-story dormitory completed in September of that year, one block south of Wieboldt Hall.

74. Untitled manuscript in the Ira D. Anderson Papers, Northwestern University Archives. Anderson also noted the effort of Delbert Duncan in securing the cooperation of the 12 Chicago retail firms. Duncan, along with Elizabeth M. Paine, previously a member of the research staff at Harvard's Graduate School of Business, was responsible for working out the program's initial details, according to Anderson. By 1942, the war had created "an urgent

need [for] executive and semi-executive material," Duncan wrote to Professor Henry J. Ryskamp of Calvin College in a letter soliciting recommendations for prospective students. "Because of the number of men being called into military service, many retail stores are placing women in supervisory positions formerly held by men," Duncan stated.

75. Students were required to keep a professional journal detailing their contributions at the stores. Here is a typical student entry: "Nov. 22. I think the credit dept. is swell! Worked this morning for two hours filing open account cards—then the rest of the morning and all afternoon I interviewed—it's very interesting so far, and I'm beginning to feel that I'm really part of the dept.—I can now see the various definite jobs that I can do—had to handle several people who had accounts already in other Sears stores—did it O.K. sans *too much* help."

76. "Delbert J. Duncan," John S. Wright, *Journal of Marketing,* Vol. 32 (April 1968), p. 73. Wright also observed that Duncan was "constantly selling the better and more advanced thoughts from academia to the business man . . . through [Duncan's] extensive contacts with trade associations and his large consulting practice with business firms." Duncan also consulted for government and remained active in the American Marketing Association from 1925 on, serving as its national director as well as committee member and chairman. He was elected to the Hall of Fame in Distribution in 1953.

77. *Printout* (Fall-Winter 1983), p. 22. See also *History of Management Education,* pp. 79–80.

78. *History of Management Education,* p. 82.

79. The letter is among the documents in the Ira D. Anderson Papers, Northwestern University Archives.

80. *The Evolution of Management Education,* Michael W. Sedlak and Harold F. Williamson, p. 79. The authors also noted that so many returning veterans took advantage of the GI Bill that Northwestern was overwhelmed by the demand. "The faculty was forced, because of crushing enrollment pressures, to turn away a large number of civilian applicants. Vanderblue recalled that this restriction precipitated 'angry mobs of doting mothers' whose sons had been refused admission." The comment appeared in correspondence between Vanderblue and Fagg, May 16, 1946, Fagg Papers, Northwestern University Archives.

81. "Significant Current Trends in Marketing," L. D. H. Weld, Paul Nystrom, Fred E. Clark, et al., *Journal of Marketing,* Vol. 6, No. 4, Pt. 2 (April 1942), pp. 20–21.

82. For additional detail, see http://www.advertisinghalloffame.org/members/member _bio.php?memid=564.

83. "Lyndon O. Brown," James Smith, *Journal of Marketing,* Vol. 29, No. 4 (October 1965), p. 56.

84. Reviewers regarded the book as "a very welcome addition to a field of growing importance" (see Roland S. Vaile in *Annals of the American Academy of Social Science,* Vol. 197, p. 293) and "an important contribution to the literature of this field" (see Richard R. Mead in *Journal of Marketing,* Vol. 20, No. 2, p. 206). Paul T. Cherington advised both novices and experienced market researchers to seek out the text and "read [it] with care" (see *Public Opinion Quarterly,* Vol. 2, No. 3, p. 511).

85. "Toward a Profession of Marketing," Lyndon O. Brown, *Journal of Marketing,* Vol. 13, No. 1 (July 1948), pp. 27–31. See also "Towards a Theory of Marketing," W. Alderson and R. Cox, *Journal of Marketing,* Vol. 13, No. 2, p. 137; "Can Marketing Be a Science?" Robert

Bartels, *Journal of Marketing*, Vol. 15, No. 3, p. 310; and "Marketing as a Science: An Appraisal," Kenneth D. Hutchinson, *Journal of Marketing*, Vol. 16, No. 3, pp. 286–293. The consensus, though varied in the details and qualifiers, was that marketing was indeed a science or at least tending that way. Hutchinson, however, disputed the claim, saying: "Marketing is not a science. It is rather an art or a practice . . . resembling engineering, medicine, and architecture than . . . physics, chemistry, or biology." Further, he observed that little progress had been made in elevating marketing to a science. "One should expect far more in the way of results if the venture is to prove successful, and the dearth of progress to date lends the suspicion that the project is ill-advised." Some dozen years later, Weldon J. Taylor added some nuance to the debate with "'Is Marketing a Science' Revisited" in the *Journal of Marketing*, Vol. 29, No. 3, pp. 49–53. "The act of marketing is an art," he wrote. "The practitioner is not a scientist. Yet in . . . his work he may publish observations and conduct experiments. To the extent that he does so and contributes to the fund of conceptual schemes that are fruitful . . . he functions as a scientist."

86. "The course will cover the entire subject of radio advertising and prominent men in radio advertising work will deliver lectures on their specific work," according to a *Chicago Daily Tribune* notice of September 10, 1933.

87. "Toward a Profession of Marketing," p. 29.

88. Westfall was awarded two Bronze Stars and the Philippine Liberation Ribbon for his service. He would remain in the army reserve for 30 years, retiring as a colonel. Westfall would also build a career at Northwestern that lasted until 1975, when he was named dean of the College of Business at University of Illinois–Chicago, where he remained until his retirement in 1985. From 1965 until 1975, he served as associate dean for academic affairs at Northwestern's School of Business, which had changed its name in 1953. The name would change again in 1969, to the Graduate School of Business, a decision that Westfall helped bring about. See chapter 3.

89. Clewett's contributions, balanced as they were between teaching and research, resulted in the American Marketing Association honoring him with its Distinguished Service Award in 1964. In addition to serving as chair for several AMA committees, Clewett was on the *Journal of Marketing*'s editorial board. In 1979, the year he retired, his students bestowed the "Professor of the Year" award upon him, and faculty colleagues adopted a unique resolution of professional praise for him. "Above and beyond his substantial contributions to the academic and practical sides of marketing," read the faculty's resolution, "Professor Clewett has made even more remarkable contributions as a teacher of young people and as a colleague." When Clewett died on December 1, 2006, longtime friends recalled his personal and professional qualities. Among those doing so was Kellogg School marketing legend Philip Kotler, who said, "When I first met Dick Clewett in 1961 upon joining the faculty, he greeted me with such warmth and interest that I remember the moment vividly to this day." Kellogg School dean emeritus Donald P. Jacobs, whose 26-year tenure extended from 1975 until 2001 but who arrived at Northwestern as a finance professor in 1957, considered Clewett a significant figure in the Marketing Department's history. "Dick Clewett was certainly among the people who built and maintained the marvelous franchise the Kellogg Marketing Department has become," said Jacobs, "and he was crucial in making it the world leader." Personal interviews with the author, 2006.

90. The doctoral program also emphasized economic theory and intensive research methods along the lines of the core curriculum in the MBA program, reducing specialization and electives. By 1965, enrollment in the doctoral program overall reached 76 students, with 7 degrees awarded that year. By 1969, the numbers would jump to 107 students enrolled and 14 degrees awarded. Two years later, 133 students were enrolled, with 26 degrees conferred. Information from the Office of Doctoral Studies, Kellogg School.

91. Personal interview with author, 2006. Stasch also remembered teaching the school's "Marketing Policy" course with Clewett. "He was the primary instructor, and I was the secondary instructor," said Stasch. "We also worked together for three or four years studying product managers in consumer products companies. We published a well-received article in *Harvard Business Review* ["The Shifting Role of the Product Manager," *HBR*, Vol. 53 (January-February 1975), pp. 65–73] and presented a mini conference on the subject at the Marketing Science Institute. Regarding the *Marketing Policy* course, Dick Clewett taught me a wonderful method to use when teaching students how to undertake the analysis of complex marketing case situations. I considered that lesson invaluable and continue, to this day, to pass that knowledge on to students whenever the opportunity arises."

92. "The General Theory of Marketing," Robert Bartels, *Journal of Marketing*, Vol. 32 (January 1968), pp. 29–33.

93. "The Development of the Science of Marketing: An Exploratory Survey," Paul D. Converse, *Journal of Marketing*, Vol. 10, No. 1 (July 1945), pp. 14–23.

94. *History of Marketing Thought*, p. 126.

95. Ibid.

96. "Channels of Distribution for Consumer Goods in Egypt," Harper W. Boyd Jr., Abdel Aziz El Sherbini, and Ahmed Fouad Sherif, *Journal of Marketing*, Vol. 25, No. 6 (October 1961), pp. 26–33.

97. "Review: For a First Course," Raymond F. Barker, *Journal of Marketing*, Vol. 29, No. 1 (January 1965), pp. 114–115. In their preface, Westfall and Boyd noted that the cases were developed carefully over several years. "They are analytical in substance and require the student to 'take action.' They represent typical problems, and many offer the student the opportunity to use quantitative tools of analysis as well as his knowledge and awareness of concepts from the behavioral sciences."

98. "Review," Ralph F. Breyer, *Journal of Marketing*, Vol. 19, No. 1 (July 1954), pp. 107–108.

99. Ibid., p. 108.

100. "Review," Harry A. Lipson, *Journal of Marketing*, Vol. 22, No. 4 (April 1958), pp. 455–456.

101. "Steuart Henderson Britt," *Printout* (September 1979), p. 16. See also "Leaders in Marketing: Steuart Henderson Britt," Darrell B. Lucas, *Journal of Marketing*, Vol. 38, No. 1, p. 69. George R. Frerichs, a member of the Northwestern School of Business class of '57, is today president of Chicago-based GRFI, Ltd.

102. Britt's responsibilities included discovering unusual talents and developing a new Science Aptitude Examination each year. The competition was founded in 1942 by Science Service, a nonprofit organization whose mission is to "advance the understanding and appreciation of science," according to its press materials. The top prize in the annual event is a $100,000 college scholarship. Beginning in 1998, the contest has been sponsored by Intel

Corporation. See "Science Talent in American Youth," Steuart Henderson Britt and Harold A. Edgerton, *Science*, Vol. 101, No. 2619 (March 1945), pp. 247–248, for more details about the annual Westinghouse contest.

103. "The Consumer Is King," D. B. Lucas, *Journal of Marketing*, Vol. 25, No. 4 (April 1961), p. 110.

104. "Bookshelf: Consumer Emerges; His Power as Factor in Economy Comes as a Surprise," Elizabeth M. Fowler, *New York Times*, January 9, 1961, p. 126. "Like the discovery of America, the revelation of the power of the consumer came as a surprise," wrote Fowler. "Few economists had sailed these uncharted seas, discouraged by the consumers' vagaries, unpredictable as the wind, they thought. Then in 1958 came recession and much to most everyone's astonishment the consumer became the power that wafted the nation out of the doldrums by providing some stalwart buying momentum. . . . It should be hoped that economists will make more use of psychology and marketing research in the future. The surprise is that it was not done sooner." Among Britt's valuable observations in the text was that American advertisers were confronted by the fact that only some 8 percent of new products introduced each year manage to become successful, and 80 percent of products never even reach the market. Of 100 leading brands, about 30 would lose their market leadership within about five years. See the chapter titled "Are They Tops or Flops?" in Steuart Henderson Britt's *The Spenders*.

105. *Consumer Behavior in Theory and Action*, Steuart Henderson Britt (New York: John Wiley & Sons, 1970), pp. 150–151.

106. "Leaders in Marketing: Steuart Henderson Britt," *Journal of Marketing*, Vol. 38 (January 1974), pp. 67–69, and *Printout* (September 1979), p. 16.

107. *New York Herald Tribune*, October 30, 1956.

108. For more details, see "Leaders in Marketing: Steuart Henderson Britt," p. 67, and *Printout* (September 1979), p. 16.

109. Interview with author, 2005.

110. Ibid. Britt also served on the *Journal of Marketing*'s editorial board for a decade prior to becoming its editor.

111. This work was coauthored with former Kellogg School colleague Sidney J. Levy. The article appeared in the *Journal of Marketing*, Vol. 33, No. 1 (January 1969), pp. 10–15.

112. See the November 18, 2005, edition of *Financial Times*.

113. Interview with Philip Kotler, 2006. Additional details from "Mr. Marketing," Jon Marshall, *Northwestern Magazine* (Winter 2003).

114. Interviews with author, 2005.

115. Ibid. Kotler also stated that earlier efforts in the 1930s to create a more inclusive model to capture such factors as advertising and sales promotion were "just pushed to the side and ignored, since the mathematical representation of these forces was considered too difficult in the minds of most people."

116. Kotler earned the Converse Award in 1978, when a jury of 90 peers bestowed it upon him for his "landmark textbook," *Marketing Management*, and seminal articles, including "Broadening the Concept of Marketing." In addition, Kotler was the first recipient of the American Marketing Association's Distinguished Marketing Educator Award in 1985, one of many other distinctions he attained.

117. The books have also been widely translated into languages other than English.

118. Interview with author, 2005.

119. *Brands, Consumers, Symbols, and Research: Sidney J. Levy on Marketing,* Sidney J. Levy and Dennis W. Rook, eds. (London: Sage Publications, 1999), p. xv. Among these early articles referenced by Rook are Levy's *Harvard Business Review* contributions titled "The Product and the Brand" (1955) and "Symbols for Sale" (1959).

120. Levy would remain at the Kellogg School until 1997, when he became chair of the Marketing Department at the University of Arizona's Eller College of Management, a position he held until he became a special assistant to the head of the department in 2004.

121. Interview with author, 2005

122. "General Theory of Marketing," pp. 29–33. According to the American Marketing Association, the history of the Four P's can be traced to Neil Borden's 1953 presidential address to the AMA. He would further elucidate the idea in a 1964 *Journal of Advertising Research* article, "The Concept of the Marketing Mix." E. Jerome McCarthy's 1960 text, *Basic Marketing: A Managerial Approach,* also addressed the Four P's. Both P. J. Verdoorn, with his 1956 article "Marketing from the Producer's Point of View," in the *Journal of Marketing,* Vol. 20, and Albert W. Frey's 1956 publication, "The Effective Marketing Mix: Programming for Optimum Results," articulated the framework as well.

123. "Review: Three Emphases," Edward J. Fox, *Journal of Marketing,* Vol. 31, No. 3 (July 1967), pp. 103–104.

124. "Leaders in Marketing: Philip Kotler," Gerald Zaltman, *Journal of Marketing,* Vol. 36, No. 4 (October 1972), p. 60.

125. "Marketing Management," Michael J. Thomas, *Journal of Business,* Vol. 40, No. 3 (July 1967), pp. 345–347.

126. Interview with author, 2006.

127. "Review," Adel I. El-Ansary, *Journal of Marketing,* Vol. 35, No. 4 (October 1971), p. 108.

128. *Journal of Marketing,* Vol. 33, No. 1 (January 1969), pp. 10–15.

129. Ibid., p. 10.

130. "Broadening the Concept of Marketing. Too Far," David J. Luck, *Journal of Marketing,* Vol. 33, No. 3 (July 1969), pp. 53–55.

131. "Broadening the Concept of Marketing," Philip Kotler and Sidney J. Levy, *Journal of Marketing,* Vol. 33, No. 1 (January 1969), pp. 10–15.

132. "A New Form of Marketing Myopia: Rejoinder to Professor Luck," Philip Kotler and Sidney Levy, *Journal of Marketing,* Vol. 33, No. 3 (July 1969), pp. 55–57.

133. Ibid., p. 56.

134. *Fifty Key Figures in Management,* Morgen Witzel (London: Routledge, 2003), p. 177.

135. Interview with author, 2006.

136. "A Generic Concept of Marketing," Philip Kotler, *Journal of Marketing,* Vol. 36, No. 2 (April 1972), pp. 46–54.

137. Ibid., p. 47.

138. *History of Marketing Thought,* p. 31.

139. Interview with author, 2005.

140. "Distribution Channels as Political Economies: A Framework for Comparative Analysis," Louis W. Stern and Torger Reve, *Journal of Marketing,* Vol. 44, No. 3 (Summer 1980), p. 61.

141. Stern said this issue has probably been attacked in the most compelling fashion by Oliver Williamson of Berkeley, a transaction-cost economist who has drawn on British economist Ronald Coase's seminal work, "The Nature of the Firm" (1937), at the University of Chicago Law School. Coase earned the 1991 Nobel Prize in Economic Sciences for his contribution. Williamson explored the nature of markets and hierarchies, Stern explained. "Do you deal with a market, across a market, preserve a marketplace, or make it into a hierarchy and do you become a firm?" Answering such questions raises issues that surround power and conflict "because those are critical issues in the management of distribution," said Stern.

142. Interview with author, 2005.

Chapter 3

1. "You'll Hire This Man in '65," *Nation's Business,* Vol. 45, No. 7 (July 1957), p. 34.

2. The concept of using a card for purchases, however, had earlier roots, dating to 1887 and Edward Bellamy's utopian novel *Looking Backward: 2000–1887.* The popular book showcased its author's concerns with a society strongly influenced by competition and commerce. Among other cards being used for purchases was the Diners Club card, created in 1950 by Ralph Schneider and Frank McNamara. Western Union had also produced a card for use by its best customers in 1914.

3. "Business in 1958," *Time,* December 29, 1958.

4. "Gain Is Fantastic in Mutual Funds," *New York Times,* January 12, 1959, p. 86.

5. "Business in 1958."

6. See the "economic indicators" section at the Federal Reserve Archival System for Economic Research (FRASER), available at http://fraser.stlouisfed.org/publications/ei/.

7. *The Education of American Businessmen,* Frank C. Pierson, p. xvi.

8. *The Evolution of Management Education,* Michael W. Sedlak and Harold F. Williamson, pp. 104–105.

9. "Minutes of the Faculty of the School of Commerce," March 6, 1953, p. 2. (This material is currently located in unofficial Kellogg archives.)

10. "You'll Hire This Man in '65."

11. "Ford Grants $250,000 to N.U. School," *Chicago Tribune,* January 23, 1957, p. 19.

12. *Evolution of Management Education,* p. 82.

13. "Ford Grants $250,000 to N.U. School."

14. "1,230 to Enter N.U. Business School's New Term," Chesly Manly, *Chicago Tribune,* September 2, 1962, pp. A1–A2.

15. Northwestern University, *Register,* 1950–1963.

16. Interviews with author, 2005.

17. "You'll Hire This Man in '65."

18. Pierson noted the course's focus on the political, economic and moral aspects of various cultural conflicts, approached as case studies for analysis. In addition, he called attention to the course's eclectic reading material, including selections from Robert Heilbroner's *The Worldly Philosophers,* Northcote Parkinson's *Parkinson's Law* and Alvin Hansen's *The American Economy.* See pp. 207–208 in *Education of American Businessmen.*

19. Lavengood recalled that his classroom in the old building once served as the seminary's chapel.

20. Overton was recruited by Dean Vanderblue in 1945 to help support the school during a postwar enrollment boom and to assist in curriculum development. In particular, he was instrumental in bolstering the course "American Business History," which in 1946 was expanded from the original "Introduction to Business" course to reflect a more comprehensive offering. A railroad history expert, Overton served as chairman of the Business History Department from 1949 until 1954, when he accepted a position at the University of Western Ontario. "Overton was a historian I had admired long before I even met him," said Lavengood. "His work on railroads—the Burlington in particular—was groundbreaking and he had a talent for presenting his story vividly, winningly. When he invited me to come here, I felt I was going to be working with a major figure in the historical profession, and that turned out to be. We had a sense that we were creating history, that we were going to embark on something that, if successful, would be a historic reinvention of both business education and management practice." Bennett joined Northwestern in 1946, but he would interrupt his academic career to enlist in the U.S. Naval Reserve in 1951, remaining on active duty as an air intelligence officer until 1953, when he returned to the School of Commerce. Earlier, he had been in the reserves during his Harvard studies. In World War II, he served in various capacities, from company officer in the student flight battalion to instructor in air navigation and air combat intelligence officer on the USS *Essex* in the Pacific Fleet. At Northwestern, he was made chairman of the Business History Department in 1955, and he remained at the school through 1968, when a serious automobile accident resulted in partial paralysis and forced Bennett to suspend all professional duties. His history of the Bodine Electric Company was published as *Precision Power* in 1959 and is considered a pioneering example of business history. For additional information, see the Howard F. Bennett and Richard C. Overton Papers, Northwestern University Archives, the source of these biographical details.

21. "Recruiting Business History Teachers," Herman E. Krooss, *Business History Review,* Vol. 36, No. 1 (Spring 1962), pp. 44–60.

22. Perkins's book in particular was "an eye-opener," said Lavengood. Most of Lavengood's students came from conservative backgrounds and homes where Perkins was considered "the devil's disciple" for her labor sympathies and other efforts, such as advancing legislation to improve the minimum wage and investigating factory abuses. "We had an interesting time as teachers helping these students appreciate what Frances Perkins's contribution to the political history of this country had been, and what principles she attempted to incorporate into the legislation she had anything to do with," said Lavengood. "She came off, finally, as a very important, interesting person to these students, even though they could continue to believe with part of their souls that she had views and goals that they would not entirely endorse themselves." Interview with author, 2005.

23. "Review of the Year: Economic Development and Administration," *Ford Foundation Annual Report, 1957.* Ford money also supported economic research at Northwestern during the summer of 1957, when a $15,000 grant enabled professors from 29 colleges to get together and share their insights. All told, during the 1957–1958 school year, the Ford Foundation provided grants and appropriations totaling $5.6 million to support the "searching re-examination" of American business schools.

24. The proposed MBA program was discussed in detail in the May 18, 1960, faculty minutes. The proposal was voted on by the faculty and approved at the June 1, 1960, meeting.

25. "Minutes of the Faculty of the School of Commerce," March 6, 1953, p. 1.

26. The Northwestern program became known as the Advanced Executive Program, or AEP.

27. "N.U. to Hold an Institute on Management," John Astley-Cock, *Chicago Tribune*, July 8, 1951, p. E10.

28. "Minutes of the Faculty of the School of Commerce," May 9, 1952, p. 10. Indeed, an American Management Association study conducted about the time the Northwestern program opened claimed that nearly 50 percent of the 500 leading companies had some sort of executive development program.

29. "Is Executive Development Coming of Age?" Robert K. Stolz, *Journal of Business*, Vol. 28, No. 1 (January 1955), pp. 48–49. Beginning in the 1930s, the demand was accelerated by a marked separation of the ownership and the management of enterprises, resulting in the rise of a large managerial class that nevertheless had not benefited from formal management education before being thrust into this rather new commercial role. See "How to Develop General Managers," Lyndall F. Urwick et al., in *How to Increase Executive Effectiveness*, Edward C. Bursk, ed. (Cambridge, Mass.: Harvard University Press, 1954).

30. "Executive Development Programs (Panel Discussion)," Franklin Folds, Hoke S. Simpson, Howard Johnson, Richard Donham, and Billy E. Goetz, *Journal of the Academy of Management*, Vol. 1, No. 2 (August 1958), pp. 34–49. But in the same article, Donham also stated his belief that business schools had "shirked their proper responsibilities" in developing students' abilities to make good value judgments. He cautioned against "a mania for the scientific method and for the specious accuracy of figures [that] leads us to emphasize quantitative data and the quantitative approach to problems and to eschew qualitative data and subjective judgments," which, he said, were unavoidable. But educators and students, he added, had better establish their values firmly. "I believe in right and wrong, in good and bad, in beauty and ugliness, in truth and falsity," said Donham. "I believe, too, that it is an educator's responsibility to help his charges find ways to make such distinctions accurately in all circumstances. I do not believe we are trying very hard to do this today."

31. "Minutes of the Faculty of the School of Business," May 4, 1960.

32. Interviews with author, 2006.

33. Tabatoni would also be asked to assume the deanship of Northwestern's Graduate School of Management in the early 1970s, an offer he refused (see chapter 5). Jacobs noted that the British faculty member was rotated. Initially, this person was Professor J. H. Brian Tew of Nottingham University.

34. The topics of executive education and lifelong learning have enjoyed much support and engendered lively discussion as they've developed since the mid-1950s. Typical of the discourse surrounding these topics were the remarks of Robert D. Calkins, president of the Brookings Institution and former dean of the business schools at Columbia and the University of California–Berkeley, as reported in the *Wall Street Journal* for July 3, 1962: "No branch of higher education is more neglected today than the re-education of the educated. And no neglected branch of education is more important at this time to the future of this country. I am less disturbed by the conditions and problems facing this country . . . than I

am by the intellectual unpreparedness of our people, and especially our thinking people, to face these problems in an informed and responsible way . . . No one in these times can go far on the intellectual capital he acquires in youth. Unless he keeps his knowledge or skill up to date, revises it, adds to it, enriches it with experience and supplements it with new ideas . . . he is soon handicapped for the duties of the day."

35. Dean Heilman had appointed Davies, a CPA and accounting professor at the school, as assistant dean of the Chicago division in 1923. Davies had graduated from the Northwestern School of Commerce the year before. He served as acting dean after McDaniel left the position to join the Ford Foundation as an assistant director. McDaniel had assumed the deanship shortly after the resignation of Homer Vanderblue, who retired in 1949, citing ill health. During the four years prior to Donham becoming dean, the school had relocated its graduate division to the Chicago campus in 1950, begun an executive education program in 1951 and started a commercial and secretarial education program known as the Gregg Division in 1952.

36. For instance, by 1928, Wallace Donham, a graduate of Harvard Law School and a onetime banker, had already broached the differences between traditional methods of management education, rooted in apprenticeships, and the requirement for more formalized training at the college level. See "Current Problems in Management Development," Walter A. Thompson, *Business Quarterly,* Vol. 24, No. 3 (Fall 1959), pp. 157–163. Donham brought both an academic perspective and a practical perspective to his work, and he believed the businessperson's objective primarily was to make decisions in various situations. At the core of his perspective on the case method was the opinion that business decisions more closely resembled art rather than science, having few, if any, principles that could be taught. Therefore, traditional lectures and readings were considered inappropriate or even damaging to the student. See *Education of American Businessmen,* pp. 48–49.

37. Some faculty members, including Donald P. Jacobs, a member of the Finance Department at the time, recalled Donham's case study efforts, saying that faculty members were not entirely receptive to the strategy despite the fact that nearly a quarter of them had Harvard degrees themselves. "Northwestern wasn't that kind of culture," said Jacobs in an interview with the author, 2006.

38. The Carnegie study noted that a student in the Harvard program worked through some 1,000 cases in the two-year curriculum, whereas formal study in disciplines such as economics, statistics and psychology was "reduced very much to a supporting role." The framework at Chicago, conversely, viewed the best academic preparation for business as being "a thorough grounding" in "basic business disciplines—accounting, statistics, economics, and law." See *Education of American Businessmen,* pp. 246–247.

39. Alfred Chandler's work, particularly *Strategy and Structure: Chapters in the History of the Industrial Enterprise* (1962) and *The Visible Hand: The Managerial Revolution in American Business* (1977), provide great insight into the development of large-scale enterprises. Vertically integrated, multidepartmental entities had arisen before World War I as a structural response to market changes resulting from the Second Industrial Revolution, whose innovations (e.g., steam and electricity) produced more capital-intensive industries. In Chandler's thesis, this development required more capital to exploit the new systems, which in turn demanded bigger enterprises and more people to manage them. This trend continued after 1918 with a "higher-level development," according to Cambridge professor

of economic history Barry Supple, producing "multidivisional enterprises coordinated by general offices and senior administrators whose functions were confined to finance and long-sighted strategy"; he described this as a reaction to a postwar economy in flux as well as "product diversification and the extension of business to a national or even international level." See "Chandler and the Dynamics of Industrial Capitalism," *Economic History Review,* Vol. 44, No. 3 (August 1991), pp. 500–514.

40. Operations research (OR) advocates distinguished themselves by their ability to examine and improve an entire system, rather than only concentrating on individual elements (although such parts were also examined frequently). Joseph McCloskey nicely detailed the roots of management science: "Operations research was born of radar on the eve of World War II. But its advent was forecast before and during World War I in connection with three technologies introduced during that war; the dreadnaught [a large battleship armed with large-caliber guns], the aeroplane and the submarine." See "The Beginnings of Operations Research," Joseph F. McCloskey, *Operations Research,* Vol. 35, No. 1 (January-February 1987), pp. 143–152. Prior to the Gordon and Howell and Pierson reports were others, sponsored by the American Association of Collegiate Schools of Business: Richard L. Kozelka's 1954 report, *Professional Education for Business,* and the AACSB's 1956 *Faculty Requirements and Standards in Collegiate Schools of Business.* These studies echoed some educators' concerns about the "inferior academic ability" of business students and about standard business curricula that offered too few challenges. Such soul-searching observations had their roots in broad economic and political transformations that, for some 20 years, had affected the United States. Said one dean of a Canadian business school in 1950: "Depression and war have materially altered the old [business] concepts; government intervention in trade has expanded; business managements, once chiefly concerned with profits, are becoming increasingly involved with 'human relations' and employee welfare; new political, social and economic demands press upon the businessman from every side." See "University Training for Careers in Business," Lloyd W. Sipherd, *Business Quarterly,* Vol. 15, No. 2 (Summer 1950), pp. 69–76.

41. Although the studies themselves are detailed, informative and intriguing, the casual reader may find a useful gloss in Leonard S. Silk's *The Education of Businessmen* (1960), a 44-page overview by the senior editor of *Business Week* that provides intelligible insights.

42. Gordon and Howell noted the dramatic increase in business degrees over that time. In the 1919–1920 academic year, they reported, U.S. schools produced 1,576 undergraduates with bachelor's degrees and 110 with master's degrees. By the 1957–1958 term, those numbers were 50,090 bachelor's degrees and 5,205 master's degrees. But even those figures were down from the historical postwar high point for the 1949–1950 year, when more than 72,000 undergraduates earned bachelor's degrees in business administration. See *Higher Education for Business,* R. A. Gordon and J. E. Howell (New York: Columbia University Press, 1959), p. 21, for a detailed table that also includes doctoral degrees.

43. These questions raised others, including those set out by Leonard Silk: "Is there any good reason why hundreds of thousands of young people should be devoting their college years mainly to vocational training for the relatively low-level jobs in large business concerns which they are likely to get—or for the sorts of business responsibilities in small organizations which their fathers handled without the benefit of a collegiate business education?" But the overriding question for Silk transcended mere employment. He wanted to know, "Are we

going to waste our human resources, or develop them to their greatest potential?" See his *Education of Businessmen*, p. 11.

44. Ibid., p. xii.

45. Gordon and Howell, *Higher Education for Business*, pp. 69–70.

46. Undoubtedly, Donham had long had a privileged opportunity to give the subject consideration: his father, Wallace B. Donham, was the founding dean of the Harvard Business School.

47. "Minutes of the Faculty of the School of Business," April 6, 1960, p. 3.

48. "Progress report on the study of education," memo to Deans Donham and Anderson, December 30, 1958, in the Ira D. Anderson Papers, Northwestern University Archives. Lavengood also noted in the progress report that "the liberalization of business courses has been from the first a principal goal of this experiment in liberal education for business." He concluded the detailed, six-page memo with a characteristically frank remark: "I am wondering . . . whether there should be plans to visit other business schools. Such visits might prove helpful, but only, I believe, if the schools are carefully selected, the visits are planned well in advance, and the questions to be asked are wisely framed. Otherwise, jaunting about would be a great waste of money and time."

49. The committee consisted of Lavengood, Frederick Ekeblad, Richard Clewett, T. Leroy Martin, H. Barrett Rogers, Ira Anderson and Leon Bosch.

50. "Minutes of the Faculty of the School of Business," March 3, 1960. Lavengood's detailed report, dated February 24, 1960, was distributed to all faculty members and included as an addendum to the March 3 minutes.

51. "Minutes of the Faculty of the School of Business," December 7, 1960, p. 3.

52. Members of a task force that spearheaded this effort included Leon Bosch (serving as chair), Harper Boyd, Virgil Boyd, John Larson, Ken Myers and John O'Neil.

53. "Minutes of the Faculty of the School of Business," May 18, 1960, p. 2.

54. "Minutes of the Faculty of the School of Business," June 1, 1960, p. 9.

55. Interview with author, 2005.

56. *Evolution of Management Education*, p. 103.

57. Ibid, p. 104.

58. "Schools, Top Graduates View Business Education," Chesly Manly, *Chicago Tribune*, June 24, 1962, pp. 1–2.

59. Ibid.

60. "1,230 to Enter N.U. Business School's New Term."

61. Ibid. The article went on to note that among the outstanding alumni of the school were Herbert V. Prochnow, president of First National Bank of Chicago; Willis D. Gale, chairman of the board at Commonwealth Edison Company; Melvin E. Dawley, president of Lord and Taylor; and George Esterly, dean of Rutgers University's school of business. A few years later, Donham would still be working to articulate the school's innovations. Responding to a *Nation's Business* article focused on recruiting practices at business schools and the resulting boost to student quality, Donham wrote to highlight the hard work on the curriculum that schools such as Northwestern had done over the previous five years to create a liberal education. "Liberal, in our terms, includes not only traditional courses in the liberal arts but general education courses within the framework of the curricula of the School of Business," stated Donham. "It includes seeing things as wholes, searching across the borders of separate

disciplines to discover relevancies, a sense of personal integration, a feeling of social responsibility." See *Nation's Business,* Vol. 52, No. 6, p. 10.

62. "Minutes of the Faculty of the School of Business," December 5, 1962, p. 2.

Chapter 4

1. "I am aware of the ever increasing expenditure of energy, resolve and self-discipline required to maintain the high level of activity which for many years was one of my greatest assets," Donham wrote to university president J. Roscoe Miller in his letter of resignation dated October 14, 1964. Donham indicated that he no longer had such reserves of energy and recognized that there was a "particular need of an abundance of such resources in the Dean of the School of Business in the years immediately ahead." The letter is included in the faculty minutes for October 14, 1965.

2. "Colleges Ponder Student Drift Away from Business," *Chicago Tribune,* December 5, 1965, p. D8.

3. Ibid.

4. Westfall would serve as associate dean until 1972. He would leave Northwestern in 1975 to assume the deanship of the University of Illinois–Chicago business school.

5. In addition to the council's advisory influence, some of its members also supported the school with financial gifts: original board members Gaylord Freeman Jr. and John D. Gray endowed professorial chairs at the school. In 1990, Donald Jacobs reflected on 25 years of the council's service, saying: "The Advisory Council was established at a pivotal time in the history of the Kellogg School. Its earliest recommendations—to focus on graduate management education—had a profound effect on the School as we know it today. So the celebration of Kellogg Advisory Board's 25th anniversary is also a celebration of the quality of its guidance." See *Kellogg World,* Summer 1990, p. 16.

6. Other distinguished executives who would lead the council included Charles Lee Brown, president and later chairman of Illinois Bell; William Smithburg '62, CEO of Quaker Oats; and Patrick G. Ryan '59, founder and executive chairman of Aon Corporation.

7. "Minutes of the Faculty of the School of Business," December 8, 1965. (This material is currently located in unofficial Kellogg archives.)

8. Interview with author, 2006.

9. "Minutes of the Faculty of the School of Business," April 13, 1966, p. 2.

10. "Minutes of the Faculty of the School of Business," April 20, 1966.

11. Interview with author, 2005.

12. Interview with author, 2006.

13. Interview with author, 2005.

14. Interview with author, 2005.

15. "Ward's New Chief Is an Outdoor Man; Barr Likes to Hunt and Fish and Raise Roses—Worked Way through College," *New York Times,* May 10, 1955, p. 39.

16. "John Andrew Barr: Modern Retailer," *Time,* October 19, 1959.

17. "Barr Named N.U. Business School Dean," William Clark, *Chicago Tribune,* December 7, 1964, p. 1.

18. "John Andrew Barr." Barr began opening new stores, something the company had not done in years, and he closed unprofitable ones. He also introduced more than a dozen

new executives from companies like Marshall Field's and Macy's. In his first year, Barr opened 141 catalog stores. In 1957, Ward's bought The Fair, a large Chicago department store, along with three of its suburban outlets. Barr also strengthened employee benefits and pensions even as he announced a five-year expansion costing $84 million. When shareholders complained, Barr noted that these expenditures would result in increased future profits—something proven with an almost immediate 7.8 percent sales increase in 1956. Three years later, the company reported a 14 percent increase over 1958 sales figures, with earnings jumping to $10.6 million from $8.6 million. Details are in the April 8, 1957, and October 19, 1959, editions of *Time* magazine.

19. "Barr Named N.U. Business School Dean," William Clark, *Chicago Tribune,* December 7, 1964, p. 1.

20. "Barr Explains Shift to Academic Role," *New York Times,* December 7, 1964, pp. 65–66.

21. Interview with author, 2006.

22. "Minutes of the Faculty of the School of Business," May 25, 1966, p. 16.

23. "Minutes of the Faculty of the School of Business," October 4, 1967, p. 5.

24. Interview with author, 2006.

25. Interview with author, 2005.

26. "Five Million Given to N.U. by Leverone," *Chicago Tribune,* August 16, 1968, p. 3.

27. Ibid.

28. See the *Northwestern Business Reporter* (Winter 1968), p. 26.

29. Other factors contributed to the oil shock, of course, not the least of which were political tensions arising from the 1967 Arab-Israeli Six Days' War. The war contributed to the formation of the Organization of Arab Petroleum Exporting Countries, a subgroup of OPEC, formed in 1960. Additional conflict in the Yom Kippur War of 1973 led to an embargo on Arab oil going to the United States, Western Europe and Japan.

30. "Management in the 1970s," John Barr, *Northwestern Business Reporter,* Vol. 3, No. 2 (Fall 1970), pp. 2–6.

31. "Minutes of the Graduate School of Management," January 20, 1971, p. 2. In September 1970, President Strotz had addressed the business school faculty to alert them to a $1,800,000 deficit that was "expected to grow for the next five years." Despite these economic concerns, the university had been developing its facilities. It expanded its Evanston campus 1,200 feet eastward onto a lakefill and introduced facilities such as the Vogelback Computing Center (in 1965) and the Rebecca Crown Center (in 1968). Northwestern also built a new library (in 1970) and the Norris University Center and the Francis Searle Building and Foster-Walker Complex (in 1972), among other projects.

32. Interview with author, 2005.

33. Interview with author, 2005.

34. Interview with author, 2005.

35. Kamien was department chair through 1975 and then associate dean for academic affairs in three separate periods: from 1976 to 1978, from 1982 to 1984 and from 1986 to 1989.

36. The group advised the dean "on any matter relating to the school and its programs," according to a document describing the committee's function. In addition to Jacobs, other department chairmen in the 1970–1971 academic year were: Leon A. Bosch, Policy and

Environment; Richard M. Clewett, Marketing; Thomas R. Prince, Accounting and Information Systems; Michael Radnor, Organization Behavior and Industrial Relations; and Stanley Reiter, Quantitative Methods, Operations Management and Managerial Economics.

37. Interview with author, 2006.

38. Interview with author, 2005.

39. Interview with author, 2005.

40. Interview with author, 2006.

41. Interview with author, 2007.

42. *Northwestern Business Reporter* (Spring 1970), pp. 26–27.

43. Jacobs gave a speech on "Banking Automation and the Bank Structure" at Princeton University's Conference on Banking in the Next Decade, December 7–8, 1967. In his remarks, Jacobs forecast the type of automation the banking system would develop, noting that unless regulatory prohibitions interfered, "the commercial banking system during the next decade will operate a funds transfer mechanism which, if not checkless, will use a substantially smaller amount of paper per dollar of money transferred than is now the case." He also saw the "credit card [as] a first step on the road to an electronic transfer system." With respect to the computer, Jacobs predicted that this technology could also be expected "to lessen the locational advantage of neighborhood banks operating in local markets. The need to visit the bank premises is diminished by use of a credit card or a prearranged line of credit and further reduced by automatic debiting and crediting of accounts." See the reprinted speech in *Northwestern Business Reporter* (Fall 1968), pp. 17–21.

44. "1969–1994: Banking Center Strikes Silver," Matt Carey, *Kellogg World* (April 1995), pp. 10–11.

45. Ibid.

46. *The Evolution of Management Education,* Michael W. Sedlak and Harold F. Williamson, p. 135.

47. Interview with author, 2006.

48. Interview with author, 2005.

49. Graduate School of Management catalog, 1972–1973, p. 4.

50. "Management Education—The School of Management Concept," *Bulletin of the American Association of Collegiate Schools of Business* (April 1970).

51. Graduate School of Management catalog.

52. Ibid. In a report from the Environment Curriculum Task Group in March 1972, its members, including Lawrence Lavengood, Hervey A. Juris, John A. Nicholls, Charles W. Hofer, Samuel I. Doctors and chairman Richard W. Barsness, noted: "Environment is a relatively recent academic field, and one in which the Graduate School of Management has been a major innovator." The report traced the school's historical interest in the subject to 1950 and the "Management Responsibilities" segment of the Institute for Management Program. From this offering came the "Social Problems in Administration" course later that decade, as well as the "Competition of Ideas in a Business Society" course taught by Lavengood and others. Committee members stated that despite the "persisting problems of definition," environment as an area of study had, over the previous 15 years, evolved into a conventional part of curricula. "Serious dispute no longer exists regarding the relevance of such courses for aspiring managers," stated the report, "indeed, the external complexities to which institu-

tions increasingly must relate suggest that the need for Environment courses in professional school curricula is more urgent than ever before." Course readings in the area of environment included a range of economic and cultural sources, including Friedman's *Capitalism and Freedom,* Galbraith's *New Industrial State,* Heilbroner's *Limits of American Capitalism* and Schon's *Technology and Change.* See "Addenda to Minutes of the Faculty of the Graduate School of Management," April 26, 1972.

53. Graduate School of Management catalog, p. 6.

54. "New '3–2' Program Yields Bachelor/Master Degrees," *Printout* (Spring 1974), p. 6.

55. "A New Way to Start the MBA," Eugene Lerner, *Northwestern Business Reporter,* Vol. 3, No. 1 (Spring 1970), pp. 15–18.

56. Ibid. Student comments ranged from thoughtful to glib. One student reported: "The CIM program was 100 per cent great. It was very rewarding to see that the faculty cares so much about the school and the student that they would take the extra time to develop this program. It was very gratifying to meet many members of the staff and to see how helpful all of them are." Another student noted: "I enjoyed getting a view of the many professors that are available at NU. I may avoid some."

57. "C.I.M. for New Students Hints at What's Ahead," *Printout* (Fall 1973), pp. 2–3.

58. Graduate School of Management catalog, p. 8.

59. These sections were given numbers ranging from 61 to 65.

60. Serving with Lavengood were a number of other faculty members, including Robert B. Duncan, Hervey Juris, John Nicholls and Samuel Doctors. In addition, three MBA students were nominated to participate by the Graduate Management Association.

61. "Minutes of the Faculty of the Graduate School of Management," September 30, 1970.

62. The proposal appears as an addendum to the faculty minutes for May 24, 1972.

63. "The Saturday MBA Program is very similar to the Evening MBA Program in that the faculty, the student profile, admissions and degree requirements, and networking opportunities are the same," Lyons said in a February 22, 2007, press release from the school. "We've identified a gap in the marketplace that we had not served before. This new program allows us to reach out to an entirely underserved group of people, both in the Chicago region and throughout the country." Press release available at www.kellogg.northwestern .edu/news/whatsnew/parttime-saturday.htm.

64. Interview with author, 2006.

65. Interview with author, 2006. Lyons also noted the gradual improvement in the Part-Time MBA Program's academic strength. One metric he used to measure this advance was scholarships bestowed on the school's participants. For instance, the First Scholars Program, offered by the First National Bank in Chicago, was designed for prospective graduate students whom the bank hoped would pursue management education. Only the University of Chicago and Northwestern's Graduate School of Management garnered these scholarships. Lyons recalled his effort to attract more of these scholars. "During that time, First National Bank would want to recruit about 15 of these students. We would get maybe two or three of them," said Lyons. "The rest would go to Chicago because people perceived they had a better program. One of my main objectives was to reverse this trend. If I could reverse this, I knew that the perception of our program was shifting. By the 1990s, the numbers were

reversed: We would get 11 or 12 out of 15 students. The bank eventually wanted more parity. . . . That was sort of my barometer in terms of gauging our dominance in the Chicago area."

66. Jacobs recalled a visit from the dean of the London School of Business, who, he said, remarked, "You know, if I could keep our administration down to your numbers, I wouldn't have to go out and fund raise."

67. Interview with author, 2006.

68. "Dean's Council Turns Focus on GSM," *Printout* (Fall 1974), p. 1. See also "Alumni Set $110,000 Goal" in the same edition, as well as "Alumni Support Drive to Begin," *Printout* (Summer 1974), p. 2. Alumni also took part in various other fund-raising initiatives, including a phone-a-thon in the fall of 1975 that resulted in 131 pledges of financial support from alumni in the Chicago area.

69. "Alumni Form Area Chapters," *Printout* (Spring 1974), p. 1.

70. "Report," Business Advisory Council, a special supplement in the faculty minutes for April 1966.

71. Interview with author, 2005.

72. Graduate School of Management catalog, p. 4.

73. Interview with author, 2005.

74. "Letter from Dean Dipak Jain to the Kellogg Community," February 6, 2002, available at www.kellogg.northwestern.edu/news/whatsnew/wilson.htm.

75. Wilson provided insights into the application process in a fall 1973 *Printout* article, "GSM Enrollment in Evanston, Chicago Up from Year Ago." There, he indicated that enrollment had increased nearly 10 percent year after year from 1972 on, to a record total of 1,238 students. Vennie Lyons '72, director of the school's Evening Program, noted in the same article that enrollment goals for the part-time curriculum targeted 800 students by 1975.

76. One of those expressing mixed feelings about the increase in student numbers was Frank Hartzfeld, as he related in an October 1974 lecture. He reflected that, starting in 1972, the total number of students taking the admissions test had gone up dramatically. "The upshot of all that is our enrollment is actually greater than what the [Leverone] building was designed to accommodate," he said, noting the current student body numbered 652 in a facility intended to hold 600. "[A couple years ago] when there were 400 students here, I could reach around and really get to know them," said Hartzfeld. "Going beyond that, it breaks down and I simply can't do that."

77. Interview with author, 2006.

78. "Barr Reviews GSM Growth, Future Needs," *Printout* (Summer 1974), p. 3.

Chapter 5

1. "Mr. Business-School Boom: What Jacobs Wrought," David Leonhardt, *New York Times,* May 3, 2000. About the same time, Northwestern president Henry Bienen also was paying tribute to Jacobs's informality. "He's not one who stands on ceremony. He's not a stuffed shirt," said Bienen. "He has a very easy yet forceful manner. He has a copious memory, but also a very strong analytical mind." Quoted in "Saluting the 'Dean of Deans," *Kellogg World* (Spring 2000), p. 18.

2. "Building the Brand," Rebecca Lindell, *Kellogg World* (Spring 2000), p. 10.

3. From 1970 to 1971, Jacobs served as co–staff director of the Hunt Commission, formally called the Presidential Commission on Financial Structure and Regulation. President Richard Nixon established the commission in June 1970 to recommend legislative and regulatory changes to improve the financial system's performance. The commission determined that it would concentrate on "problems relating to commercial banks, savings and loan associations, mutual savings banks, credit unions, reserve life insurance companies and private pension funds," wrote Jacobs in a 1972 journal article describing the commission. The basic reason for the body's formation, he wrote, was twofold: it was the result of "inflation-induced movements" in interest rates and the "effects of new technologies available to financial institutions." See "The Commission on Financial Structure and Regulation: Its Organization and Recommendations," *Journal of Finance,* Vol. 27, No. 2 (May 1972), pp. 319–328. Among his other publications, Jacobs authored *Financial Institutions* and edited *Regulating Business: The Search for an Optimum.*

4. "Saluting the 'Dean of Deans.'" Tabatoni's remarks were among those compiled for Jacobs's twenty-fifth anniversary as dean. Tabatoni, an influential and well-respected French intellectual and onetime candidate for the Kellogg School deanship, met Jacobs in 1965, beginning a long friendship that encompassed not only academics and but also leisure pursuits, such as sailing. Tabatoni, who occasionally taught at Kellogg, died in 2006 at the age of 83.

5. Interview with author, 2005.

6. Martha died in 1999.

7. Strotz, a 1951 graduate of the University of Chicago's doctoral program, served as Northwestern's president from 1970 until 1985 and its chancellor from 1985 until 1990.

8. This view was predicated on Jacobs's experiences with the school's Institute for Management, some 20 years earlier. Quoted in "Allen Center Cornerstone Unveiled," *Printout* (Winter 1979), p. 3.

9. "James L. Allen Lecture Series Established," *Printout* (Winter-Spring 1981), p. 49.

10. Today, it is known as the Kellogg School Executive MBA Program. James Fyffe '76 was among those students in the first EMP class. "Northwestern put its very best team forward to develop that program," he recalled in a 2006 *Kellogg World* interview. "They were very much in listening mode, and very respectful and supportive of the students in the program." He remembered the spirit of that initial class and the stimulating lectures on the sixth floor of Leverone Hall, three years before the Allen Center opened as the school's modern EMBA facility. "It was an honor to be part of that program," Fyffe said. "I'm still talking to people about it."

11. IIM classes were scheduled six days a week, including most afternoons and evenings, with seminars running from 8:30 a.m. until 3 p.m. and resuming from 4:30 p.m. until 6 p.m. The academic focus of the program examined a wide range of multinational strategies, including organizational structure and staffing; political relations; and national differences with respect to employment, economics, education and foreign policy.

12. "The Allen Center's Origin," *Kellogg World* (Summer 1988), pp. 2–5.

13. "The Allen Center," *Printout* (Fall 1977), pp. 1–4.

14. Interview with author, 2005.

15. "Executives Head Back to School," Joanna R. Cook, *Kellogg World* (Summer 1987), pp. 4–7.

16. "James Allen: A Great Man and a Great Friend," *Kellogg World* (Spring 1993), p. 7.

17. Interview with author, 2005. In addition to Allen, a host of donors, corporate and individual, supported the building's construction, including: Abbott Laboratories, Borg-Warner Corporation, Commonwealth Edison Company, Kraft Foods Inc., Walgreen Corporation, Northern Trust Company, Jewel Companies Inc., Quaker Oats Foundation and General Motors Foundation, as well as Mrs. John A. Barr, John Darling, Raymond F. Farley, Robert R. Graham Jr., Gregory P. Jorjorian, Susan M. Miller, James E. Nall, James O'Keefe, James A. Peponis, Martin J. Pregenzer, Edward A. Ravenscroft, David Warshauer, May and Sidney Warshauer, Myron Warshauer, Herbert S. Wilkinson Sr., Joyce D. Wisemiller and Kenneth Zwiener.

18. Interview with author, 2005.

19. "'Finest Facility of Its Kind,'" *Printout* (Spring 1980), pp. 10–15.

20. Maddox was inducted into the Interior Design Hall of Fame in 1992. Her Chicago-based firm worked closely with Jacobs during the Allen Center's design. Jacobs recalled their warm relationship and Maddox's ambitious design goals—some that the dean told her frankly might be out of his budget. "Eva just dismissed the concern," he related with a laugh. The designer said that she was more concerned with producing exemplary results than with the school's ability to pay for these amenities.

21. The sculpture was designed by the Italian-born artist Harry Bertoia but completed by his son Val after Bertoia died in November 1978. Bertoia, who achieved an international reputation, designed the wind-chime sculpture located in Chicago's Standard Oil Building. He also designed modern furniture, including the "diamond chair" introduced in 1952. See www.hbrp.net for more details on the artist. Among the other original art works in the Allen Center were a 16-foot-by-6$\frac{1}{2}$-foot woven tapestry that hung in the reception hall adjacent to the lobby. Hughes, a faculty member at the School of the Art Institute of Chicago, had created several commissioned fiber sculptures. Richard Hunt's 6-foot-tall bronze sculpture *Windover* was also commissioned for the Allen Center. Hunt had already acquired an international reputation in 1979, one that has only grown in the intervening years.

22. As Jacobs's personal art collection grew, he began bringing select pieces into the Allen Center for permanent display. Alumni also began making gifts to the school in support of the collection.

23. "As Allen Center Grows So Do Its Programs," *Kellogg World* (Spring 1988), pp. 24–27.

24. AEP was created for executives "near the top of the leadership structure," according to Nancy Hartigan, who outlined the program in ibid. The monthlong program was housed at the Allen Center and staffed by senior Kellogg faculty.

25. More recently, Burnett has been directing the Kellogg Management Institute, a nine-month nondegree general management curriculum that he founded.

26. "A Plan Comes Together," *Kellogg World* (Spring 1994), pp. 18–21.

27. "As Allen Center Grows."

28. "A Plan Comes Together."

29. "Remembering Nancy," Cheryl Dahle, *Kellogg World* (November 1994), pp. 16–17.

30. Ibid.

31. "Getting Wired," Lynn Sherman, *Kellogg World* (November 1995), pp. 20–25. "The Internet is the transport system for tools such as electronic mail and the World Wide Web,"

the article stated helpfully. "It provides nearly instantaneous communication as well as a vast, constantly updated, interactive reference library that can provide up-to-the-minute stock quotes, breaking news, travel information, even scores and highlights from sporting events."

32. Ibid.

33. "Dean's Letter," *Kellogg World* (Fall 1993), p. 33.

34. "The State of the School," Donald P. Jacobs, *Kellogg World* (Winter 1980), pp. 17–19.

35. See "Family Friendly," Mayrav Saar, *Kellogg World* (Summer 1994), p. 10.

36. Interview with author, 2007.

37. "From Local to Global," Rebecca Lindell, *Kellogg World* (Winter 2006), pp. 22–24.

38. "James L. Allen Lecture Series Established," *Printout* (Winter-Spring 1981), p. 49.

39. "Charles L. Brown: Why AT&T Had to Go on the Chopping Block," *Printout* (Winter 1982), p. 39. Among those present for Brown's lecture were James Allen and James B. Farley, chairman of Booz Allen Hamilton. After his remarks, Brown met informally with the Kellogg School's Austin Scholars.

40. Interview with author, 2006.

41. Though he remained involved in the school's leadership until the search committee found a new dean in 1975, Barr, along with Professor Ira D. Anderson, retired in 1974. In a resolution dated May 29, 1974, and appearing in the faculty minutes for that day, Professors Richard Clewett and Leon Bosch traced the arc of Anderson's 37 years of service to the school, concluding: "We will all remember his high sense of loyalty to the School, his tireless efforts to do well any task given to him and his continuing aim to accomplish the unassigned in School purpose and effect. His sympathetic understanding, ready cooperation and consistent cheerfulness, as well as his knowledge and judgment, will be missed by all of us." A similar resolution honoring Barr noted his "sure, demanding leadership [that] has lifted the School to higher levels of public and academic esteem." His "thrust for excellence permeated the School and generated changes and improvements," and his "courage, confidence and courtly concern quickened and enhanced academic virility throughout the School."

42. "'It was time to move, to step down . . . ,'" *Printout* (Winter 1974), p. 2.

43. Interview with author, 2006.

44. A scholar of the humanities, law and economics, Tabatoni began his career as a law professor at the University of Algiers in 1950. Over his illustrious professional life, he was instrumental in founding educational institutions, such as the Institute for the Administration of Enterprise at the University of Aix-Marseille and the University of Paris IX Dauphine. His accomplishments were many and included service in numerous educational posts in France, such as rector of the Academy of Paris and chancellor of universities. In 1995, he was elected to the Académie des Science Morales et Politiques, holding the seat once occupied by Talleyrand-Périgord. He was also instrumental in establishing the European Institute for Advanced Studies in Management, which played a critical role in the development of management research throughout Europe.

45. Interview with author, 2006.

46. "I told them I would take the job for a year or so and I would keep looking for a new candidate," Jacobs said. Interview with author, 2005.

47. NBER is among the largest economics research organizations in the United States; almost half of the 31 American Nobel Prize winners in economics have been NBER associates.

48. Juris, professor of management and human resources, joined Northwestern's Graduate School of Management in 1970. A graduate of the University of Chicago's doctorate and MBA programs, Juris would remain at Kellogg until his retirement in 2001. His contributions to the Policy and Environment Department and the Management and Strategy Department are discussed elsewhere in this chapter.

49. Duncan proved adept in the role, particularly since his research involved organizational behavior and aligning incentives to create effective and efficient hierarchies. In a *Kellogg World* (Fall 1985, pp. 13–17) interview with Harry Dreiser, the school's director of public affairs, Duncan said that structuring an organization was only part of what his discipline studied. In addition, scholars such as Duncan explored how to establish an organizational strategy and execute it. "What kinds of incentives—what reward systems—do you set up to reinforce what you are trying to do?" he offered as an example of a key consideration. "What kind of culture do you need to accomplish your strategy?" He also noted the challenges of trying to "get creative things accomplished within a traditional organizational structure," since established rules can short-circuit innovation in favor of minimizing costs. "If you're really interested in creativity and innovation you have to make sure that you get people with different backgrounds and different perspectives, give them some leeway to operate, and then make sure the organization rewards innovation and risk-taking," said Duncan, articulating an approach that had served the Kellogg School exceptionally well within its own organization.

50. "Three to Share Deanship," *Printout* (Fall 1975), pp. 1–2.

51. Ibid.

52. In 1976, Fargo would be promoted to assistant dean. The Northwestern graduate had been part of the Evanston community since 1942.

53. Interview with author, 2005.

54. Donald Cahill played an important fund-raising role at Kellogg, having been associate director of corporate relations in the Northwestern University Development Office starting in 1978, a position similar to one he previously held at Case Western Reserve University in Cleveland. Upon leaving Northwestern in 1986, Cahill, a 1982 graduate of the Kellogg Part-Time MBA Program, assumed the presidency of the Northwestern Memorial Foundation. According to former colleague Robert Duncan, Cahill, who died in 2007, was a "real catalyst" and a person who "really had a big impact" at the school, particularly in "mobilizing alumni and friends to be [financially] supportive." Interview with author, 2007.

55. Interview with author, 2006.

56. Interview with author, 2005.

57. Neuschel died in February 2004 at the age of 84. The former McKinsey & Company executive (1949 to 1977) became a partner and director at the firm. Neuschel authored more than 125 articles on many management subjects and wrote *The Servant Leader: Unleashing the Power of Your People.* He was credited with designing the first managerial leadership course at Kellogg in 1983, and he was also a governance expert. From 1979 to 1992, Neuschel directed the Transportation Center. Many at Kellogg grew to know the friendly, dapper professor through his daily rounds, when he would proudly wear his military pins, a reminder of his service in the Philippines under General Douglas MacArthur in World War II. "The Kellogg School family has lost not only a premier educator, but a beloved leader, colleague

and dear friend," said Dean Dipak C. Jain in a February 19, 2004, *Observer* obituary of Neuschel.

58. Interview with author, 2005.

59. Interview with author, 2006.

60. "We're #1," *Printout* (Summer 1976), p. 9.

61. "The Rating Game, or Onward and Upward in the Polls," *Printout* (Spring 1977), pp. 19–21.

62. "Donald P. Jacobs Appointed Dean," *Printout* (Summer 1975), pp. 1–2.

63 Interview with author, 2005.

64. "GSM Faculty Roster Boasts 31 New Members," *Printout* (Fall 1975), pp. 6–7; "20 New Faculty Members Join GSM," *Printout* (Fall 1976).

65. "20 New Faculty Members Join GSM."

66. Interview with author, 2007.

67. Interview with author, 2007.

68. Ibid.

69. "Chair Honors Freeman," *Printout* (Spring 1976), p. 1. The First National Bank of Chicago provided the endowment funds for the chair. Freeman served on the executive and investment committees of the university's Board of Trustees.

70. Facsimile from Park of the original letter to the Kellogg Foundation, dated July 29, 1978, p. 7.

71. Ibid., p. 8.

72. Interview with author, 2005.

73. The proposal also provided a gloss of management education's macro trends since World War II and set the school in context among its peer institutions. Before 1950, Harvard's case method proved popular for bringing contemporary examples into the classroom but "broke no new ground," a major limitation. In the late 1950s, the University of Chicago argued that "economic doctrine was basic to the education of students planning to enter business, and that the major principles of management were maximization and Adam Smithian self-interest," noted the proposal's authors. Carnegie Mellon rose as the next major innovator by the early 1960s, when it combined economic principles with the emerging behavioral field. Stanford then combined cases, economics and behavioral approaches to gain prominence. Northwestern's general management concept, indicated the proposal, was among the frameworks that distinguished it from the competition.

74. Facsimile from Park of the original letter to the Kellogg Foundation, dated January 12, 1979, p. 1.

75. Ibid., pp. 1–2.

76. "A Proposal to the John L. and Helen Kellogg Foundation," January 1979, pp. 14–15.

77. Ibid., p. 15.

78. Ibid., p. 17. The proposal also offered details of the planned MEDS center. Outlining a variety of economic complexities, including increased government regulation, resource scarcity and globalization, the appeal noted: "Our present situation derives from a variety of past economic-political decisions based on doctrines that do not take account of modern realities. Likewise, the modern corporation, beset by a multitude of new rules and regulations, and often unable to effectively analyze the consequences of its actions, has been forced

to resort to ad hoc responses. All these problems suggest the need for a rationalization of our decision making processes, both with regard to overall institutional choices and within the modern corporation." The school's MEDS Department, the document noted, was particularly well positioned to address such concerns.

79. Ibid., p. 18.

80. Correspondence from John L. and Helen Kellogg Foundation to Thomas G. Ayers, dated March 12, 1979, and signed by Dale Park Jr.

81. Jacobs noted that the Kellogg Foundation money was not spent but invested. In 2006, the gift was worth more than $55 million.

82. Interview with author, 2005.

83. The school completed the conversion in two stages, with 137 of the 208 planned apartments ready for the fall of 1981 because the university still required a part of the building for undergraduates, due to delays in construction of new dormitories for those students who had been displaced.

84. "Contractors Set to Remodel Building for Kellogg Students," *Printout* (Winter-Spring 1981), pp. 18–19. Other members of the conversion committee were: Carole Bruning, manager of administration; Mary Corbitt Clark, assistant dean and director of admissions; K. M. Henderson, associate dean; Daniel Feldman, assistant professor of organization behavior; two students—John Monson, president of the Graduate Management Association, and Karen Snepp '81—and a recent alumnus, Daniel Kinsella '80, who had served as resident hall director at Northwestern Apartments while a student. Monthly rental rates for the facility were initially about $150 per person (double- or triple-occupancy rooms) and $475 for a two-bedroom shared apartment. These figures included all utilities except telephone.

85. "Education Is the Best Investment," *Kellogg World* (Fall 1989), p. 17.

86. Interview with author, 2005.

87. Letter to author from Dale Park Jr., dated November 3, 2005.

88. "Northwestern's School of Business Scrambles onto the Fast Track," Frederick C. Klein, *Wall Street Journal*, January 20, 1981, p. 1.

89. Interview with author, 2005.

90. Interview with author, 2005.

91. *The Evolution of Management Education*, Michael W. Sedlak and Harold F. Williamson, p. 158.

92. "Advisory Council Considers Its Role," *Printout* (Summer 1978), pp. 2–5. The council's membership at the time consisted of 45 senior leaders, among them Karl D. Bays, chairman and CEO of American Hospital Supply Company, who served as the Advisory Council's chairman. Other figures included: Thomas G. Ayers, chairman and CEO of Commonwealth Edison; James F. Beré, chairman and CEO of Borg-Warner Corporation; Alan S. Boyd, president of Amtrak; Lester Crown, president of Material Service Corporation; Robert H. Malott, chairman and CEO of FMC Corporation; Robert Neuschel, director, McKinsey & Company; William D. Smithburg, executive vice president, U.S. grocery products, Quaker Oats Company; and E. Norman Staub, chairman of Northern Trust Company.

93. "Kellogg School Rated Best in U.S.," *Kellogg World* (Winter 1986), pp. 2–5.

94. One important measure of the Marketing Department's strength was the number of doctoral students who continued winning top prizes in prestigious dissertation competitions sponsored by the American Marketing Association. Figures for 1984 showed Kellogg

graduates in marketing had compiled a total of 13 wins and 11 honorable mentions since 1967, when the awards were started. Stanford was second on the list with 5 wins and 4 honorable mentions.

95. "Kellogg Pushes through Ivy to Top of League," Matt O'Connor, *Chicago Tribune,* October 27, 1985, p. D1.

96. Interview with author, 2005.

97. "General Motors Foundation Awards $500,000 to Kellogg School," *Kellogg World* (Winter 1986), p. 38.

98. "PepsiCo Finances Fellowships," *Kellogg World* (Winter 1987), p. 7.

99. "Quaker Oats Endows Scholarships," *Kellogg World* (Winter 1987), p. 17.

100. "Building the Brand," Rebecca Lindell, *Kellogg World* (Spring 2000), p. 13.

101. Interview with author, 2007.

102. Interview with author, 2007.

103. Correspondence with author, 2007.

104. Interview with author, 2007.

105. Interview with author, 2007.

106. Today, Montgomery is a professor at the Harvard Business School, Wernerfelt is a professor at MIT's Sloan School of Management and Amit is a professor at the Wharton School.

107. Interview with author, 2007.

108. Interview with author, 2007.

109. Interview with author, 2007.

110. The six-year "tenure clock" was modified in 2001 after Kellogg and Northwestern negotiated adding an additional year under certain circumstances. See chapter 6 for details.

111. Interview with author, 2006.

112. "Building the Brand," p. 14.

113. Interview with author, 2007.

114. Interview with author, 2007.

115. Ibid.

116. Nancy Schwartz, a graduate of Purdue's doctoral program, would chair the Managerial Economics and Decision Sciences Department and serve as director of the school's doctoral program until her death in 1981. Under her guidance, the program attracted some 85 students each year beginning in 1975, according to the Kellogg School's Office of Doctoral Studies records. Schwartz's academic output included more than 40 papers and coauthorship of two textbooks. At the time of her death, she was associate editor of *Econometrica,* on the board of editors of the American Economic Review and on the governing councils of the American Economic Association and the Institute of Management Sciences.

117. Interview with author, 2007.

118. Interview with author, 2007.

119. "The Campaign for Kellogg," *Kellogg World* (Winter 1987), pp. 2–6.

120. "And Now, Hobbs Hall," *Kellogg World* (Summer 1988), pp. 6–7. H. Wendell Hobbs '29 was a graduate of Northwestern's School of Commerce, majoring in finance. He credited the education's "excellent training" with enabling his professional success. The son of a physician, Hobbs was born in Galesburg, Michigan, and went on to enjoy a career in finance

until 1929, when the market crash temporarily interrupted this professional pursuit. He bought a fruit farm and managed it successfully for several years before returning to banking with a position on the New York Stock Exchange. For more details, see "The Hobbs Saga," *Kellogg World* (Summer 1988), p. 8.

121. "The Campaign for Kellogg."

122. "A Great Day for Kellogg," *Kellogg World* (Fall 1989), pp. 2–3. To cite some specifics: funding from Mr. and Mrs. Morris A. Kaplan (both graduates of the school, in 1935 and 1936, respectively) created the Morris and Alice Kaplan Chair to encourage business ethics; the DeWitt W. Buchanan Jr. Chair was endowed; the James B. Farley/Booz Allen Hamilton Research Professorship was established; the Merrill Lynch Capital Markets Research Professorship honored the division's campaign commitment; First Chicago Corporation augmented the First Chicago Research Professorship, established in 1983; Allstate Insurance Company endowed the Dispute Resolution Research Center; and Hartmarx Corporation initiated a research professorship in conjunction with other companies.

123. Ibid.

124. Interview with author, 2005. Weber also noted Jacobs's entrepreneurial approach to negotiating financial support with the university. Though dealings were sometimes challenging, Weber stated that the central administration and Kellogg arrived at arrangements that were mutually agreeable and equitable. Said Weber: "When I came in [as university president], we had a highly centralized budget process, and the previous four years we had run deficits and there wasn't a lot [of money] around. Everybody knows, unlike a state university, [a private university like Northwestern must] look at the different colleges and schools in their market contexts. So you could get away with, at that time, an average [Northwestern] professor's salary of $75,000 and 3 percent increase annually. You couldn't do that at Kellogg, in a business school context, where you were starting to have professors break $100,000 or [if you did not meet their salary requirements] they'll go somewhere else. I'm trying to balance the budget and Don is coming in . . . [telling me] he's got to have 7 percent. 'No you can't have 7 percent. I just gave Arts and Sciences, the lumpen proletariat, 3 percent. And besides I don't have it.' At certain times it got fairly tense because Don obviously had this great sense of ownership, and justifiably so, in his school. We did come to an agreement: We froze the university's contribution to the school, which was like $7 million. Don then wouldn't ask us for any more, for any construction. But he kept 70 percent of the increment in tuition; the university got 30 percent. That was the deal. It took the burden off the central budget and reduced the potential sense of inequity among the other schools. It also said, you can keep 70 percent of tuition, and that's a lot of money. So Don ran the enrollment up. And incidentally, he kept 100 percent of these special programs [like Executive Education] at the Allen Center. It was a sensible deal. It created his incentives to grow and enhance quality."

125. "The Best B-schools," *BusinessWeek,* November 28, 1988, p. 76.

126. Ibid.

127. Kellogg School professors serve in leadership roles on dozens of peer-reviewed journals across all management disciplines.

128. "The Best B-schools," p. 79.

129. Interview with author, 2006.

130. Jacobs noted that this practice raised some eyebrows. "The response from people outside Kellogg was one of horror," he said in a 2000 *Kellogg World* interview. "In academic mores, it wasn't appropriate."

131. "They Say We're Number One," *Kellogg World* (Spring 1989), pp. 4–9.

132. The *Wall Street Journal* had ranked Kellogg number one in its 1985 survey.

133. Interview with author, 2006.

134. Interview with author, 2005.

135. "Building the Brand," p. 15.

136. Ibid.

137. Interview with author, 2005.

138. Interview with author, 2005.

139. Interview with author, 2006. See also "Building the Brand," p. 15.

140. "Feeling the Impact," Aaron B. Cohen, *Kellogg World* (Spring 1989), p. 9. Applications had increased steadily over the preceding two decades, according to data in the article. In 1970, the school had 923 applicants. By 1976, that figure had more than doubled to 1,932. In 1988, the number of applicants stood at 3,679. Similarly, the GMAT test scores for these applicants had risen sharply, from an average of 535 in 1970 to 630 in 1988. Not surprisingly, during that same time, grade point averages also jumped, from 2.8 to 3.4.

141. "How Kellogg Responds to Change," Donald P. Jacobs, *Kellogg World* (Spring 1989), p. 2.

142. Ibid.

143. The school's Full-Time MBA Program was ranked number four by *U.S. News* that year, a fraction of a percentage behind number three Wharton. Stanford and Harvard, respectively, occupied the top two spots. In the survey article, the author wrote: "Greed is out. Ethics in. For many of the nation's top business schools, it's back to the drawing board to figure out how to educate today's students so that they meet the demands of a changing world." Some 700 graduate business programs were in operation at the time, producing about 70,000 MBAs each year, up from 21,400 in 1970, according to *U.S. News,* which noted that "Wall Street's allure [was] fading fast," resulting in a shift of student interest to subjects other than finance. At Kellogg, for instance, among the most popular courses was one focused on negotiations and dispute resolution. See "America's Best Graduate and Professional Schools," Eva Pomice, *U.S. News & World Report,* March 19, 1990.

144. In the film, Gekko said: "The point is, ladies and gentlemen, that 'greed'—for lack of a better word—is good. Greed works. Greed clarifies, cuts through, and captures the essence of the evolutionary spirit. Greed, in all of its forms—greed for life, for money, for love, knowledge—has marked the upward surge of mankind." Though the film's director had intended to fashion Gekko as a nemesis, he became more like a hero to those in investment banking and those looking to break into the industry. Kenneth Lipper, former managing director at Salomon Brothers, served as script adviser for the film, after initially rebuffing Stone's request to be chief technical adviser, on the grounds that the film, as originally written, was a one-sided portrayal that gave the impression Wall Street was "a charade or a cesspool," according to Lipper. See "The Platoon of Pros Who Helped Out on 'Wall Street,'" Chris Welles, *BusinessWeek,* December 21, 1987, p. 38.

145. For detailed background and bibliography on the savings and loan failures, see www.fdic.gov/bank/historical/s&1.

146. "The MBA World Revisited: What Corporations Are Doing Now," Barbara Ettorre, *Management Review* (September 1992), pp. 15–20. The concerns raised in the article applied primarily to second- and third-tier schools, rather than schools such as Kellogg. "Downsizing is shrinking the layers of middle management into which most MBAs are hired," wrote Ettorre. "But more and more companies—many of them smaller, midsized ones—are entering the arena of MBA hiring because this training is still considered vital. They are, however, targeting their searches carefully." They were also recommending that business schools revise their curricula to include more emphasis on ethics and global business. Some were calling for graduates who were "more mindful of the external world and how to work on integrated problem solving, as well as team management, communications and global management," all areas of focus at Kellogg.

147. "What Business Schools Aren't Teaching," Anita Bruzzles, *Incentive* (March 1991), pp. 29–31.

148. "Ivy and Innovation: B-schools That Try Harder," Amy Dunkin, *BusinessWeek*, June 7, 1993, pp. 113–114.

149. "Business Backlash Snares MBAs in Catch-22," Charles Haddad, *Chicago Tribune*, January 17, 1993.

150. "Shaking Up the MBA," Robert L. Jacobsen, *Chronicle of Higher Education*, December 15, 1993, pp. A18–19.

151. "The Best B-schools," John A. Byrne, *BusinessWeek*, October 26, 1992, p. 60.

152. "Kellogg Holds On to No. 1 Rank," Hollee Jo Schwartz, *Daily Northwestern*, October 16, 1992, p. 1.

153. Ibid., p. 7.

154. Ibid.

155. "MBAiling," *Economist*, April 20, 1991, pp. 13–14.

156. "The Best B-schools," October 26, 1992.

157. "Kellogg Extends Its Global Reach with New MBA Programs," *Kellogg World* (April 1996), p. 3.

158. "Kellogg Global Footprint Expands with Strategic EMBA Partnerships," Matt Golosinski, *Kellogg World* (Winter 2006), pp. 31–32.

159. Ibid.

160. "Thirty Years of Executive MBA Experience: A World of Difference," Rebecca Lindell, *Kellogg World* (Winter 2006), pp. 18–20.

161. Chulalongkorn itself is the oldest university in Thailand, established in 1917 by King Vajiravudh and named in honor of his father, King Chulalongkorn, an influential ruler who advanced modern education in Thailand.

162. Interview with author, 2006. See also "A Golden Venture: Partnership between Sasin and Kellogg Flourishes," Zachary Coile, *Kellogg World* (Spring 1991), pp. 30–32. "Few business schools have succeeded so well, so fast," *AsiaWeek* magazine wrote of Sasin in 1990. In fact, the school expanded so quickly that it soon outgrew its original quarters at Chulalongkorn, which required the school's directors to raise funds for a $4.7 million, 11-story building, completed in 1990. This facility has since been augmented by an adjacent expansion. The school's success prompted His Majesty the King of Thailand, Bhumibol

Adulyadej, to confer the name *Sasin* on the institution in 1987. The word, roughly translated from the Sanskrit, means "chief of the rabbits."

163. "Building the Brand," p. 16.

164. Wilson served as admissions director for the school's first class; Dardes, then director of admissions at Kellogg, screened 145 applicants to arrive at the 35 who constituted the school's second cohort. See "Kellogg Helps Create Thai Business School," *Kellogg World* (Winter 1985), pp. 16–17.

165. "The World Is Their Classroom," Rebecca Lindell, *Kellogg World* (Winter 2004), pp. 20–23.

166. Interview with author, 2006.

167. "Bumpy Takeoff Didn't Ground Innovative GIM Course," Rebecca Lindell, *Kellogg World* online, spring 2006, available at www.kellogg.northwestern.edu/kwo/spr06/indepth/gim.htm.

168. Interview with author, 2007.

169. Correspondence with author, 2007.

170. "Study at Kellogg . . . and See the World," Elizabeth Leech, *Kellogg World* (Fall 1991), pp. 2–5.

171. Interview with author, 2007.

172. "The World Is Their Oyster," *Kellogg World* (Spring-Summer 1992), pp. 10–11.

173. Ibid.

174. "Study at Kellogg . . . and See the World."

175. "The World Is Their Classroom."

176. "Kellogg Team a Life-Saver with Global Health Initiative," *Kellogg World* (Spring 2007), p. 5.

177. Interoffice correspondence from Wilson to McGann and Jerome, dated May 2, 1979.

178. Letter from William A. Jerome, dated February 26, 2006.

179. Copy of original memo from William A. Jerome.

180. "Bummertime," 1980 KGSM Business Revue script. The song was sung to the music of "Summertime."

181. "Dramatic Presence," Rebecca Lindell, *Kellogg World* (Spring 2006), pp. 30–31. The script featured an interchange between "Jacobs" and an offstage voice intended to be Helen Kellogg.

182. "Up for Sale," Lisa Weirich, *Merger,* May 22, 1980, p. 7.

183. 1980 KGSM Business Revue script.

184. 1980 KGSM Business Revue Program, p. 1.

185. "Rites of Spring: The Special K Revue," *Printout* (Summer 1984), pp. 19–21.

186. "Dramatic Presence."

187. "Kellogg Graduate School of Management Dean Donald P. Jacobs Announces Plans to Retire," Kellogg press release, September 27, 2000.

188. "Letter from the Dean," *Kellogg World* (Spring 2000), p. 2.

189. During the April 27, 2001, ceremony to name the atrium, Jacobs praised Levy for his many contributions to Kellogg over the years. "Joe Levy is the ultimate entrepreneur," said the dean to about 100 individuals gathered for the event. "A lot of people have great faith in his good judgment."

190. "Kellogg Graduate School of Management Dean Donald P. Jacobs Announces Plans to Retire."

191. Interview with author, 2006.

192. "Salute to the 'Dean of Deans' Caps Illustrious Jacobs Tenure," Matt Golosinski, *Kellogg World* (Summer 2001), p. 24.

193. "Saluting the 'Dean of Deans.'"

194. "Dipak Jain Named Dean of the Kellogg Graduate School of Management," Northwestern University press release, May 7, 2001.

Chapter 6

1. Jain recognized this "very humble beginning" and said that during a visit to Tezpur in March 2007, he returned to his grade school and met with teachers and students there as part of a two-day Shaping Young Minds Conference. More than 700 students participated. "People were very excited," Jain recalled, adding that his example of earning international distinction in education served as an inspiration for the students. "The best thing was they said, 'I also have a future.'" Jain noted that the classroom where he studied in the tenth grade had hardly changed since his time there. "It was almost the same classroom I left in 1971," he said. Interview with author, 2007.

2. Nevertheless, at one point, Jain's father wanted him to become an officer in the Indian Administrative Service.

3. "'You cannot ask for a better life': Dean Journeys across Continents to Build Success at NU's Business School," Marisa Maldonado, *Daily Northwestern,* February 27, 2002.

4. The school's motto is "Be a jewel among men"; it has described its mission as "serving as an instrument of change and development for the society by producing individuals who are well equipped to meet the challenges of time." See darrangecollege.org/mission.

5. Interview with author, 2003. He also has emphasized the importance of good teachers and classmates, especially in the absence of physical resources or facilities. "When you go to India from the U.S.," Jain has noted, "you have an appreciation for both countries. You appreciate what you have when you return to the States, but you also appreciate how people living in such tough conditions can also excel." Interview with author, 2007.

6. The letter is just three lines long, but Jain called it his "most precious" document.

7. Bass introduced the diffusion model in 1969 as an empirical generalization. See "A New Product Growth for Model Consumer Durables," *Management Science,* Vol. 15 (January 1969), pp. 215–227. Also see "The Future of Research in Marketing: Marketing Science," *Journal of Marketing Research,* Vol. 30 (February 1993), pp. 1–6. Bass's original paper was selected in 2004 as one of the 10 most frequently cited works in the 50-year history of *Management Science.* It was ranked number five. See *Management Science,* Vol. 50, No. 12 (December 2004 supplement). Bass died on December 1, 2006, at the age of 79.

8. "Transition at the Top," Matt Golosinski, *Kellogg World* (Summer 2001), pp. 10–15.

9. "Letter from the Dean," *Kellogg World* (Summer 2001), p. 2.

10. "Northwestern Names Insider to Lead Kellogg," Jim Kirk, *Chicago Tribune,* May 8, 2001, Business Section, p. 3.

11. "New Business School Deans See Future Built on Basics," James O'Shea, Greg Burns, and Delroy Alexander, *Chicago Tribune,* June 10, 2001, Business Section, p. 1.

12. Just as some had expressed doubts a decade earlier about the value of pursuing an MBA, certain critics, including Jeffery Pfeffer, Henry Mintzberg and Warren Benes, again raised questions of the degree's worth as the new century began, particularly with respect to its economic cost. Jain soon would formulate his response to the concerns raised (see the "MBA Life Cycle" section in this chapter), but early in his deanship, issues related to the MBA's value proposition were not far from his mind. For comparison, see, e.g., "Business Schools Hit Hard Times amid Doubt over Value of M.B.A.," William Celis III, *New York Times,* May 12, 1993, p. 6: "'There's a growing realization that an M.B.A. is not a ticket to the gravy train,' said Charles Hickman, director of projects and services for the American Assembly of Collegiate Schools of Business in St. Louis, which accredits graduate schools of business." In addition to questioning the value proposition of the graduate business degree, more recent critics, such as Mintzberg and Pfeffer, have argued that conventional methods of teaching in MBA programs fail to deliver the results promised.

13. Interview with author, 2007. The committee consisted of Kellogg professors Morton Kamien, Jeanne Brett, Artur Raviv, Robert Magee and Greg Carpenter. Joining them was Wade Fetzer '61, former Goldman Sachs limited partner and member of the Kellogg Alumni Advisory Board; Miles Marsh '76, former chairman and CEO of the Fort James Corporation and member of the Dean's Advisory Board; David van Zant, dean of the Northwestern University School of Law; Penelope Peterson, dean of Northwestern's School of Education; Michele Rogers, assistant dean of admissions and financial aid; John Margoles, assistant provost; and Brian Poger '01, a Kellogg student.

14. "Northwestern Names Insider to Lead Kellogg," Jim Kirk, *Chicago Tribune,* May 8, 2001, p. 3. The perennial debate among those recruiting business school deans is whether an academic or a corporate candidate is most capable of running the institution. The question is of particular concern with respect to the individual's fund-raising ability. "That is a metric we'll always be measured against," Jain told the *Chicago Tribune.* "There's always the myth that a corporate person . . . will do a better job of fundraising because he has better corporate contacts. I'm not sure that is right, because we have more credibility with our students. I have taught for 15 years at Kellogg. We get most of our funds from students and their friends. If I go back to this student body, they know how capable and credible I am. We academics can do as good a job as the corporate guys." See "New Business School Deans See Future."

15. Jain was instrumental in helping shape ISB, telling the *Chronicle of Higher Education,* "We really need this for India. Given the changes in India's economy, we need schools that are more globally focused. We need to specialize in e-commerce as well as emerging markets like India and China." See "Indian Business School Seeks to Give Students a Reason to Stay Home," Martha Ann Overland, *Chronicle of Higher Education,* November 3, 2000. Both Jain and Jacobs are members of the school's Governing Board.

16. Jain's research includes the study of marketing technology products, market segmentation and competitive market structure analysis; cross-cultural issues in global product diffusion; new product diffusion; and forecasting models. His work, including papers coauthored with Frank Bass, has been highly regarded. In 1991, he won the Society for Marketing Science's prestigious John D. C. Little Best Paper Award for "Investigating Household Purchase Timing Decisions: A Conditional Hazard Function Approach," *Marketing Science,* Vol. 10 (Winter 1991). (With this distinction, Jain joined Kellogg marketing colleagues

Lakshman Krishnamurthi, Robert C. Blattberg and Vincent R. Nijs, who have also earned the prize.) Teaching excellence has been equally important to Jain, and he has earned the Kellogg School's Sidney Levy Award for Excellence in Teaching. He has also been recognized by his home country: during the 2004 Pravasi Bharatiya Divas celebration, the government of India bestowed the Pravasi Bharatiya Samman Award on Jain in acknowledgment of his professional success as part of the Indian diaspora.

17. "Jain Takes on New Role as Associate Dean for Academic Affairs," Carlotta Mast, *Kellogg World* (November 1996), p. 4.

18. Oh Be Joyful was an annual Kellogg event to recognize faculty and staff accomplishments over the previous year.

19. "Transition at the Top."

20. Ibid.

21. The Guanghua arrangement included a grant from Procter & Gamble and some 30 other companies, as well as an invitation from Kellogg for Guanghua professors to visit Evanston and observe teaching practices there. As dean, Jain would continue developing these international relationships, and he entered into a three-year partnership with Guanghua in 2003 that established an MBA student and faculty exchange program between the two schools. The agreement also called for the schools to create joint executive development programs. "Asia, and in particular China, will continue to present opportunities for business leaders," said Jain at the time. Guanghua's enrollment had grown to more than 3,000 students by 2003, and it remains one of China's top business schools.

22. "Minutes of the Department/Chairpersons Committee Meeting," December 5, 1996.

23. Interview with author, 2007.

24. "Curriculum, Curriculum, Curriculum," Ryann Plinska, *Kellogg World* (July 1995), pp. 6–7.

25. Ibid.

26. "An Academic Affair," Eric Trott, *Kellogg World* (Summer 1994), pp. 18–19.

27. Among his responsibilities, Jain emphasized the need for rigorous departmental review of junior faculty members. In particular, he noted the importance of the three-year review. "Minutes of the Department/Program Chairpersons Committee Meeting," February 12, 1997.

28. Interview with author, 2007.

29. Interview with author, 2007.

30. "If you don't have the leadership pushing for something like this, it doesn't happen. These changes do not happen bottom-up," said Greenbaum. "There's a favorite expression that Donald [Jacobs] and I use often: 'The fish stinks from the head back.' That's the negative expression, but the positive analogue is equally true. That is, change has to be led. You can't have a complacent person at the top and expect to see revolutionary changes, and this was a revolutionary change." Interview with author, 2007.

31. Today, the center is known at the Financial Institutions and Markets Research Center, codirected by Ravi Jagannathan, the Chicago Mercantile Exchange/John F. Sandner Distinguished Professor of Finance, and Robert McDonald, the Erwin P. Nemmers Distinguished Professor of Finance. The center seeks to promote scholarly research and stimulate dialogue between academic and financial communities, by sponsoring a variety of

educational and research activities and disseminating knowledge through its Working Paper Series.

32. Interview with author, 2007.

33. Interview with author, 2007.

34. "'You cannot ask for a better life': Dean Journeys across Continents."

35. "Prime Minister of India Commends Dean Jain's Leadership in Education," Kellogg School press release, 2004.

36. His honors include the Paul E. Green Best Paper Award in 1999 from the *Journal of Marketing Research,* the Best Paper Award in 1991 from the American Marketing Association Summer Educators' Conference and the John D. C. Little Best Paper Award in 1988 from *Marketing Science.*

37. Interview with author, 2007.

38. For instance, he was twice honored with the William F. O'Dell Award bestowed by the American Marketing Association to distinguish outstanding contributions to marketing. He has also won the Paul E. Green Best Paper Award from the *Journal of Marketing Research.*

39. Interview with author, 2007.

40. Interview with author, 2006.

41. Interview with author, 2007.

42. Interview with author, 2007.

43. Correspondence with author, 2007.

44. Interview with author, 2007.

45. Interview with author, 2007.

46. Interview with author, 2007.

47. Besanko recalled being among those who spearheaded this effort. "I was the department chair in management and strategy at the time and we were having a dinner to honor the occasion of Gene's retirement. We had the idea that we should have something to announce in conjunction with this, so I proposed to the department chairs that we name the Professor of the Year Award after Gene. That took about half a second to be approved. I thought naming the award after him was perfect. He embodied great teaching. Gene was naturally gifted, but he worked at it too, and he cared about his students." Interview with author, 2007.

48. "Students Name Sergio Rebelo and Julie Hennessy Professor of the Year," Matt Golosinski, *Kellogg World* online, June 1, 2007, available at www.kellogg.northwestern .edu/news/whatsnew/lavengood2007.htm.

49. Interview with author, 2007.

50. Interview with author, 2007.

51. Interview with author, 2007.

52. Interview with author, 2006.

53. Interview with author, 2007.

54. "The Spirit of Kellogg," Matt Golosinski, *Kellogg World* (Winter 2001), p. 14.

55. Interview with author, 2007.

56. "Family Valuation," Matt Golosinski, *Kellogg World* (Spring 2001), p. 16.

57. "Kellogg Establishes Center for Family Enterprises," *Kellogg World* (Winter 1999), p. 29.

58. Ibid.

59. "Kellogg and Ford Motor Company Partner to Create Center for Global Citizenship," Matt Golosinski, *Kellogg World* (Spring 2001), p. 4.

60. Among the topics serving as case studies for the nascent center were racial discrimination in bank lending practices; hidden biases in personnel and admissions standards; and potential privacy violations of computer databases. Upon launching the center, Messick expressed his desire to provide practical applications for ethical study. "One goal of the center is to try to solve real ethical problems in business, to understand the dilemmas that real humans face and to design ways to resolve them," he said in a 1994 interview. "Business ethics training can equip young managers to identify and cope with moral and ethical aspects of their business." See "Doing the Ethical Thing," Rosaland Briggs, *Kellogg World* (Summer 1994), p. 15.

61. Messick retired from the Kellogg School in 2007.

62. "Doing the Ethical Thing."

63. "Kellogg Helping Women Unlock Corporate Boardrooms," Rebecca Lindell, *Kellogg World* (Spring 2003), p. 24.

64. "Brave New Business," Matt Golosinski, *Kellogg World* (Winter 2000), p. 12.

65. "Mergermania," Matt Golosinski, *Kellogg World* (Spring 2003), pp. 30–33.

66. "A Dollar Short," Rebecca Lindell, *Kellogg World* online, summer 2003.

67. For more detail, see "Ripe for Reform," *Kellogg World* online, summer 2004.

68. "Kellogg School Professor Leading the Way in Derivatives Research," Deborah Leigh Wood, *Kellogg World* online, spring 2004.

69. "Mixed Messages," Kari Richardson, *Kellogg World* online, spring 2006.

70. "Healthcare Gets a Check-Up," Romi Herron, *Kellogg World* online, winter 2006.

71. "Majority Rules," Romi Herron, *Kellogg World* online, spring 2006.

72. "It Is a Small World after All," Adrienne Murrill, *Kellogg World* online, summer 2007.

73. Interview with author, 2007.

74. "The Spirit of Kellogg," pp. 10–14.

75. Ibid.

76. "Transition at the Top."

77. "Three Years of Success," Bayo Adeniyi and Jason Miller, *Merger,* June 2004, pp. 12–13.

78. "Bringing the Kellogg Spirit to the World," Matt Golosinski, *Kellogg World* (Winter 2001), pp. 20–21.

79. See "Behind the Scenes in the Office of the Dean," Matt Golosinski, *Kellogg World* (Winter 2001), pp. 22–25. The roles were designed to rotate periodically, with new faculty members joining the dean's office as others returned to their full-time teaching and research activities. In 2003, Besanko stepped down, and Robert Korajczyk, the Harry G. Guthmann Distinguished Professor of Finance, assumed the role of overseeing curriculum and teaching. He held the position until 2006, when Sunil Chopra, the IBM Distinguished Professor of Operations Management, took over the role. Meanwhile, Magee served as senior associate dean until 2005, when he returned to the faculty; Kathleen Hagerty, the First Chicago Distinguished Professor of Finance and codirector of the Financial Institutions and Markets Research Center, filled the position.

80. Ibid.

81. Interview with author, 2005.

82. "Three Years of Success."

83. "Dipak's Indian Values Light Up Kellogg Campus," Malini Bhupta, *Economic Times* (India), October 21, 2002.

84. One myth in particular suggests why the city has become known as a place of eternal love and romance. Long ago, Aniruddha, grandson of Krishna, became the target of a young princess's affections. Princess Usha used magical influence to bring Aniruddha to her. Upon learning this, her father, Bana, a powerful thousand-armed deity, became enraged, and a great battle between his forces and those of Aniruddha commenced, with the young suitor eventually emerging triumphant and carrying off his bride. The blood shed over the matter gave Tezpur its name, which literally means "city of blood." More recently, the Sino-Indian War of 1962, sparked by a dispute over the Himalayan border in Arunachal Pradesh, looked as if it would be a modern incarnation of the mythic battle. The conflict was settled in a matter of weeks, but Jain recalled the citizens of Tezpur being forced to pack up and relocate when the Chinese People's Liberation Army marched near the town. Jain, five years old at the time, was forced, along with his family, to flee to his grandfather's home near Delhi, where they remained for three months. "I remember that day very well," he said. "I was in school and the teacher came to us and said, 'The government has asked to vacate the city by 6:45 p.m.'" Interview with author, 2007.

85. "Behind the Scenes in the Office of the Dean."

86. "New Business School Deans See Future Built on Basics."

87. "Where in the World Is Dipak Jain?" Matt Golosinski, *Kellogg World* (Summer 2005), p. 36.

88. "Gala Launch for Kellogg-Miami Executive MBA Program," Matt Golosinski, *Kellogg World* (Spring 2006), p. 4.

89. "Thirty Years of Executive MBA Experience: A World of Difference," Rebecca Lindell, *Kellogg World* (Winter 2006), pp. 18–20.

90. Hori and others, including Melinda Cervantes, director of corporate relations at Kellogg, noted Jain's remarkable ability to maintain a full travel schedule—including teaching at partner schools and then meeting with alumni and recruiters—while sleeping very little. "He would spend hours on the phone and sending email, sleep briefly and then head back to the classroom," said Cervantes, referring to one trip Jain took to Thailand in 2004. Said Hori, "Traveling with Dean Jain is not for the faint of heart." Indeed, Jain and his family narrowly escaped death during the tsunami that devastated Phuket in December 2004. Only a rare lapse of memory on Jain's part, which resulted in a return to their hotel room, prevented them from being swept away by the colossal wall of water that struck the beach where the family was headed that morning. See "Where in the World Is Dipak Jain?"

91. "Three Years of Success."

92. "The content and delivery of the core curriculum changed a lot over time," Besanko noted. "What has not changed, until now, is the structure of it—which courses go before which other courses." See "How the Best Gets Better: The Kellogg School Fine-Tunes Its Curriculum," Matt Golosinski, *Kellogg World* (Spring 2003), pp. 8–9.

93. For more details, see ibid.

94. Correspondence with author, 2007.

95. "New Kellogg School Associate Dean Delivering 'The Lift of a Driving Dream,'" Matt Golosinski, *Kellogg World* (Summer 2004), p. 3.

96. "Be True to Your School," Matt Golosinski, *Kellogg World* (Spring 2005), pp. 16–17.

97. "Kellogg Enjoys Record Year for Fund Raising," *Kellogg World* (Winter 2001), p. 9.

98. "That Great Alumni Weekend," *Printout* (Fall 1977), pp. 13–18.

99. Ibid.

100. The students themselves raised nearly $920,000. In honor of their generosity and efforts, Dean Jain contributed additional funds from his own discretionary account—money generated through his appearances and lectures around the world—to push the overall gift to $1 million.

101. The laptop went to Patricia Ozaki '97. In addition, clubs were encouraged to have their members log on, with prizes ranging from $500 to $1,000 for clubs that generated the most alumni activity on the network. The Benelux, United Kingdom and Brazil clubs all tied for top honors, followed by the clubs in Boston and the Bay Area.

102. "Enhanced Kellogg School Alumni Web Portal to Invite Grads to 'PowerUp,'" Rebecca Lindell, *Kellogg World* (Winter 2003), pp. 6–7.

103. "Profile," Danielle Anderson, *Kellogg World* (November 1995), pp. 14–15.

104. Dead in the tragic day's events were Edward "Ted" Hennessy '93, David S. Lee '90 and Patrick Jude Murphy '97. Hennessy and Lee perished in the attacks on New York; Murphy died at the Pentagon, where the U.S. naval reservist had been on two weeks of active duty. In addition, the father of one alumnus and the son of another both died. See "In Memoriam," *Kellogg World* (Winter 2001), p. 40.

105. The orientation was renamed Complete Immersion in Management in 2006. CIM's three components included the orientation itself, a required core class called "Leadership in Organizations" and the technology training program, known as TEKcamp.

106. "Taking Hold of Terror," Rebecca Lindell, *Kellogg World* (Winter 2001), pp. 37–39.

107. Interview with author, 2007.

108. "CIM Week 2001 Confronts Sept. 11 Tragedy with Kellogg Spirit," Rebecca Lindell, *Kellogg World* (Winter 2001), pp. 6–7.

109. Interview with author, 2005.

110. "Marketing Guru, 'Stone Age' Man: Jain's All That," Dipayan Baishya and Candice Zachariahs, *Economic Times Online*, December 3, 2005, available at www1.economictimes .indiatimes.com.

111. "Dipak's Indian Values Light Up Kellogg Campus."

112. Interview with author, 2007.

113. J. Keith Murnighan, the Harold H. Hines Jr. Distinguished Professor of Risk Management, supports this view. The social psychologist's research has included analysis of how a crisis can become an opportunity to try new strategies. Recessions, for instance, can become "a chance to get back to basics and understand your mission, your competencies and your threats," he said in a 2002 interview. See "Leadership in Volatile Times," Mike Golosinski, *Kellogg World* (Spring 2002), pp. 10–16.

114. Interview with author, 2007.

115. "Career Help for Kellogg Alums Is Just a Click Away," Kari Richardson, *Kellogg World* (Spring 2003), p. 29.

116. "Landing Jobs for Kellogg MBAs," Mica Schneider, *BusinessWeek Online,* June 19, 2003, available at www.businessweek.com/bschools/content/Jun2003/bs20030619_9777 _bs003.htm?chan=search.

117. Kellogg School Office of Admissions statistics.

118. "Landing Jobs for Kellogg MBAs."

119. See "Employees Train for the Long Haul: Companies Trim, Not Slash, Funds for Education," T. Shawn Taylor, *Chicago Tribune,* September 29, 2002.

120. Dean Jain explained the realignment, saying: "Increasingly, our customers are demanding MBA-type programs without the degree. We must continually evolve to meet this demand and remain on the cutting edge of programming, both on-site at the Allen Center and off-site, through customized programs at corporate locations around the globe." See "Kellogg School Executive Education Leadership Evolves to Meet Market Demand," *Kellogg World* (Spring 2003), p. 3.

121. Interview with author, 2007.

122. Ibid. Burnett said that it is difficult to make industry comparisons of the economic downturn's effects on other schools' executive programs, since there are no reliable industry statistics. However, anecdotal evidence suggests most other schools were struggling, he said, "even to the point that some have completely exited from the open enrollment business (great for us). This being said, Kellogg executive education (degree and nondegree) is one of the largest shops in the world, and the absolute impact of 9/11 on Kellogg had to be much greater than on much smaller shops."

123. See kellogg.northwestern.edu/research/tech/index.htm for more details.

124. "Technology's Promise," Matt Golosinski and Kari Richardson, *Kellogg World* (Spring 2003), p. 12.

125. Interview with author, 2006. Sawhney compared the Internet boom and bust to a "Precambrian kind of explosion of new species formation." But what is interesting, he noted, is that in an evolutionary sense, the Precambrian era was also a time of massive extinction. "Whenever there is a lot of experimentation on any frontier, there's a lot of attrition," he said. "Only a few things make it. With the early Internet era, we saw an explosion of activity that was really [a series of] experiments. The problem was that people expected every experiment to succeed. Every company and every idea and every business model was supposed to be equally successful, and that's certainly not going to be the case."

126. "Technology's Promise," p. 12.

127. One such executive education course is called "Doing Marketing@Microsoft," initiated in 2002. About the effort, Microsoft's CEO, Steve Ballmer, said in 2003: "The training our partnership with Kellogg is bringing to Microsoft is a cornerstone of our efforts to develop our marketing profession. Through their contact with hundreds of our marketers around the world, Kellogg is showing us how to become more customer-centric." See "Technology's Promise," pp. 16–20. In addition, the school formed partnerships with companies such as Motorola to produce the Motorola Research Scholars Program in 2002. The initiative allowed Kellogg students to work on research problems of mutual interest to academics and real-world managers.

128. "eCulture@Kellogg," Rebecca Lindell, *Kellogg World* (Winter 1999), pp. 10–16.

129. Interview with author, 2006.

130. The technology program was not the only aspect of the school's curriculum undergoing change. Innovation was taking place throughout the school, including in the Kellogg executive programs, which had some 5,800 participants in 134 different programs in 1999, twice the number of offerings in 1994. Also, the school's Career Management Center had expanded its efforts, including introducing an online resource for alumni job-seekers in 1997. Similar efforts were under way in the school's Department of Alumni Relations, which launched a variety of online resources for the school's graduates, including e-mail forwarding, listservs and a directory. Communications technology was also enabling alumni to remain connected, regardless of geographic distances—a development that also contributed to the school's ability to recruit more international applicants, according to Megan Byrne, who was then the director of alumni relations. Other critical innovations occurred with the addition of the analytical finance major in 2001.

131. "eCulture@Kellogg," p. 14.

132. Ibid, p. 13.

133. Ibid.

134. Visits by such corporate leaders are routine at Kellogg. Every year brings top executives from an array of industries.

135. "The Internet: A Blessing for Many, a Curse for Some," Philip Kotler, *Kellogg World* (Winter 1999), p. 25. Kotler cautioned, however, that merely putting up a Web site was hardly the solution to meeting the challenges posed by the emerging technology. In fact, he said "creating an e-commerce site is the smallest part of the investment." Companies needed systems for building customer databases that aggregated critical information; firms also needed tech-savvy employees who could quickly answer electronic mail and provide other services. Kotler advised companies: "Make and implement your Internet decisions before you need to. Because when you need to, it may be too late."

136. Interview with author, 2006.

137. "Silicon Summit," Matt Golosinski, *Kellogg World* (Spring 2000), pp. 4–5.

138. "Nothing Is Sacred," Michael Chung, *Kellogg World* (Spring 2001), p. 6.

139. Ibid.

140. "Student Conferences: Meeting of the Minds," Matt Golosinski, *Kellogg World* (Spring 2002), p. 7.

141. "The New B2B," Rebecca Lindell, *Kellogg World* (Spring 2001), p. 12.

142. Interview with author, 2006.

143. "Leadership in Volatile Times."

144. Ibid.

145. Among these alumni were Jerome Kenney '67, vice chairman of Merrill Lynch; Avi Nash '81, founder of Avi Nash LLC; Malcolm Jones '82, principal at Trinity Partners; and Jeff Ubben '87, founding partner of Valueact Capital. Kenney noted that the new Kellogg program "will produce an educated group with a clear advantage who will advise others around the world."

146. "Wall Street Smarts," Romi Herron, *Kellogg World* (Spring 2007), pp. 38–39.

147. Kellogg professors assessed the carnage in an article titled "Black Monday: The View from Kellogg," *Kellogg World* (Spring 1988). Steven DeKrey, assistant dean and director of

admissions and financial aid, reported the implications the crash had for the school's enrollment, which saw an early upsurge of nearly 20 percent over the previous year. DeKrey explained the phenomenon: "Those interested in the MBA are generally intelligent, sophisticated people. If they lose a job as a specialist in the financial services field, their response is often to broaden and improve their abilities in order to enhance their employability. They're motivated to success. Rather than take a step-down job, their reaction is to get better credentials by attending graduate management school. The MBA is becoming a prerequisite to success in management."

148. "Leadership in Volatile Times."

149. Ibid.

150. Kellogg School accounting experts weighed in on the matter, explaining what had gone wrong with financial reporting. Among the problems was a too-cozy relationship between companies and the firms providing supposedly objective assessments of those companies' financial reports. "The auditor is not your friend," said Professor Thomas Lys. "The auditor is supposed to make sure the numbers are correct and that the company does not defraud the shareholders." Both Lys and Professor Lawrence Revsine noted several weaknesses in the U.S. financial reporting structure, including some not addressed by the Sarbanes-Oxley Act of 2002. See "Cover by Numbers," Matt Golosinski, *Kellogg World* (Winter 2002), pp. 28–31.

151. He was invited to Choate Rosemary Hall in Wallingford, Connecticut. The lecture series was designed to "bring preeminent national and international educators to the school" and was underwritten by Barbara Olin Taylor '78, a leader in public school reform. "Professionalism means not only standards of skill but an organization of ethical sensibility that can be trusted—by fellow professionals and by the affected public," said Lavengood. "What is it we really are professionals in doing? What are we experts in? . . . Thinking along these lines leads me to conclude that, as teachers, we are first of all professional mediators between students and certain bodies of knowledge. The implication is that our primary interest must be the student's appreciation of a subject—and not the student's relationship with us. . . . I have come to believe that great teaching requires a passion for learning a subject and imparting it" with great skill.

152. "Doing Well by Doing Good," Ed Finkel, *Kellogg World* (Winter 2002), pp. 18–21.

153. Ibid.

154. Ibid.

155. "Dipak Jain, Dean of the Kellogg School of Management, Explains Why His School Was Ranked the Number One Business School in the Country," Ron Insana, *CNBC News Transcripts,* October 11, 2002.

156. "'Best Citizens' Unite for Change," Romi Herron, *Kellogg World* (Spring 2006), pp. 24–25.

157. Correspondence with author, 2007.

158. See "Seeds of Change: Kellogg Alum's One Acre Fund Helps Families Grow out of Poverty," Aubrey Henretty, *Kellogg World* (Summer 2006), p. 13.

159. "A Return to Real Entrepreneurship to Create New Markets for MBAs," Dipak C. Jain, *AACSB International,* June 2003.

160. "Gift Enables Establishment of Larry and Carol Levy Entrepreneurial Institute," Matt Golosinski, *Kellogg World* (Summer 2003), p. 20.

161. *Entrepreneurship Is in Your Future,* DVD produced by the Larry and Carol Levy Institute for Entrepreneurial Practice, 2006.

162. The figure is from the Levy Institute for Entrepreneurial Practice.

163. The figures are according to a study sponsored by Adam Caplan '01, founder and president of Chicago-based Model Metrics, a customer relationship management company, and conducted by the Kellogg School.

164. "Culture of Collaboration," Matt Golosinski, *Kellogg World* (Spring 2007), pp. 14–16.

165. Rogers's early experiences with entrepreneurship included delivering newspapers and milk on Chicago's South Side, restocking groceries in a neighborhood store and helping his mother, a single parent of four children, sell furniture at flea markets on the weekends. See "Steven Rogers: A Better Chance," in the December 2001 edition of the *Harvard Business School Bulletin,* as well as "The Soul of Entrepreneurship," Kari Richardson, *Kellogg World* (Summer 2003), pp. 14–20.

166. "Soul of Entrepreneurship."

167. Interview with author, 2007.

168. Interview with author, 2007.

169. Interview with author, 2007.

170. *The Republic,* Book 7.

DEANS OF THE NORTHWESTERN UNIVERSITY BUSINESS SCHOOL

List of Northwestern Business Schools Names

School of Commerce (1908–1956)

School of Business (1956–1969)

Graduate School of Management (1969–1979)

J. L. Kellogg Graduate School of Management (1979–2002)

Kellogg School of Management (2002–present)

List of Northwestern Business School Deans

Willard E. Hotchkiss (1908–1917)

Arthur E. Swanson (1917–1918)

Ralph E. Heilman (1919–1937)

Fred D. Fagg Jr. (1937–1939)

Homer B. Vanderblue (1939–1949)

Joseph M. McDaniel Jr. (1950–1951)

Ernest C. Davies (1951–1953)

Richard Donham (1953–1965)

John A. Barr (1965–1975)

Donald P. Jacobs (1975–2001)

Dipak C. Jain (2001–)

Willard E. Hotchkiss (1874–1956)
Deanship: 1908–1917

A professor of economics who arrived at Northwestern University from the Wharton School of Finance and Commerce in 1905, Willard Eugene Hotchkiss was one of two professors who took the idea of starting a school of commerce to university president Abram Winegardner Harris. In turn, Harris solicited support for the venture from members of the Chicago business community. When the School of Commerce formally opened on October 5, 1908, as a part-time evening program in downtown Chicago, the university appointed the 35-year-old Hotchkiss as dean. The school boasted a $5,000 budget, 6 professors and 255 students.

Success was immediate, and soon the school, which was open to both men and women, was practically self-supporting. Hotchkiss would oversee a rapid expansion of the curriculum, which was rooted in economic theory but also provided real tools that practitioners could use. As dean, Hotchkiss pushed the university and its trustees to expand the program, which granted a diploma of commerce to graduates, so that it could offer full-time undergraduate study, culminating in a university degree. In the end, he compromised with the central administration, which expressed doubts about whether sufficient funding existed for such a program. Consequently, in 1912, the school began a five-year curriculum that bestowed a bachelor of business administration degree. This offering, though more comprehensive than the diploma course of study, did not fully meet the dean's expectations. Meanwhile, the market at the time demonstrated little enthusiasm for either the diploma or the BBA, as many students preferred to pursue courses on an "à la carte" basis and with hopes of improving their immediate professional fortunes.

Born in Amber, New York, in 1874, Hotchkiss earned his doctorate from Cornell University in 1905, building upon his 1897 undergraduate degree from the same institution. He was awarded a President Andrew D. White Fellowship for the 1902–1903 academic year and another fellowship for the 1903–1904 term. Before going to Northwestern, Hotchkiss was a teacher and, later, assistant supervisor at George Junior Republic School in Freeville, New York, from 1897 to 1900. Between 1904 and 1905, he was an instructor in political science at the Wharton School.

Hotchkiss was attuned to a sense of public-spiritedness. He believed the professional business student should master the fundamentals of organization and management, including functional subjects such as accounting and finance. But these elements, valuable as they were, were to be marshaled within yet another, overarching framework. "All of these studies would be pursued with constant reference to the fact that business is carried on in a community in which certain public policies are enforced and in recognition of the fact that business should conform to these policies and help to make them effective in contributing to public welfare," wrote Hotchkiss in 1918, reflecting on his tenure as dean of the commerce school.

Though he was an advocate of academic rigor and an analytical approach to problem solving, Hotchkiss did not believe that those tools by themselves were sufficient for success. "Analysis is not all," he said. "Following analysis must come synthesis . . . all the facts and conclusions must be assembled . . . into a working plan." By connecting theory with practice, Hotchkiss helped establish a philosophical and pedagogical framework that has continuously informed the way Northwestern's business school has instructed its students.

Hotchkiss resigned his deanship in 1917 to become the founding dean of business education at the University of Minnesota. In 1925, he served as the first dean of the business school at Stanford University. From 1932 to 1937, he was president of Armour Institute of Technology (today known as the Illinois Institute of Technology), and he then taught at the Carnegie Institute of Technology until he retired to California in 1944. Hotchkiss died in an automobile accident in 1956.

J. D. TOLOFF

Arthur E. Swanson (1855–1945)
Deanship: 1917–1918

Arthur Swanson, the second dean of the School of Commerce, arrived at Northwestern in 1911 from the University of Illinois, where he had earned a doctorate in economics. He was instrumental in developing courses in industrial administration and commercial organization; he also taught the school's initial marketing course in 1912, in which he employed a real-world "problems method" to convey the lessons—a strategy that had previously been used there in courses on accounting and commercial law. He told the marketing scholar Paul D. Converse in 1945 that he had used 30 or more problems gathered from his work as a market consultant, among other things. Swanson's initiative also helped create a course on management policy—the school's first—to complement most of the other offerings whose focus tended to present a functional analysis of business operations. In addition to his position in the commerce school, he was a founding member of the American Association of Collegiate Business Schools, an organization whose objectives included the establishment of national professional standards in business education.

Swanson served as the school's acting dean in 1916, while Willard Hotchkiss was on leave teaching at Stanford University. Swanson's formal tenure as dean was brief, for with the onset of World War I, he was called to New York to serve on the War Shipping Board, which built non-combatant ships and helped coordinate arms shipments. After the war, Swanson moved into private business, becoming senior partner in Swanson, Ogilvie and McKenzie, although he remained a part-time professor at Northwestern from 1921 to 1927.

During his deanship, Swanson and his administration demonstrated the school's continued desire to bring practitioners and academics together, offering a series of public lectures on business organization. Hosted in the university's downtown Chicago building, these lectures addressed an array of topics and were delivered by School of Commerce faculty members in conjunction with Chicago business leaders. The most important action taken during Swanson's administration, however, was the 1917 decision to establish a separate bachelor of science in commerce program on the Evanston campus. World War I prevented its implementation until 1919.

MELVIN SYKES

Ralph E. Heilman (1886–1937)
Deanship: 1919–1937

An authority on labor relations and public utility management, Ralph Heilman arrived at Northwestern in 1916 after serving as an economics professor at the University of Iowa and the University of Illinois from 1913 to 1916. He became the third dean of the School of Commerce in 1919, pledging to the university trustees that he would fulfill his duties with "loyalty and enthusiasm," a statement that was apparently deemed necessary after the brief tenure of his predecessor.

Heilman distinguished two prime objectives in the mission of commerce schools: to train business technicians and specialists and to train executives. In a 1931 essay titled "Personal Qualities Requisite for Success in Business and the Role of the School of Business in Their Development," he would lay out his view regarding various factors—tools, information, character traits—required for business leadership.

His deanship was marked by several important developments at the school, not the least of which was the establishment of a full-time undergraduate commerce program in Evanston in 1919. This offering, which led to a bachelor of science in commerce degree, was designed to be less technically oriented than the curricula in either the evening diploma program or the bachelor of business administration program. Heilman's administration also introduced other innovations, including the Bureau of Business Research in 1919, which was created to help increase Northwestern's national presence as a research institution focused on both theoretical and applied study. Dean Heilman recruited faculty who could deliver a curriculum that emphasized functional and technical subjects, and starting in April 1920, he reorganized the school into eight departments to reflect business specialization. Heilman also oversaw the establishment of a master of business administration degree in 1920 and a doctorate in commerce in 1926.

Other significant moves during Heilman's tenure included facilities changes. In 1923, the School of Commerce moved its administrative offices in Evanston from Harris Hall, where they had been located since the building's construction in 1915, to Memorial Hall (known as "the Little

Red Schoolhouse"). Facilities downtown on the Chicago campus also underwent a transformation during Heilman's deanship, with the school moving into a new building, Wieboldt Hall, in October 1926. The dean's proposal for an institute for executives in 1929 could not be realized due to the Depression, but the Austin Scholars Program did begin during Heilman's tenure. The educational experiment was launched in 1929 as a way to provide broad, liberal arts training in an accelerated curriculum. This initiative, though successful on balance, also suffered from economic setbacks brought about by the Depression.

Born in Ida Grove, Iowa, in 1886, Heilman graduated from Morningside College in 1906. He earned his master's degree in economics from Northwestern University one year later, before going on to earn a doctorate in economics from Harvard in 1913. After months of illness, Heilman died in February 1937.

PAUL STONE

Fred D. Fagg Jr. (1896–1981)
Deanship: 1937–1939

An economist, attorney and aviation expert, Fred D. Fagg Jr. first went to Northwestern in 1923 as an instructor in economics and a student in the School of Law, from which he earned his juris doctorate in 1927. After graduation, he served on the faculty of the University of Southern California's Economics Department, and he was also an assistant dean. He would return to Northwestern as a professor of law in 1929, the same year he founded the Air Law Institute in Chicago, serving as its managing director. His interest in aviation developed during his service as a second lieutenant in the 92nd Aero Squadron during World War I, flying night missions over the English Channel in 1918.

During his tenure as dean of the School of Commerce from 1937 to 1939, he maintained the status quo established by his predecessor, Dean Heilman. Fagg resigned his deanship at the commerce school to become vice president and dean of faculties for Northwestern, a position he held until 1947, when he was named president of the University of Southern California, a role he held for another 10 years.

Among other distinctions, Fagg would receive the Federal Aviation Administration's Distinguished Service Award in 1976. The award cited his founding of the first air law institute and journal in the United States.

Born on July 30, 1896, in Brooklyn, New York, Fagg attended San Diego Army and Navy Academy before entering the University of Redlands in Redlands, California. He left school during his sophomore year to join the U.S. Army Signal Corps and subsequently enlisted for service in World War I. Upon returning to the United States after the war, he completed his undergraduate degree at Redlands in 1920. The following year, he earned a master's degree from Harvard, where he then taught economics until moving to Northwestern two years later. Fagg died on October 14, 1981, in Portland, Oregon.

EUGENE L. RAY

Homer B. Vanderblue (1888–1952)
Deanship: 1939–1949

Homer B. Vanderblue assumed the deanship of the School of Commerce in 1939, bringing experience as both an academician and a businessman. An expert in federal regulation of commerce and industry, Vanderblue would leave a legacy that included maintaining the school's strength despite the economic pressures of World War II, which forced some other institutions to close.

During his tenure, which favored a liberal arts approach to business study, Vanderblue shifted the curriculum away from excessive specialization by adding breadth to the faculty, including the hiring of several Harvard professors, one of whom was future dean Richard Donham. He also instituted a "core" set of fundamental courses, featuring business policy as the capstone. In addition, Vanderblue consolidated power in the dean's office, limiting the authority of departmental chairmen to influence the budget. He also oversaw the expansion of the two-year undergraduate commerce program into a four-year program in 1942, a move that conferred several advantages upon the school, among them an increase in tuition revenue. In 1943, under Vanderblue's deanship, the school acquired a program in home economics and launched a program in hospital administration, which would become nationally recognized.

Despite his experience in business, Vanderblue did not concentrate on maintaining intimate ties with the local business community but instead focused on his academic agenda. That agenda took a more "managerial" approach to business study and emphasized more advanced concepts rather than functional ones.

Trained in economics, Vanderblue earned both a bachelor's degree (1911) and a master's degree (1912) from Northwestern University, before earning his doctorate in economics from Harvard in 1915. In the same year, he joined Northwestern as an assistant professor in the School of Commerce and the College of Liberal Arts. He became a professor at Northwestern in 1920, but later that year, he left Evanston to become research director at the Denver Civic Commercial Association for 12 months. After that, he returned to Harvard in 1922 as a business economics professor and director of the school's Economic Service. In 1929, he became vice president of Tricontinental Corporation, a major investment firm; he held that position until 1937.

Born in Hinsdale, Illinois, on December 24, 1888, Vanderblue retired in 1949 because of deteriorating health. He died of a heart attack in 1952.

Joseph M. McDaniel Jr. (1902–1980)
Deanship: 1950–1951

A professor of business administration who was recruited by Dean Vanderblue in 1946, Joseph M. McDaniel Jr. earned both his bachelor's degree (1924) and his doctorate (1930) from Johns Hopkins University.

McDaniel's tenure as dean was brief—less than a year—for he resigned the position to join the Ford Foundation as an assistant director. During his deanship, however, the school moved its graduate division from Evanston to downtown Chicago, taking up residence in Wieboldt Hall. In addition, plans were made to organize the Institute for Management, which began in 1951. The groundwork for establishing the Gregg Division, a secretarial and commercial education program that began in 1952 and was terminated in 1959, was also laid. As dean, McDaniel created uniform admissions standards for the day and evening programs.

McDaniel also served as vice president of the National Institute for Commercial and Trade Organization Executives in 1950. He coauthored the book *Don't Bank on It* in 1970, and he earned a distinguished alumni award from Johns Hopkins in 1974.

Ernest C. Davies (1888–1962)
Deanship: 1951–1953

As dean, Ernest C. Davies oversaw the transfer of the graduate program to downtown Chicago: the division of programs was intended to impart a more distinctive character to the graduate program. Under Davies, a professor of accounting, the school also was one of the first to develop a standardized admissions test for the graduate business school. In addition, the school's Institute for Management was launched in 1951, making Northwestern the first university to offer nondegree executive education programs.

Previously, Davies and James R. Hawkinson had served as assistant deans of the Chicago and Evanston divisions of the School of Commerce during Dean Heilman's tenure. With Heilman's death in 1937, they each assumed responsibility for the school's administration while the university sought a new dean. Davies also had served as acting dean in 1949 and associate dean in 1950.

Born in 1888 in Somonauk, Illinois, Davies earned a bachelor's degree from Ohio State University before receiving his bachelor of science in commerce from Northwestern in 1922 and his CPA accreditation in 1923. He began lecturing in accounting at Northwestern in 1922, going on to become assistant dean in 1923, assistant professor in 1925 and associate professor in 1930. He was on leave from the university between 1938 and 1939 while he served at Wolf and Company, an accounting firm. Davies died in 1962.

HERB COMESS

Richard Donham (1905–1970)
Deanship: 1953–1965

The son of Wallace B. Donham, founding dean of the Harvard Business School from 1919 to 1942, Richard Donham sought to replicate the Harvard experience at Northwestern, where he arrived in 1940 at the inducement of Homer Vanderblue. The effort included making the case method a central part of the curriculum, as well as placing greater emphasis on teaching as opposed to research.

Although Donham would remain on leave throughout much of the 1940s, serving as commercial research director for Gisholt Machine Company as well as manager and education director at Price Waterhouse & Company, he is credited as dean with strengthening the MBA program and the Institute for Management by recruiting senior executives to the program. He also made efforts to bring the school closer to the business community, and he persuaded distinguished professors with considerable experience and interest in commerce to become part of what was then called the School of Business. Donham created a more distributed leadership at the school, turning to three colleagues in particular (Leon A. Bosch, Ira D. Anderson and Frank T. Hartzfeld) to play significant administrative roles. When national attention was focused on business schools and their methods during the late 1950s, a massive upheaval in education resulted. Because Northwestern had already begun making the necessary strides to remain in the vanguard of business education, the effect of the national publicity was not as pronounced at the school, though Donham's administration did take steps to bolster the undergraduate curriculum to produce an elite program at a time when many questioned the fate of middling undergraduate offerings.

Continuing the direction set by Vanderblue, Donham encouraged a liberal arts approach in both the undergraduate and graduate programs, using case methods and other teaching strategies. During his tenure, the MBA and doctoral programs were opened up to applicants whose undergraduate training was in liberal arts or engineering.

Born in Newton Highlands, Massachusetts, on March 18, 1905, Donham earned his bachelor's degree (1927), his MBA (1930) and his doctorate in commercial science (1934) from Harvard. He taught corporate organization and management at Harvard Business School and Yale Law School. In 1964, he resigned as dean, citing health reasons and a desire to return to teaching; after taking a year's leave between 1965 and 1966, he would continue to teach until his death in 1970.

PHOTO BY BACHRACH

John A. Barr (1908–1979)
Deanship: 1965–1975

John Barr, an attorney and former chairman of Montgomery Ward & Company who had served as a Northwestern University trustee since 1957, was nominated as dean of the School of Business and assumed its leadership on June 1, 1965.

Barr's tenure would be marked by significant and daring changes in the school. The faculty voted by a margin of two to one in the spring of 1966 to discontinue the undergraduate program. The school also created the Business Advisory Council, headed by James L. Allen, a founder of Booz Allen Hamilton and a business associate of Barr's, to help guide its strategic development. Other members of the council, which initially numbered 33, included top corporate leaders from diverse industries. Although he was a businessman, Barr also oversaw a considerable expansion of the school's faculty, particularly in ways that deepened its research orientation in areas of quantifiable study.

As dean, Barr created a committee, chaired by Ralph Westfall, associate dean for academic affairs, to study phasing out the undergraduate curriculum, which would be done in 1966. In its place, the school, which would become the Graduate School of Business and then the Graduate School of Management, pursued a more advanced curriculum in line with the complexity of contemporary market needs. At the same time, the school's programs championed what came to be known as the general management approach, providing education for leaders in public, nonprofit and for-profit organizations. In parallel with this decision, the school changed its degree from the MBA to the master of management, in order to emphasize the general application of the school's education. Also during Barr's tenure as dean, new facilities were constructed, with Leverone Hall in Evanston becoming home to the program in 1972.

Born on September 10, 1908, on a farm near Akron, Indiana, Barr earned his bachelor of law degree from Indiana University in 1930 and went on to practice law in Gary, Indiana. From 1933 to 1935, he served on the legal staff of Montgomery Ward, where he would be named assistant secretary in 1940 and vice president, general counsel and secretary in 1949. One year later, he was elected director of the board, and in 1955, he became chairman, a position he retained until 1965 when he resigned to become dean at Northwestern's School of Business. He retired from that role in 1975, in part because of declining health. He died on January 16, 1979, in Evanston.

EVANSTON PHOTOGRAPHIC STUDIOS

Donald P. Jacobs (1927–)
Deanship: 1975–2001

With his tenure extending over fully half of the Kellogg School's history, Donald P. Jacobs would play a dramatic part in charting the school's course, both as a scholar and as dean. He began his Northwestern career in 1957, joining the Finance Department of the School of Commerce.

Born in Chicago in 1927, Jacobs earned his bachelor's degree from Roosevelt University in 1949 and both a master's (1951) and a doctorate (1956) in economics from Columbia University. He began his Northwestern tenure as an assistant professor of finance and then became an associate professor in 1960, a professor in 1965 and chairman of the Finance Department in 1969. The next year, he was made the Morrison Professor of Finance. He was appointed dean in 1975 and named the Gaylord Freeman Distinguished Professor of Banking in 1979. He was integral to establishing the International Institute for Management in 1965, participated in the Institute for Management beginning in 1967 and served as founder and codirector (with Eugene Lerner) of the Banking Research Center in 1970.

In addition to his academic roles, Jacobs had been a member of the research staff at the National Bureau of Economic Research from 1952 to 1957 and a research associate at the bureau from 1966 to 1970. He was senior economist for the Banking and Currency Committee of the U.S. House of Representatives from 1963 to 1964 and co–staff director of the Presidential Commission on Financial Structure and Regulation (the Hunt Commission) from 1970 to 1971. From 1975 to 1979, he was chairman of the board of Amtrak. Jacobs's research has been published in many articles on capital markets and banking, and he is the coauthor of *Financial Institutions*.

His deanship, longer than that of any other business school dean in the country, resulted in many pivotal developments that helped Kellogg become one of the world's most prestigious business schools. Among the initiatives that Jacobs led was the creation of the school's team-oriented culture; further, he renewed the focus on research-based faculty by hiring very promising but young professors who would then be groomed for success in the school's collaborative environment. He also championed "lifelong learning," as manifested in the school's Executive MBA Program that was launched in 1976, as well as the construction of a renowned, dedicated facility—the James L. Allen Center—built in 1979 to house the executive offerings.

Jacobs also oversaw innovations such as the school's strategy of personally interviewing all prospective students, a process that allowed the resource-constrained institution to discover talented people whom other schools overlooked. Critical to the school's rise in the rankings during Jacobs's tenure was a $10 million gift from the J. L. Kellogg Foundation in 1979, which resulted in a new name for the institution: the J. L. Kellogg School of Management. With this financial support, Jacobs bolstered teaching, research, facilities and the school's overall culture, ultimately taking Kellogg to the number one spot in several national rankings, starting with the 1988 *BusinessWeek* survey. Along with Dipak C. Jain, he was instrumental in establishing global joint-degree partnerships with schools around the world.

Jacobs retired as dean in 2001, returning to the classroom as a finance professor.

EVANSTON PHOTOGRAPHIC STUDIOS

Dipak C. Jain (1957–)
Deanship: 2001–

Born in Assam, India, in 1957, Dipak C. Jain became dean of the Kellogg School in 2001, consolidating the advances made by his predecessor while delivering many of his own innovations designed to meet new market challenges.

Jain has undertaken an ambitious global branding effort in order to expand the school's footprint, while also enhancing the Kellogg alumni network through a renewed commitment to lifelong learning and engagement with the school's graduates. A distinguished teacher and scholar whose expertise includes strategic marketing and new products and services, Jain also has reasserted the centrality of academics, bringing rigor and relevance to the curriculum. To strengthen the school's organizational structure, he has created the Office of the Dean, bringing together the insights of top professors who serve in three senior associate dean roles. The positions, which rotate about every three years, have brought great flexibility and depth to the school's leadership and served as a model of the team-oriented culture at Kellogg. These and other efforts resulted in Kellogg again being ranked number one in national surveys of business schools in 2002 and 2004.

Jain joined the Kellogg School's Marketing Department as an assistant professor in 1986, having earned his bachelor's (1976) and master's (1978) degrees in mathematics and statistics from Gauhati University in India. He received his master's degree in management science in 1986 and a doctorate in marketing in 1987, both from the University of Texas–Dallas, where he studied under the esteemed marketing scholar Frank M. Bass. Jain became associate professor in 1990, professor in 1993 and the Sandy and Morton Goldman Professor of Entrepreneurial Studies in 1994. He served as senior associate dean for academic affairs from 1996 to 2001 and was named dean in 2001.

As senior associate dean, Jain worked closely with Donald Jacobs to set the agenda for the school's curriculum, faculty and research, including the development of joint-degree programs with schools in Asia, Europe and the Middle East. The recipient of numerous teaching and research honors, he continues to champion theory and practice in management education, as well as the need to cultivate the leadership and people skills required for success in the contemporary global marketplace. He also brings his keen analytical mind to bear on the challenges facing practitioners and scholars in business, continuously striving to refine the Kellogg School experience. The principal framework that has shaped this experience during Jain's deanship has been a fourfold approach emphasizing intellectual depth, experiential learning, leadership and social responsibility and global perspectives. Jain himself continues to bring his passion for teaching into the classroom, despite his leadership responsibilities.

With Jain in the Office of the Dean, the Kellogg School has remained among the world's most prestigious business schools.

Appendix B

KELLOGG SCHOOL OF MANAGEMENT CHAIRED, TENURED AND EMERITUS FACULTY

Marcus Alexis, Professor Emeritus of Management and Strategy

Torben Andersen, Nathan S. and Mary P. Sharp Professor of Finance

Eric T. Anderson, Hartmarx Research Associate Professor of Marketing

James Anderson, William L. Ford Professor of Marketing and Wholesale Distribution

David Austen-Smith, Peter G. Peterson Professor of Corporate Ethics

Bala Balachandran, J. L. Kellogg Professor of Accounting Information and Management

Haskel Benishay, Professor Emeritus of Managerial Economics

David Besanko, Senior Associate Dean: Planning and External Relations; Alvin J. Huss Professor of Management and Strategy

Henry S. Bienen, President of Northwestern University, Professor of Management and Strategy

Robert Blattberg, Polk Bros. Professor of Retailing

Galen V. Bodenhausen, Professor of Marketing

William J. Breen, Professor Emeritus of Finance

Jeanne Brett, DeWitt W. Buchanan Jr. Professor of Dispute Resolution and Organizations

Bobby Calder, Charles H. Kellstadt Professor of Marketing

Gregory Carpenter, James Farley/Booz Allen Hamilton Professor of Marketing Strategy

Sunil Chopra, Senior Associate Dean: Curriculum and Teaching; IBM Professor of Operations Management and Information Systems

Anne Coughlan, Professor of Marketing

Sudhakar D. Deshmukh, Charles E. Morrison Professor of Decision Sciences

Daniel Diermeier, IBM Professor of Regulation and Competitive Practice

David Dranove, Walter J. McNerney Professor of Health Industry Management

Allan Drebin, Professor of Accounting and Information Systems

Ronald A. Dye, Leonard Spacek Professor of Accounting Information and Management

Janice Eberly, John L. and Helen Kellogg Professor of Finance

Linda Emanuel, Professor of Medicine

Timothy Feddersen, Wendell Hobbs Professor of Managerial Economics and Decision Sciences

Michael J. Fishman, Norman Strunk Professor of Financial Institutions

Adam Galinsky, Morris and Alice Kaplan Professor of Ethics and Decision in Management

Aaron Gellman, Professor of Management and Strategy

Shane Greenstein, Elinor and H. Wendell Hobbs Professor of Management and Strategy

Ranjay Gulati, Michael Ludwig Nemmers Professor of Strategy and Organizations

Kathleen Hagerty, Senior Associate Dean: Faculty and Research; First Chicago Professorship in Finance

Donald Haider, Professor of Management and Strategy

Paul Hirsch, James L. Allen Professor of Strategy and Management and Organizations

Thomas N. Hubbard, John L. and Helen Kellogg Professor of Management and Strategy

Edward Hughes, Professor of Health Industry Management

Donald P. Jacobs, Dean Emeritus; Gaylord Freeman Professor of Banking

Ravi Jagannathan, Chicago Mercantile Exchange/John F. Sandner Professor of Finance

Dipak C. Jain, Dean; Sandy and Morton Goldman Professor of Entrepreneurial Studies

Hervey Juris, Professor Emeritus of Human Resources Management

Ehud Kalai, James J. O'Connor Professor of Decision and Game Sciences

Morton Kamien, Joseph and Carole Levy Professor of Entrepreneurship

Robert Korajczyk, Harry G. Guthmann Professor of Finance

Philip Kotler, S. C. Johnson and Son Professor of International Marketing

Lakshman Krishnamurthi, A. Montgomery Ward Professor of Marketing

Arvind Krishnamurthy, Harold Stuart Professor of Finance

Angela Lee, Mechthild Esser Nemmers Professor of Marketing

Sidney Levy, Charles H. Kellstadt Professor Emeritus of Marketing

Alicia Löffler, Professor of Biotechnology

Deborah Lucas, Donald C. Clark/HSBC Chair in Consumer Finance Fund

Thomas Lys, Eric L. Kohler Chair in Accounting

Robert Magee, Keith I. DeLashmutt Professor of Accounting Information and
    Management

Robert McDonald, Erwin P. Nemmers Professor of Finance

Therese McGuire, ConAgra Foods Research Professorship in Strategic Management

Victoria Medvec, Adeline Barry Davee Professor of Management and Organizations

David Messick, Professor Emeritus of Management and Organizations

Edwin Mills, Professor Emeritus of Real Estate and Finance

Joseph Moag, Professor Emeritus of Organization Behavior

J. Keith Murnighan, Harold H. Hines Jr. Professor of Risk Management

William Ocasio, John L. and Helen Kellogg Professor of Management and
    Organizations

Jonathan Parker, Professor of Finance

Mitchell A. Petersen, Glen Vasel Professor of Finance

Stephen Presser, Professor of Business Law

Thomas R. Prince, Professor of Accounting Information and Management

Michael Radnor, Professor of Management and Organizations

Artur Raviv, Alan E. Peterson Professor of Finance

Sergio Rebelo, Tokai Bank Professor of Finance

Stanley Reiter, Morrison Professor Emeritus of Economics and Mathematics

Steven Rogers, Gordon and Llura Gund Family Professor of Entrepreneurship

Mark Satterthwaite, A. C. Buehler Professor in Hospital and Health Services
    Management

Mohanbir Sawhney, McCormick Tribune Professor of Technology

Constantinos Skiadas, Harold L. Stuart Professor of Finance

Daniel Spulber, Elinor Hobbs Professor of International Business

Swaminathan Sridharan, John L. and Helen Kellogg Chair of Accounting Information and Management

Louis Stern, John D. Gray Professor Emeritus of Marketing

Brian Sternthal, Kraft Foods Chair in Marketing

Leigh Thompson, J. Jay Gerber Professor of Dispute Resolution and Organizations

Alice Tybout, Harold T. Martin Professor of Marketing

Brian Uzzi, Richard L. Thomas Professor of Leadership and Organizational Change

Jan A. Van Mieghem, Harold L. Stuart Professor of Managerial Economics

Rakesh Vohra, J. L. and Helen Kellogg Professor of Managerial Economics and Decision Sciences

Robert Weber, Frederick E. Nemmers Professor of Decision Sciences

Edward Zajac, James F. Beré Professor of Management and Organizations

Andris Zoltners, Professor of Marketing

INDEX

Heron, Alexander, 64
Herrold, Lloyd D., 69, 82, 306n5
Hickman, Charles, 341n12
Hillman, Sidney, 22, 297n31
Himmelblau, David, 34, 44, 51,
    299–300n70
Hinman House, 58
Hobbs, H. Wendell, 335–336n120
Hofer, Charles W., 154, 326n52
Holden, Betsy, 245
Holgate, Thomas Franklin, 17, 21
Honack, Richard P., 261, 264
Hori, Roxanne, 256, 266, 267, 268,
    345n90
Hospital and Health Services
    Management Program, 158, 161, 164
Hotchkiss, George Burton, 76, 309n34
Hotchkiss, Willard Eugene, 4, 7, 9, 10, 21,
    23, 25, 28, 34, 36, 37, 39, 44, 46, 47,
    62, 63, 75, 296n26, 298n45, 303n122,
    351, 352–353, 352(photo)
Houri, Francis J., 155
Howard, Delton T., 58, 59
Howard, Earl Dean, 16, 21, 22–23, 24, 25,
    36, 42–43, 44, 48, 56–57, 58, 59, 63,
    64, 74, 294n2, 296nn25, 29, 297n31,
    298nn45, 48, 303n122
Howard, Liz Livingston, 258
Howell, James E., 110, 121, 123, 322n42
Hubbard, Gurdon Saltonstall, 19
Hulburd, C. F., 28
Hunt, Richard, 330n21
Hutchins, Robert Maynard, 61
Hutchinson, Kenneth D., 314n85
H. Wendell and Elinor Hobbs Hall, 175,
    207

Ichan, Carl, 213
Ickes, Harold, 296n22
IIM. *See* Institute for International
    Management
Independent Study Plan, 59
Indian Business Conference, 216
Innes, George, 27
Insana, Ron, 276

Institute for Advanced Study in
    Managerial Economics and Decision
    Sciences, 192
Institute for Executives, 56–57
Institute for International Management
    (IIM), 118, 170, 171, 329n11, 360
Institute for Management, 115, 116, 168,
    170, 175, 329n8, 357, 360
Institute for Mathematics, 117
Institute for Research in Land Economics
    and Public Utilities, 53
Integrated Study Plan, 59
International Advanced Executive
    Program (IAEP), 175
International Business and Markets
    Program, 202
International Business and Markets
    Research Center, 202
Isenman, Al, 199
Ivey, Paul W., 6, 68, 75, 77, 80

Jackson, Matthew O., 250
Jacobs, Celia, 168
Jacobs, Donald P., viii, 6–7, 92, 93, 95, 96,
    117, 118, 119, 126, 134, 137–138,
    141, 143, 146, 148, 149, 152, 157,
    161, 164, 166(photo), 167, 168,
    169–177, 177–178, 179, 180, 181,
    182, 183, 184, 185, 186, 187, 189,
    190, 193, 194, 195, 196, 203, 204,
    206, 207–208, 209, 210, 211–212,
    214, 215, 216, 217, 218, 219, 220,
    224–225, 226, 227, 229, 231,
    232–233, 234, 241, 244, 251, 262,
    263, 267, 270, 273, 282, 314n89,
    320n33, 321n37, 324n5, 326n43,
    328n66, 329nn3, 4, 8, 330nn20, 22,
    331n46, 334n81, 336n124, 337n130,
    339nn181, 189, 341n15, 342n30, 351,
    360–361, 360(photo), 362
Jacobs, J. L., 47
Jacobs, Mary, 182
Jagannathan, Ravi, 247, 342n31
Jain, Dipak Chan, viii, 7, 11, 69, 96, 106,
    204, 227, 228(photo), 229, 230, 231,